DEEP LEARNING FOR IMAGE PROCESSING APPLICATIONS

Advances in Parallel Computing

This book series publishes research and development results on all aspects of parallel computing. Topics may include one or more of the following: high speed (HPC) and high throughput computing (HTC) architectures, including grids, clouds, clusters, Service Oriented Architectures, etc., network technology, performance measurement, system software, middleware, algorithm design, development tools, software engineering, services and applications from all scientific and engineering fields, including data science and analytics.

Series Editor:
Professor Dr. Gerhard R. Joubert

Volume 31

Recently published in this series

Vol. 30. G. Fox, V. Getov, L. Grandinetti, G. Joubert and T. Sterling (Eds.), New Frontiers in High Performance Computing and Big Data

Vol. 29. M. Mittal, D. Jude Hemanth, V.E. Balas and R. Kumar (Eds.), Data Intensive Computing Application for Big Data

Vol. 28. C. Trinitis and J. Weidendorfer (Eds.), Co-Scheduling of HPC Applications

Vol. 27. G.R. Joubert, H. Leather, M. Parsons, F. Peters and M. Sawyer (Eds.), Parallel Computing: On the Road to Exascale

Vol. 26. L. Grandinetti, G. Joubert, M. Kunze and V. Pascucci (Eds.), Big Data and High Performance Computing

Vol. 25. M. Bader, A. Bode, H.-J. Bungartz, M. Gerndt, G.R. Joubert and F. Peters (Eds.), Parallel Computing: Accelerating Computational Science and Engineering (CSE)

Vol. 24. E.H. D'Hollander, J.J. Dongarra, I.T. Foster, L. Grandinetti and G.R. Joubert (Eds.), Transition of HPC Towards Exascale Computing

Vol. 23. C. Catlett, W. Gentzsch, L. Grandinetti, G. Joubert and J.L. Vazquez-Poletti (Eds.), Cloud Computing and Big Data

Vol. 22. K. De Bosschere, E.H. D'Hollander, G.R. Joubert, D. Padua and F. Peters (Eds.), Applications, Tools and Techniques on the Road to Exascale Computing

Vol. 21. J. Kowalik and T. Puźniakowski, Using OpenCL – Programming Massively Parallel Computers

Vol. 20. I. Foster, W. Gentzsch, L. Grandinetti and G.R. Joubert (Eds.), High Performance Computing: From Grids and Clouds to Exascale

Vol. 19. B. Chapman, F. Desprez, G.R. Joubert, A. Lichnewsky, F. Peters and T. Priol (Eds.), Parallel Computing: From Multicores and GPU's to Petascale

Volumes 1–14 published by Elsevier Science.

ISSN 0927-5452 (print)
ISSN 1879-808X (online)

Deep Learning for Image Processing Applications

Edited by

D. Jude Hemanth

Karunya University, India

and

Vania Vieira Estrela

Universidade Federal Fluminense, Brazil

Amsterdam • Berlin • Washington, DC

ISBN 978-1-61499-821-1 (print)
ISBN 978-1-61499-822-8 (online)
Library of Congress Control Number: 2017959841

Publisher
IOS Press BV
Nieuwe Hemweg 6B
1013 BG Amsterdam
Netherlands
fax: +31 20 687 0019
e-mail: order@iospress.nl

For book sales in the USA and Canada:
IOS Press, Inc.
6751 Tepper Drive
Clifton, VA 20124
USA
Tel.: +1 703 830 6300
Fax: +1 703 830 2300
sales@iospress.com

LEGAL NOTICE
The publisher is not responsible for the use which might be made of the following information.

Preface

Deep learning and image processing are two areas that interest many academics and industry professionals. The main objective of this book is to provide concepts about these two areas in the same platform. Professionals from academia and research labs have shared ideas, problems and solutions relating to the multifaceted aspects of these areas.

The first chapter deals with an interesting introduction to deep learning: the relation between man, mind and intelligence, which is dealt with here. This provides an excellent foundation for subsequent chapters. The second chapter demonstrates the application of deep neural networks for image classification. A wide range of images are used in this application, proving the robustness of the proposed approach. Hand gesture recognition with deep neural networks is analyzed in the third chapter. An interesting aspect of this chapter explains how recognized hand gestures are used to control the robotic arm.

Deep learning techniques for image retrieval are discussed in the fourth chapter. The significance of increasing multimedia data in real time and the necessity for efficient search processes is also stressed in this chapter. The fifth chapter concentrates on from human images using deep learning techniques. The sample disease used in this approach is a form of diabetes commonly found in humans. The sixth chapter deals with the application of tuberculosis detection in the human body through deep learning approaches. Experimental results show promising results for the proposed technique.

Object retrieval from images using deep convolutional features are discussed in the seventh chapter. Convolutional neural networks are used for the experimental analysis in this work. The eighth chapter highlights the application of hierarchical object detection with deep reinforcement learning approaches using different variations of the images. A comparative analysis of deep data and big data are discussed in the ninth chapter which adds a different dimension to the preceding content.

Vehicle type recognition using sparse filtered convolutional neural networks is discussed in the tenth chapter. Images from publicly available database are used for the experimental analysis in this work. The application of deep learning approaches for surveillance and security applications is discussed in the eleventh chapter. The final chapter talks about the possibility of enhancing the quality of images captured from a long distance using deep learning approaches. The variety of content in these chapters provides an excellent platform for researchers working in these areas.

We would like to express our gratitude to all of the authors who submitted chapters for their contributions. We also acknowledge the great efforts of the reviewers who have spent their valuable time working on the contents of this book. We would also like to thank Prof. Gerhard Joubert, Editor-in-Chief, Advances in Parallel Computing series and IOS Press for their constant guidance throughout this book project.

D. Jude Hemanth
Vania Viera Estrela

About the Editors

Dr. D. Jude Hemanth received his B.E degree in Electrical and Computer Engineering (ECE) from Bharathiar University in 2002, as well as an M.E degree in communication systems from Anna University in 2006 and a Ph.D from Karunya University in 2013. His research areas include computational intelligence and image processing. He has authored more than 100 research papers in reputed international journals such as Neurocomputing, Neural Computing and Applications, Neural Network World, etc. He has authored a book with VDM-Verlag, Germany, and many book chapters with reputed publishers such as Springer and Inderscience. He is the guest editor of the book series "Lecture Notes in Computational Vision and Biomechanics" with Springer, and "Advances in Parallel Computing" with IOS Press. He has also served as an associate editor for various international journals with publishers such as IEEE (IEEE Access Journal), Springer (Sensing and Imaging), Inderscience (IJAIP, IJICT, IJCVR, IJBET), IOS Press (Intelligent Decision Technologies), etc. In addition, he has been an organizing committee member for several international conferences across the globe. He holds professional membership of the IEEE Technical Committee on Neural Networks (IEEE Computational Intelligence Society) and the IEEE Technical Committee on Soft Computing (IEEE Systems, Man and Cybernatics Society). He has completed a funded research project from CSIR, Govt. of India, and acts as the research scientist for the Computational Intelligence and Information Systems (CI2S) Lab of Argentina and the RIADI Lab of Tunisia. He is currently working as Associate Professor in the Department of ECE, Karunya University, Coimbatore, India.

Prof. Vania V. Estrela received her bachelor degree in ECE from the Federal University of Rio de Janeiro, Brazil, her first master degree from the Instituto Tecnologico de Aeronautica, Brazil, her second master degree from Northwestern University, USA, and her Ph.D in ECE from the Illinois Institute of Technology, USA, in 2002. She is an Associate Professor of the Department of Telecommunications in the Universidade Federal Fluminense, Brazil. She is currently editing a book on Deep Learning, and has authored or co-authored over 30-refereed publications. She has also co-guest-edited 2 Special issues of international refereed journals and edited over 12 international peer-reviewed international conference and workshop proceedings. She is currently a reviewer for more than 20 journals and magazines, including IET Image Processing. She is an associate editor/editorial board member for 8 journals and magazines and is a member of IEEE, ACM, and IASTED.

Contents

Preface   v
D. Jude Hemanth and Vania Viera Estrela

About the Editors   vii

Mind, Machine, and Image Processing   1
Subhash Chandra Pandey

Deep Neural Networks for Image Classification   27
A. Vasuki and S. Govindaraju

Virtual Robotic Arm Control with Hand Gesture Recognition and Deep Learning
Strategies   50
*K. Martin Sagayam, T. Vedha Viyas, Chiung Ching Ho
and Lawrence E. Henesey*

Intelligent Image Retrieval via Deep Learning Techniques   68
*Rajeev Kumar Singh, Suchitra Agrawal, Uday Pratap Singh
and Sanjeev Jain*

Advanced Stevia Disease Detection Using Deep Learning   94
S. Lakshmi and R. Sivakumar

Analysis of Tuberculosis Images Using Differential Evolutionary Extreme
Learning Machines (DE-ELM)   111
E. Priya and S. Srinivasan

Object Retrieval with Deep Convolutional Features   137
*Eva Mohedano, Amaia Salvador, Kevin McGuinness, Xavier Giró-i-Nieto,
Noel E. O'connor and Ferran Marqués*

Hierarchical Object Detection with Deep Reinforcement Learning   164
*Miriam Bellver Bueno, Xavier Giro-i-Nieto, Ferran Marques
and Jordi Torres*

Big Data & Deep Data: Minding the Challenges   177
Madhulika Bhatia, Mamta Mittal and Madhurima

Sparse-Filtered Convolutional Neural Networks with Layer-Skipping
(SF-CNNLS) for Intra-Class Variation of Vehicle Type Recognition   194
Suryanti Awang and Nik Mohamad Aizuddin Nik Azmi

On the Prospects of Using Deep Learning for Surveillance and Security
Applications   218
Shuo Liu, Vijay John and Zheng Liu

Super-Resolution of Long Range Captured Iris Image Using Deep
Convolutional Network 244
  Anand Deshpande and Prashant P. Patavardhan

Subject Index 271

Author Index 273

Deep Learning for Image Processing Applications
D.J. Hemanth and V.V. Estrela (Eds.)
IOS Press, 2017
doi:10.3233/978-1-61499-822-8-1

1

Mind, Machine, and Image Processing

Subhash Chandra PANDEY

Computer Science & Engineering Department
Birla Institute of Technology, Mesra, Ranchi
(Allahabad Campus)
B-7, Industrial Area, Naini, Allahabad (UP), India
subh63@yahoo.co.in

Abstract. Image processing (IP) and artificial intelligence (AI) is an exciting research area in cognitive and computer science. This chapter deals with the image processing and attempts have been taken to illustrate the intertwining among mind, machine and image processing. Further, different subtle aspects pertaining to mind and intelligence are also presented. In fact, intelligence acts as a substrate of mind to engage it in consciousness. Indeed, mind is distinct from the consciousness and both are subtler than the body. The chapter also elucidates the comparison of mind machine, and intelligence in image processing. Moreover, attempt has been made to envision the core issues related to different aspects like: (1) intelligence is the means to engage the mind in consciousness (2) Brain is analogous to a feed forward hierarchical state machine and acts as a substrate for mind and possesses vital relationship with intelligence. Indeed, there are two important approaches to develop an artificially intelligent device. These are the conceptual understanding of mind and the computational framework of brain. This chapter emphasizes that the agent in which embryonic artificial intelligence is to be created must have the capacity of embodied experience and it must possess sensory components to establish relations between it and the external world. Further, this chapter also renders the philosophical perspectives of some intuitive questions such as: Can mind be explained in terms of machines? Can mind be replicated on machines? Do machines can ever be intelligent? In fact mind or intelligence cannot be reflected by physical means. In addition, this chapter preludes that mainly there are two approaches pertinent to the philosophy of mind. These are the dualism and functionalism. However, it is hard to explain the true nature of mind with the help of only these two approaches because mind displays the characteristics like and dislikes a machine simultaneously. Moreover, the concept of machine seems to be based on dichotomy between these two approaches. Various difficulties pertaining to image processing have also been incorporated.

Keywords. Mind, Machine, Artificial Intelligence, Image Processing, IP and AI

1. Introduction

Vision can be considered as the most formidable sense organ of the humans. Indeed, majority of the problem solving abilities emanates from the vision. It provides the ability to visually simulate the effects of actions in mind. AI researchers have been created vision system in machines. The vision system of machines augments the various abilities of machine including its ability to process the images. Human being is biologically intelligent agent and it is intuitive to think that "can machines process the images like human mind?" There are numerous parameters which vividly influences this question. Within the realm of classical artificial intelligence and cognitive science it is obvious to think that cognition can be reproduced by the machines and it also plays vital role in image processing. It is imperative to mention that animal intelligence displays extremely effective functioning in image processing. Animals live in an open world and researchers are trying to overcome the closed world hypothesis of the machine. In fact, many simple animals such as insects, fish, and frogs exhibit intelligence behavior yet have virtually no brain. Therefore, they must be doing something that avoids the frame problem. Further, it is assumed that sensors would give an accurate representation of the world. However, this is not often true. Sensors are always noisy and have vulnerabilities. Therefore, it is obvious that images are processed in the presence of uncertainty.

In fact, in different stream of science e.g., cognition, computation, psychology, philosophy, linguistic, anthropology, neuroscience etc, the term intelligence has varying implications. Genesis of the word intelligence is supposed to be from Latin word "intelligere" and is also associated with the Greek philosophical terms "nous". The meaning of "intelligere is to perceive or comprehend. In medieval period, the word "intellectus" were used for understanding. In past, these terms were used as impetus for explaining the metaphysical and cosmological theories of immortality pertaining to the soul. The common definition of intelligence assimilates different abilities to acquire, understand and apply knowledge. It can also be considered as the ability to exercise thought and reasoning process. Moreover, it is a beautiful amalgamation of thought, imagination, sight, and sound perception. Precisely we can say that intelligence encompasses the knowledge and facts acquired during the conscious and unconscious states. Further, one can express and feel emotions and perhaps much more through intelligence and it is acquired through study and experience.

Philosophically, intelligence displays a dual attribute with mind. It is subtler than the mind and at the same time acts as a substrate of mind to engage it in consciousness which in turn further strengthen the mind together with senses. It is obvious that rationality and irrationality, right and wrong of action are differentiated by means of intelligence. Intelligence is also pertinent to brain which is the substrate of mind. Brain can be considered analogous to the hardware of computing machines. Moreover, the hierarchical regions of the brain possess the ability to learn as well as to predict its future input sequence. The hierarchy of intelligence, mind, working senses, and dull matter is shown in Figure 1.

There are many implicit aspects related to mind. However, the insight to such related aspects is still obscure. In [1], the modern version of identity theory was proposed by Herbert Feigl. Further, it is inquisitive to think the relationship between mind, brain, and body. Perhaps, when we discuss the theory of mind philosophically, this relationship and other implicit aspects related to mind are of the paramount interest and deserve to discuss. Moreover, these questions also generate many other questions. Indeed, mind has always been a topic of interest for philosophers and different inquisitive questions related to mind still need philosophical explanation. In [2], attempt has been made to elucidate the different questions i.e. what is mind and brain and how is it related to body and how it affect the physical world? Moreover, in [2] a fundamental question is raised that whether the mind resides inside the head or in environment. Logically, it is hard to know about the others mind whether it is a living being or machine and it is also not easy to get the true recognition of the self. In [2], substantial attempt has been taken to elucidate all these inquisitive questions. An extensive literature survey reveals the fact that the views on these issues can be categorized into different domain. These are the:

- Dualism
- Materialism.
- Idealism
- Functionalism
- Anomalous monism

As per the canon of dualism, mind, brain and body are distinct entity. Moreover, there is dichotomy between mental and physical states. However, mind, brain, and body are associated in some fashion. In lieu of dualism, materialists consider the mind as a physical entity. Materialists believe that mental states are derivative of physical states. The idealism theory contradicts the materialists' theory. The idealism theory states that physical states are derivative of mental states. Further in [3], a theory was proposed which was against the dualism. Functionalism stems from behaviorism and the identity theory. Functionalism states that mental states implicate functional states anyway. These functional states play peculiar act within the purview of cognitive system. Functionalism was developed in the 1960s by David Armstrong [4]. Furthermore, anomalous monism view connects mental events with physical events. This theory further emphasizes that there are no strict laws for governing of the mental events themselves. In [5], it is argued that in general, the high level concept of an entity cannot be obtained in a low-level concept of the same entity. This is the reason behind the fact that when three dimensional images transformed in two dimension considerable information loss occur. If one is trying to capture the high level concepts in low level then it will become complex and arbitrary. This concept is more viable particularly in the domain of psychology. Within the purview of metaphysics, mental causation and the way mind influence the physical world is the central point of consideration. This issue is considered as the tangible difficulty for any form of dualism and materialism [6].

The mind and consciousness are two different entities. We can perceive that consciousness connects the mind with body as shown in Figure 1. In fact, a conscious system has to be aware as well as intelligent. It is a common phenomenon that unconscious state cannot convey pain or pleasure of the body to mind and vice versa. In [2], different phenomena pertaining to consciousness like what is consciousness and could a purely physical system be conscious are discussed. Further, it is obvious to think that is it possible to explain subjective experience in objective terms and how does the mind represent the world? These issues are discussed in [2]. The nature of belief and desire is also elucidated in [2]. Indeed, philosophy deals substantially and extensively with the intricacies of human mind. In fact, the oriental philosophy tries to establish the correlation between the thought process concerning the human's well being and mind.

Rest of the chapter is organized as follows: Section 2 gives the brief description of artificial intelligence (AI). Section 3 presents the brief literature survey of image processing. In section 4 attempts have been made to analysis the different aspects of mind, machine and images. Further, section 5 proposes different reasons which make image processing difficult. Section 6 renders the analytical view of limitations of image processing in case of machine mind and human mind. Finally, concluding remarks are given in section 7.

2. What is Artificial Intelligence?

It would be appropriate to define the term "intelligence" before defining the artificial intelligence. In [7], a profound definition of intelligence is given. However, in this definition of intelligence the relationship between intelligent agent and environment is missing. It is obvious that agent will be influenced by the external world and the action of agent will also influence its environment. From Dreyfus' point of view, this is the 'situatedness' of intelligence.

Indeed, it is not easy to define the term "Artificial Intelligence" (AI). Perhaps, it is a weird philosophical question and its systematic answer will require foundational details of AI.

Indeed, different definitions of AI reveal many new questions such as what are intelligent behavior and its characteristics, what exactly is the definition of mind and what are the essential components of mind. It is also inquisitive to think that how to develop mind in artificial agent for various purposes including performing the image processing and how artificial agent mimics the way human being manage to behave intelligently. Further, the nature of last question is not deterministic. Perhaps, the phenomenon of last question is empirical in nature and to answer this question requires the canon of psychology and cognitive science. Further, it is obvious that without having insight of the human thought process it would be difficult to build the intelligent machine. As a matter of fact, a deep philosophical contemplation of all these questions will certainly influence the course of AI.

In fact, there is no common globally accepted definition of Artificial intelligence. Perhaps, this is the reason researchers declare the belongingness of their work from the domain of "intelligent system" or "knowledge-based systems". However, it can be consider as the science of making machines whose act is usually referred as artificial intelligence. In [8], it is defined as "the study of ideas that enable computers to be intelligent". Further, in [9, 10], AI is defined in a simple and elegant manner.

Further, some researchers believe it is possible that machine cognition can perform many tasks more efficiently than the human intelligence including processing of the images. However, some researchers do not believe this phenomenon and they state that there is need to reset and redefine the philosophy and theories of AI as well as the relationship of AI and cognitive science. Indeed, there is need to redesign the modified version of AI from the realm of technical AI. Furthermore, some researchers also emphasizing the replacement of classical cognitive science with embodied cognition theory. We should also incorporate innovative approaches of AI like neuroscience and system theory and undoubtedly this will require reconsideration of basic questions related to computing, cognition, and ethics pertaining to AI.

2.1. History of AI

AI is considered as a recent field of study in psychology, computation, and cognition. Cognitive science is an interdisciplinary field which includes the computer models from the domain of AI and experimental techniques from Psychology and thus constructs the pragmatic theories pertaining to the working of human mind. Many ancient philosophers considered intelligence as a rational part of mind. Furthermore, the concept of logic which was a science of reasoning was commenced by Aristotle. It yielded the conclusion of a problem by proceeding in a step by step manner starting from a fixed set of prepositions. However, Rene Descartes (1596-1650), a French philosopher and mathematician pointed out a problem which was purely related to the physical and mechanical conception of mind. The development of logic paved the way of understanding the functioning of mind mathematically. Subsequently, George Boole (1815-1864) preludes the mathematical foundation of symbolic logic to Aristotle's system of reasoning as we understand it today. Further, Kenneth Craik (1914-1945) developed the domain of cognitive psychology.

The notions of today's computers have been formalized by Alen Turing (1912-1954) and he also rendered the mathematical characteristics regarding the functioning of computer program. Furthermore, the substantial concept of Decision Theory has been proposed by Von Neumann (1903-1957). Indeed, the Decision Theory was precursor of a new theory to distinguish the good and bad actions as was hypothesized by Socrates. In [11], McCulloch and Pitts introduced that how neurons might work in the brain. They used an electrical circuit to model a simple neural network and thus the sub-field of neural computing commenced its use in the AI.

Norbert Wiener compared the different characteristics of human and machine including the study of communication in human and machine which in turn emerged the cybernetics as an active area of research [12]. Cybernetics hybridized the concepts from information theory, feedback control systems (both biological and machine), and electronic computers. Further, the developments which have been made in formal grammars and logic during the early 1900s helped to provide new approaches of language theories. Further, several prototype systems have been developed including the Mark I Harvard relay computer (1944), the University of Pennsylvania Moore school of Electrical Engineering's ENIAC electronic computer (1947), and subsequent development of the Aberdeen Proving Ground's EDVAC and Sperry-Rand's UNIVAC. In this conjunction, it is genuine to say that the introduction of information theory which is mainly due to the work of Claude Shannon [13], neurological theories and models of the brain originated by psychologists, as well as the introduction of Boolean algebra, switching theory etc. further augmented the efficacy of AI. In fact, AI is not just the outcome of this century. Much ground work had been laid by many earlier researchers dating back several hundred years. These were the Aristotle, Leibnitz, Babbage, Hollerith, and many others which played significant roles in building of a foundation that eventually led to what we now know as AI. One of the first programs for automatic theorem proving was completed by Newell, Shaw, and Simon [14]. Further, Newell and Shaw developed programming for the logic theory machine [15]. The consequence of this development was completion of the processing language called IPL (Information Processing Language). Moreover, the development of FORTRAN (begun in 1954) and Noam Chomsky's work had a strong impact on AI.

The pattern recognition and self-adapting systems were the central area of interest by the researchers. During this period Rosenblatt's perceptron were receiving much attention [16]. Perceptrons are types of pattern recognition devices that have a simple learning ability based on linear threshold logic. Further, McCarthy developed the LISP programming language [17] which was the recognized programming language of A.I.

Furthermore, references on early work in AI include Newell and Simon's Human Problem Solving [18] and McCorduck's Machines Who Think [19].

2.2. Approaches of AI

Artificial intelligence is inter-linked with many other subjects. An inter-relation among different subjects as proposed by Gardner [20] is given in Figure 2. The two dichotomies of AI are summarizes in [21] as follows:

- Acting Humanly: It takes the Turing test approach [22]. If a machine passes the idea of Alan Turing's (1912-1954) "imitation game" it is said to be intelligent. In this game, both the interrogator and computer can communicate to each other by textual message. If the interrogator would not detect by questioning that a computer is there in the next room then we can consider that computer intelligent.
- Thinking Humanly: It is based on the cognitive modeling approach.
- Thinking Rationally: This approach is based on the logic and is incepted by the Greek philosopher Aristotile (384-322 B.C.).
- Acting rationally: It takes the rational agent approach. Agent can change its state by performing a set of pre-defined actions. For example, navigating robot has sensors and it can perform actions such as "turn left" and "go ahead".

In fact, there are many associated problems with the achievability of these tasks. These problems are mainly related with how to render intelligence that could be useful in applications. There are many factors which influence the usefulness of intelligence in applications such as background knowledge, intractability of computations, and structural limitations of the knowledge representation. The problems related with the achievability of these tasks are of diversified nature that arose from design community as well as from philosophical community.

In fact, many philosophers observed a clear rationalist view in the artificial intelligence. However, Dreyfus did believe in anti-rationalist paradigm. Further, the rational approach of AI is considered as the foundation stone of classical AI. Furthermore, Dreyfus analyzed this as a combination of three fundamental hypotheses:

- Psychological hypothesis
- Epistemological hypothesis
- Ontological hypothesis

Psychological hypothesis states that human intelligence is rule-based symbol manipulation and epistemological hypothesis states that all knowledge is formalizable. Further, Dreyfus critically analyzed these hypotheses and also propounded some new indispensable concepts for intelligence. He stated that intelligence is embodied and situated. However, it is difficult to visualize the embodiment in this sense. Perhaps, it is implicit that whether intelligence requires a body or it can only develop with the help

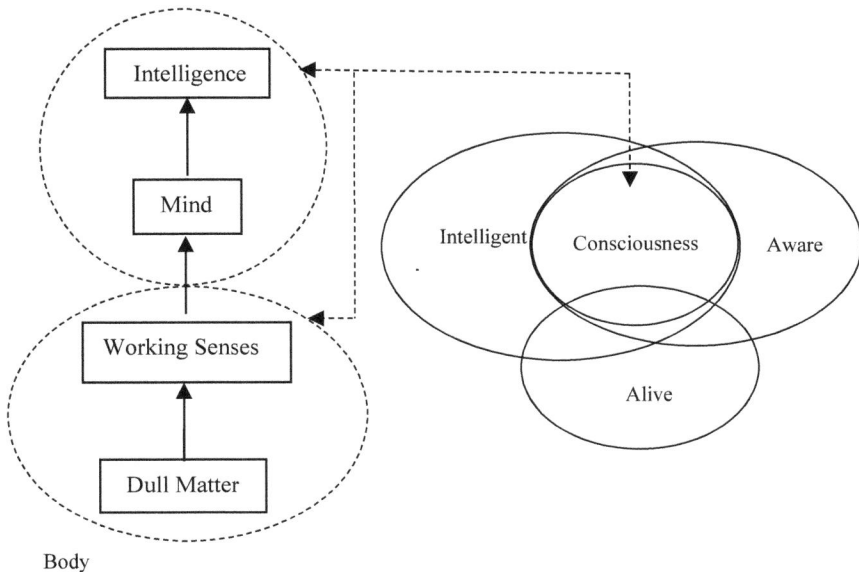

Figure1. Hierarchy of different components of intelligence

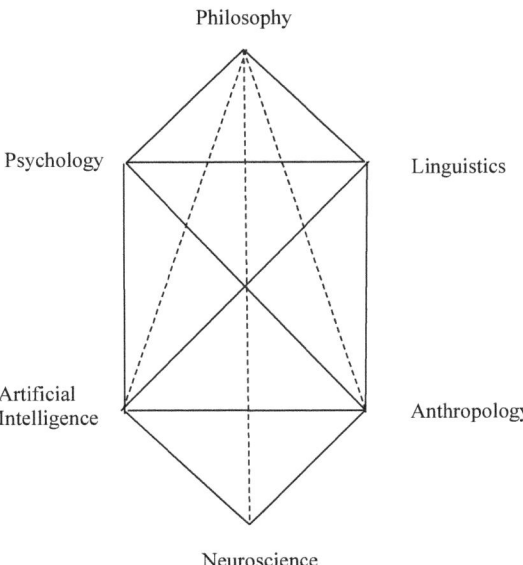

Figure2. Connection among the artificial intelligence, based on the Gardner, 1985, p. 37 [19]

of body [23]. Furthermore, in connectionist approach it is assumed that the intelligent behavior emanates from simulated structure and the simulated structure resembles the neuron and connections in the human brain. However, it is doubtful that whether a complexity of human brain is ever feasible in such machines.

Indeed, Dreyfus presented formidable work which offered substantial debate pertaining to the feasibility of AI goals. There are two limitations of Dreyfus approach. First, he mainly focused on strict symbolic approaches of AI and revealed the fact that it is not possible to construct real intelligent machine with the help of symbolic AI. In recent past, several attempts have been made regarding the construction of hybrid intelligent systems and in all these endeavor attempts have been made to incorporate non-rule based approaches in symbolic AI. These systems presented an exotic view of intelligence, which cannot be analyzed entirely by Dreyfus hypothesis. Second limitation of Dreyfus approach is based on the skepticism view on AI.

3. Image Processing: Brief Literature Survey

Image processing is supposed to commence in 1960s. In [24], it is given that image processing was used in different applications. Image processing is also used in electronic speckle pattern interferometry [25]. Further, in [26] the progresses in image processing during the past ten years have been discussed. The application of image-processing in computer system for automation of fringe analysis is proposed in [27]. Furthermore, in [28], the image processing aspects are discussed in phenomenon of data transmission. A survey of thresholding techniques are proposed in [29]. In [30], a new scheme has been proposed for image compression. This scheme takes into account the psycho visual features and it entails two steps. The first perform the wavelet transformation and a second step uses Shannon's rate distortion theory. Over and above, an image compression method using auto-associative neural network and embedded zero-tree coding is proposed in [31]. The method proposed in [31], the role of the neural network (NN) is to decompose the image stage by stage and thus render the analysis akin to wavelet decomposition. Working principle of this method is principal component extraction (PCE). The work given in [32] reflects a fully automated approach for segmentation of lungs in CT datasets. Moreover, a novel image compression technique is proposed in [33]. Indeed, there are mainly two categories of compression techniques. These are (a) Lossless Compression and (b) the compression which includes loss also. Some of these techniques displayed excellent results in certain applications whereas some other techniques perform well on different applications. A novel technique has been developed for image-processing which uses a multi resolution massive training artificial neural network [34]. This is highly nonlinear filter and it can be trained by using training images. In [35], a ridge detection algorithm is presented. This algorithm correctly diagnoses the indeterminate nodules. Further, an enhancement technique which is based on contrast limited adaptive histograms on transform domain coefficients called logarithmic transform coefficient adaptive histogram equalization is developed in [36]. A currency classification system which works using image processing technique is proposed in [37]. The processing effect and recognition accuracy is an important aspect in this work. In addition, a defect extraction approach for image segmentation has been proposed in [38]. The research given in [39] presents a contrast enhancement technique for X-Ray images. This technique uses Adaptive Neighborhood technique for contrast enhancement. The adaptive histogram equalization (AHE) is used as an enhancement capability on the soft tissue [40]. In this method, due to the high resolution, the images were cropped before being processed using adaptive histogram equalization. In [41], a diffraction-enhanced imaging is given and the capability of this method is observed for different types of tissues. This technique generates high spatial resolution and contrast of calcified and soft tissues. Indeed, it is a synchrotron based imaging technique. The method of medical image enhancement based upon non-linear technique and the logarithmic transform coefficient histogram equalization is proposed in [42]. It has been observed that the method given in [42] improves visual quality of images. Experimental results render its superiority over other commonly used enhancement techniques. The gray level co-occurrence matrix based image processing method is introduced for face recognition in [43]. Furthermore, a shape "break-and-repair" strategy is presented for medical image segmentation and it is applied to the segmentation of human lung and pulmonary nodules [44]. In this strategy, the regions that may cause any problems in segmentation are removed and then estimated using implicit surface fitting based on radial basis function. Moreover, a novel predictive model called active volume model is proposed in [45] for object boundary extraction. In [46], the use of software with edge detection and segmentation methods is given. This method produces the edge pattern and segment of brain and the brain tumor. Further, medical imaging is expensive and very much sophisticated because of proprietary software and expert personalities. In [47], the tasks of image analysis have been reviewed. In [48], it has been reported that in order to achieve an effective way to identify skin cancer at an early stage without performing any unnecessary skin biopsies, digital images of melanoma skin lesions can be investigated. Feature extraction plays vital role for image analysis in this approach. Moreover, a method is described for detecting effectively the presence of cancer cells in [49]. This method also reduces the overall time taken for diagnosis by carrying the whole process under biotelemetry. In addition, the work given in [50], describes an application for digital image processing and analysis. This method is substantially beneficial to healthcare domain to predict some major diseases of human beings. In the image processing system given in [50], the images of human palm are given as input to the system. This is why this method is supposed to work on medical palmistry.

4. Mind, Machine and Images

It is intuitive to think that can mind be explained in terms of machine? Can mind be replicated on machine? Very often the artificial intelligence (AI) researchers consider the mind as software and brain as hardware. They also consider the mind as pattern and the brain as a substrate. Further, researchers have been tried to establish the analogy of "senses as inputs", and "behavior as outputs". Neurons are considered as the smallest processing units of the brain and synapses as "circuitry". Indeed, this analogy is simply based on some casual presumption and is not justified by the actual working of the computer. It is important to analyze if there is any philosophical base under this analogy. It is also important to envisage the implication of this analogy from the subject point of view whether it correctly reveals the present state of AI research. Further, it is pragmatic to think whether the metaphor "mind-as-machine" can be treated as a discipline or it is merely a dogma. Broadly speaking, computer is a machine that can perform many different procedures rather than just one or few and this procedure is known as algorithm whereas nature of biological mind is more versatile.

Many researchers consider mind as computer metaphor [51] and presented substantial theories. It is explicit that storing of structured data in the memory for the purpose of image processing is the characteristics of machine. Further, attempts have been made to solve the interesting problems related to image processing by manipulating the stored data in systematic ways. The entire task can be accomplished by executing appropriate instructions. Perhaps a similar model could explain and eventually help to duplicate human thought.

In this sequel, author would like to put forth the Turing-machine functionalism which can be considered as the natural extension of CTM [52]. Indeed, the Turing-machine functionalism visualize mind as a giant Turing machine and its working is specified by a set of instructions. These instructions dictate that if mind receives certain input in certain state then a state transition will occur and output is produced. Further, it is pertinent to mention that probabilistic transitions are also allowed in some versions of Turing-machine functionalism. These models of Turing-machine formalism are substantially popular but least implausible. In [51], one more model is proposed which is closely related to CTM. This model is called 'Physical Symbol System Hypothesis (PSSH)'. Further, the machine based on physical symbol system can be considered similar to variety of syntactic operations. Moreover, there have been various internal disagreements such as questions of innateness among different models like CTM, PSSH, and Turing-machine functionalism. These models also loosely characterize "classical" or "symbolic" AI. In [53], these models are also termed as "good old-fashioned AI" (GOFAI).

In the sequel of mind and machine, it is pertinent to mention that matter is only reality in the universe. However, non-materialist neuroscientists have a different ideology. The materialist scientists claim that the brain produces consciousness and perhaps memory is the most important aspect of consciousness. The canon of materialist philosophy claims that our memories behave as repositories of brains. Perhaps, decay and change is the law of nature irrespective of mind and machine. Therefore, it is obvious to think that do the dying cells transfer the memories to the new cell? I would like to express this analogy to write a message on a wall and then gradually replace the particles that comprise the wall. Suppose we replace all the surface particles of that wall and find that the resulting surface of the wall still reads the same message written on it. It is obvious that such phenomenon cannot be explained by virtue of materialistic philosophy because mechanistic and purely materialistic philosophy has its own associated constraints. Perhaps, non-materialistic philosophy seems to be more pragmatic.

The philosophy of "transcends biology" is substantially helpful in explaining this complexity. According to this philosophy, memories are stored in brain as well as in mind simultaneously. Memories are made available to newly formed brain cells from mind when the old cells die out.

4.1. Machine and Images

Human are able to perceive and understand the world surrounding them, while machine aims to duplicate the effect of human vision by electronically perceiving and understanding on image. It is difficult task to make machine able to see, perceive, and understand the images of the world. Further, human beings live in a three-dimensional world and human mind has developed through the process of evolution the efficacy to analyze the world around them with incredible efficiency, accuracy, and precision. However, when machines try to analyze objects in 3D space, the visual sensors usually produce two-dimensional images. The transformation of images from 3D space to 2D space causes huge amount of substantial information loss. In some peculiar cases, some devices can produce 3D images but this might be a debatable issue and even more analyzing 3D datasets is explicitly more complicated than 2D.

Indeed, the scientific evidences obtained so far are in favor of the "transcends biology" and is against the materialistic approach. The perception that we can create a machine which has a mind to process the image is not a new one. It has featured in entertaining and frightening fictions since long. In early to mid-twentieth century, this fiction has emerged the term of "mechanical men" or robots. In present scenario, the idea of a mechanical mind has paved the way to the new stream of computational artificial intelligence. Indeed, the enhancement of artificial intelligence domain comprises of technological as well as philosophical advancement. In twentieth century, the philosophy of mind has observed a substantial enrichment and thus the currently dominant theory becomes the precursor for the possibility of machine mind which can process the images like human mind. In fact, different philosophical theories also require a sound understanding of what a machine is? It is author's candid view that mind, intelligence, consciousness, emotions etc, all are the outcome of vivid intensity of bio-chemical reactions which are taking place inside the brain cells and it is inquisitive to think that is it possible to get the same outcome from mechanical means that we are getting from bio-chemical reaction that too even when we do not know exactly about that bio-chemical reactions. This is what we really trying for advancement of mechanical mind for the pursuit of image processing. Further, we must have to impose some necessary conditions on the development of artificial intelligence and subsequently on mechanical mind e.g., embodied experience is a must for advancement of semantics which, in turn, are necessary for having a mind.

There are two substantial ways for exogenous development of machine mind for image processing. These are (1) conceptual understanding of mind so that a machine mind can be developed and (2) the computational framework of brain. As it has already been stated that the machine in which embryonic artificial intelligence or mind is created for image processing must have the capacity of embodied experience and this is motivated by the fact that biological being also possess the capacity of embodied experience. Therefore, the machine in which mind is to be inculcated must possess sensory components to establish relations between it and the external world so that machine can receive the images of the world as an input. Perhaps, to develop a machine mind for the purpose of image processing similar to human mind is still in the primitive stage and much philosophical and technical advancement is required in this pursuit.

Indeed, human mind is surprisingly effective to perform the sequence of operations such as image capturing, early processing, segmentation, model fitting, motion prediction, qualitative and quantitative inference etc. However, in case of machine it is highly complicated to perform these tasks effectively. Each of these tasks requires number of efficient algorithms and intelligence. Moreover, there are two pertinent issues in realm of image processing. There are: (a) the closed world assumption and (b) frame problem. The closed world assumption says that the world model contain everything the machine need to know. If the closed world assumption is violated, the machine may not perform correctly the image processing task. But, on the other hand, it is easy to forget to put all necessary details into the world model. As a result, the success of the machine depends on how well the human programmer can think of everything.

Further, the manner of processing and distribution of sensory data is an important phenomenon in image processing. It is intuitive to think that how much a person or machine or animal is influenced by what it senses. In some paradigms, use of sensor information is bounded in a specific or dedicated way. In such situation the image processing is local to each machine function. However, in other paradigms it is assumed that entire sensory information will be first processed into one global world model and subsequently subsets of the model will be distributed to other machine functions as needed. But it is highly difficult for the programmer to entail all the details in program because resulting world model is likely to be huge. The opposite of the closed world paradigm is known as open world paradigm. In this paradigm, it is believed that closed world hypothesis cannot be applied to that particular domain. No doubt, machines are good at tedious algorithm but the formal representation of the world and to maintain every change about it is really hard. This renders the image processing by machine difficult. Furthermore, it is also intuitive to think that how difficult it would be to modify the planning algorithm if the world model could suddenly change. The algorithm could get lost between recursions. In addition, the facts and axioms which frame the world very often become too numerous for realistic domain and thus make image processing difficult for the machine. In the following sub-section 4.2, attempt will be made to analyze the intuitive question; could machine have a mind?

4.2. Could Machine Have a Mind?

Indeed, the question of whether a machine could ever think, could it experience emotions, or to have a mind: is not really new one. These questions touch upon deep issues of philosophy. In this sub-section attempt has been made to give new impetus to these aspects.

There are mainly two approaches pertinent to the philosophy of mind as mentioned in section 1. These are the dualism and functionalism. The dualism and functionalism are substantially endowed by René Descartes and B.F. Skinner respectively. Within the realm of dualism, mind and intelligence is considered as non-physical and spiritual and thus it creates doubt to understand or imitate human mind purely on the basis of the physical means. In lieu of this, the philosophy of functionalism renders the mind analogous to a computing machine. Functionalism asserts that mind is an information processing machine like computer and it receives inputs by sensory organs as well as from existing mental state. Further, mind processes all these information and produces new behavior and mental states. The two important concepts which can distinguish dualism and functionalism are ontological and epistemic concept. The ontological concepts describe the nature of mind and epistemic concepts describe how mind can be known.

Turing test have substantial impact on cognitive science and his work seems to fall within the purview of behaviorism. In [54], the Turing's proposal has been challenged and it was concluded that a program in execution i.e. process could not understand the conversation. Two important limitations are worthy to consider (1) is it possible to know with certainty that any other being thinking? (2) Is the conversation only the paramount way to assess the person's intelligence?

In fact, from Turing's perspective the question "Can machines think?" does not deserve discussion. He asserted that passing the Turing Test constitutes thinking and perhaps it is a yardstick to measure the substantiality of AI research from experimental to philosophical level. However, it is my candid view that it is not meaningless to discuss "Can machine think"? Some time author feels that belief network is a good attempt to cause machine think. However, it is paramount to dwell upon what does it mean to think or to feel? What is a mind? Does mind really exists? Perhaps, philosophy is indispensable for study of mind. However, it is a fact that philosophy does not provide foundations for core study of mind but its contribution cannot be underestimated.

Moreover, the knowledge about mind can be obtained by means of introspection. Contrary to this, Skinner's approach consider mind as an entity to study the behavior. Undoubtedly, some AI researcher will not like to use a computer metaphor to describe the mind but they would prefer to say that such description is not sufficed to understand the mind. However, the term "mentality" which I would like to replace by the term "mental process" is chiefly understandable entirely in computational terms. Perhaps, mental processes display behavior which relies upon observation and experimentation.

Indeed, physical means cannot create tangible reflection of mind and intelligence because these are the subtle entity. However, philosophically it is possible to have mind in a machine. Indeed, the concept of machine seems to be based on dichotomy between dualism and functionalism and neither dualism nor functionalism can explain the true nature of mind. It requires an alternative approach that considers behavior as evidence for the existence of non-reductive, semiotic modes of mentality. This approach is usually treated as "Computational conception of mind". Further, in the realm of computation a program is independent of the hardware but it is also a fact that it depends on some physical representation just to execute. Therefore, comparison of mental process with computer process leads the question that is there any entity which if in execution produces "mental process" like program in execution produces computer process? In this approach "mentality" is treated as "computer process" i.e., program in execution and thus human and machines are supposed to operate in similar ways. However, since the inception of the AI, the replication of 'mentality' in machine was an inquisitive domain. However, certain pitfalls were always associated with domain. Perhaps, to conclude that whether machine could have mind one should envisages on following issues:

- How do we define that machine has a mind?
- Is there any method to identify or prove that machine does have a mind?

The experiment given in [54] tried to differentiate between the syntactic and semantic properties of the symbols. This experiment attempted to extract the syntactic properties of the symbol and consequently concluded that a program cannot impart mind to a computer irrespective of how intelligently it may programmed. Precisely, functioning of the machines depend on the syntactic properties of the symbols and is independent of the semantic properties. As a matter of fact, if a computer is manipulating the syntactic features of the symbols only and is entirely oblivious of the semantic features could not have a mind because semantic property is of the paramount importance for the mind.

Mind is closely associated with the learning process in which the mind irrespective of biological or artificial establishes connections between syntactic and semantic properties. This connection is established by using a set of commands or methods. In fact, learning process is a sort of mental process during which different attributes e.g., acquiring new knowledge, modify existing knowledge, values, behavior, or synthesizing of the different information takes place. The new knowledge produced can be stored for the further retrieval to percept the things. We can compare this phenomenon with the natural evolution which looks like a program rewriting itself. Precisely, learning is a mapping from syntactic properties to semantic properties.

Further, the functioning of machine is based on the syntactic properties of symbols instead of semantic properties. Perhaps, it is not possible to inculcate the semantic properties in a machine obliviously. It could be possible only when the input information is fetched into the machine's memory by human mind. Indeed, perception of a symbol incorporates both the syntactic and semantic properties. Syntactic properties allow minds (biological or artificial) to recognize particular symbol whereas semantic properties let the mind to retrieve the meaning of that symbol from the archive. Obviously, it is a point to ponder that: (1) Do the semantic properties of symbols stored in DNA? Does the mind retrieve these properties from DNA? (2) Does mind possess any specific part or function to understand the semantic properties? As on date, there is no any evidence for the first case. The second case is more viable instead of the fact that storage capacity of the human brain is finite. We can consider learning process as a tradeoff between these two cases. Indeed, construction of artificial agent is a sensor dependent process and as author has already stated in section 4 that agent in which AI is to be inculcated must possess sensory components to establish relations between it and the external world. Author's view is that the true perception of any object is beyond the limit of sensory inputs of the artificial agent. Perhaps, the true perception can be obtained by the inference, not by the inference which deals with sense data of the input images and frames concepts on their basis but inference which works in its own right.

All true intelligence is intelligence by identity. Our intelligence through physical contact or mental symbols is indirect and approximate because the true knowledge of the things is perceived by the intelligence and it is beyond the reach of the senses. Therefore, the author doubt that the artificial intelligence created in an agent is really intelligence. However, attempt has been made to discuss this issue philosophically in sub-section 4.3.

Neurobiologists believe that it is paramount to identify the actual relationship between the biological neural network and consciousness which is an ensemble outcome of mind, experience and understanding. This relationship is termed as "neural correlates of the consciousness". It is given in [55] that human nature and mind is profound and unknowable. Further, mind cannot be described simply in procedural or computational terms. However, this "neural correlates of consciousness" plays vital role in all the problems pertaining to the learning process as well as the set of the order of execution. In fact, if the semantic properties are not in the archive of brain, we cannot perceive symbols e.g., learning of a language is the process of establishing the connections between syntactic and semantic properties of symbols used in that language. In order to argue the non-mechanical nature of mind; its highest level components such as consciousness, emotion, and intelligence seem to be more pragmatic. This type of argument is given in [55].

Since long, philosophers and theologians have speculated about the nature of human mind using the functionalism [56]. This theory produces an essence of mental states. Indeed, functions can also be implemented on the machines and thus functionalism states that mental states are similar to the software states of a machine. Therefore, it can be asserted that a machine could have mental states and seems to have a mind, belief, hope etc. Further, it can again be asserted that machine could have intelligence.

There are two important theories to describe the nature of mind. One is the given by Joseph Weizenbaum [52] and second is given by Rodney Brooks [57]. In [55], higher level of mind is used to describe its nature whereas in [33], lowest levels of mind are described to assert its mechanical nature. In [57], it is asserted that mind is also a machine and thus it must be described in computational terms like brain is supposed to be.

Indeed, both the theories given in [55] and [57] fail to acknowledge that the mind may be simultaneously like and dislike a machine and it depends on the level at which it is being described. In [58], it is argued that human intelligence and expertise depends basically on unconscious instincts. Perhaps, human intelligence and expertise does not depend on conscious symbolic manipulation. It is an obvious fact that some phenomenon like meditation cannot possible to describe in computational terms. Many robots mimic humans and animals. However, human and animals have feeling or experience of making unconscious decision. It is obvious to think that can a robot make unconscious decision? It is also important to think whether the functioning of mind depends upon its physical structure and if the answer is affirmative how are they associated?

It is also possible that mind might be able to function independently of such structures. We also have to ponder that is it necessary the relevant structures be biological in nature (brains) associated with bio-chemical reactions or might mind be equally well associated with pieces of electronic equipments? Indeed, the quality of human judgment and understanding emerges from the consciousness.

It is intuitive to think is there any "machine soul" inside the machine which can create the "machine consciousness" in the machine. Sometime I tempted to envisioned operating system as the "machine soul" and different system programs as the "machine consciousness" of different aspects. The author does not know is it genuine to establish this analogy? And the author would like to leave this aspect on reader to decide whether this analogy seems comical or sound serious.

From extensive literature survey this fact has been observed that research towards the philosophical aspects of machines conscious was an active area of research. However, very limited works have been done in this pursuit by various researchers [59, 60]. Further, some more authors have done substantial work in this direction [61-69]. Moreover, if we assume that the mind is similar to a program even it would not be possible to conclude that what's inside the mind is irrelevant [70-74]. Perhaps limited work in this domain is due to the complex and provocative nature of the related terms like thought, awareness, attention etc.

4.3. Could Machine Really Have Intelligence?

Do machines can ever be intelligent? Today, computers are being used in different domain even to improve the human intelligence. Researchers are constantly toiling to embed the ability and flexibility of human intelligence into the machine while it still requires lot of efforts. Undoubtedly, AI trailed substantial effort in this pursuit but it is yet to think whether this rapidly evolving technology can challenge human intellect? As on date, the most intelligent computer in the world is perhaps as smart as an ant. In 1960, researchers obtained substantial success in the domain of AI and they predicted that truly intelligent machines might follow in recent future. In [75], statement of Herbert Simon is quoted: "Machines will be capable, within twenty years, of doing any work a man can do". However, true machine intelligence is still not a reality as on date. Perhaps, it might be materialized in distant future.

Extensive literature survey revealed the fact that by the early 1950's the primitive question that 'is it possible for machine to thin?' is changed by other question that "is it possible for machine to deal with physical symbol?'. Further, it is also intuitive to think that can machine perform structure-sensitive rules thinking? It seems logical that this question renders an improvement. It is because of the fact that formal logic and computational theory observed major developments in past five decades. Many researchers give affirmative answer in response to question could a machine think? Perhaps, the first reason behind affirmation is related with computability of the function. Indeed, if a function is effectively computable then it implicates that function will also be recursively computable. Author would like to elaborate that here the term effectively computable implicates a procedure which determines the output for a given input within finite time interval. The second reason behind this is the important result given by Alan M. Turing. A recursive computable function can be computed in finite time by Turing machine. Such Turing machine is also called as "Universal Turing Machine". Moreover, the Turing machine is a symbol-manipulating machine. Precisely, these two results implicate that a symbol-manipulating machine is considered as consciously intelligent machine provided it passes the Turing test. However, these two results assure that a suitable symbol-manipulating machine could compute an effective function. Thus, the challenging task before the researcher is two-fold. First challenge is to identify the complex function. This complex function is supposed to control the human pattern of response in lieu of environment. Further, the second task is, writing of the program by which the symbol-manipulating machine can compute it. In fact, these goals are fundamental in the domain of classical AI. Moreover, these goals create fundamental research program pertaining to AI.

In fact, there are two profound topic of interest in the realm of AI. These are 'Can machine perform intelligently'? Or 'can computer think and perform action like human being or other biologically intelligent agent?" depends on how we envisage ourselves and the machines considered. It is highly complicated and skeptical to believe that machine which is a man made physical object could possess intelligence like biological agent which has something mysterious and special. Classical AI and cognitive science do claim that cognition is computable. Therefore, it is explicit from the perspective of classical AI and cognitive science that cognition can be reproduced by the machine and perhaps machine surpasses the abilities of human intelligence. However, it is ridiculous to believe because the functioning of machines depends strictly on logic; they can do the things for which they are programmed. Therefore, it seems to be paradoxical that a man made machine touch the ability of its creator.

It is explicit that AI algorithms are consistently finding the solution of given problem by applying the heuristic approach in which the form of reasoning is not logical. Researchers have invented innovative designs for problems which have never been visualized by the system programmer [76]. Computer has learnt to play chess and perhaps computers can play a provably perfect game [77]. However, can we impart sixth sense to a machine? Sixth sense or subtle perception is the ability of biological beings to perceive the subtle-dimension or the unseen world. Sixth sense also facilitates us to understand the subtle cause and effect relationship behind many events. Moreover, this ability is beyond the understanding of the intellect and thus it appears that there is a need to re-establish the philosophy and theory of AI and cognitive science.

Brains are poorly designed for calculation and information storage purposes. However, in case of machine there is no such limitation. There is plethora of algorithms for different types of problems which can vividly be used in machines. From the subject point of view of some peculiar acts, human brain which can also termed as a 'meat machine' is certainly not as efficient as machines. The author would like to assert that the construction of such intelligent machine which can replicate the brain's design might be a reality. Perhaps the brain's algorithm is close to optimal for some things, but it is certainly not optimal for all the problems. However, it is likely to perceive the possibility of improvement over brain regarding the algorithm, hardware and scale. In fact, it is obvious that brain is highly complex system and is still incredible to any other man-made objects in many ways. Indeed, we can perceive such objections as a particular stream of philosophy known as "vitalism" i.e. we suppose that some supreme power is at work when science could not explain some unusual phenomenon.

The author wish to point out that if the brain is essentially just a machine, which appears to be the case then it, is certainly not the most intelligent machine that could exist. This idea is reasonable once we think about it: machines can easily carry more, fly higher, move faster and see further than even the most able animals in each of these categories. Why would human intelligence be any different? Perhaps, machine can perform many tasks with great precision and effectiveness yet machine could not be treated more intelligent than humans. This is because of the fact that it is highly complex to develop micro level phenomena such as mood, mentality, emotions etc in machines.

Composition of poem by an AI computer is a common phenomenon. This fact created different orientations from different researchers and they insisted that machine possesses intelligence. Contrary to this, another group of researchers have different opinion they think that machine has accomplished this task in a mechanical manner without understanding the real essence of the poem. In fact, processing of a program which is based on a successful algorithm does not implicate that understanding is taking place. Therefore, it is obvious that just composing a poem does not implicate that machine has intelligence.

Indeed, philosophy reveals the fact that the intelligence of human being can not be generated through a mechanical process rather its impetus is consciousness. Further, within the purview of Indian philosophy the brain is treated as non-intelligent and consciousness uses the brain as a computing instrument.

For decades, researchers did believe that computer can be intelligent provided when it is powerful. However, the author is individually not agreeing with this view.

Indeed, brain and computers perform substantially in different manner. It is true that brain constitutes a network of neurons and it can perform variety of tasks in efficient manner and it also requires a huge quantity of memory to model the world. Brain is able to predict the future event with great accuracy with the help of this memory based model. Undoubtedly, future prediction is the important attribute of intelligence. It is also obvious that simple neural networks can create intelligent more easily and successfully in comparison to computer program.

It is author's view that machine can perform action intelligently but author doubt that a machine percept intelligently and philosophically. Therefore, from this philosophical kaleidoscope, machine can be asserted non-intelligent. Indeed, intelligence is a component of the subtle material entity. Further, the material entity that composes this world is highly complex and infinite and it is impossible to understand all these by finite intellect. Perhaps this is the reason we try to classify and categorize this material entity in smaller granules to make it lucid, comprehensive and easy to imbibe in our finite intellect. Therefore, it is vacuous to attempt to make a machine as intelligent as human brain because the human brain in itself is not absolutely intelligent. Perhaps, this may be the reason that we could not develop any machine which possesses intellect equivalent to human being.

The author would like to incorporate that philosophically there are amazing variety of ways in which one may approach the true consciousness and intelligence. However, it is impossible for any effort of logical reason to percept the true scenario of ultimate reality. The philosophical perspective of metaphysics entails that no manifestation is to be taken as absolute true, while from the stand point of experience, every one of them has some validity. Therefore, this is the author's view that whatever we trying to inculcate in an agent is not "intelligence" in true sense. Indeed, the pure and transcendent intelligence is different from scientific intelligence, though it is not discontinuous from it. Further, every science expresses in its own fashion and within a certain order of things and thus reflects the higher immutable truth in which everything of any reality must be incorporated. Scientific or discriminative intelligence prepares us for the higher wisdom. However, scientific intelligence when inculcated inside the machine, it displays very limited and confined behavior. The miscellaneous limitations of AI are discussed philosophically in the forth coming section.

5. Why is Image Processing Difficult?

Image processing is an important paradigm in the domain of computer science and it is deeply related with the artificial intelligence, machine cognition, and machine vision. Perhaps, computer vision is difficult. In this section author will try to render some philosophical insight regarding this question. The first and foremost reason behind the difficulty of machine vision is due to the loss of information when three dimensional entity is converted into the two dimensional entity. Further, interpretation of the images requires a substantial degree of intelligence and as on date artificial intelligence of the machine is very less than human intelligence. Moreover, when a biologically intelligent creature like human being tries to interpret the image his previous experience and knowledge also plays a vital role. Human beings are able to apply their stored knowledge in an excellent manner to solve the new problem. The domain of AI is still in developing phase and lot of research is still requiring augmenting the capacity of machine vision so that effective image processing can be performed. From several decades, AI is trying to enrich the machine with the ability to understand observations. No doubt the progress in this pursuit is substantial yet the practical ability of machine to understand observations is still very limited. In fact, researchers are trying to solve the related multidisciplinary scientific problems. The systems capable of solving the multidisciplinary scientific problems are termed as "cognitive systems" and this characteristic is paramount for the development of intelligent machine. The concept of interpretation is considerably advantageous in the realm of image processing. Indeed, it paves the way for the application of syntax and semantics of propositional and first order predicate logic. In image processing image observations is often consider as an instance of formal expressions and semantics reveals the relationship between expressions and their meaning. It is explicit that interpretations of images require high degree of AI and interpretations can be treated as an instance of semantics.

Further, second reason behind this question is noise. In fact, noise is an unavoidable fact in any measurement of the real world and machines are not properly equipped with AI to deal with these short comings. Noise incorporates certain degree of uncertainty in the image and thus it demand different mathematical tools such as fuzzy logic and probability theory to deal the uncertainty involved. Presence of noise also renders the analysis of images stochastic in nature. Moreover, application of complex mathematical tools makes the entire process of image analysis complex in comparison to deterministic method used for the analysis. It is also obvious that accuracy of image analysis will not be more in case of stochastic analysis. In addition, application of complex mathematical tool for noise removal may also require high degree of AI and machine learning. Thirdly, in the image processing task the machine has to tackle huge quantity of data associated with image and video and it requires considerable degree of machine perception, machine cognition, and AI. Furthermore, the real time processing of huge data is a challenging task and it requires suitably designed algorithm besides intelligence, perception, cognition, and hardware support. Fourthly, the brightness measurement is an important task in the image analysis. Indeed, the brightness and intensity of the image depends on many factors such as type and position of the light source, the position of the observer relative to the source etc. Image brightness also depends on the surface and geometry of the object as well as reflexive properties of the object's surface. The brightness measurement is also stochastic in nature and it requires a machine with substantial intelligence. Further, as on date the AI of machine is sufficiently less than the human intelligence which in turn render the image analysis difficult. Moreover, in image processing the phenomenon of image understanding can be envisage as an attempt to find a relation between input image(s) and previously established models of the observed world. It is to some extent similar to the working of associative memory neural network. Further, in the phenomenon of image understanding the transition from the input image data to the previously established model of the observed world substantial quantity of relevant information is lost. In fact, the process of image understanding is performed in many steps and several levels of image representation are used. The lower most layers entail raw image data whereas the upper most levels attempt to interpret the data. The artificial intelligence of machine plays vital role in this intermediate representation of image.

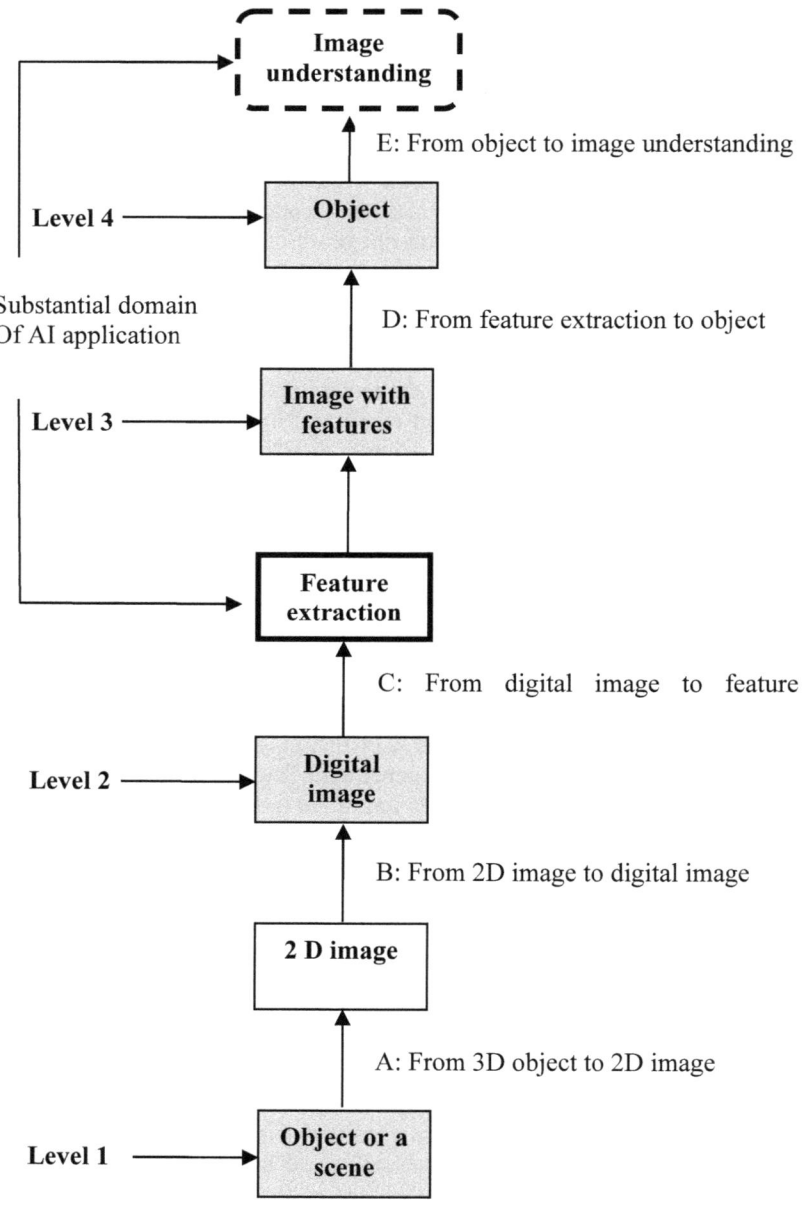

Figure3. Four levels of image representation with substantial domain of AI

The machine vision designs these intermediate representations of the images. It is the crucial role of AI to establish and maintain relations between entities within and between layers.

Data organization is an important task in machine intelligence and it is of the paramount importance in the classification of image representation. Four possible levels of image representation with the domain where artificial intelligence has substantially been used are shown in Figure 3. Figure 3 renders a bottom up approach of the information processing. This bottom up approach entails the flow of information from low level i.e., from signals which have zero or least abstraction to high level abstraction. It is indispensable to mention that this transition of low level abstraction to high level abstraction requires substantial degree of AI. It is also pertinent to mention that the flow of information is not necessarily unidirectional. Very often feedback loop is also introduced and it creates the requirement of suitably designed machine learning algorithm. Further, image processing can be broadly classified into two categories. These are:

- Low level image processing
- High level image processing

The low level image processing generally requires little knowledge and intelligence. Different tasks performed in low level image processing are image compression, pre-processing of images, edge extraction, image sharpening etc. Moreover, low level image processing is mainly associated with the input images. Perhaps, the first step in the low level image processing is digitization of the image and thus machine must possess a suitably designed machine learning algorithm for this purpose. In contrast high level image processing requires high degree of AI in machine. High level image processing is based on knowledge, goals, and plans of how to achieve those goals. Further, AI methods are widely used for high level image processing. Moreover, high level image processing also requires artificial cognition which mimics the functionality of human cognition. Indeed, high level image processing starts with some form of formal model of the world, and then the "reality" perceived in the form of digitized images is captured to the model [78]. Furthermore, machine vision is expected to solve very complex tasks and thus it is formidable to have sufficient potential of AI in the machine.

Perhaps, image processing cannot be accomplished without image segmentation. It is a core step of image processing in which machine tries to separate objects from the image background and from each other. In addition, image segmentation can be total or partial as per the requirement. However, total segmentation is possible only for very simple tasks but in case of partial segmentation AI plays vital role. Low and high-level image processing differs in many respects. One important differentiation between these two is that they both use different data. Low- level image processing use the data associated with original image whereas in high level image processing, the data originates in the image as well, but only those data which are relevant to high-level goals are extracted and thus reducing the data quantity considerably. Therefore, it is obvious that machine must entail the various characteristics of AI and cognition for this purpose. The ordering of low-level steps to solve a specific task is a complicated and open problem. The automation of ordering of low-level steps has not yet been achieved. This task is even today completed by human operator. In this task the human operator obtain the domain specific knowledge. Moreover, the uncertainty involved depends on the operator's intuition and on his previous experience [78]. Furthermore, image understanding is of the paramount importance in high-level image processing and the role of AI formidable in this pursuit. Perhaps, this task is very complicated and computationally intensive.

6. Limitations in Image Processing: Machine Mind versus Human Mind

It is obvious that the role of AI is of the paramount importance for the task of image processing. Further, whatever the restriction of AI might be will also be render as the limitations of image processing. It is intuitive fact that provably whatever is imagined and hypothesized cannot be happen in AI. This fact is also true for the task of image processing. Indeed, the functioning of AI and thus of the image processing is always associated with some inevitable and inherent limitations. One such limitation is given in [79]. Mathematical explanation of these limitations is hard. However, philosophically these limitations are easily explainable. In fact, any scientific theory commenced and based on a set of assumptions. This is called axioms and these axioms are self-evident truths. The subsequent proof of any theorems relies upon these axioms. The Godel's first completeness theorem given in [79] says:

> *"Given any axiom system, there will always be some true statement which the system will not be able to prove".*

The foundation stone of artificial intelligence is that the human mind is understandable by means of mathematical and logical tools. Perhaps, this is not a complete truth even as on date. We know only some facts and partial facts regarding our mind. Moreover, we could never be able to know complete reality of our mind. In fact, human being knows only a part of his being and that is only the surface reality. There is a good deal beneath the surface of which he has no knowledge though it has effects on his conduct. We are sometimes completely overcome by emotions, instinctive and involuntary reactions that upset the rule of conscious reason. In [79], Godel propounded his first and second theorem. Godel's first law creates the susceptibility that there exist some truths about our mind. However, it is not ever possible for us to know these truths. Certainly, this will influence the power of AI adversely and thus creates limitations in the realm of image processing. This is due to the fact that without knowing and understanding our own mind it would be unjustified to say that we can develop a machine which would be as intelligent as the human being. Moreover, it would also be wrong to say that machine can perform the task of image processing utterly as effective and efficient as humans can.

In [79], incompleteness theorem is given. This theorem deals with consistency. Indeed, a formal system which contains axioms is said to be consistent if any stamen proved by the system is either true or false. Contrary to this system is said to be inconsistent if the statement proved by the system is true and false both. We can further elaborate the theorem of incompleteness as follows:

> *"If an axiom system is consistent, then it cannot verify its own consistency".*

The influence of this law is severe and it causes adverse implications on AI. It implicates that if we design a machine for image processing, then that machine cannot justify its own consistency. It is due to the fact that robot has been designed and developed by means of a set of scientific axioms. Further, as per this theorem, human mind is not just a system which suppose to work on as set of axioms. Perhaps, the functioning of human mind is beyond the axioms. Therefore, it is explicit that machine cannot usher human mind in image processing.

7. Conclusions

Mind is closely associated with the learning process and can perform numerous tasks including image processing. Learning processes are also associated with machines to perform the image processing tasks vividly. The learning process for image processing requires establishing connections between syntactic and semantic properties so that feature extraction and image understanding can be done precisely and efficiently. In fact, learning process for the image processing of the machine mimics the mental process during which information processing is taking place in human mind for the very purpose of image processing. Indeed, the philosophical question that 'can machine be intelligent?' or 'can machine think and act like human being or other biologically intelligent agent are discussed in the light of images and there processing. It is highly complicated and skeptical to believe that machine can process the images as efficiently as human mind. After all, machine is a man made physical object. The Gödel's first and second theorem which deals with consistency also supports this ideology. In fact, a machine could have a mind or does machine possesses intelligence is still a skeptical discussion. However, it can be asserted that machine can be as intelligent as human being if it can achieve the feature of self-learning and self-improving process and then machine would be supposed to perform the task of image processing similar to human beings. These two are the essential attribute of the intelligence. The trail of advancement in science and technology which have been observed in past are emanating the possibilities that machines could perform the task of image processing excellently like human mind will be a reality in near future.

References

[1]   Feigl, H., *The 'Mental' and the 'Physical'*, University of Minnesota Press, 1958, reprinted 1967.

[2]   David J. Chalmers, *Philosophy of Mind: Classical and contemporary readings*, Oxford University press, 2002.

[3]   Ryle, G., *The concept of mind*, Hutchinson and Co., 1949.

[4]   Armstrong, D. M, *A Materialist Theory of the Mind*, Routledge and Kegan Paul, 1968.

[5]   Fodor, J., Special sciences: Still autonomous after all these years, *Philosophical Perspectives* 11(1997), 149-63.

[6]   Kim. J., *Mind in a Physical World*, MIT Press, 1998.

[7]   McCarthy, John, and Hayes, Patrick J., *Some Philosophical Problems from the Standpoint of Artificial Intelligence*. In: Meltzer, B. and Michie, D., Machine Intelligence 4, Edinburgh University Press, pp. 463-502,1969. .

[8]   Winston P.H., *Artificial Intelligence*, Addison-Wesley, 1992.

[9]   Rich E., and Knight K., *Artificial Intelligence*, McGraw Hill Text, 1991.

[10] Penrose Roger, *The Emperor's New Mind: Concerning computers, Minds, and law of Physics*, Oxford University Press, Oxford, 1989.

[11] Warren S. Mcculloch, Walter Pitts, A logical calculus of the ideas immanent in nervous activity, *Bulletin of mathematical biology*, Vol. 52, No. ½, pp. 99-115, 1990. Pergamon Press plc, Great Britain, 1990. Reprinted from the *Bulletin of Mathematical Biophysics*, Vol.5, (1943), 115-133, 1943.

[12] Norbert Wiener, *Cybernetics or control and communication in the animal and the machine*, second edition, MIT Press, Cambridge, Massachusetts, 1985. Reprinted from 1948.

[13] C.E. Shannon, A Mathematical Theory of Communication, *The bell system technical journal*, Vol. 27, (1948), 379-423, 623-656, July, October, Copyright 1948 by American telephone and telegraph co., USA.

[14] Newell A., Shaw J., and Simon H. A., Empirical explorations of the logic theory machine: A case study in heuristics, *Proceedings of the 1957 western joint computer conference February* 26-28, pp. 218-230, 1957.

[15] Newell A., Shaw J.C., Programming the logic theory machine, Proceedings of the 1957 *Western Joint Computer Conference*, February 26-28, pp. 230-240, 1957.

[16] Rosenblatt F., The perceptron: A probabilistic model for information storage and organization in the brain, *Psychological Review*, 65 (1988), 386-407.(Reprinted in Neuro-computing (MIT Press, 1988).

[17] John McCarthy, , Recursive functions of symbolic expressions and their computations by machine, MIT, 1960. http://edge.cs.drexel.edu/regli/Classes/Lisp_papers/McCarthy-original-LISP-paper-recursive.pdf

[18] Herbert A. Simon, Allen Newell, *Human problem solving*, American psychologist, prentice Hall, 1972.

[19] Pamela McCorduck, *Machines who think, A personal inquiry into the history and prospect of artificial intelligence*, San Francisco, California, Freeman, pp. 375, 1979.

[20] Gardner, H., *The mind's new science*, New York: Basic Books, 1985.

[21] Russel S., and Norvg P., *Artificial Intelligence: A modern approach*, Prentice Hall, Second edition, 2002.

[22] Turing, A.M., Computing machinery and intelligence, *Mind*, 59 (1950), 433-460.

[23] Brey, Philip, Hubert Dreyfus, *Humans versus computers*. To appear in: Achterhuis, H. (ed.), American philosophy of technology: The empirical turn , Indiana University Press, 2001.

[24] Azriel Rosenfeld, *Picture Processing by Computer*, New York: Academic Press, 1969.

[25] SuezouNakadate, ToyohikoYatagai, and Hiroyoshi Saito, Electronic speckle pattern interferometry using digital image processing techniques, *Applied Optics*, 19,Issue 11 (1980),1879-1883.

[26] William H. Carter San Diego, Evaluation of Peak Location Algorithms With Subpixel Accuracy For Mosaic Focal Planes, *Processing of Images and Data from Optical Sensors*,Conference Volume 0292, 1981.

[27] David W. Robinson, Automatic fringe analysis with a computer image-processing system, *Applied Optics*, 22, Issue 14 (1983), 2169-2176.

[28] S. V. Ahamed ,V. B, An image processing systemforeye statistics from eye diagrams, *Lawrence IAPR Workshop on CV- SpealHarclware and Industrial Applications* October 12-14. 1988. Tokyo.

[29] P. K. Sahoo, S. Soltaniand A. K. C. Wong, A Survey of thresholding Techniques, *Computer vision, graphics, and image processing*, 41(1988), 233-260.

[30] Marc Antonini, Michel Barlaud, Image Coding Using Wavelet Transform, *IEEE transactions on image processing*, vol. 1,no.2.APRIL 1992.

[31] Patnaik, S.Pal, R.N, Image compression using auto-associative neural network and embedded zero-tree coding, IEEE Third Workshop on Wireless Communications (2001) 388-390.

[32] Shanhui Sun Christian Bauer and ReinhardBeichel, Robust Active Shape Model Based Lung Segmentation in CT Scans, LOLA11 Challenge pp.213 -223, 2011.

[33] Sonal, Dinesh Kumar , *A study of various image compression techniques*. www.rimtengg.com/coit2007/proceedings/pdfs/43.pdf

[34] Suzuki K, Abe H, MacMahon H, Doi K, Image-processing technique for suppressing ribs in chest radiographs by means of massive training artificial neural network (MTANN*), IEEE Transactions on Medical Imaging.*, vol. 25,no.4, (2006), 406-416.

[35] WeixingWang,Shuguang Wu, A Study on Lung Cancer Detection by Image Processing, *international conference on Communications,Circuits and Systems Proceedings*,(2006) 371-374.

[36] Md. FoisalHossain, Mohammad Reza Alsharif, Image Enhancement Based on Logarithmic Transform Coefficient and Adaptive Histogram Equalization, *International Conference on Convergence Information Technology*, 21-23 November,(2007), 1439–1444.

[37] Wenhong Li,Yonggang Li,KexueLuo, Application of Image Processing Technology in Paper Currency Classification System, *IEEE transactions* 22-24 Oct. (2008), 1-5.

[38] Li Minxia, ZhengMeng A Study of Automatic Defects Extraction of X-ray Weld Image Based on Computed Radiography System, *International Conference on Measuring Technology and Mechatronics Automation* - ICMTMA, 2011.

[39] Kanwal, N. , Girdhar, A. ; Gupta, S "Region Based Adaptive Contrast Enhancement of Medical X-Ray Images", Bioinformatics and Biomedical Engineering, (ICBBE), *5th International Conference*, (2011), 1-5.

[40] Noorhayati Mohamed Noor, Noor Elaiza Abdul Khalid, Fish Bone Impaction Using Adaptive Histogram Equalization (AHE), *Proceedings of the Second International Conference on Computer Research and Development* , IEEE Computer society Washington, (2010),163-167.

[41] Lu Zhang, Dongyue Li, ShuqianLuo ,"Information extraction of bone fracture images based on diffraction enhanced imaging" International Conference of Medical Image Analysis and Clinical Application (MIACA) 10-17 June 2010, pp. 106-108.

[42] Md.FoisalHossain, Mohammad Reza Alsharif, and Katsumi Yamashita"Medical Image Enhancement Based on Nonlinear Technique and Logarithmic Transform Coefficient Histogram Matching", IEEE/ICME International Conference on Complex Medical Engineering July,2010, pp.13-15.

[43] HasanDemirel, Co-occurrence matrix and its statistical features as a new approach for face recognition, Turk J Electrical Engeneering and Computer Society, vol.19, No.1(2011), 97-107.

[44] Pu J, Paik DS, Meng X, Roos JE, Rubin GD"Shape , Break-and-Repair" Strategy and Its Application to Automated Medical Image Segmentation, *IEEE transactions on visualization and computer graphics*, vol.17, no. 1, january 2011.

[45] TianShen, Hongsheng LiXiaolei Huang, Active Volume Models for Medical Image Segmentation, IEEE Transactions on medical imaging vol. 30, Issue 3 (2011), 774–791.

[46] KimmiVerma, AruMehrotra, VijayetaPandey, Shardendu Singh, Image processing techniques for the enhancement of brain tumour patterns, *International journal of advanced research in electrical, electronics and instrumentation engineering*, 2(4) (2013),1611-1615.

[47] Pallavi T. Suradkar , Detection of Malarial Parasite in Blood Using Image Processing, *International Journal of Engineering and Innovative Technology* (IJEIT) ,vol. 2, Issue 10, (2013), 124-126.

[48] Md.AmranHossenBhuiyan, Ibrahim Azad, Md.KamalUddi, Image Processing for Skin Cancer Features Extraction, International Journal of Scientific & Engineering Research,Volume 4, Issue 2 (2013), 1-6.

[49] S.Kannadhasan, N.BasheerAhamed, M.RajeshBaba , Cancer Diagonsis with the help digital Image Processing using ZIGBEE Technology, *International Journal of Emerging Trends in Electrical and Electronics* (IJETEE), Volume 1, Issue 2, 2013.

[50] HardikPandit ,Dr. D M Shah, Application of Digital Image Processing and Analysis in Healthcare Based on Medical Palmistry, *International Conference on Intelligent Systems and Data Processing* ICISD,Special Issue published by *International Journal of Computer Applications (IJCA)*, (2011), 56-59.

[51] Newell, A. and Simon, H. A., Computer Science as Empirical Inquiry: Symbols and Search, *Communications of the ACM* 19 (1976), 113–126.

[52] Putnam, H., Minds and machines, in S. Hook (ed.), *Dimensions of Mind*, New York University Press, pp. 138–164, 1960.

[53] Haugeland, J, *AI: The Very Idea*, MIT Press, 1985a.

[54] Searle John. R., Minds, brains, and programs, *Behavioral and brain sciences*, 3(3) (1980), 417-457.

[55] Joseph Weizenbaum, *Computer Power and Human Reason: From Judgment to Calculation*, W. H. Freeman, 1976.

[56] David L. Anderson, *Introduction to functionalism, Consortium on cognitive science instruction*, 2003. http://www.mind.ilstu.edu/curriculum/functionalism_intro/functionalism_intro.php

[57] Rodney Brooks, *Flesh and Machines: How Robots Will Change Us*, Vintage, Reprint edition 2003.

[58] Hubert L. Dreyfus, *Body and world: a review of What Computers Still Can't Do: A Critique of Arti cial Reason* , MIT Press, Cambridge, MA, 1992.

[59] Anderson, M. L., and Oates, T., A review of recent research in metareasoning and metalearning. *AI Magazine, 28*(1) (2007), 7-16.

[60] Baars, B. J., *A cognitive theory of consciousness*, Cambridge University Press, 1998.

[61] Blackmore, S., There is no stream of consciousness, *Journal of Consciousness Studies*, 9(5-6) (2002),, 17-28.

[62] Chrisley R., Embodied artificial intelligence. [Review*]. Artificial Intelligence*, 149(1) (2003), 131-150.

[63] Clowes, R., Torrance, S., and Chrisley, R., Machine consciousness-embodiment and imagination. [Editorial Material*]. Journal of Consciousness Studies*, 14(7) (2007), 7-14.

[64] Dennett D.C., *Consciousness Explained*, Penguin Press, 1993.

[65] Densmore, S., and Dennett D., The virtues of virtual machines. [Article]. *Philosophy and Phenomenological Research*, 59(3) (1999), 747-761.

[66] Gamez D., Progress in machine consciousness, *Consciousness and Cognition*, 17(3)(2008), 887-910.

[67] Haikonen P. O. A., Essential issues of conscious machines, *Journal of Consciousness Studies*, 14(7)(2007), 72-84.

[68] Rolls E. T., A computational neuroscience approach to consciousness. [Review], *Neural Networks*, 20(9)(2007),, 962-982.

[69] Rosenthal D. M., *The nature of Mind*, Oxford University Press, 1991.

[70] Sloman, A., and Chrisley, R., Virtual machines and consciousness, *Journal of Consciousness Studies, 10*(4-5) (2003), 133-172.

[71] Sun R., Learning, action and consciousness: A hybrid approach toward modelling consciousness. [Article], *Neural Networks*, 10(7)(1997), 1317-1331.

[72] Taylor, J. G., CODAM: A neural network model of consciousness, *Neural Networks*, 20(9)(2007), 983-992.

[73] Velmans, M., Making sense of causal interactions between consciousness and brain, *Journal of Consciousness Studies*, 9(11)(2011), 69-95.

[74] Velmans, M., How to define consciousness: And how not to define consciousness, *Journal of Consciousness Studies*, 16(5) (2009), 139-156.

[75] Crevier D., *AI: The tumultuous search for artificial intelligence*. New York: Basic Books, 1993.

[76] Koza, J. R., Keane, M. A., Streeter, M. J., Mydlowec, W., Yu, J., and Lanza, G., *Genetic programming IV: Routine human-competitive machine intelligence*, Kluwer Academic, 2003.

[77] Schaeffer, J., Burch, N., Bj¨ornsson, Y., Kishimoto, A., M¨uller, M., Lake, R., Lu, P., and Sutphen, S., Checkers is solved, *Science*. 19 July, 2007.

[78] Milan Sonka, Vaclav Hlavac, Roger Boyle, *Image Processing, Analysis, and Machine Vision*, Cengage learning, 2008.

[79] Godel K., *Under formal unentscheidbare satze der principia mathematica und physic*, 38 (1931), pp. 173-198. Translated in English by Van Heijenoort: *From Frege to Godel*, Harvard University Press, 1971.

Deep Learning for Image Processing Applications
D.J. Hemanth and V.V. Estrela (Eds.)
IOS Press, 2017
doi:10.3233/978-1-61499-822-8-27

Deep Neural Networks for Image Classification

Vasuki. A[a,1] and Govindaraju. S[b]

[a] *Department of Mechatronics Engineering, Kumaraguru College of Technology, Coimbatore – 641 049.*
[b] *Department of Electronics and Instrumentation Engineering, Kumaraguru College of Technology, Coimbatore – 641 049.*

Abstract. This chapter gives an insight into Deep Learning Neural Networks and their application to Image Classification / Pattern Recognition. The principle of Convolutional Neural Networks will be described and an in-depth study of the algorithms for image classification will be made. In artificial intelligence, machine learning plays a key role. The algorithm learns when exposed to new data or environment. Object / Pattern Recognition is an integral part of machine learning and image classification is an integral part of such algorithms. The Human Visual System efficiently classifies known objects and also learns easily when exposed to new objects. This capability is being developed in Artificial Neural Networks and there are several types of such networks with increasing capabilities in solving problems. Neural networks themselves have evolved from evolutionary computing techniques that try to simulate the behavior of the human brain in reasoning, recognition and learning. Deep neural networks have powerful architectures with the capability to learn and there are training algorithms that make the networks adapt themselves in machine learning. The networks extract the features from the object and these are used for classification. The chapter concludes with a brief overview of some of the applications / case studies already published in the literature.

Keywords. Artificial Intelligence, Convolutional Neural Networks, Deep Learning, Image Classification, Machine Learning, Neural Networks.

1. Introduction

Machine Learning (ML) is a part of Artificial Intelligence (AI) that enables computer algorithms to learn from input / training data [1]. Learning can be categorized as supervised, unsupervised or semi-supervised. If the learning happens with a set of known (training) data and the algorithm is trained for a particular task, it is supervised learning [2]. If the learning happens with unknown input data, it is unsupervised learning. Semi-supervised learning falls in between these two categories. In supervised learning, the training inputs and the desired outputs are given and the relation of input to output is learnt by the algorithm. The mapping between the input and output are already known. In unsupervised learning, the inputs are given and the algorithm learns to find patterns or features to produce the output. The number of

---

[1] Corresponding Author.

outputs need not be known earlier by the algorithm. In semi-supervised learning, the training inputs and desired outputs are partially given and the algorithm learns to find the missing relations and patterns.

Neural Networks (NN) play a key role in the development of machine learning algorithms in AI. NNs have been developed, inspired by the working of biological neurons in the human brain. Each neuron is a processing element and an interconnection of such neurons leads to huge computing power that can solve complex tasks. Warren McCulloch and Walter Pitts (1943) created a computational model for neural networks based on mathematics and developed algorithms called threshold logic. This model paved the way for neural network research to take two approaches - one for biological processes in the brain while the other for application of neural networks to artificial intelligence. Neural networks have been developed primarily for solving complex problems that might not fit in with rule based algorithms or programs. In real world problems, some data might be missing or all the rules might not be known. Heuristics play a large role in artificial intelligence and hence in neural networks.

Artificial Neural Networks (ANNs) are computing systems inspired by the biological neural networks that constitute human and animal brain. An ANN is constructed from a collection of connected units called artificial neurons. Each connection between neurons can transmit a signal from one to another. The receiving neuron can process the signal(s) and then transmit to downstream neurons connected to it. Neurons have states, generally represented by real numbers, typically between 0 and 1. Neurons also have weights that vary as learning progresses, which can increase or decrease the strength of the signal that it sends downstream to other neurons. Further, they might have a threshold such that only if the aggregate output is below (or above) that threshold level the downstream signal is sent. Typically, neurons are organized in layers. Different layers perform different kinds of transformations on their inputs. Signals travel from the first (input) layer, to the last (output) layer, possibly after traversing the layers in between them multiple times.

Such neural networks learn to do tasks, with progressive improvement in performance, by considering examples, generally without task-specific programming. They have found more use in applications difficult to express in a traditional computer algorithm using rule-based programming. The original goal of the neural network approach was to solve problems in the same way that a human brain would. Over time, attention focused on matching to specific mental abilities, leading to deviations from biology such as back propagation, or passing information in the reverse direction and adjusting the network to reflect feedback information. Neural networks have been designed for a variety of tasks, including computer (machine) vision, speech recognition, pattern / object recognition, image classification, machine translation, social network filtering, playing video games, medical diagnosis and in many other domains.

Neurons are organized in layers with interconnections between the layers. Signals are transferred across the layers, after processing. Mostly, signals travel from the input layer to the output layer in the forward direction and such networks are called feedforward networks. In certain networks, signals also travel in the reverse direction, leading to recurrent networks and the development of the back propagation algorithm. All layers of neurons other than input and output are called 'hidden' and their number varies depending on the problem to be solved. When the number of hidden layers is more than two or three, it becomes a deep neural network. Such deep neural networks have the capacity to learn to solve problems and the learning is called deep learning.

Such deep neural networks and learning algorithms are developed for solving complex tasks such as machine vision, pattern recognition, object recognition / identification, surveillance, image classification, character recognition, speech / speaker recognition, etc.

Image Classification is one of the toughest tasks to be learnt and solved by an algorithm. When several images are available, the human brain learns and classifies existing as well as new images with almost 100% accuracy. Machine learning algorithms have been developed to mimic exactly this behavior of human brain. The problem becomes more difficult when the images are taken under different conditions such as change in illumination, rotation or translation of objects in the image, incomplete or hidden objects, different postures if the object is a face, etc. Such conditions lead to hundreds of different images (image sets) containing the same object, adding to the complexity of the recognition / classification problem.

Many algorithms have been developed in the past for image classification such as Minimum Distance Classifier, *k*-means clustering, Bayes Classifier, Maximum Likelihood Classifier, Support Vector Machines (SVM), Principal Component Analysis (PCA), Kernels, etc. These algorithms are based on a fixed logic and they cannot learn. They are either parametric or non-parametric. If the classification algorithm requires the computation of statistical parameters such as mean, covariance, etc., it is parametric; otherwise it is non-parametric. Parametric classifiers require training samples / data from which the parameters have to be estimated. More number of training data, more accurate the parameter estimation will be.

Image classification can be pixel-based or object-based. In pixel-based classification, the attributes of every pixel is extracted to label it as belonging to a particular class. In object-based classification, segmentation is done to extract regions or objects in the image and their attributes evaluated. Features or attributes have to be extracted in order to do classification. The efficiency of the algorithm depends on the number of features used in the process. This leads to the problem of 'curse of dimensionality'. Dimensionality reduction has to done which is equivalent to feature reduction and hence reduced time consumption. More the number of features, more processing and storage of data are required. This increases the time complexity of the algorithm. The algorithms that classify objects with minimum number of features with less time consumption are more efficient.

Neural Networks are also developed for image classification and they are inculcated with the capability to learn. A set of training data is available and relationships between training inputs and the desired outputs (or pattern classes) have to be fed into the network. The network gets trained on these known data and learns to recognize / classify new data. Machine learning algorithms have been developed to make learning happen, with the logic being learnt by the algorithm during training. The data or patterns are given as inputs, the outputs are specified and the algorithm learns to find the relationship between inputs and outputs. When the problem is complex such as in image classification, more hidden layers are required and this makes the neural network 'deep'. Hundreds of hidden layers improve the accuracy of the classification and the learning becomes 'deep learning'.

Deep Learning Neural Networks are covered in Section 2. Image Classification is discussed in Section 3. Some of the applications of Deep Neural Networks to image classification problems are briefly described in Section 4. The chapter concludes with Section 5, followed by the bibliography.

2. Deep Learning Neural Networks

Machine learning algorithms generate their own logic based on the input data. The algorithm learns by itself and code need not be written to solve every problem. Typical example is categorization of emails into various bins such as input, spam, etc. Another important classification is for objects present in images. For example, an image contains the picture of an animal. The problem is to categorize the animal as deer, dog, cat, lion, etc, which is equivalent to object / pattern recognition. Large number of images with pictures of animals has to be fed as input to the algorithm from which it can learn to classify. If the images are already classified and fed, it is supervised learning. If not, it is unsupervised learning. The simplest case is that of classifying a pattern into two classes such as identifying whether the animal in the picture is elephant or not. Then it becomes a two class problem. Basically, machine learning algorithms classify based on patterns in the data. The data can be text, sound, image, etc.

Neural networks have been found to be best suited for implementation of machine learning algorithms. Traditional neural networks have one input layer, one output layer and two or three hidden layers. Deep neural networks have one input layer, one output layer and hundreds of hidden layers, typically as shown in Figure 1 [3]. More number of hidden layers, deeper the network. The layers are interconnected, with the output of the previous layer being the input of the current layer. The inputs / outputs are weighted, and the weights determine the performance of the network. Training of the network involves obtaining the appropriate weights for the various layers. Deep networks require higher processing power, computing speed, large database and the appropriate software with parallel processing.

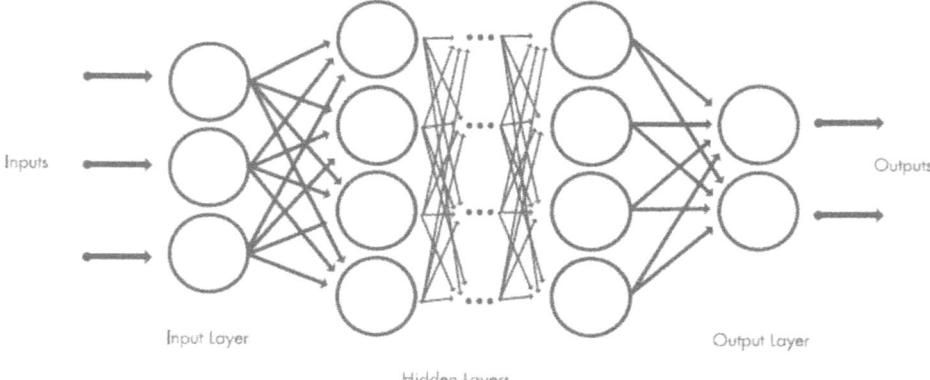

Figure 1. Typical Deep Neural Network [Cited from Ref. 3]

Convolutional Neural Network (CNN) is a type of deep learning network that has become popular for image classification. Three examples of CNN architectures are given in Figure 2 [4], Figure 3 [5] and Figure 4 [3]. It consists of an input layer and hundreds of feature detection layers. Feature detection layers perform one of the following three operations: Convolution, Pooling, Rectified Linear Unit (ReLU). Convolution puts the image through convolution filters that activate certain features in the image. Pooling performs non-linear down sampling in order to reduce the number of data to be handled. Rectification Linear Unit maintains positive values and maps negative values to zero. The classification layer is the one before the output layer. It is a fully connected layer with N-dimensional output, N being the number of classes to be categorized. This layer outputs a N-dimensional vector, each element of the vector is the probability that the input image belongs to one of the N classes. The final output layer uses a *softmax* function to give the classified output. To produce accurate results, thousands or millions of images have to be fed into the network. It requires higher computing power with several Graphics Processing Units (GPUs) operating in parallel.

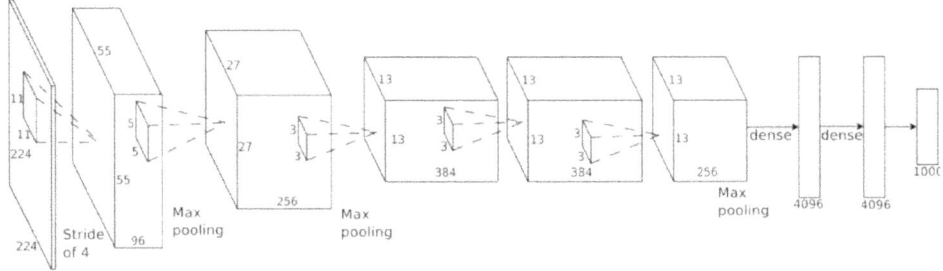

Figure 2. Convolutional Neural Network 1 [Cited from Ref. 4]

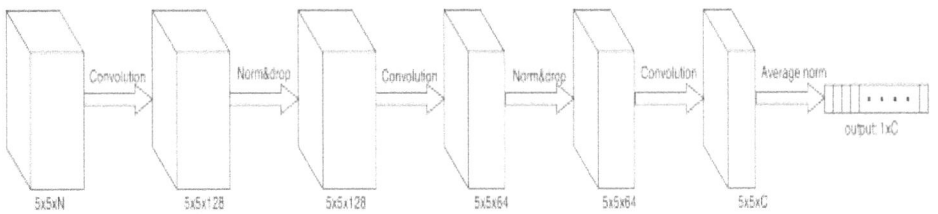

Figure 3. Convolutional Neural Network 2 [Cited from Ref. 5]

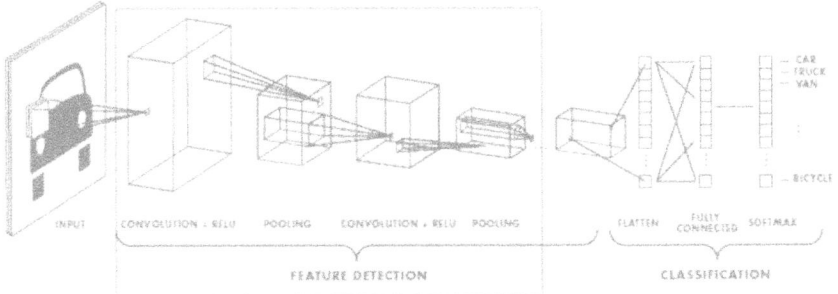

Figure 4. Convolutional Neural Network 3 [Cited from Ref. 3]

When millions of training images are fed into the deep learning network, the network starts to identify features of the data that can be used in categorization. Processing takes place at each layer of the network and this is fed to the next consecutive layer. CNNs have been designed based on biological structure of the visual cortex. The simple and complex cells of visual cortex activate based on the subregions of a visual field, called receptive field. The neurons of a layer in CNN connect to the subregions of the previous layer instead of being fully connected. The neurons are not responsive to other subregions. The subregions are allowed to overlap and hence produce spatially correlated outcomes, unlike traditonal neural nets. This is the fundamental difference between CNN and other neural nets. The CNN reduces the number of parameters to be handled by reducing the number of connections, sharing the weights and by downsampling.

2.1. Functioning of CNN

The functioning of a typical CNN is pictorially indicated in Figure 5 [6].

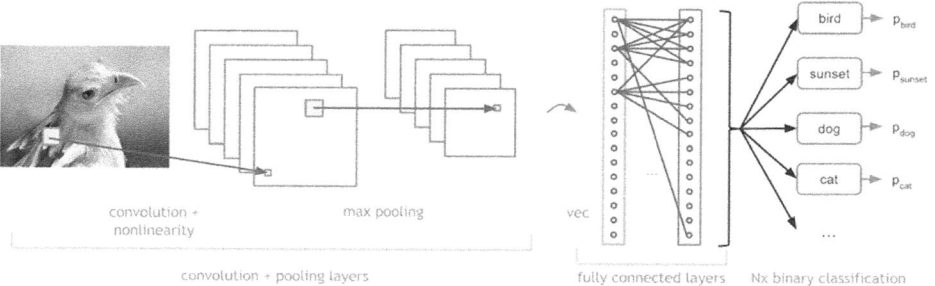

Figure 5. Functioning of CNN [Cited from Ref. 6]

The input to the CNN will be an image containing one or more objects to be classified. The number of input values will depend on the image size and the depth of the pixels (3 in the case of RGB). These are simply numbers that have to be translated or identified as objects belonging to a certain class. CNN tries to imitate the human visual cortex that has sensitivity to certain regions of the visual field in small regions of cells. Some of the neurons in the brain are sensitive to certain content in the visual images, for example, edges, curves, etc.

The first layer in CNN is the convolution layer that performs spatial convolution of a pre-defined mask with the pixel values. This is equivalent to linear filtering operation and the convolution output depends on the pre-defined mask. For example, the image size might be 256 x 256 x 3 and the mask size could be 5 x 5 x 3; so it has to multiply the pixel values and mask values (element by element multiplication) and sum it up to get the convolved output at the position of the mask placed over the image. The mask is moved over the image from left to right and top to bottom and the convolution is repeated to cover the entire image. The shape that is to be detected determines the mask values so that higher convolved values are obtained if the shape is present in the image at that location. This produces a feature map which will be another array of numbers, as shown in Figure 6 [6].

When the activation output (feature map) of the first layer is input to the second hidden layer and the convolution operation is repeated, another feature map that is at a higher level than the first is obtained. This process produces different activation maps for different features in the image, including complex features.

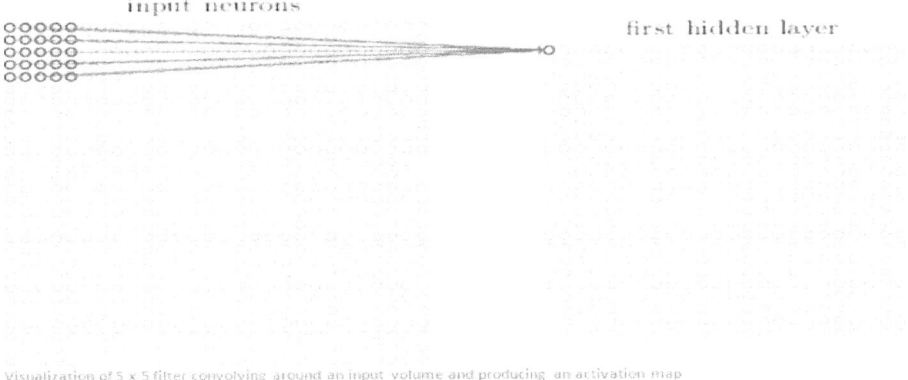

Figure 6. Convolution in a CNN mapping from input to hidden layer [Cited from Ref. 6]

There is a fully connected layer at the end of the network that takes its input from the preceding layer and produces N-dimensional output. For N-class problem, it could possibly output N different probability values, representing the probabilities that the object could belong to that class. In the image containing bird as shown in Figure 5, the probability for class bird could be 0.72, for class dog could be 0.17, for class flower could be 0.15, etc. This is the *softmax* approach, contrary to the hard approach where the probability of one of the classes is 1 and all others are 0. The CNN needs to be trained by the back propagation algorithm on millions of images for the classification to be accurate.

Each convolution layer is followed by an activation ReLU (Rectified Linear Unit) Layer that makes the operation non-linear. It makes the negative activation values zero and retains the positive activation values. The ReLU layers are followed by pooling layers, popular being the max pooling layer, that takes the activation inputs and produces a down sampled output. For example, if the layer is max pooling and the filter size is 2 x 2, it takes the maximum value from the 2 x 2 activation region and the composition from all the regions is the array output of this layer. Instead of maximum value, other possibilities such as averaging are also done. There are also dropout layers that drops out certain activation outputs during the training phase of the network. This prevents overfitting.

2.2. Software for Implementing Deep Neural Networks

Several software are available to design and implement deep neural networks. Some of them are open source and an overview of the available software is outlined.

Tensorflow [7, 8] is an open source software that has been developed specifically for machine learning. Its built-in functions ease the design of deep neural networks in a modular manner. The software also adapts to the use of multiple Central Processing Units (CPUs) / GPUs in execution. The Application Programmer Interface (API) is built in layers that provide control to the user at different levels.

R [9, 10, 11] is a programming environment composed of software utilities that are available at no cost. It is a GNU that provides functions, libraries, debuggers and other modules that make things easier for algorithm development. *R* follows a graphical approach and provides a set of tools for data storage, manipulation, analysis and other computations. It is an extension of _S_ Language that was developed earlier and most of the codes in _S_ run under _R_.

MATLAB [12, 13]: Deep learning requires substantial amount of data and computations. So it requires high computing power with parallel architectures. The neural network and other allied toolboxes in _MATLAB_ allow users to create, train and use neural networks for various applications. The allied toolboxes facilitate the image to be acquired, input to the neural network and the processed output to be displayed.

Caffe [14, 15, 16, 17] is a deep learning framework that has been designed with C++, Python and MATLAB. It is an open source framework from UC Berkeley that let researchers design and train deep neural networks. _Caffe_ has an expressive architecture, extensible code and high speed that has created a community of users for industrial and research applications.

Torch [18, 19] is an open source software for machine learning based on LuaJIT script with C implementation. It has a library that can be used for developers for applications in deep learning. The core object of the library is _Torch_ that is tensor based. Complex neural networks can be built with ease and flexibility with high execution speed.

Microsoft Cognitive Toolkit [20, 21, 22] allows users to develop, train and apply their own neural networks. It is an open source library for deep learning supported by Windows and Linux. It runs in different environments – from CPUs to GPUs and it is compatible with existing programming languages.

Keras [23, 24, 25] is a high level neural network programming API intended for fast development of algorithms and applications. It can run on top of Theano, Microsoft Cognitive Toolkit (CNTK) and Tensorflow, seamlessly on CPUs and GPUs. It is a collection of modules placed in a library developed in Python.

Deeplearning 4j [26] is a programming library written for Java. The algorithms include programs for various types of deep neural networks. The basic neural network layers are stacked on top of each other to create deep networks. These networks have artificial intelligence and can produce astounding results for complex problems that were solvable only by humans until now.

MXNet [27, 28] is an open-source software for training and deploying deep neural networks. It is scalable and flexible suitable for fast training, and supports programming model and multiple languages (C++, Python, Julia, Matlab, JavaScript, Go, R, Scala, Perl, Wolfram Language).

ConvNetJS [29] is a Javascript library for training Deep Neural Networks. It allows the users to formulate and solve Neural Networks in Javascript and has been extended since inception by contributions from the community.

Several CNNs have been implemented to classify thousands of pattern classes [30]. The error rates achieved were lesser than the already existing versions of CNN. One typical network has around 650,000 neurons and GPUs have been used in training. Currently, deep neural networks are being trained on CPUs, GPUs and in the cloud. CPUs are the cheapest option but they can be used only for pre-trained networks. GPUs can be used for training the deep neural networks as well as for classification. Cloud based resources can be utilized for both training and classification, without procurement of expensive hardware.

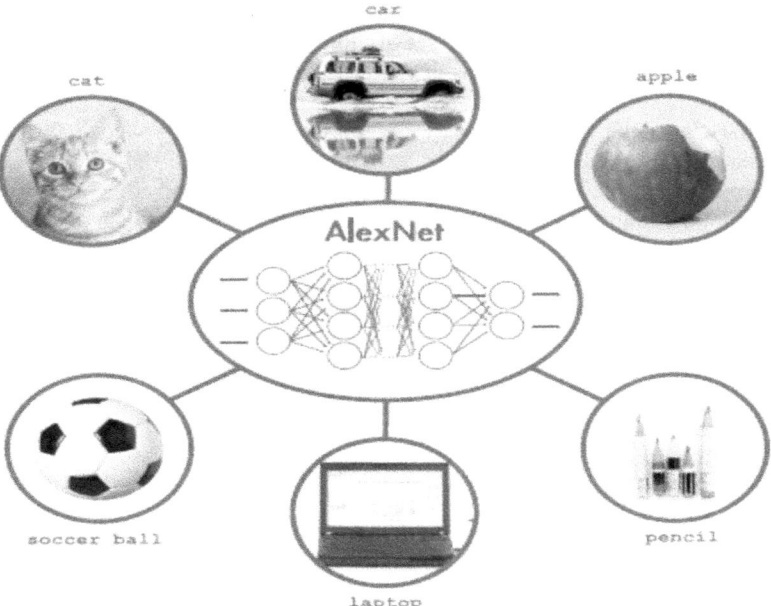

Figure 7. AlexNet [Cited from Ref. 3]

One of the successful CNNs developed is AlexNet that has been trained on more than million images. It was first published in 2012 and can classify various objects and several breeds of animals, as shown in Figure 7. AlexNet can be used along with webcam for image acquisition and the associated packages in MATLAB. It can also be used to classify images for which it is not trained by *transfer learning*. ZF Net was developed in 2013 by Zeiler and Fergus which is a modified version of AlexNet. VGG net was created in 2014 by Karen Simonyan and Andrew Zisserman of the University of Oxford with error rate less than the previous CNNs. GoogLeNet and Microsoft ResNet were developed in 2015 with incredibly reduced error rates.

3. Image Classification

Image classification refers to the classification of various objects in images such as persons, crops, trees, soil, minerals, water bodies, etc. The different objects or regions in the image have to be identified and classified. The classification algorithm determines the accuracy of the result. It is usually based on a single image or sets of images. When sets of images are used, the set will contain multiple images of the same object with different views and under different conditions. It will be more effective in classification when compared to classifying with single images, since the algorithm can accommodate varying conditions like differences in background, illumination, or appearances. It can also be invariant to image rotation and other transformations.

The input to the algorithm will be the pixels of the image that are numeric in nature. The output will be a value or set of values indicating the class. The algorithm will be a mapping function that maps the pixel values to the appropriate class. It can be a single output multi-valued function or it can be multi-output single valued function to indicate the class. Classification can be supervised or unsupervised. In supervised classification, the number of classes is known and a set of training data with information on their class is given. It is like learning from a teacher. In unsupervised classification, the number of classes is not known and the training data are not available. The relationship (or mapping) between the data to be classified and the various classes has to be learned. It is like learning without a teacher. If some information is available regarding the mapping of data to classes, then supervised and unsupervised methods can be combined and it becomes semi-supervised.

Features are the most important parameters associated with input data based on which the data are classified. Defining certain attributes of the object as features plays a crucial role in classification. Extraction of features from the objects in the image is used for classification.

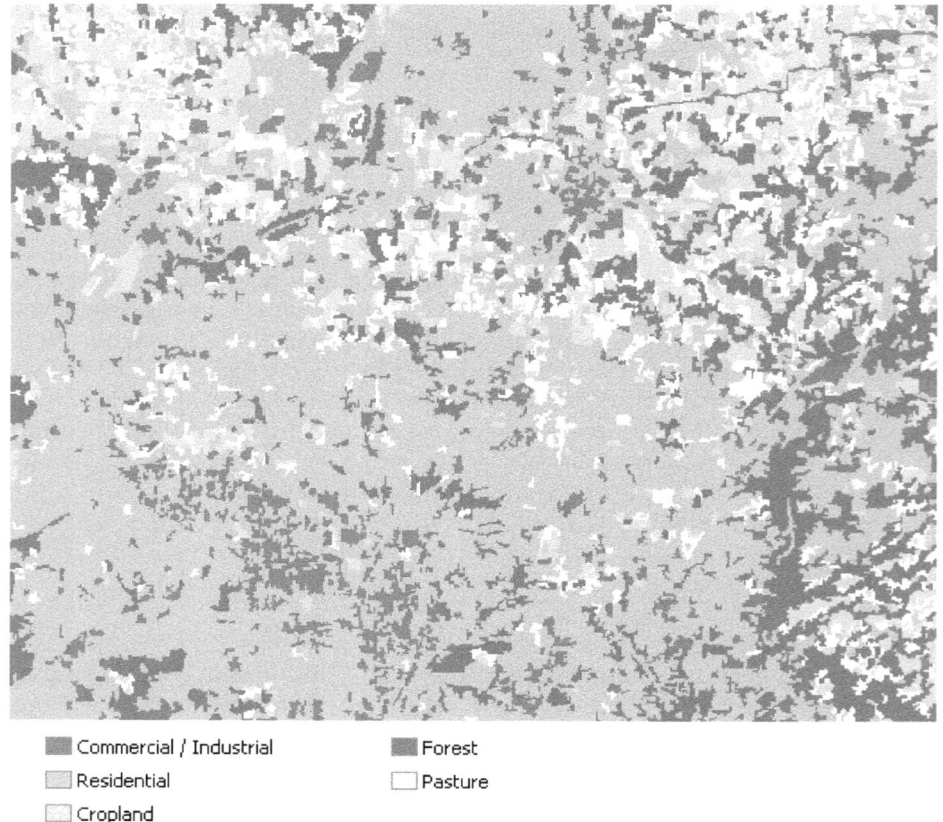

■ Commercial / Industrial   ■ Forest
▨ Residential   ☐ Pasture
☐ Cropland

Figure 8. Satellite Image Classification – Example 1 (Cited from Ref. 31)

Example:

- Satellite image is the input for which classification has to be done.
- Problem is to identify or classify the pixels into land, desert, crop coverage, water, mountains, minerals, etc.
- Land cover can be classified into different themes called thematic mapping.
- Supervised learning: information on the relationship between pixel values in different bands and the classes has to be known based on training data.
- Unsupervised learning: information on the relationship between pixel values in different bands and the classes has to be learnt.
- Features: attributes of the pixels that could possibly be numerical values in different bands of a multispectral image.

Examples of categorization of satellite images are given in Figure 8 [31] and Figure 9 [32]. A mathematical function (discriminant function) has to be defined for each categorization to which the inputs are the features and the output will be a numerical value that indicates the class to which the data belongs. So it has be a multi-valued function that maps the feature set to classes. One method of extracting features is by doing a statistical analysis of the pixels to obtain parameters like mean, correlation, covariance, etc. If the mapping information of the parameters with the classes is known or expertise is available, then it is supervised; otherwise it is unsupervised. Training data can be used in developing these relations or mapping.

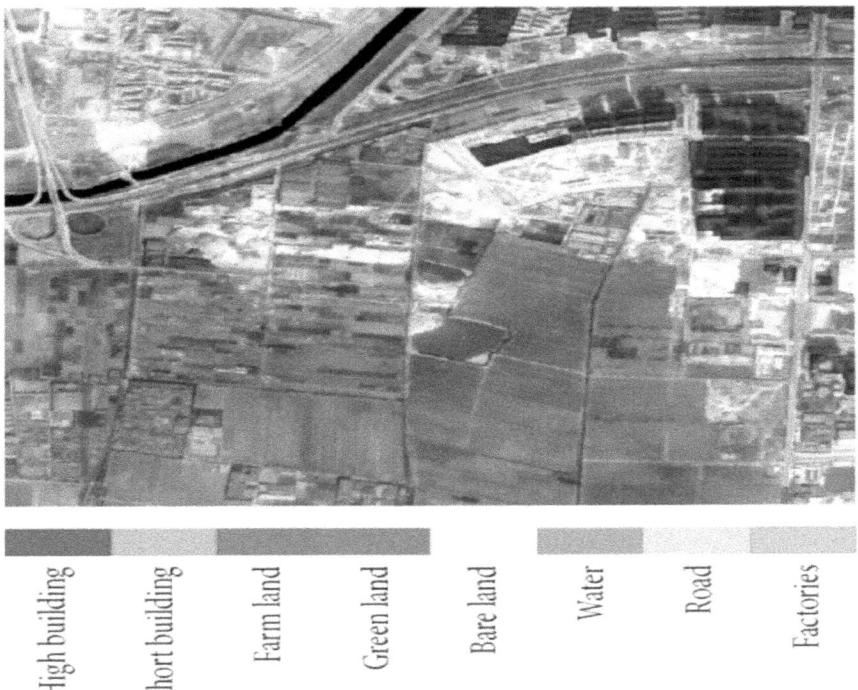

Figure 9. Satellite Image Classification – Example 2 (Cited from Ref. 32)

Character recognition is another classical example of classification where different alphabets or digits map to different classes [33]. The input is the pixel values of a region in the image containing the alphabet and the output is the recognized character. In classical character recognition problems, the image containing the characters to be identified is the input. The image has to be first segmented to identify the region containing each character. The attributes of each character has to be known earlier. Features are extracted from the segmented image, and applied to the classification algorithm. The algorithm recognizes the characters and gives the appropriate output. Typical images of handwritten characters are given in Figure 10 [33].

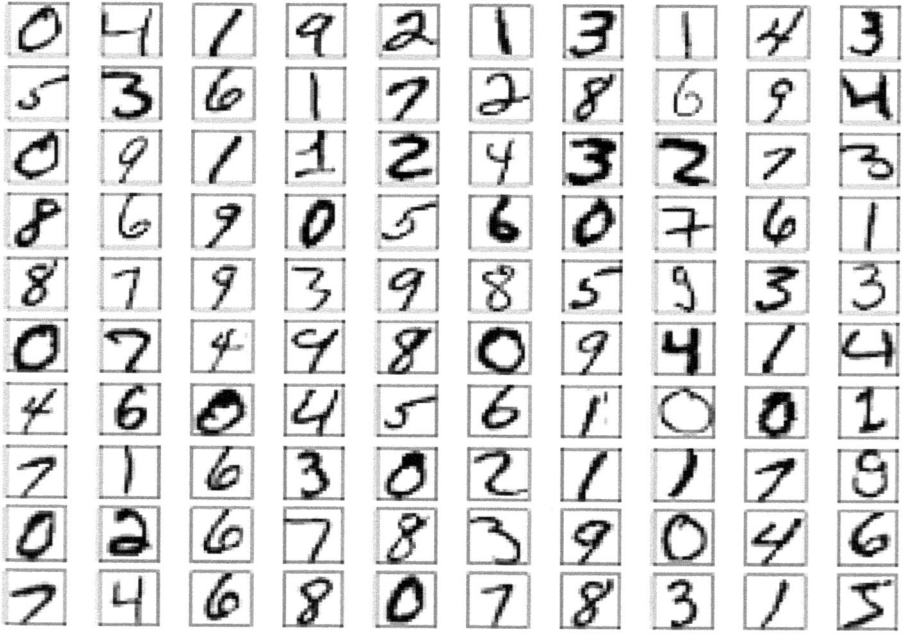

Figure 10. Training Samples of Handwritten Digits [Cited from Ref. 33]

In Figure 11 the image of an animal is taken and it is classified into four different categories with varying probabilities [34]. In Figure 12, images are given and the classification has to be done under different illuminations, view points, etc. In Figure 13, image set classification has to be done.

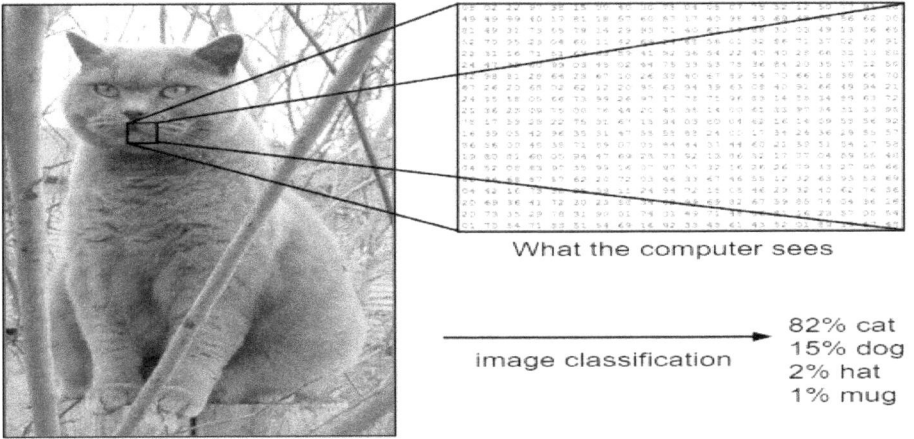

Figure 11. Classification of a single image [Cited from Ref. 34]

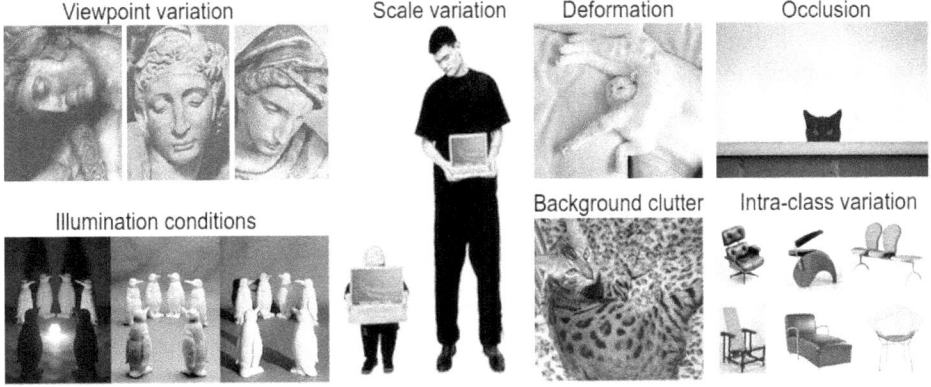

Figure 12. Classification from an image(s) under different conditions [Cited from Ref. 34]

Figure 13. Classification from an image set [Cited from Ref. 34]

Several classification algorithms are available and some of them are listed below:

- Minimum Distance Classifier
- Bayes Classifier
- Neural Networks
- Support Vector Machines (SVM)
- Principal Component Analysis (PCA)
- *k*-means algorithm

Minimum Distance Classifier

Classification is done based on the minimum distance between the unknown pattern vector and the prototype pattern vector that represents the mean of a pattern class [35]. The distance measure is the Euclidean distance computed using the feature vectors. Each pattern class has a set of features that have to be extracted to make pattern matching or recognition easier and more accurate. The features are represented in terms of numbers in order to make mathematical computations.

Let **x** be the vector representing the features of a pattern. Let **x**$_i$ be the pattern vector of the ith pattern in a pattern class. Then **x**$_i$ = [x_{i1} x_{i2} x_{i3} .... x_{in}], where n is the dimension of the feature vector (number of features used to represent the pattern). Hence **x**$_{ij}$ stands for the jth feature in the ith pattern in the given pattern class. The mean vector of a pattern class is computed to obtain the prototype vector of that class. It is given by,

$$m_r = \frac{1}{N_r} \sum_{i=1}^{N_r} x_i, \quad r = 1, 2, ... N \tag{1}$$

where **m**$_r$ is the mean vector of the rth pattern class, N_r is the number of vectors in the rth pattern class and N is the number of pattern classes. The Euclidean distance of a given vector **x** with the mean of a pattern class is defined as,

$$D_r = \|x - m_r\| \quad r = 1, 2, ... N \tag{2}$$

where $\|x\| = (x^T x)^{\frac{1}{2}}$ is defined as Euclidean norm of vector **x**. The Euclidean distance of pattern vector **x** to the mean of various classes is computed, as shown in Figure 14 and Figure 15. The pattern represented by **x** is assigned to class r if D_r is the smallest distance.

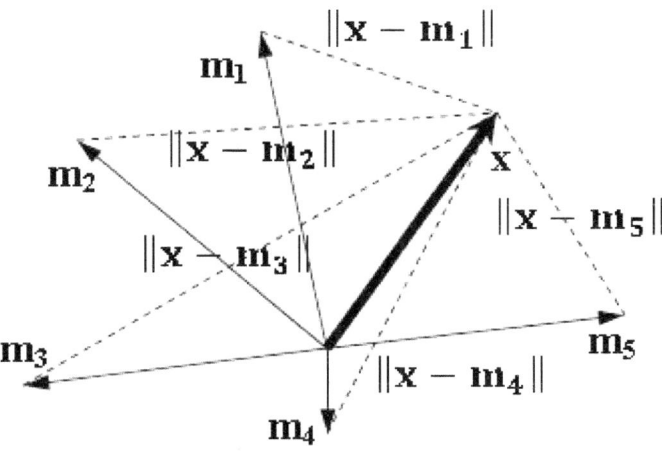

Figure 14. Distance of pattern vector **x** to the mean of various pattern classes – Example 1 [Cited from Ref.36]

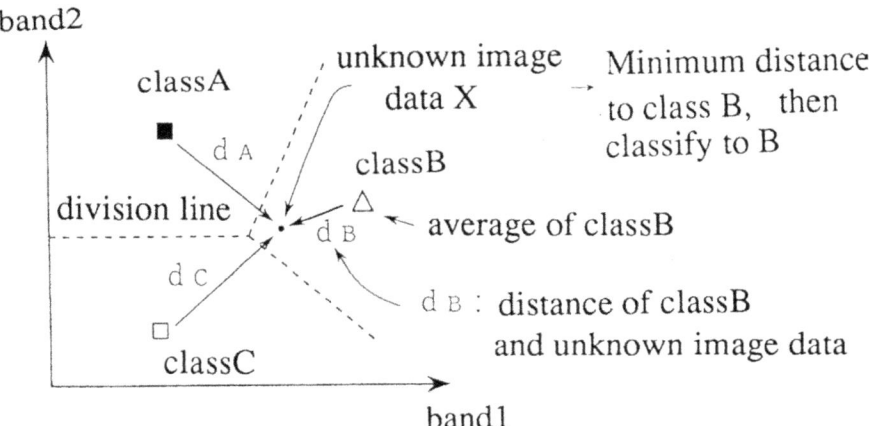

Figure 15. Distance of pattern vector **x** to the mean of various pattern classes – Example 2 [Cited from Ref. 37]

Bayes Classifier

The Bayes classifier is based on statistical parameters of probabilities [35]. The probability that a pattern vector **x** belongs to class ω_i is given by,

$$p\left(\frac{\omega_i}{x}\right) \tag{3}$$

When the pattern $\mathbf{x}$ is wrongly classified as belonging to class ω_j the loss incurred is L_{ij}. The average loss incurred by the input pattern $\mathbf{x}$ is when it is classified as belonging to class ω_j is,

$$r_j(x) = \sum_{k=1}^{N} L_{kj} p\left(\frac{\omega_k}{x}\right) \tag{4}$$

By applying Baye's theorem, the average loss is rewritten as,

$$r_j(x) = \frac{1}{p(x)} \sum_{k=1}^{N} L_{kj} p\left(\frac{x}{\omega_k}\right) p(\omega_k) \tag{5}$$

The loss functions $r_1(x), r_2(x) \ldots r_N(x)$ are computed for the N pattern classes and the pattern $\mathbf{x}$ is classified as belonging to the class j that has the minimum value among all the $r_j(x)$. The pattern is classified as class ω_j if,

$$\sum_{k=1}^{N} L_{kj} p\left(\frac{x}{\omega_k}\right) p(\omega_k) \leq \sum_{p=1}^{N} L_{pi} p\left(\frac{x}{\omega_p}\right) p(\omega_p) \tag{6}$$

for all pattern classes. This is equivalent to the condition,

$$p\left(\frac{x}{\omega_i}\right) p(\omega_i) > p\left(\frac{x}{\omega_j}\right) p(\omega_j) \tag{7}$$

leading to decision functions of the form,

$$d_j(x) = p\left(\frac{x}{\omega_j}\right) p(\omega_j) \tag{8}$$

$j = 1, 2, \ldots N$, and the pattern $\mathbf{x}$ is assigned to the pattern class with the largest decision value. The accuracy of the classification depends on the estimation of the probabilities $p\left(\frac{x}{\omega_j}\right)$ and for n-dimensional pattern vectors, the Gaussian distribution is assumed.

Neural Networks

Neural networks [35] are composed of a network of neurons which are tiny processing elements that are similar to biological neurons. The neurons are placed in an order such that they form a layer. The perceptron is a simple neural network shown in Figure 16. The input vector $\mathbf{x} = [x_1\ x_2\ x_3\ \ldots\ x_n]$ is applied to the neurons forming the input layer. The output of each neuron x_k is weighted by a factor w_k and they are summed. The weighted sum of inputs is given to an activation function that gets activated whenever the sum crosses a fixed threshold.

The response of this network is given by,

$$d(\mathbf{x}) = w_o + \sum_{k=1}^{n} x_k w_k ,$$ (9)

where w_o, w_1, w_2, ... w_n are weights and $d(\mathbf{x})$ is the linear decision function. The output $O = +1$ if $d(\mathbf{x}) > 0$ and $O = -1$ if $d(\mathbf{x}) < 0$. The final output is determined by an activation function which determines the threshold. This simple perceptron can be used to differentiate between two pattern classes. The vector $\mathbf{x}$ is equivalent to the feature vector of the given pattern and the output of the neural network can take one of two levels, either +1 or -1. The two levels are indicative of two different pattern classes. The weights can be varied which will vary the decision function, the activation function can be varied which will determine the activation threshold of the output, as shown in Figure 16.

This basic concept of pattern classification with a simple perceptron can be extended further to higher level neural networks with more number of input nodes, output nodes and hidden layers between the input and output. More neurons in the output can differentiate more number of pattern classes. Hidden layers can help in the design of the network to be more accurate in the classification process. The weights can be modified by applying a training algorithm with patterns belonging to known pattern classes. More the number of training data, better the network will classify unknown input patterns.

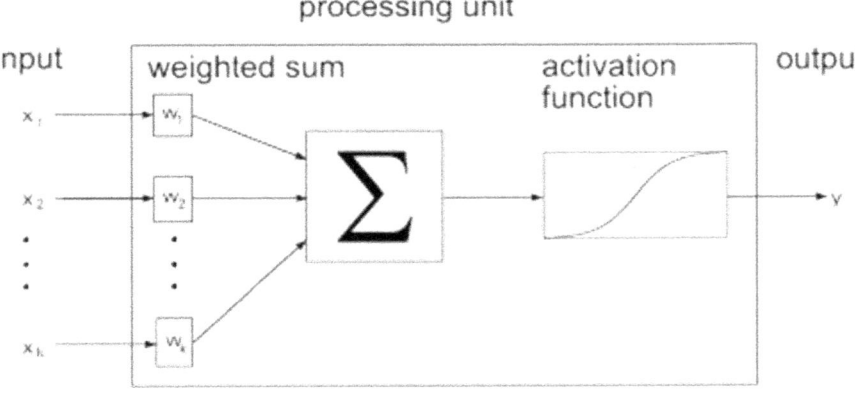

Figure 16 Perceptron [Cited from Ref. 38]

The patterns can be differentiated into separable and non-separable classes. In the separable case, the pattern classes can be easily differentiated with a decision boundary separating them. In the non-separable case, the pattern classes are not exactly separable and there is some amount of overlap between them that makes exact separability difficult. Multilayer feedforward neural networks with layers of neurons –

one input layer, one output layer and multiple hidden layers – have been designed and trained to classify patterns that are not linearly separable. The activation function can be hard limiting step function or soft limiting sigmoid function. Different activation functions can be used for different layers or for different nodes in the layer. The squared error between the desired output and the actual output of the network is to be minimized. The training of the network is done by back propagation that adjusts the weights of the network such that the error in the output is minimum.

Support Vector Machines (SVM)

SVMs are non-parametric classifiers originally proposed by Vapnik and Chervonenkis (1971). SVM is a classification algorithm that was proposed originally for linear separable classes and later modified to include non-linear separability. Basically SVM takes a set of input training data (each data point x_i is a n-dimensional vector) and constructs a hyperplane separating two classes. This is for binary classes, where the output y $\in$ [+1, -1]. Figure 17 (a), (b), (c) shows three possibilities for location of hyperplane separating class 1 and class2. [39]

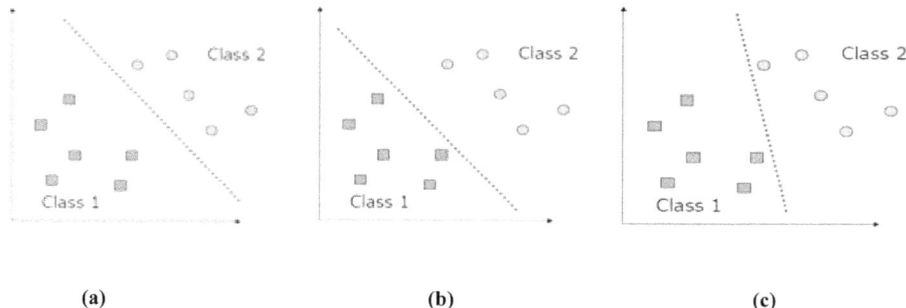

(a)   (b)   (c)

Figure 17(a) – (c). Hyperplanes separating two classes [Cited from Ref. 39]

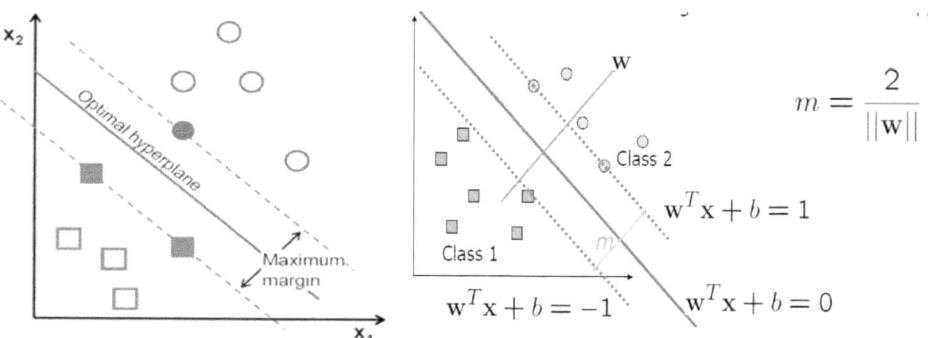

Figure 18. Location of optimal hyperplane   **Figure 19.** Equation of hyperplane [Cited from Ref. 40]
[Cited from Ref. 40]

The optimum location of the hyperplane will be such that the distance from the hyperplane to the input vectors of each class should be maximum, as shown in Figure 18. The input vectors closest to the hyperplane are called support vectors. The location of the support vectors determines the hyperplane and the classification accuracy of the algorithm. The separation between the hyperplane and the support vectors determines the margin. For good classification, the margin should be maximized, as shown in Figure 18 [40].

The hyperplane can be represented by the equation $\mathbf{w}^T\mathbf{x} + \mathbf{b} = \mathbf{0}$, where $\mathbf{x}$ represents all the training input vectors lying on the hyperplane, $\mathbf{b}$ is the bias, representing the displacement from the origin, $\mathbf{w}$ is a vector that is perpendicular to the hyperplane and $\mathbf{m}$ is the functional margin of the hyperplane, as shown in Figure 19 [40]. For good classification and separability, all training vectors belonging to class 1 should satisfy $\mathbf{w}^T\mathbf{x} + \mathbf{b} \leq \mathbf{-1}$ and all training vectors belonging to class 2 should satisfy $\mathbf{w}^T\mathbf{x} + \mathbf{b} \geq \mathbf{+1}$.

In 1995, Corinna Cortes and Vladimir N. Vapnik proposed a *softmargin* method for maximum margin hyperplane where it is not possible to cleanly separate the two classes. If the input vectors are not linearly separable, SVM allows the mapping of the finite dimensional input vector space to a higher dimensional feature space that makes separability easier. Kernel functions of the form K(x, y) are suitably selected so that the dot product of the variables takes minimum computation load. In a higher dimensional space, the hyperplane is defined as the one where the dot product of the input vectors lying on the hyperplane with a vector in that space is constant. [41, 42]

Principal Component Analysis (PCA)

PCA extracts the important information from the data and represents it in terms of principal components that are orthogonal to each other [43, 44]. The pattern or relationships between the various data can be extracted and visualized. The statistical components are obtained from the data using Singular Value Decomposition (SVD). PCA is a statistical technique that has wide range of applications such as object detection, face recognition, image compression, pattern recognition, classification, etc. When there is a large set of data to be analyzed, PCA can be applied for computing the statistical parameters. Mean refers to the statistical average of a set of data. Standard Deviation is a measure of the spread of the values of a given set around the mean. Variance is also a measure of the spread of the data about the mean and it is square of standard deviation. Covariance is a measure of the spread of data in two dimensions.

PCA can find patterns in data and by analyzing these patterns, dimensionality can be reduced. The covariance matrix of the given set of data is computed after subtracting the mean in each dimension. The Eigen vectors and Eigen values of the covariance matrix are calculated. The Eigen vector with the highest Eigen value is the principal component of the data set. Ordering the data in terms of Eigen values and choosing the first p components from the set of n-dimensional data reduces the dimension. The feature vector is constructed by forming a matrix with the Eigen vectors forming the columns of the matrix. Finally the input data is expressed in terms of these Eigen vectors instead of the original basis functions. This makes the data to be expressed in terms of the patterns existing among them, thus making pattern classification possible.

k-means algorithm

A set of data is given in an n-dimensional space R^n. The problem is to find k data points among them that can be the centers of k clusters such that the mean squared distance from any data point in the cluster to the cluster center is minimum. The k cluster centers should be chosen such that the average distance among all the data points should be minimized. Lloyd's algorithm is one of the popular clustering algorithms available to solve such problems. The *k-means* algorithm [45] is one of the simple iterative techniques for finding the k cluster centers so that the squared error distortion is minimized.

According to Lloyd's algorithm, the optimum center of a cluster is the centroid. Initially, a set of k points is identified, that is represented by z. The region around z is called Voronoi region $V(z)$. Each iteration of the algorithm computes the centroid of the Voronoi region such that the mean squared error reduces. The algorithm stops when the error reduces below a pre-defined threshold or the maximum number of iterations is reached.

Some of the popular classification algorithms have been discussed. Dimensionality reduction is another problem associated with classification. When more number of features are extracted, they have to be properly represented and processed. For example, in 7x5 image, the number of pixels to be processed for each segmented region is 35. If there are 10 characters in the image, then 350 pixels have to be processed in one component of the image. If it is a color image, then there will be three components for each pixel (RGB) and the number of values to be processed will be 350 x 3 = 1050. When there are thousands of training samples in a database, it could lead to increased time and computational complexity. This complexity in computations leads to the concept of feature reduction. Feature reduction refers to extracting minimal number of features among the existing ones that are necessarily required for classification. The representation of features also plays a major role in dimensionality reduction.

4. Applications

In the paper by Munawar Hayat et. al. [46] deep learning has been applied for image set classification. The main contributions of this work are : (i) Deep Reconstruction Models (DRMs) that discover the underlying geometry of the data. (ii) Three voting strategies – majority, weighted, preferentially weighted – take the inputs from the DRMs (reconstruction error information) and decide the class of image data set. (iii) Using automatic pose group approximation, classification performance is further refined. Face recognition from Kinect data is formulated as RGB-D based image classification problem. The performance of the algorithm has been evaluated on various data sets and it has been found to be superior.

In [47] Convolutional Neural Network (CNN) has been developed for image superresolution (SR). High resolution (HR) image is obtained from a low resolution (LR) image using deep convolutional neural networks. The input to the network is LR image and the output is a HR image. Deep learning based CNN and sparse CNN have been compared. Deep learning achieves good quality and speed. Bicubic interpolation is applied on the low resolution image as a pre-processing step. From the interpolated LR image, overlapping patches are extracted and each patch is a high dimensional vector comprising of feature maps. The number of feature maps is equal to the dimension of the vector. The vectors are mapped to another set of high dimensional vectors which form another set of feature maps. The vectors representing the patches are aggregated to reconstruct the HR image.

In [48], the acceleration of test-time computation of deep CNNs has been proposed. It has achieved a speed-up of 4x at the cost of slight increase in imageNet classification error. The focus is on non-linearity enabling an asymmetric reconstruction without the application of stochastic gradient descent algorithm. In [49], Deep Dynamic Neural Networks (DDNN) has been applied for segmentation and multimodal gesture recognition. A semi-supervised architecture with Hidden Markov Model has been developed. Skeleton joint information along with depth and RGB images has been used as inputs for classification and gesture recognition. The performance is on par with other learning based algorithms. Kaiming He et al. [50] have proposed spatial pyramid pooling (SPP-net) in their work. In conventional CNNs, the input images have to be of fixed size. Spatial Pyramid Pooling has eliminated this requirement and it generates a fixed length representation for whatever size of the input image applied. The algorithm is robust to scaling and deformations of the input image. The feature maps are extracted from the image once and they are pooled for the sub-images. It has been found to improve detection and classification accuracy compared to existing methods.

In [51], object detection based on region based CNNs has been proposed. Supervised pre-training followed by domain specific fine tuning has been applied. First, category independent region proposals are generated. They are the candidate detections available. Second, a CNN extracts features from the regions. Third, a set of class-specific SVMs are applied. Accuracy has improved by more than 50% relative to the best result on VOC2012. Deep CNNs can learn task-specific features, which improves the performance in computer vision [52]. Since acquiring labeled data can be quite challenging, training CNNs using unlabeled data is proposed in this work. The classification results have been found to outperform existing unsupervised learning on several popular data sets. In [53], Hybrid CNN – Restricted Boltzmann Machine model has been proposed for face verification. The uniqueness of this work is in learning high level relational visual features with rich identity similarity information. It is processed through the multiple layers of the network to extract high level features and the Restricted Boltzmann Machine does the classification. Zifeng Wu et. al. [54] have proposed deep CNNs for gait based human identification through similarity learning. Changing gait patterns can be used for identifying persons and it has achieved good results.

5. Conclusion

This chapter has given an insight into deep learning neural networks, image classification methods and overview of deep learning applications to image classification / computer vision / object identification. It is found that deep neural networks are an integral part of machine learning that constitutes artificial intelligence. Such deep learning techniques are required for solving complex tasks which the human brain does automatically with ease. In trying to imitate or uncover the intricacies of human intelligence, deep neural networks have paved the way for developing artificial intelligence applications that have proved difficult in the past. Further research in this field is required for doing complex tasks that the human brain accomplishes without visible effort.

References

[1] http://www.deeplearningbook.org/
[2] Remote Sensing Classification Algorithms Analysis Applied To Land Cover Change, *Master in Emergency Early Warningand Response Space Applications*. Mario Gulich Institute, CONAE. Argentina, 2014.
[3] www.mathworks.com
[4] https://medium.com/@ageitgey/machine-learning-is-fun-80ea3ec3c471
[5] S. Yu, S. Jia, C. Zu, Convolutional Neural Networks for Hyperspectral Image Classification, *Neurocomputing,* **219** (2017), 88–98.
[6] https://adeshpande3.github.io/adeshpande3.github.io/A-Beginner%27s-Guide-To-Understanding Convolutional-Neural-Networks/
[7] https://www.tensorflow.org/tutorials/wide_and_deep
[8] https://www.tensorflow.org/tutorials/
[9] https://www.r-project.org/about.html
[10] http://www.r-tutor.com/deep-learning/introduction
[11] https://en.wikipedia.org/wiki/R_(programming_language)
[12] https://in.mathworks.com/help/nnet/ug/deep-learning-in-matlab.html
[13] https://in.mathworks.com/discovery/deep-learning.html
[14] http://caffe.berkeleyvision.org/
[15] http://caffe.berkeleyvision.org/tutorial/
[16] https://devblogs.nvidia.com/parallelforall/deep-learning-computer-vision-caffe-cudnn/
[17] http://adilmoujahid.com/posts/2016/06/introduction-deep-learning-python-caffe/
[18] https://en.wikipedia.org/wiki/Torch_(machine_learning)
[19] http://torch.ch/
[20] https://www.microsoft.com/en-us/cognitive-toolkit/
[21] https://www.microsoft.com/en-us/cognitive-toolkit/blog/2017/06/microsofts-high-performance-open-source-deep-learning-toolkit-now-generally-available/
[22] https://channel9.msdn.com/Shows/Microsoft-Research/Microsoft-Cognitive-Toolkit-CNTK-for-Deep-Learning
[23] https://keras.io/
[24] https://www.datacamp.com/community/tutorials/deep-learning-python#gs.IipBCuo
[25] https://machinelearningmastery.com/tutorial-first-neural-network-python-keras/
[26] https://en.wikipedia.org/wiki/Deeplearning4j
[27] http://mxnet.io/
[28] https://en.wikipedia.org/wiki/MXNet
[29] http://cs.stanford.edu/people/karpathy/convnetjs/
[30] A. Krizhevsky, I. Sutskever, G. E. Hinton, ImageNet Classification With Deep Convolutional Neural Networks, *Proceedings of the 25ᵗʰ International Conference on Neural Information Processing Systems*, 1097 – 1105.
[31] http://desktop.arcgis.com/en/arcmap/latest/extensions/spatial-analyst/image-classification/what-is-image-classification-.html
[32] D. Lin, X. Xu, F. Pu, Bayesian Information Criterion Based Feature Filtering for the Fusion of Multiple Features in High-Spatial-Resolution Satellite Scene Classification, *Journal of Sensors,* **2015** (2015), 1 – 10.
[33] M. Nielson, *Neural Networks and Deep Learning,* http://neuralnetworksanddeeplearning.com/, 2017.
[34] http://cs231n.github.io/classification/
[35] R.C. Gonzalez, and R.E. Woods, *Digital Image Processing*, Prentice Hall of India Pvt. Ltd., 2007.
[36] L. G. Martins, Introduction to Pattern Recognition, UCP, Porto, Portugal, (2011), http://artes.ucp.pt.
[37] http://www.jars1974.net/pdf/12_Chapter11.pdf
[38] E. Rogers, Y. Li, *Parallel Processing in a Control Systems Environment*, Prentice Hall, 1993.
[39] M. Law, A Simple Introduction to Support Vector Machines, Department of Computer Science and Engineering, Michigan State University, https://www.cise.ufl.edu/class/cis4930sp11dtm/notes/intro_svm_new.pdf
[40] http://docs.opencv.org/2.4/doc/tutorials/ml/introduction_to_svm/introduction_to_svm.html

[41] C. J C Burges, A Tutorial on Support Vector Machines for Pattern Recognition, *Data Mining and Knowledge Discovery*, **2** (1998), 121–167.

[42] P.-H. Chen, C.-J, Lin and B. Schölkopf, A tutorial on *v*-support vector machines. *Applied Stochastic Models in Business and Industry*, **21** (2005), 111–136. doi:10.1002/asmb.537.

[43] H. Abdi and L. J. Williams, Principal Component Analysis, **2** (2010), *Computational Statistics*, John Wiley and Sons, 433 – 459.

[44] L. I Smith, A Tutorial on Principal Components Analysis, (2002), http://www.iro.umontreal.ca/~pift6080/H09/documents/papers/pca_tutorial.pdf

[45] T. Kanungo, D. M. Mount, N. S. Netanyahu, C. D. Piatko, R. Silverman, and A. Y. Wu, An Efficient k-Means Clustering Algorithm: Analysis and Implementation, *IEEE Transactions on Pattern Analysis And Machine Intelligence*, **24** (2002), 881 – 892.

[46] M. Hayat, M. Bennamoun, S. An, Deep Reconstruction Models for Image Set Classification, *IEEE Transactions on Pattern Analysis and Machine Intelligence*, **37** (2015), 1 – 15.

[47] C. Dong, C. C. Loy, K. He, X. Tang, Image Super-Resolution Using Deep Convolutional Networks, *IEEE Transactions on Pattern Analysis and Machine Intelligence*, **38** (2016), 295 – 307.

[48] X. Zhang, J. Zou, K. He, J. Sun, Accelerating Very Deep Convolutional Networks for Classification and Detection, *IEEE Transactions on Pattern Analysis and Machine Intelligence*, **38** (2016), 1943 – 1955.

[49] D. Wu, L. Pigou, P. J. Kindermans, N. D. Le, L. Shao, J. Dambre, and J. M. Odobez, Deep Dynamic Neural Networks for Multimodal Gesture Segmentation and Recognition, *IEEE Transactions on Pattern Analysis and Machine Intelligence*, **38** (2016), 1583 – 1597.

[50] K. He, X. Zhang, S. Ren, and J. Sun, Spatial Pyramid Pooling in Deep Convolutional Networks for Visual Recognition, *IEEE Transactions on Pattern Analysis and Machine Intelligence*, **37** (2015), 1904 – 1916.

[51] R. Girshick, J. Donahue, T. Darrell, J. Malik, Region-Based Convolutional Networks for Accurate Object Detection and Segmentation, *IEEE Transactions on Pattern Analysis and Machine Intelligence*, **38** (2016), 142 – 158.

[52] A. Dosovitskiy, P. Fischer, J. T. Springenberg, M. Riedmiller, T. Brox, Discriminative Unsupervised Feature Learning with Exemplar Convolutional Neural Networks, *IEEE Transactions on Pattern Analysis and Machine Intelligence*, **38** (2016), 1734 – 1747.

[53] Y. Sun, X. Wang, X. Tang, Hybrid Deep Learning for Face Verification, *IEEE Transactions on Pattern Analysis and Machine Intelligence*, **38** (2016), 1997 – 2009.

[54] Z. Wu , Y. Huang, L. Wang, X. Wang, T. Tan, Comprehensive Study on Cross-View Gait Based Human Identification with Deep CNNs, *IEEE Transactions on Pattern Analysis and Machine Intelligence*, **39** (2017), 209 – 226.

Deep Learning for Image Processing Applications
D.J. Hemanth and V.V. Estrela (Eds.)
IOS Press, 2017
doi:10.3233/978-1-61499-822-8-50

Virtual Robotic Arm Control with Hand Gesture Recognition and Deep Learning Strategies

K. Martin Sagayam[a,1], T. Vedha Viyas[b], Chiung Ching Ho[a,2], Lawrence E. Henesey[b]

[a,b,1] *Department of ECE, Karunya University, Coimbatore, India.*
[a,2] *Department of Computing and Informatics, Multimedia University, Malaysia.*
[b,2] *Deparment of Systems and Software Engineering, Blekinge Institute of Technology, Sweden.*

Abstract. Hand gestures and Deep Learning Strategies can be used to control a virtual robotic arm for real-time applications. A robotic arm which is portable to carry various places and which can be easily programmed to do any work of a hand and is controlled by using deep learning techniques. Deep hand is a combination of both virtual reality and deep learning techniques. It estimated the active spatio-temporal feature and the corresponding pose parameter for various hand movements, to determine the unknown pose parameter of hand gestures by using various deep learning algorithms. A novel framework for hand gestures has been made to estimate by using a deep convolution neural network (CNN) and a deep belief network (DBN). A comparison in terms of accuracy and recognition rate has been drawn. This helps in analyzing the movement of a hand and its fingers which can be made to control a robotic arm with high recognition rate and less error rate.

Keywords. Deep learning, convolution neural network, Deep belief network, virtual reality, hand gesture recognition, spatio-temporal feature, kinetic, Restricted Boltzmann Machine

1. Introduction

Deep learning (DL) is viewed to be a part of a broader terminology of machine learning methods based on learning data representations, where the results generated are comparable to and in some cases superior to human experts. This method is used in many applications, such as in mobile phones for the estimation and detection of weather and traffic forecasting. It is used in enhancing systems; DL is a credible technology to use based on the foundations of Artificial Intelligence (AI). By combining virtual reality (VR) with DL techniques, we can achieve a lot more in realizing various real time applications and make work much easier. Currently, the use of VR is gaining traction and acceptance by industry, which is leading the development at a fast rate. Some examples where VR is currently well developed and being used are

---

[1] K. Martin Sagayam, Department of ECE, Karunya University, Coimbatore 641 114, India; E-mail: martinsagayam.k@gmail.com.

in the field of health care, gaming, mobile phones and almost in every filed. The development of VR was realized with the deployment of two technologies. The first was the development of Kinect sensor by Microsoft Corporation© [2]. Kinect sensor features an RGB camera, a multi array microphone and depth sensor that is capable of tracking body movements. In using this technology both color and depth information is obtained. This results into an improved experience on human computer interaction (HCI). One limitation is that it is very challenging to achieve 100% accurate results due to low resolution and sometimes interference due to other objects. The second technology that has lead to VR development is known as Deep Neural Networks (DNN). It is also known as Deep Learning (DL). It mimics the functionalities of the human brain. It acts as a platform for AI. It contains neuron-like structure and predicts the output like the way a human brain behaves.

The use of DL is becoming popular as major companies such as Facebook, Google, Microsoft, and Amazon are further developing and applying techniques from DL. In applying DL, we can predict various outcomes and this activity is useful in various applications. Many industries are adopting techniques and solutions from DL as a mean for prediction. In various applications, it is viewed that AI can "think for itself" by simplifying the work of human beings. It is viewed that DL should be considered as the starting point of AI.

1.1. Outcome

Based upon our research in which is presented in this book chapter, we plan to overcome the difficulties faced by hand gesture recognition and improve the accuracy rate of hand gestures. The difficulties that we aim to improve are as follows:

- Using a single camera to capture the picture of the hand gestures and then estimating other parameters to lower the total cost.
- To improve the overall detection of various hand gestures.
- Extracting the features of a hand in precise manner that is more precise, in a fixed lighting background condition.

1.2. Literature Survey

The VR arm is a concept, which is achieved, can be used for various real-time applications [23]. The VR arm is a robotic arm, which is portable and can be controlled from a distance. It can be controlled by using DL techniques, which involves the usage of DL algorithms. Normally, to obtain a 3-D image of a hand, a multi-camera setup or GPU acceleration is deployed. It is practically challenging, and it limits to the public, which makes it impossible for the common man to use it. The realization of this multi-camera setup is very expensive [10]. In this chapter, we present a more robust technique for the purpose of building a robotic arm operated via hand gestures and deep learning, by utilizing just a single camera and estimating the other parameters [22].

1.3. Related works on hand detection and segmentation

There are many approaches to implement hand gesture recognition and estimation. To detect the image of a hand, three types of methods are utilized:

- Color based method
- Depth based method

- Methods combining both depth and color information

Color-based (CB) methods are used to differentiate between the colors of a hand from the background of that particular image. A skin colored model was taken into consideration [24], where the skin colors and their particular surrounding region had been found by thresholding in YC_bC_r color space. According to Micheal Van den Bergh and Luc Van Gool [25], they have presented a trained Gaussian mixture model; that is incorporating with histogram feature points. The property of using edge detection and motion detection was realized [26]. The accuracy rate of CB methods is not satisfactory as it mostly relies on background color and stability.

In depth-based (DB) methods often a camera is used to obtain depth data by time of flight camera. Depth techniques consider that hands are closer to the acquisition device and therefore must be kept a slight distance away from the user, which is not possible in all cases. Combining both CB and DB methods can, leads to superior performances of the system. In a study by Lu Xia et al [26] have proposed hand overlapping with the help of ToF camera and RGB camera. However, calibration is necessary. Therefore, it must be combined with other predictions methods to improve the accuracy rate.

1.4. Related work on hand gesture recognition

Hand gesture recognition can be classified based on shape such as:

- Feature-based
- Appearance-based

The main property of feature based methods is detection using position and number of fingers. In a study of Chuging Cao and Ruifeng Li [29] they have proposed a hand pose recognition (HPR) algorithm based on topological features. Calculations and estimation using topological features resulted with an accuracy rate of 95.4%. This method was experimented on nine static gestures. The feature points which are extracted from recognition of hand gestures that are used are curvature extremes, valleys and peaks [30]. The feature point values are perfectly matched with a high rate image pair using fuzzy neural network. The main disadvantage of these methods is that the number of recognized hand gestures is limited to a particular number.

Using appearance-based method, Poonam Suryanaryanan et al [27] have presented a technique for detection of hand poses using 3D volumetric shape descriptions. This method uses recognition of scale and volumetric shape descriptors. The accuracy of this method was found to be from 80% to 95%. This method was experimented with six hand gestures. In a study by Malassiotis and M G Strinzis [28] have described a range data for recognition of static hand postures. This method was tested with 20 hand postures and the accuracy rate range between 70% - 90%.

2. Framework of Hand Gesture Recognition System

In Fig. 1 have described about the framework with four main stages is presented beginning with image acquisition stage, then leads to pre-processing stage and segmentation stage with classification being the final stage.

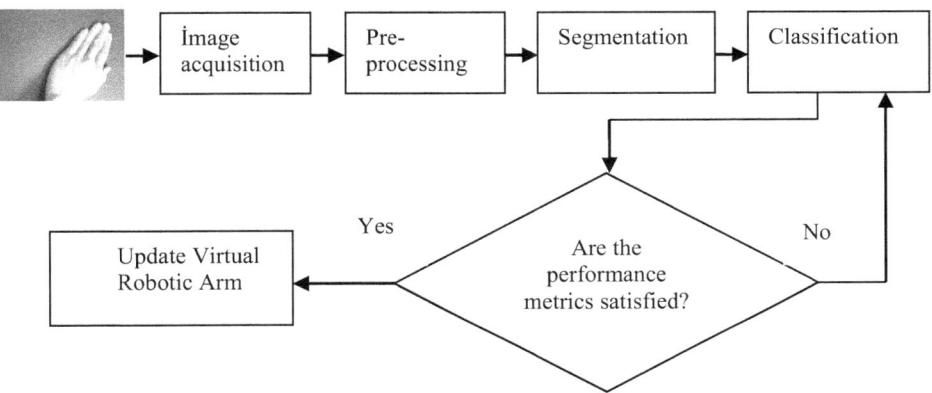

Fig.1 Framework of the hand gesture recognition system

2.1. Image Database

The dataset consisting of various images of different hand gestures were obtained from the Website of Imperial College of London [34]. Five datasets, each corresponding to different gestures are considered in this book chapter. The five hand gesture deployed are: a) Center-to-left, b) Compress hand, c) V-Shape center-to-left, d) V-Shape center-to-right, and e) Left-to-right. Each class corresponds to each actions of hand gesture, and each comprises of 100 images. Each sequence was filmed in front of a stationary camera having roughly isolated gestures. Thus, substantially large intra-class variations in spatial and temporal alignment reflect the datasets. Each hand image is of size 320 x 240 and is available in jpeg format. Fig. 2 represents the typical sample sequences of the five different hand datasets.

Center to left

Compress hand

V-shape center to left

V-shape center to right

Left to right

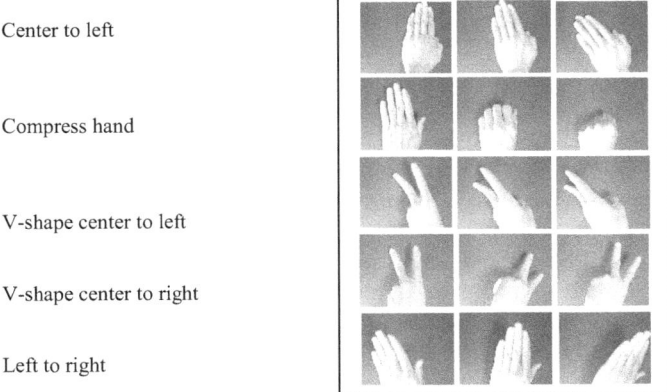

Fig.2 Sample sequences of five gesture datasets

2.2. Image Acquisition

Under image acquisition, images are captured with camera and with the help of various sensors. The sensors presents in the camera further process the image, process various values based on image acquisition methods, and then these values are directed to the pre-processing unit.

2.3. Pre-processing

The hand gesture parameters are obtained from the image acquisition in a fixed background. By using various edge detection techniques like Sobel, Canny, Prewitt, etc., the appropriate edges of the image are detected and then these edge values are sent to the further process such as feature extraction and segmentation.

2.4. Segmentation

The hand gesture parameters obtained may contain a lot of values. Therefore it takes a lot of time to process these values. Therefore, to reduce time and to improve latency, feature extraction is done. Important parameters are extracted and then processed. Then these parameters are further segmented using occlusion techniques.

2.5. Classification

In this work, have presents two deep learning classifier realizations: DBN and CNN. The parameters have normalized in terms of scale, translation and rotation to train from the hand posture image using Deep Belief Network (DBN). CNN has an effective parallel computation to those parameters than DBN [5]. After processing through various layers of the neural network, the final output of an image is obtained. By using DL techniques, it shows that the improved results in terms of accuracy and recognition rate.

3. Image Acquisition

Image acquisition can be acquired by two methods are capturing and pipelining, it has been described in section 3.1 and 3.2 detailed.

3.1. Image Capturing

The gesture of a hand is captured with the help of a webcam or any camera connected to a computer or laptop. Mostly all webcams work generally in the same manner. Every camera has an image sensor chip build into it. These image sensors are used to capture moving images and convert them into streams of digits. The image sensor chip is considered to be the heart of a camera. Camera sources present today are mostly based on two types of sensors: Complementary Metal Oxide Semiconductor (CMOS) technology and Charged Coupled Device (CCD) sensor are used in recent approaches. In tradition, to detect and track hand gesture using Kinect sensor, accelerometer, etc., [1,

2]. It captures the raw stream data and skeletal data to the system. The main drawback of Kinect sensor is ineffectiveness, easily hacked and privacy issues.

3.2. Image Pipelining

The image acquisition by the sensors is processed and the acquired signal is sent to the next building block for processing. CMOS sensors has gives yield to a digital signal in parallel streams of pixel segments in either YC_bC_r or RGB design, along vertical and horizontal synchronization and a clock of pixel [7]. There are odds of permitting an external clock and adjusting signs to control the exchange of image from the sensory nodes. A CCD utilizes an analog front-end chip, for example AD9948, will handle the simple processed analog data, quantized into digital form and creates a suitable timing to check the CCD cluster [8, 9]. The parallel computing yields a digitalized output from AFE in 10-bit, or 12-bit determined output values per pixel. Nowadays, low voltage differential (LVD) signaling, has turned into a vital option to the simultaneous bus information approach. LVD's is an easy, low pin-count, fast serial interconnector that has better commotion invulnerability and low control utilization than the standard approach. The process of the input data does not stop at the sensory node. There are a few calculations determined by the processing element before the shutter catch is discharged. The concentration and presentation frame work with the assistance of mechanical camera segments to control the focal point position in light scene attributes. Auto-exposure algorithm has determined the illumination over scene locales to make up for exposed regions by controlling either shade speed or gap estimate or both. The fundamental reason here is to keep up the relative difference between various locales in the input data and to accomplish an objective normal luminance. Auto-focus calculations are isolated into two classes active techniques which come under the main classification utilize infrared or ultrasonic emitters/ beneficiaries to gauge the separation between the cameras and object being acquired by the device. Inactive strategies, which come under the previous, on acquiring the data from the acquisition device, settle on the centering choices. The media processor controls different focal points and screen engines by means of PWM yield motions in both of the above prototypes. It also alters the automatic gain control (AGC) sensory circuits for automatic control unit. The final stage is the outcome of the desired data from the camera sensor has been obtained.

4. Image Pre-processing

Pre-processing is a strategy used to evacuate commotion or an undesirable recurrence segment from an input data. This procedure includes identification of edges by recognizing the sharpness in the input data, which portrays the limitations of the patterns in the hand gesture image. Pre-processing is the typical concept for processing the input data at the least level of reflection with both information and yield high intensity [11]. Edge detection has shown up excessively troublesome in uproarious data on the grounds that both the input data and commotion deliver high recurrence content [10]. There are various issues in edge detection operators such as Sobel, Canny, Prewitt and Robert. Kernel functions are by and large used to identify flat, vertical and corner-to-corner edge of an image [12].

4.1. Robert's edge detection method

Lawrence Robert has introduced Robert's edge detection strategy in the year 1965 [10]. It rushes to process and to compute the 2-D spatial slope on an input data by its gradient operator. This strategy accentuates areas of high spatial recurrence, which regularly edges within an image. The contribution of this kernel function towards the input is an image of gray scale type with regards to the yield is most used for this method [10]. The pixel level values in every point in the specific yield speak to the assessed, to compute the extent of the spatial domain of gradient data at that instant point.

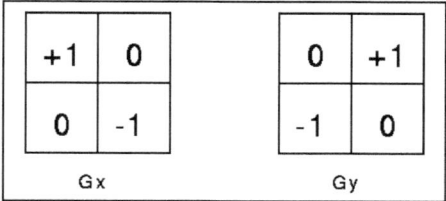

Fig.3 Robert's edge detection method used couple of 2x2 convolution kernels

4.2. Sobel edge detection method

The Sobel edge detection method was introduced in the year 1970 [32]. The image partition is the major goal in this work, Sobel edge detection technique has perceives edges utilizing Sobel operator approximates to the subordinate. It is shown by the edges at that specific focus where the gradient is most noteworthy. It represents the space of high spatial recurrence that relates to the edges by making a 2-D spatial slope amount on that specific image. It is used to find the determined total gradient size in 'n' input grayscale image at every point.

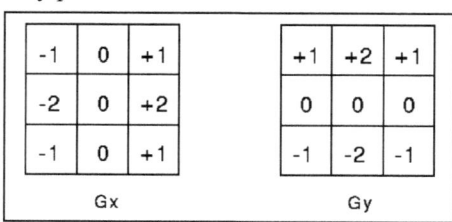

Fig.4 Sobel detection method used a pair of 3x3 convolution kernels

4.3. Canny edge detection method

Canny edge detection strategy is maintained as one of the predominant method used in industrial applications. This specific method was presented by John Canny in the year 1983, which he made for his Master's postulation at MIT. Despite the fact that it was presented numerous years prior, regardless it outperforms the majority of the newer algorithm   that have been produced. The main objective of Canny edge detection approach is to separate commotion from the input data before locating the edge point within an image. It has the attitude to find the edges and the genuine estimation of the limit without disturbing the components of the edges in the input data. It is less defenseless to commotion than the strategies for Robert and Sobel operators. The calculations required in canny edge detection technique as listed below [12]:

- Convolution of image f(r,c) with a Gaussian capacity to get smooth image f^(r,c).

$$f^(r,c)=f(r,c)*G(r,c,6)$$

- To compute edge strength, apply contrast gradient operator and afterward bearing and edge size are required.
- Exert non-maximal or basic concealment to the inclination extent.
- Finally, apply edge to the non-maximal concealment image and the edges are recognized.

4.4. Prewitt edge detection method

The Prewitt edge detection strategy was invented by Prewitt in the year 1970 [32]. Prewitt operator discovers its motivation in the estimation of greatness and introduction of an edge. Distinctive gradient operator needs a very tedious figuring to appraise the bearing from the extents in the x and y directions. In any case, the compass edge identification extricates the direction with the most astounding reaction, specifically from the kernel function. Despite the fact that it kept to 8 conceivable directions, information exhibits that the most direct course figuring's less great. This gradient operator is ascertained in the 3x3 matrix representation of neighborhood pixel for 8 consequent directions. All the 8 convolution masks are determined. One of the complicated masks is then added up, in particular with the handiness of the biggest module. It is slightly less demanding to actualize than Sobel operator; however it creates to some degree of noise outcomes.

$$H_1 = \begin{bmatrix} 1 & 1 & 1 \\ 0 & 0 & 0 \\ -1 & -1 & -1 \end{bmatrix}; H_2 = \begin{bmatrix} -1 & 0 & 1 \\ -1 & 0 & 1 \\ -1 & 0 & 1 \end{bmatrix}$$

Fig.5 Prewitt detection method used 3x3 convolution kernel

5. Feature Extraction

On completion of the pre-processing of the hand gesture image, the respective feature vectors associated to the hand gestures are calculated. Various feature extraction techniques are available, but the most suitable one depends upon the type of features to be extracted from the hand gesture. The main objective of feature extraction is to lessen the amount of variables used to explain the data under supervised learning [13, 14]. Feature extraction is used to extract derived values from an initial set of input data that should be more informative, non-redundant allowing to interpret the data which can be understood by human and also allows reduction in dimensionality of the hand image without loss of information [16, 17].

At the each time interval, large amount of data to be processed results in overloading of system; only some features that are more informative and relevant can be used for processing. Generation of too many variables is common while handling large amounts of data [15, 16]. Therefore, the system requires large amount of memory and more power, which results in failure while generalizing the data. The phenomenon, which describes the feature vector, is known as feature descriptors [14].

6. Classification

Deep neural networks (DNN) are derived from artificial neural network that include more than two layers of dominant variables in its structure called as Deep Learning (DL) [3]. The main objective of DL is used to select and extract the feature from an input hand gesture data automatically, and then classify the target set with respect to the defined trained set [5, 6]. The detailed description of deep learning techniques has been discussed in the subsections.

6.1. Hand Gesture Recognition using DL Techniques

Artificial neural networks (ANNs) has comprised with various hidden layers in the structure is also known as Deep Neural Networks (DNNs) are complex to deal with and their aim is to withdraw and close features automatically from an input data, and then sort them towards their respective classes. In recent years, the DL uses has been expanded in various research fields. Vinod Nair and Geoffrey E Hintom [31] have introduced a top-level model for DBNs, which is evaluated in the form of 3-D object recognition. In this work, DBN based hand gesture recognition has been developed. The parameters have normalized in terms of scale, translation and rotation to train from the hand posture image using Deep Belief Network (DBN). The training process of DBN's is too difficult to parallelize through the system, in order to increase the robustness of the system by computing parallel using convolution neural networks (CNN). It can be used in various pattern recognition applications such as written recognition, face recognition, action recognition etc.

6.2. Deep Belief Networks (DBN)

DBNs are considered to be productive model, which are probabilistic in natural way. It comprises a number of hidden layers over a lower layer of over units that acquire an input data. DBN set up connections that are undirected in between the upper units and connections that are directed in between the lower units as shown in Fig. 6(a) [3]. Naïve DBNs are generative neural networks that stack RBMs (resembling generative autoencoders). DBNs can be implemented as a pile of restricted Boltzmann machines (RBMs). An RBM is considered from every two adjacent layers. There are two steps involved in the training process of DBN. They are known as pre training and fine tuning [18].

(a) Structure of Deep Belief Network

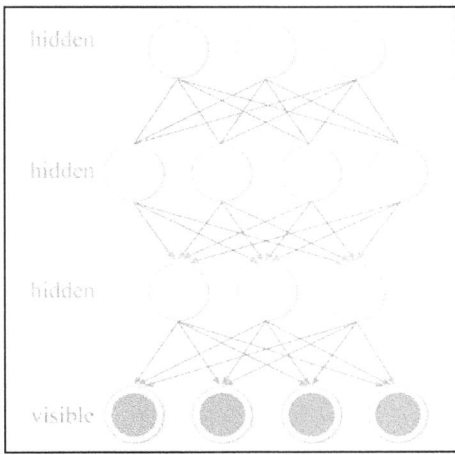

(b) Restricted Boltzmann Machine

Fig.6 DBN implementation via RBMs

6.3. Restricted Boltzmann Machines (RBM)

Restricted Boltzmann Machines (RBMs) consists of 1 hidden unit and 1 visible unit, which forms a bipartite graph without hidden-hidden 0r visible-visible connection, similar to that of displayed in Fig. 6(b). As there exists no hidden-hidden or visible-visible connection, the conditional distribution over hidden layers h and visible layers v are written in logistic functions:

$$p(h_j = 1 \mid \vartheta; \theta) = \sigma(\sum_i w_{ij}\vartheta_i + a_j) \tag{1}$$

$$p(v_i = 1 \mid h; \theta) = \sigma(\sum_j w_{ij}h_j + b_i) \tag{2}$$

Where $\theta = \{w, b, a\}$ are model quantities; w_{ij} indicates the symmetric constant between over unit j and visible unit i; b_i and a_j are bias terms; $\sigma(x)$ is a logistic function.

Algorithm 1: Contrastive Divergence
u= CD for RBM($x^{(0)}$, epoch,$\in$);
Input: Learning rate$\in$, number of iterations epoch, a sample $\upsilon^{(0)}$ from training sets.
Output: w, which represents RBM weight matrix
w is to be initialized with ergodic values from 0 to 1;
recur
gibbs sampling $h^{(0)}$ using P(h| $\upsilon^{(0)}$);
gibbs sampling $\upsilon^{(1)}$ using P(υ| $h^{(0)}$);
$$\Delta w = -P(h = 1 \mid \upsilon^{(0)})\upsilon^{(0)} + P(h = 1 \mid \upsilon^{(1)})\upsilon^{(1)};$$
$$w = w + \in \Delta w;$$
İndex++;
until index$\geq$epoch;

Algorithm 2: DBN to be Pre-trained

w= preTrainDBN($\upsilon^{(0)}$, epoch, $\in$, L);

Input: Learning rate$\in$, number of iterations epoch, number of layers L excluding the visible layer, a sample $\upsilon^{(0)}$ from training sets.

Output: Weight matrix w^i of layer i,i=1,2,......,L-1;

$h^0=\upsilon^{(0)}$ where h^i indicates the value of units in i^{th} hidden layer. h^0 represents the input layer.

Layer=1;

recur

$$w^{layer} = CDforRBM(h^{layer-1}, epoch, \in);$$

Gibbs sampling $h^{layer} \_ u\sin g \_ P(h^{layer} \mid h^{layer-1})$

until layer $\geq$ L;

- **Pre-training**

Greedy layer-by-layer algorithm, are also known as pre-training is focused on training a accumulation of RBMs, where every two layers that are adjacent is to be considered as an RBM and we use contrastive divergence to develop RBM weights. The training of the first layer of RBM using various training data is carried on. Then we utilize eqn. 2 to calculate hidden class activation probability P(h|v). For higher levels of RBM, we would be using P(h|v) as training data, which is useful in obtaining features from the output of the previous layer (i.e. each set). After completion of pre-training, the starting values for all the units of the network and the number of hidden layers are obtained which is equal to the number of RBMs.

- **Fine-tuning**

DBNs have the capacity of obtaining high-level representation from higher-level dimensional data. For the purpose of achieving hand gesture recognition, we will also attach an output layer consisting of randomly set weights at the tip of the deep belief networks after pre-training all parameters θ of DBN. Since fine-tuning comes under supervised learning, we must acknowledge the respective label towards each hand image. For that, we utilize back-propagation for the purpose of fine-tuning all the weights with labeled input data.

6.4. Convolutional Neural Networks (CNN)

Convolutional Neural Networks (CNNs) comprises of neurons that optimizes itself through training process. Each neuron will obtain an input and does an operation (such as scalar product) – the basis of limitless ANNs. The entire network will still formulate a single perceptive score function from the input raw feature vectors to the end output of the class score. The final layer consists of loss functions related with classes while still applying the usual methods developed for traditional ANNs [19]. CNNs are mainly used for the purpose of pattern recognition applications. This helps us encode image specific features into the instruction set, rendering the network more applicable for image-focused tasks, while decreasing the values needed to set up the model. CNNs comprises of three different layers. The layers are as follows: convolutional layers, pooling layers and fully connected layers. A modified CNN architecture for MNIST classification is illustrated below in Fig. 7.

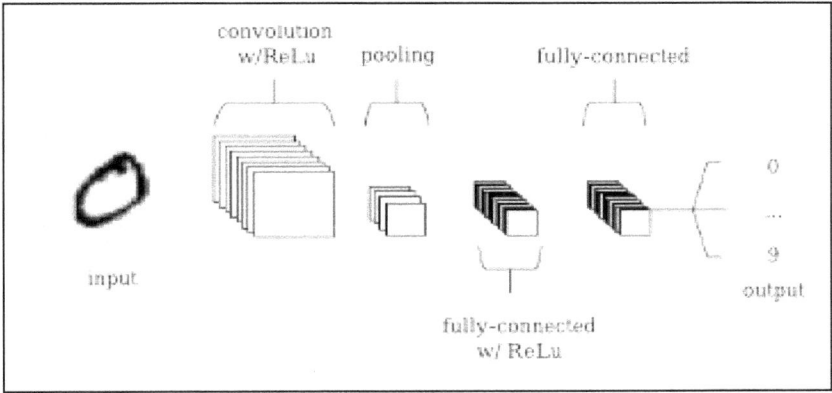

Fig.7 CNN architecture with five layers

The canonical functionality of above example of CNN can be simplified into four key areas [20]:

- The input layer will preserve the pixel parameters of that particular image.
- The convolutional layer helps in determining the outcome of neurons, which are joined with the local regions of the input by calculating scalar product between the regions connected to the input volume and their respected weights. The rectified linear unit commonly known as ReLu, aims to put in 'element-wise' activation function such as sigmoid to the output of the activation exerted by the previous layer.
- The pooling layer performs down sampling along with the spatial dimensionality of the given input, which helps in reducing the number of parameters within that activation function.
- The fully connected layers render similar to that of the standard artificial neural networks by producing class scores from the activations, to be used for classification. ReLu can be used between these layers for the purpose of improving performance.

Therefore, by the above process, CNNs are able to change the original input layer by layer with the help of convolution and down sampling techniques to exert class scores for classification purposes.

7. Results and Analysis

Various experiments have been carried out in series to examine various sectors of the proposed system. Analyses have been done on hand gestures with five different classes. These hand gestures are trained and then tested. For hand gesture training and testing experiments, first we have considered five sets of hand gestures such as center to left, compress hand, V-shape center to left, V-shape center to right and left to right [4]. We have recorder frames from video clips containing hand gestures and have collected 500 frames in the form of the images in total. All images have been transformed into grayscale and they have been rescaled into images with resolution of 32x32 pixels [3]. The intensity of each pixel is modified into (0-1).

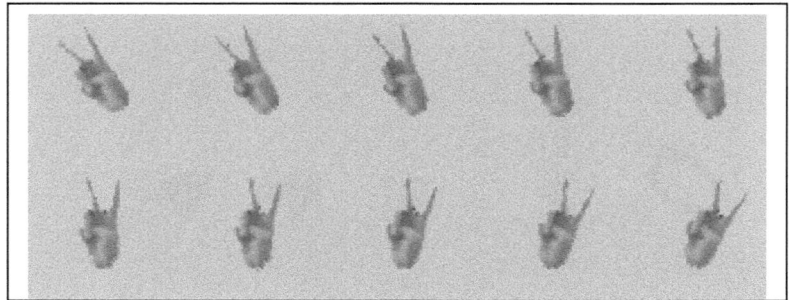

Fig.8 Hand gesture moving from left to right in V-shape

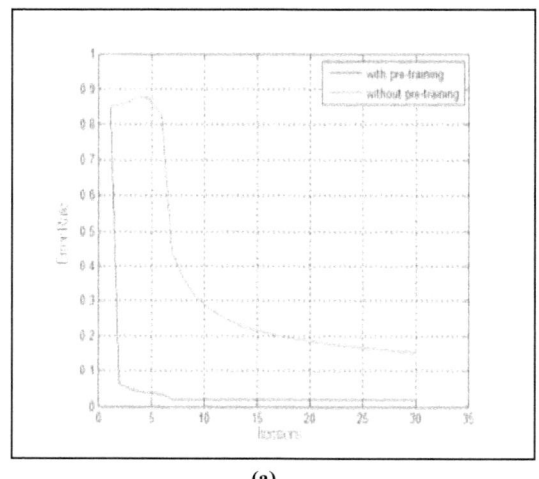

(a)

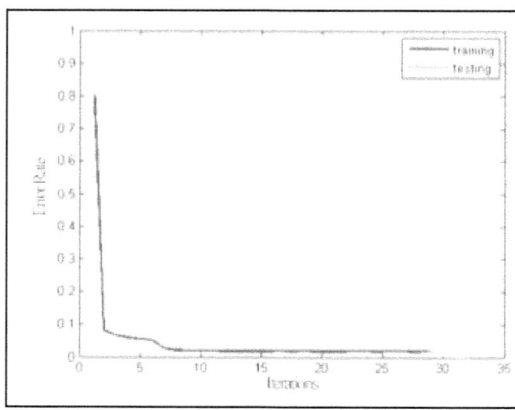

(b)

Fig.9 (a) Training and testing error rate of DBN (b) Error rate while using DBN, with and without pre-training on training set

7.1. Training with DBN

We have opted to use DBN, consisting of hidden layers, three in number, with 500, 1000, and 2000 hidden units in each hidden layer. The input units are assumed to be 1024 in number since the resolution of each input image is 32x32 pixels. The final layer consists of five units. Each unit represents five sets of hand gestures with 60 frames per seconds have been recorded. During pre-training period of the starting layer, intensities of all pixels are assumed as input units. After the pre-training of DBN on unlabeled various hand gestures, a classification unit consisting of five output units is attached to the labeled images with the final layer of the DBN model as its input. Back propagation algorithm is utilized in fine-tuning the whole network with 32 iterations. The rate of training and testing fine-tuned values are shown in Fig. 9(a). The experiments have been carried out without pre-training in DBN. The results obtained are shown in Fig. 9(b) and the pre-training process using unlabeled data has a great beneficial impact in the training process of DBN. Table 1 shows that the detailed analysis of DBN architecture with respect to layer, connections and weights.

Table 1. Comparison of Internal layer, Weights and Connections

Layer	Types of Layer	Maps	No. of Weights	Connections
Input	Input	1x(32x32)	----	----
C1	Convolution	6x(28x28)	153	12301
S2	Sub-sampling	6x(14x14)	15	5878
C3	Convolution	16x(10x10)	1512	151603
S4	Sub-sampling	16x(5x5)	30	2001
C5	Convolution	120x(1x1)	48120	48120
Output	Full connection	36x(1x1)	4356	4356

7.2. Training with CNN

According to Yann LeCun et al [33], a convolution network is also known as LeNet-5 has been proposed for pattern recognition applications which have fidelity of 99.2% developed on MNIST database. In this work, LeNet-5 is used for hand gesture recognition applications. It consists of six layers, which excludes the input. Total input units are 1024, as the resolution of images is 32x32 pixels. The information regarding LeNet-5 used in this work is shown in Table 2. There are five output layers in correspondence to five different hand gestures. It has established a colligation between C5 and the output layer. CNN are developed on the training set using 20 iterations. Fig. 10 given below represents the evaluation of training and testing of error rate using CNN, for each iteration. Table 2 compares the accuracy with various classifiers for various models such as rotate left, rotate right, front, back and catch.

Table 2. Comparison of accuracy rates between DBN, CNN and HOG+SVM

Model	Accuracy (DBN) (%)	Accuracy (CNN) (%)	Accuracy (HOG + SVM) (%)
Center to left	97.69	92.91	87.88
V-shape center to left	98.65	95.63	91.15

V-shape center to right	98.26	94.25	88.71
Left to right	98.67	94.94	88.91
Compress	98.46	95.98	91.47

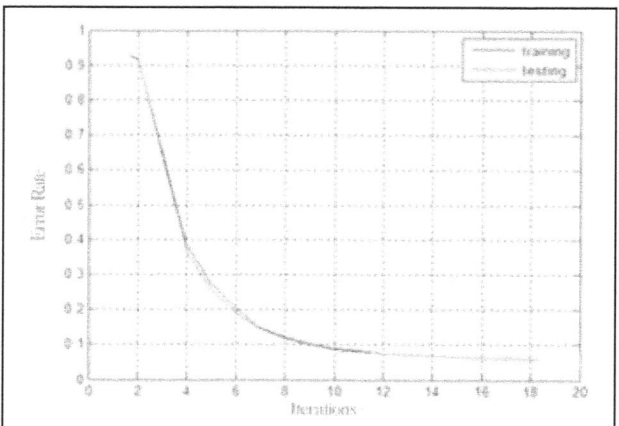

Fig.10 Error rate for training and testing of CNN as a function of the number of iterations

7.3. Comparison of Accuracies

After the completion of training, DBN and CNN are made to run on a testing set. HOG+SVM is also tested with our dataset for comparison. For each hand data, the 144-D HOD feature is extracted [21]. The image resolution of 32x32 is split into 16 cells. The gradient of a cell is split into 9 orientation bins and each cell consists of 8x8 pixels. Without overlapping, each image consists of 4 blocks. For the purpose of training multiclass SVM, LIBSVM is used with linear kernel for recognition. Table 2 shows that the results related to the accuracy rate of DBN, CNN and HOG+SVM for each hand gestures. On comparison of values from the results obtained above, it is found that both CNN and DBN obtain has high recognition rate. The total means relate to accuracy rate for all hand gestures are listed here: DBN – 98.35%, CNN – 94.74% and HOG+SVM – 89.62%. The proposed system with DBN is superior than CNN constructed result. Another result is that both DBN and CNN perform much better compared to the baseline HOG+SVM method.

7.4. Controlling 3-D model of VR arm

For implementing robotic arm control, a 3-D model of robotic arm is chosen [34, 35]. Variety of functions respective to each hand gesture movements are coded and saved in the database. Hand gestures are used to control the robotic arm, have five different movements of robotic arm related with five different actions are considered. If the captured gesture matches with that of the gesture stored in the trained database, the instruction sets are activated and passed on to the robotic arm model for execution. Fig. 11 shows that the movement of a robotic hand corresponding to five different hand gestures. Temporarily only five movements have been made corresponding to five different actions. In further, more actions are to be considered and executed by the robotic arm model. Therefore, using different hand gestures, robotic arm is controlled which in real-time can be used for various applications. As the accuracy rate is also higher from the analysis, recognition of hand gestures will be of higher recognition rate and will be error frees making way to be useful in the real world for performing complex operations.

(a) Compress

(b) Flat

(c) Center to right

(d) V-shape center to left

(e) V-shape center to right

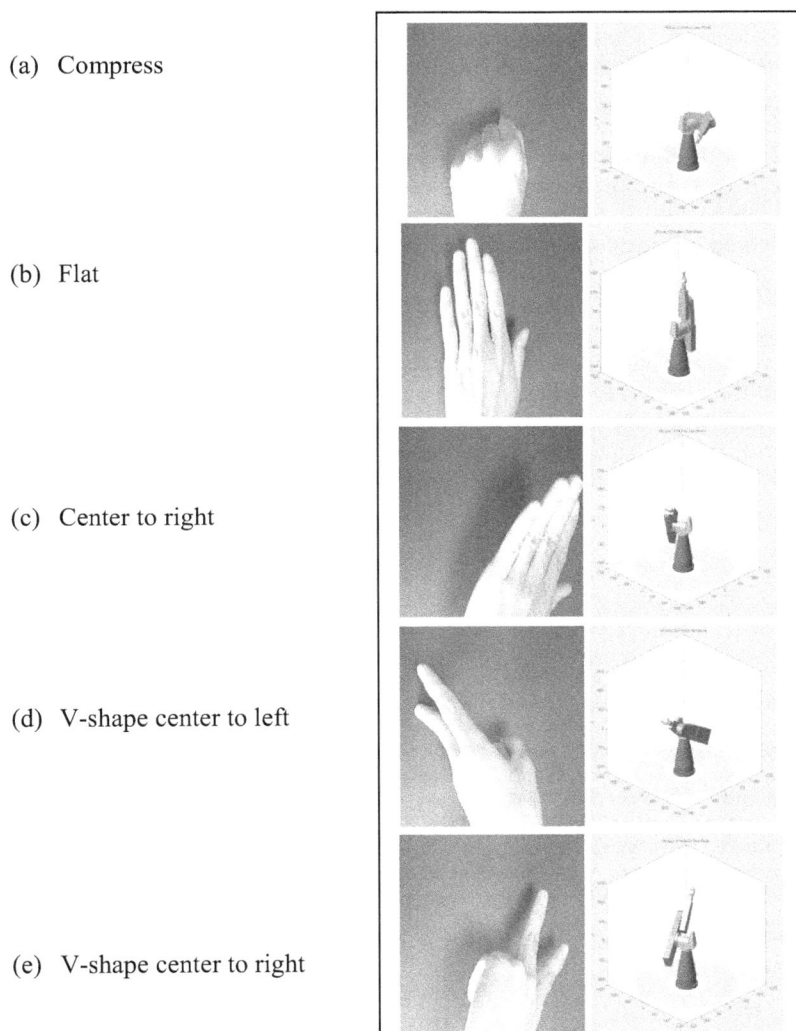

Fig.11 Movements of the VR Arm model corresponding to different hand gestures

The various actions performed by a VR arm model are as follows: (a) controlled arm bens down when hand is closed, (b) controlled arm changes into default position when hand is made flat, (c) controlled arm moves downwards backside when hand is moved from center to right, (d) controlled arm moved towards the left when hand in V-shape is moved from center to left, and (e) controlled arm moves towards the right when hand in V-shape is moved from center to right.

8. Conclusion

By this research, a real time hand gesture recognition module has been developed to control robotic arm. Firstly, we have considered hand gesture data from MNIST datasets of five different classes with 60 different frames in each class. Both DBN and CNN have greater accuracy than HOG+SVM. Instead of a normal camera, by using 3-D depth camera, we can further enhance the performance. We can obtain both 3-D spatial data and depth data from this 3-D depth camera. With this data, the prediction rate will be higher, and these parameters can be used to obtain the 3-D hand image. With these techniques, hand gesture recognition can be made efficient and realizing this system could be inexpensive. Due to higher accuracy rate, hand gesture recognition would be more effective to the system to recognize. Finally, through various experiments we have analyzed that by applying DL techniques through neural networks, the accuracy rate of hand gesture recognition has increased in greater extent. The output data obtained using DL techniques can be fed to control a robotic arm which can be employed for various real time applications like performing surgeries, driving a car from home, and doing any other tasks by being at one place. This results in to less time consumption from this experimentation. Hence, future research work tends to work on implementing this VR arm through hand gesture recognition in VR applications.

References

[1] A. El Gamal, H. Eltoukhy, *CMOS image sensors*, IEEE Circuits and Devices Magazine **21(3)** (2005), 6-20.
[2] Robert McCartney, Jie Yuan, hand-Peter Bischof, *Gesture recognition with the Leap motion controller*, published in RIT scholar works, Rochester Institute of Technology (2015).
[3] Di Wu, Lionel Pigou, Pieter-Jan Kindermans, Nam Do-Hoang Le, Ling Shao, Joni Dambre, Jean-Marc Odobez, *Deep Dynamic Neural Networks for Multimodal Gesture Segmentation and Recognition,* IEEE Transactions on pattern analysis and machine intelligence **38(8)** (2016).
[4] Natalia Neverova, Christian Wolf, Graham Taylor, Florian Nebout, *ModDrop: Adaptive multi-modal gesture recognition*, arXiv:!501.00102v2[cs.CV] (2015).
[5] Ao Tang, Ke Lu, Yufei Wang, Jie Huang, Houqiang Li, *A real time hand posture recognition system using deep neural networks*, ACM Transaction Intelligence System Technology **9(4)** Article 29 (2013).
[6] Pooyan Safari, Martin Kleinsteuber, *Deep learning for sequential pattern recognition*, Technische Universitat Munchen (2013).
[7] Nick Waltham, *Observing photons in space-CCD and CMOS sensors*, Springer publisher New York (2013), 423-442.
[8] M. Bigas, E. Cabyuja, J. Forest, J. Salvi, *Review of CMOS image sensors*, Microelectronics, Elsevier publisher **37** (2006), 433-451.
[9] Courtney Peterson, *How it works: The charged-coupled device (CCD)*, Published by George town university in the journal of young investigators, Inc. (2009).
[10] Van kasteren T., Englebienne G., and Krose B. J., *Human activity recognition from wireless sensor network data: Benchmark and software*, In activity recognition in pervasive intelligent environments (2011), 165-186.
[11] Rafael C. Gonzalez, Richard E. Woods and Steven L. Eddins, *Digital Image Processing using MATLAB*, Pearson education Ptd. Ltd., Singapore (2004).
[12] Muthukirishnan R., M. Radha, *Edge detection techniques for image segmentation*, International journal of computer science and information technology 3(6) (2011).

[13] Swapnali B., Vijay K., Varsha H., *Feature based object detection scheme*, Technovision International Conference (2014).

[14] Bay H., Tuytelaars T., VanGool L., *SURF: speeded up robust features*, ECCV 1 (2006), 404-417.

[15] Bhosale Swapnali B, Kayastha Vijay S, Harpale Varsha K., *Feature extraction using SURF algorithm for object recognition*, International journal of technical research and applications 2(4) (2014), 197-199.

[16] Bassem Sheta, Mohammad Elhabiby and Naser El-Sheimy, *Assessment of different speeded up robust features (SURF) algorithm resolution for pose estimation of UAV*, Survey (IJCSES) 3(5), 2012.

[17] Kosuke Mizuno, Yosuke Terachi, Kenta Takagi, Shintaro Izumi, Hiroshi Kawaguchi and Masahiko Yoshimoto, *Architectural study of HOG feature extraction processor for real-time object detection*, IEEE workshop on signal processing systems (2012).

[18] G. E. Hinton, R. R. Salakhutidinov, *Reducing the dimensionality of data with neural networks*, Science 313(5786) (2006), 504-507.

[19] Keiron O'Shea, Ryan Nash, *An introduction to convolutional neural networks*, Published in research gate, arXiv:111.08458v2 (2015.)

[20] Yann LeCunn et al, *Generalization and network design strategies connectionism in perspective* (1989), 143-155.

[21] Chih-Wei Hsu, Chih-Chung Chang, Chih-Jen Lin and others, *A practical guide to support vector classification*, (2003).

[22] Ganesh Choudary B., Chetan Ram B V., *Real time robotic arm control using hand gestures*, ICHPCAA International Conference, IEEE Publisher (2014).

[23] Ayan Sinha, Chiho Choi, Karthik Ramani, *Deep hand: robust hand pose estimation by completing a matrix imputed with deep features*, IEEE conference on computer vision and pattern recognition, (2016).

[24] Marco Fagiani, Emanuel Principi, Stefano Squartini, Francesco Piazza, *A new system for automatic recognition of Italian sign language – neural nets and surrounding*, Springer publisher, (2013), 69-79.

[25] Micheal Van den Bergh, Luc Van Gool, *Combining RGB and ToF cameras for real time 3D hand gesture interaction*, Applications of Computer Visions, IEEE publisher, (2011), 66-72.

[26] Lu Xia, Chia-Chih Chen, J K Agarwal, *View invariant human action recognition using histograms of 3D joints*, Computer vision and pattern recognition workshop, IEEE publisher, (2012).

[27] Pooanm Suryanaryanan, Anbumani Subramanian, Dinesh Mandalapu, *Dynamic hand pose recognition using depth data*, 20th International Conference on Pattern Recognition, IEEE publisher, (2010).

[28] S Malassiotis and M G Strinzis, *Real time hand posture using range data*, Image and Vision Computing 27(7) (2008), 1027-1037.

[29] Chuging Cao and Ruifeng Li, *Real time hand posture recognition using Haar like and topological feature*, Machine vision and human machine interface, IEEE publisher, (2010), 683-687.

[30] Balaz Tusor and A R Varkonyi-Koczy, *Circular fuzzy neural network based hand gesture and posture modeling*, Instrumentation and Measurement Technology Conference, IEEE publisher, (2010), 815-820.

[31] Vinod Nair and Geoffrey E. Hinton, *Rectified linear units improve restricted Boltzmann machines*, Published by department of computer science, University of Toronto (2009).

[32] Rafael C. Gonzalez, Richard E. Woods and Steven L. Eddins, *Digital image processing using MATLAB*, Published in Pearson Education Ltd., Singapore (2004).

[33] Yann LeCun et al, *Generalization and network design design strategies- Connectionism in perspective*, (1989), 143-155.

[34] T-K. Kim and R. Cipolla, *Canonical correlation analysis of video volume tensors for action categorization and detection*, IEEE Transaction on Pattern Analysis and Machine Intelligence 31(8) (2009), 1415-1428.

[35] Jagdish Raheja, Radhey Shyam, *Real-time robotic hand control using hand gestures*, published in research gate, publication no: 221923729 (2012).

Deep Learning for Image Processing Applications
D.J. Hemanth and V.V. Estrela (Eds.)
IOS Press, 2017
doi:10.3233/978-1-61499-822-8-68

Intelligent Image Retrieval via Deep Learning Techniques

Rajeev Kumar Singh[a,1], Suchitra Agrawal [a,1] , Uday Pratap Singh[a] and Sanjeev Jain[b]

[a] *Madhav Institute of Technology and Science, Gwalior*
[b] *Shri Mata Vaishno Devi University, Katra*

Abstract. With increase in amount of multimedia content, there arises need to retrieve it from database effectively. Several techniques have been introduced to deal with the situation efficiently. Such methods are known as Image Retrieval methods. This chapter focuses on brief review of different content based and sketch based image retrieval systems. Along with existing techniques, it also covers about what further can be achieved with these systems.

Keywords. Relevance Feedback, Content Based Image Retrieval (CBIR), Sketch-Based Image Retrieval (SBIR), Feature Selection, Semantic Gap

1. Introduction

With regards to the utilization of digitized images over the World Wide Web, it is known to everybody that there could be a huge number of clients working with digital data. This advanced data can be as computerized images as images are one of the most ideal methods for sharing, understanding and retaining the data. Image retrieval can be arranged into two sorts; exact image retrieval and relevant image retrieval. Exact image retrieval [1] can be alluded to as image acknowledgment and its genuine applications [2] has been implemented by different researchers. It obliges images to be coordinated precisely or 100 percent, though relevant image retrieval is in light of contents and there is adaptable size of importance relying on definite element values. A more prominent number of controllers of computerized data infers a more noteworthy number of advanced image handling/sharing included bringing about a more prominent measure of multifaceted nature while overseeing and controlling advanced content; in this manner, it is very frequently required from an advanced content administration framework to give an elegant interface to productively dealing with the utilization of advanced images in certain applications. The essential objective of an image administration framework is to pursuit images and to contend with the applications in the present time, image looking ought to be founded on its visual content. For this reason, numerous analysts have conceived numerous methods in view of various parameters to acquire precise outcomes with high recovery execution. The starting points of research in the field of content based image retrieval were laid in the late 70's. Database advancements for pictorial applications were talked about without precedent for that period and the scientists got fascination for this space from that point forward.

---
[1] Rajeev Kumar Singh, Suchitra Agrawal, CSE-IT Department, MITS, Gwalior (M.P.), India; E-mail: suchiagrawal0007@gmail.com.

Previous image retrieval procedures were not that clever and modern and they were not ready to scan for images in light of its visual components rather those strategies depended on content based metadata of pictures. All pictures put away in the database were initially labeled with the metadata and after that images were looked in view of the image metadata. Content based image retrieval techniques were utilized for traditional database applications. They were utilized with parcel of business applications and purposes however expanding utilization and volume of advanced images made execution and precision issues for content based image retrieval techniques.

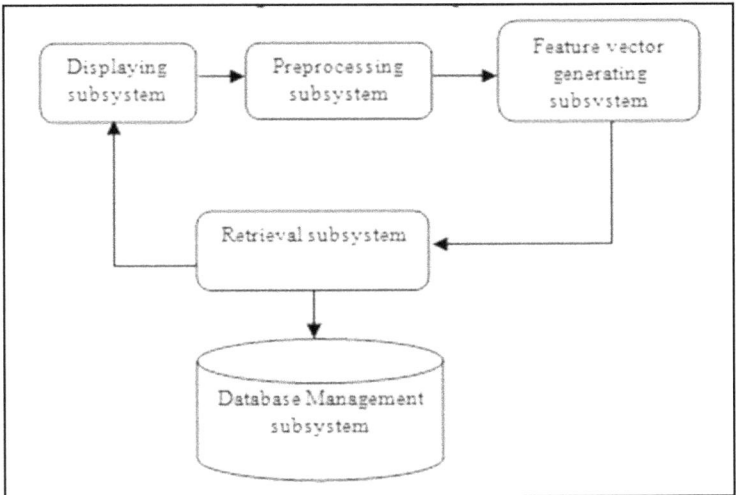

Figure 1: The global structure of the system [50]

Content Based Image Retrieval (CBIR) is known as QBIC and is technique of computer vision application to the problem of image retrieval, that is, the digital images searching problem in huge amount databases. CBIR is opposed to concept-based methods. "Content-based" means contents of an image search rather than metadata like tags, keywords, or descriptions associated with image. Textual data about images can be simply searched applying existing technology, but these need humans to manually define all images in the database. It is possible to lost images which is use quite a lot of synonyms of their descriptions.

Users sometimes do not have sufficient and/or suitable inputs to get the picture they want through Content Based Image Retrieval and the unavailable request for such query photos again led the researchers to create another better system to conduct for this purpose. Sketch Based Image Retrieval (SBIR) is a system that allows to show the user's query by a free-hand drawn sketch which the new system idea is. This system, paved the way to the user to show his ideas by drawing that facilitate the matter for those who cannot express their desires well by annotation. This system adds new interesting variety of free-hand drawing style to express the relevance and provides users with the even more flexibility of query.

The retrieval of content based image includes the following frameworks:

Color based retrieval: Among different component extraction systems, color is considered to be the most predominant and recognizing visual element. Most of the times, histograms are used to portray the color elements of an image. A color histogram allows system to depict the complete color dispersion in an image and is most utilized system for CBIR [3] on account of its proficiency and viability.

Color histograms strategy has the benefits of expediency, low request of memory space and because they are not modified with the change in size and resolution of the image, it holds the broad consideration.

Texture based retrieval: The recognizable proof of particular textures in an image is accomplished basically by considering texture as a two-dimensional gray-level variety. Textures are depicted by contrasts in brightness with high frequencies in the range of image. They are helpful in recognizing ranges of images with comparative color, (for example, sky and ocean, or water, grass). An assortment of techniques has been utilized for measuring texture likeness; the best settled rely on upon looking at estimations of what are outstanding as second-request insights evaluated from query and database pictures. Basically, these gauge the relative brightness of picked sets of pixels from every image. From these it is conceivable to measure the image texture, for example, contrast, coarseness, directionality and regularity [4] or periodicity, directionality and randomness [5].

Shape based retrieval: By utilizing the histogram of edge detection, shape information can be extracted. Strategies for shape feature extraction are elementary descriptor, Fourier descriptor, template matching, quantized descriptors, canny edge detection [6] and so on. Shape elements are less advanced than their color and texture partners as a result of the natural unpredictability of representing to shapes. Specifically, regions covered by an object must be identified so as to portray its shape, and various known segmentation algorithms are applied to identify the low-level color and texture components along with region growing or split-and-merge. In any case, for the most part it is not really conceivable to accurately fragment a picture into important areas utilizing low-level components because of the assortment of conceivable projections of a 3-D protest into 2-D shapes, the multifaceted nature of every individual object shape, the presence of shadows, occlusions, non-uniform illumination, changing surface reflectivity, etc. [7].

The remaining part of the chapter have been organized as follows: Section 2 covers the techniques introduced for retrieving images on the basis of content present in the query image. Section 3 gives a brief review about the Sketch Based Image Retrieval. Section 4 then concludes by providing future scope for image retrieval techniques.

2. Content Based Image Retrieval

The very first system developed for content based image retrieval is QBIC [8] by IBM is one the well-known commercial system. Many techniques since then have been proposed for CBIR with use of different other methodologies. Few of them are discussed in further sections.

An agent based searching framework [9] is deployed. The plan has proposed use of numerous agents to reduce the search space by utilizing an interleaving system. The neural system assumes a vital part in the creation of feature-contained vector to be utilized by the agents for image retrieval in an interleaved form. The system treats the problem as a distributed query and with the reduction in the search space; images are retrieved from the database simultaneously. It also used the concept behind Lilies to deal with multiple agents.

An online image retrieval framework that allows multiple queries has been presented in [10]. The proposed strategy has been executed over the web and test outcomes are combined with loads of various queries and tests. Neuro-fuzzy logic is used to interpret the query expressions provided by the user. Input query consists of colors to be retrieved from the database of images.

In contrast to linear relationship between different features of an image, a method of dynamically upgrading the similarities among components of an image has been proposed with the utilization of radial basis function [11] neural system which permits the collection of heterogeneous image elements for more relevant image retrieval. The intersection of histograms for feature vector of query image f_i^q and database image f_i^t is calculated as:

$$v_i = 1 - \frac{\sum_{m=0}^{M-1} \min(f_i^q[m], f_i^t[m])}{\min(|f_i^q|, |f_i^t|)} \tag{1}$$

where
$|f_i^q| = \sum_{m=0}^{B-1} f_i^q[m],$
$|f_i^t| = \sum_{m=0}^{B-1} f_i^t[m],$
$i = 1$ (*for red*), 2 (*for green*), 3 (*for blue*) and
B is used to denote the number of bins in histogram. The user's feedback is ranked as:

$$U(q) = \begin{cases} 0.9, & if \ alike \\ 0.5, & if \ similar \\ 0, & if \ different \end{cases}$$

The framework gives out better results in comparison with different strategies in the light of implemented results.

The researchers introduced a plan for altering the feature vector comparison strategy [12] at run time in view of the user's preference. The error function defined is as:

$$E = \frac{1}{2}\sum_{\mu}(d^\mu - t^\mu)^2 \tag{2}$$

where μ indexes the μth training pattern, d^μ is the rank provided by the user and t^μ is the rank obtained by system.

Thus, the framework acts like a human and takes in the similarity matching components on various queries. The algorithm was tested on the NIST Mugshot Identification Database and results obtained are quite acceptable.

To achieve the higher efficiency in retrieval results, the search space can be increased for specific features providing a more clear view to extract images from database. It can be implemented along with relevance feedback [13] where the system can learn from the user feedback mechanism. Implemented system performed experiments on database of images more than 50 k and the results showed that the increase in feature search space can retrieve more relevant results.

In [14] images of interested organs are retrieved from the database. Images of healthy and fit organs are put in the database and when performing examination on any therapeutic image comprising of various organs, the proposed system permits the user to distinguish organs as indicated by the ones put in the database. Neural systems are utilized to classify the query image and images are then retrieved from the database by calculating the distance between their features.

A relevance feedback technique [15] for updating the query with search criteria has been implemented to improve the performance efficiently. The feature vector is updated as:

$$r_i^{(k+1)} = r_i^k + \alpha \left(\frac{1}{N_R} \Sigma_{j \in D_R} D_j \right) - \beta \left(\frac{1}{N_N} \Sigma_{j \in D_N} D_j \right) \tag{3}$$

where $i = 1, 2, \ldots, N$, D_R and D_N are sets of relevant images and irrelevant images respectively, N_R and N_N are number of images in the above two sets respectively, while α and β are suitable constants [63]. The similarity between query image and database image is then calculated as:

$$Sim(R^{(k+1)}, Z) = \Sigma_{i=1}^{N} W_i^{(k+1)} m_i^{(k+1)} \left(r_{ij}^{(k+1)}, z_{ij}, W_{ij}^{(k+1)} \right) \tag{4}$$

where Z is the feature vector of the database image, $m_i^{(k+1)} \left(r_{ij}^{(k+1)}, z_{ij}, W_{ij}^{(k+1)} \right)$ is the normalized similarity measure between query image and retrieved image, W_i and W_{ij} are inter-weight and intra-weight vectors for elements updated using the Eq. (5) and (6) respectively.

$$W_i^{(k+1)} = 1 - \frac{d_i^{(k)} - D_{min}^{(k)}}{d_{max}^{(k)} - D_{min}^{(k)}} \quad (i = 1, 2, \ldots, N) \tag{5}$$

where $d_i^{(k)}$ is the average value of variance distance of ith feature vector, $D_{min}^{(k)}$ and $D_{max}^{(k)}$ are minimum and maximum variance distance among all feature vectors.

$$W_{ij}^{(k+1)} = \frac{1}{\sigma_{ij}^{(k)}} \tag{6}$$

where σ is the standard deviation. The use of simultaneous processing of moving query vectors and updating weight factors accelerated the speed of convergence for the relevance feedback retrieval system and can retrieve results effectively as compared to conventional methods of image retrieval.

The multi-label graph-cut algorithm [16] group edges according to two key Gestalt principles i.e., continuity and proximity. Perceptual edge grouping framework produces better edge groups which can be used to improve a variety of higher level tasks. During sketch generation, edge grouping is carried out via edge detection and then filtering to generate the sketch. HOG is extracted for each machine generated sketch and query sketch. Edge map is constructed and then perceptual grouping framework is applied to group salient edges together.

The dynamic incorporation [17] with user interest for a search criterion along with utilization of intelligent agents to mix along the user interested search matrix in the upcoming retrieval handle makes the procedure to work smartly. The prototype system, Locating Images Easily (LIZY) developed to test supports both query-by-sketch and query-by-example. The efficiency of the system was evaluated using the following:

$$2 * P * R * U / (P + R + E + U)$$

where P is the precision, R is recall, U is usability and E is efficiency.

In the light of working results, the framework has carried on great in comparison with different strategies of a similar kind.

The characteristics of self-organizing neural systems [18] are utilized to enhance image retrieval strategies. Self-organizing neural systems upheld working of various leveled quad tree map. The overall structure of the proposed framework is as:

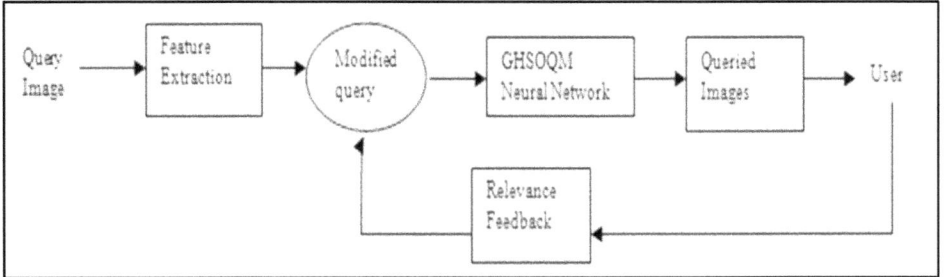

Figure 2. Architecture of GHSOQM-based CBIR system [18].

To compare similarity between two images A and B, there is need to calculate distance between the two defined as:

$$d_{mn} = \left(w_1 \sum_{i=1}^{3} \left(f_{m,i}^A - f_{n,i}^B \right)^2 + w_2 \sum_{i=4}^{6} \left(f_{m,i}^A - f_{n,i}^B \right)^2 + w_3 \sum_{i=7}^{9} \left(f_{m,i}^A - f_{n,i}^B \right)^2 + \right.$$
$$\left. w_4 \sum_{i=10}^{12} \left(f_{m,i}^A - f_{n,i}^B \right)^2 \right)^{1/2} \tag{7}$$

where $w_1 - w_4$ are weights to colors and textures. Then new query matrix is formed using:

$$R_i^x(t+1) = \alpha R_i^x(t) + \frac{\beta}{|Y|} \sum_{k=1}^{|Y|} Y'_{ki} - \frac{\gamma}{|Z|} \sum_{k=1}^{|Z|} Z'_{ki} \tag{8}$$

where α, β and γ are parameters to control the relative wrights for current query image, relevant images and irrelevant images respectively. Y and Z are the nearest regions from the regions of query image. The time complexity for growing hierarchical self-organizing quad tree map is less as compared to flat structure comparison in images.

For color-based image retrieval, multivariate measurements [19] are provided by using neural systems. Image database adopted for the experiment is from the Corel gallery as it contains wide variety of images. The mean $E[R]$ and variance $var[R|C]$ for given two multidimensional point samples X and Y of size m and n are calculated as:

$$E[R] = \frac{2mn}{N} + 1 \tag{9}$$

$$Var[R|C] = \frac{2mn}{N(N-1)} \times \left\{ \frac{2mn-N}{N} + \frac{C-N+2}{(N-2)(N-3)} [N(N-1) - 4mn + 2] \right\} \tag{10}$$

where $N = m + n$. After calculating the above parameters, for comparing color distributions, WW Test is carried out by computing:

$$W = \frac{R - E[R]}{\sqrt{Var[R|C]}} \tag{11}$$

Using the Neural-Gas network, the RGB feature vectors of images are extracted and then similarity comparison is carried out between the query image and the database images.

Multi-instance strategies [20] for learning user priorities of image scientific categorizations have been contemplated. For given set of images, the energy function of the class has been defined as:

$$E(X_t, W_t) = \ln\left(-\sum_{b=1}^{N} \sum_{t=1}^{N_b} \ln p(x_{tb}(t)|w_t) \right) \tag{12}$$

The framework proposed is prepared to order images in a database as positive and negative to lie in the intrigued class. After positive and negative sets have been formed, the learning rules are applied to the corresponding subsets:
Reinforced Learning:

$$w_i^{(m+1)} = w_i^m - \eta \nabla E(X_i^+, w_i) \tag{13}$$

Anti-reinforced Learning:

$$w_i^{(m+1)} = w_i^m + \eta \nabla E(X_i^-, w_i) \tag{14}$$

where η is a user defined learning rate and ∇E is the gradient vector.

The tests were made and the framework was prepared by providing diverse groups of input images. After a couple iterations of learning, the framework could effectively sort pictures that lie in class of user's interested images.

Another approach of image retrieval with the use of reasonable weighting [21] in performing comparability among images by relevance feedback is incorporated with image's texture elements when connected to the retrieval procedure enhances the precision. The distance between object set O_i to the query center R_i is formulated as:

$$d' = \frac{d.weight_i}{\sum_i weight_i} + \frac{d.\sum_i dist_i}{dist_i} \tag{15}$$

where d is the distance between O_{ij} and O_i, $weight_i$ applies to relevant object, $dist_i$ is the original distance between relevant object and original query center, d' is the combined distance between each object. Consequences of experiments demonstrated that the level of user satisfaction is improved.

The use of semantic tree [22] for image retrieval process with a different way of utilizing given query image has been proposed. In this, the semantic tree needs to be updated after each and every successful retrieval. The tree is updated using the following algorithm:

1) If $T = null$, initialize T; else go to Step 2.

2) For each i, if $\|f_q - f_{c_i}\| < \varepsilon$, collect all the child nodes of C_i to the set S and all its leaf nodes to set $Leaf$.

3) If $r \in S$, get all its child nodes as relevant images to q. Then move to step 8; else 4.

4) Calculate the similarity $sim(q, Leaf_i)$, where $Leaf_i$ represent the element from set. And then display the nearest K images to user.

5) Add the indexes of relevant images to r and add r to C_i which is nearest cluster to q.

6) Update f_q in r and the center of C_i, and go to step 8.

7) For each i, if $\|f_q - f_{c_i}\| < \varepsilon$, get relevant images from whole set and add r to the newly constructed cluster node C as child.

8) Continue retrieving images till the user's requirement.

The above algorithm clusters the tree in such a way that it forms different semantic categories for results. The results of the experiments have shown that the performance of the system increases gradually.

The algorithm has been proposed based on relevance feedback and selection algorithm [23] following the probabilistic scheme for image retrieval. The algorithm needs to remember the weight assigned to an image, which is done by gathering the advantages of probabilistic conceptualization and interaction of user. Further, on the basis of similarity matching algorithm, the images are classified as positive and negative cases. In case of only Positive Examples, the query likelihood needs to be maximized to select the optimal parameters as:

$$\emptyset = \log(L) = \sum_{i=1}^{I} \alpha_i \sum_{n=1}^{N_i} \log \sum_{k=1}^{K_i} P_{ik} P(X_{ni} \Theta_{ik}) \tag{16}$$

where $i = 1, \dots, I$ feature indexes, $n = 1, \dots, N_i$ data in the ith feature, $K = 1, \dots, K_i$ classes for i^{th} feature, X_{ni} is the nth data item of ith feature, Θ_{ik} represents the set of parameters. While in case of Positive and Negative Examples, the likelihood is maximized as:

$$\emptyset = \log(L) = \sum_{i=1}^{I} \alpha_i (A_i - R_i) \tag{17}$$

where A_i and R_i are given as,

$$A_i = \left[\sum_{n=1}^{N_i} \log \sum_{k=1}^{K_i} P_{ik} P(X_{ni}|\Theta_{ik}) \right] + \left[\sum_{m=1}^{M_i} \log \sum_{h=1}^{H_i} P_{ih} P(Y_{mi}|\Theta_{ih}) \right]$$

$$R_i = \left[\sum_{m=1}^{M_i} \log \sum_{k=1}^{K_i} P_{ik} P(Y_{mi}|\Theta_{ik}) \right] + \left[\sum_{n=1}^{N_i} \log \sum_{h=1}^{H_i} P_{ih} P(X_{ni}|\Theta_{ih}) \right]$$

Then the framework continues with the positive case images for further retrieval process. Tests demonstrated that the framework has a decent potential for recovery of varying images.

User log-based information for maintaining the image retrieval information [24] in user log has been proposed. To improve the retrieval performance, the preferred retrieval results from the database are maintained in log files for further retrieval process. As per user preference, this strategy tends to remove noise while performing image retrieval, as it may reduce the speed of the whole process. The proposed architecture is as:

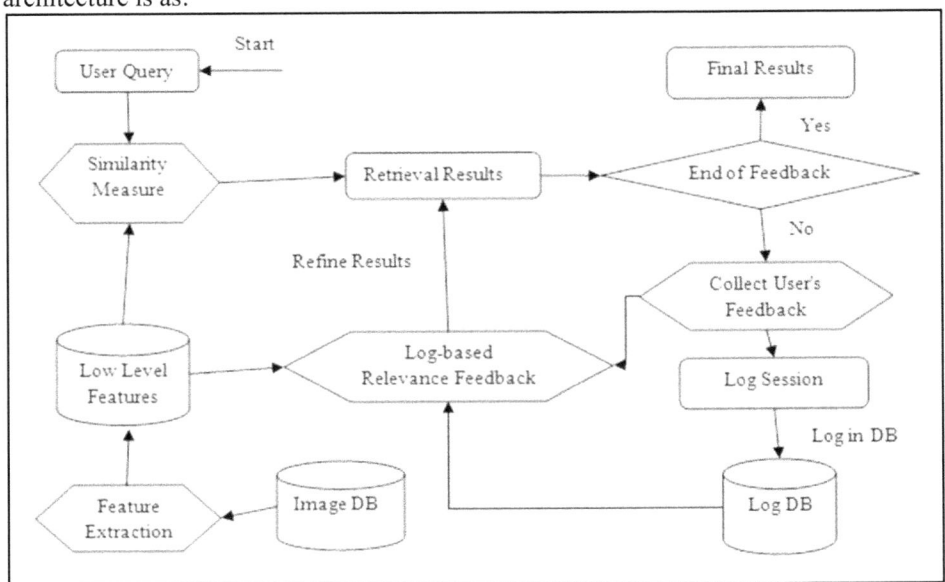

Figure 3. The architecture of the system [24].

Experiments performed on different set of images with different preference have increased the efficiency of the system.

Having so many algorithms for image retrieval based on relevance feedback, an analysis [25] was performed on these algorithms by following an abstract model for CBIR. It has been found that relevance feedback when implemented with slight modifications to the logic components and existing system results in the improvement of performance. Performance was measured by following the Rate of Ascent (ROA) as:

$$\frac{2 * precision * recall}{N * (precision + recall)}$$

where N is the Rate of Convergence of the relevance feedback network. The analysis was performed by designing a system which measured the relevance feedback based image retrieval system performance for different relevance feedback modules.

Neural networks along with the relevance feedback approach [26] have been implemented to train the system to learn user semantics. In contrast to static construction of neural network, the dynamic neural network is constructed with the help of images retrieved against the queries.

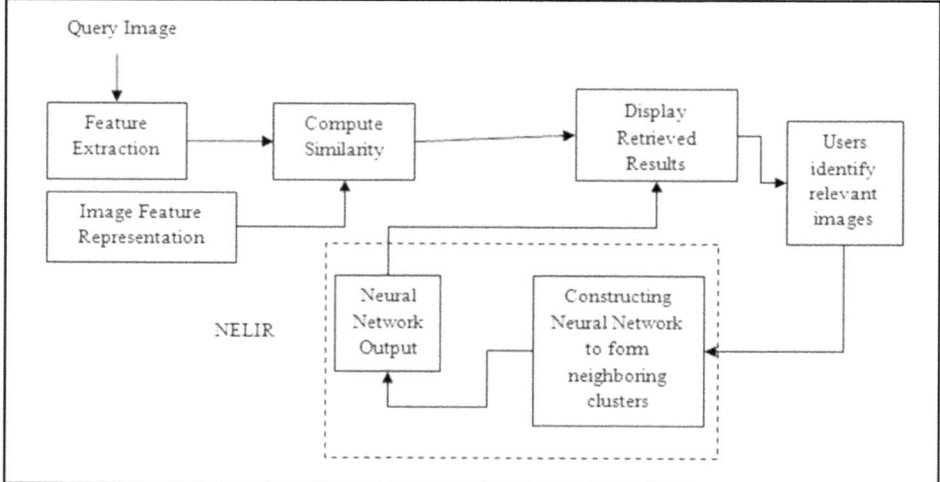

Figure 4. Relevance feedback using neural network [26].

This in result makes the framework independent of particular extracted features and matching function. It can be easily incorporated along with other image retrieval systems to improve the performance based on previous results.

Different techniques [27] for relevance feedback in image retrieval have been tried and tested along with re-weighting approach. The experiments were carried out with 4 different databases with images ranging from 1000 to 19511. Different techniques gave different results for different databases depending on factors such as feature vector, similarity measure, sample size, database size etc. Mainly two techniques have been compared by analyzing results obtained on different databases. One of them is Feature Re-Weighting Method, in which the weight factor [64] is updated as:

$$w_i^{(k+1)} = \delta_i^k * \frac{\sigma_{K,i}^k}{\sigma_{rel,i}^k} \tag{18}$$

where $\sigma_{K,i}^k$ is standard deviation over K retrieved images and $\sigma_{rel,i}^k$ is the standard deviation over relevant images in k^{th} iteration.

Another method is Relevance Score Method, in which the degree of relevance or degree of non-relevance is treated as parameter for retrieving images. The Relevance Score of an image I is given as:

$$RS(I) = \frac{1}{1+\frac{dR(I)}{dN(I)}} \tag{19}$$

where $dR(I)$ and $dN(I)$ is the maximum and minimum distance from the set of relevant and non-relevant images respectively.

Art images have altogether different style of presentation and high level of semantics with understanding. A strategy to translate the high-level style semantics [28] of art images and utilize them in effective image retrieval has been proposed. A linguistic variable is utilized to characterize the semantics of the high-level image components of each image. In view of this variable, the neural system creates the element vector. Tests demonstrated that the framework is great with art image retrieval.

Classification of images in view of image components is introduced with the strategy of grouping the images [29] for searching from database is proposed. The thought is to partition the database with specific criteria so that the search space can be minimized. Multi-layer perceptrons are utilized for training the framework and characterize pictures in the database. The image is first processed to extract its spectral histogram features and then use them to train the network. A probability p is assigned to each image I that it belongs to class i.

$$p(i|I) = \frac{e^{-\|1-out_i\|^2/2\sigma^2\tau}}{\sum_{j=1}^{P} e^{-\|1-out_i\|^2/2\sigma^2\tau}} \tag{20}$$

where $\sigma^2 = \frac{1}{P-1}\sum_{j=1}^{P}\|1-out_j\|^2$, τ is the temperature parameter similar to the simulated annealing, P is the number of classes, out is the P-dimensional output vector. Tests demonstrated that the framework is suitable for retrieving the images productively.

The semantic gap can also be reduced by utilizing query alteration which includes the hybrid technique [30] along with relevance feedback. For image retrieval, it includes the hybrid steps as feature extraction, combination and color space transformations in this framework. The flowchart of the system is as shown in fig. 5. The Empirical Mode Decomposition (EMD) thus calculated for the color histogram is based on transportation problem. Experiment results demonstrated increase in efficiency over the conventional retrieval techniques.

Neural networks not only provide a better classification framework but also guarantee the improvement in results for various systems. One such framework has been proposed as local general error model scheme [31] for image retrieval which utilizes the training capabilities of neural system to ensure that mostly higher similar feature images are shown to user for labeling. The framework has been implemented and tested and results show that the proposed system can retrieve images with higher efficiency.

A neural system based procedure is presented for superior quality of image retrieval with the use of wavelets [32]. Symlet transforms are implemented along with Euclidian distance for similarity comparison. Analyses were carried out on standard image database and productive outcomes appeared. The proficiency of image retrieval process is expanded up to 92%. In addition, no extra overhead has been observed. A subjective representation of components present in the image is the essential principal of human visual framework.

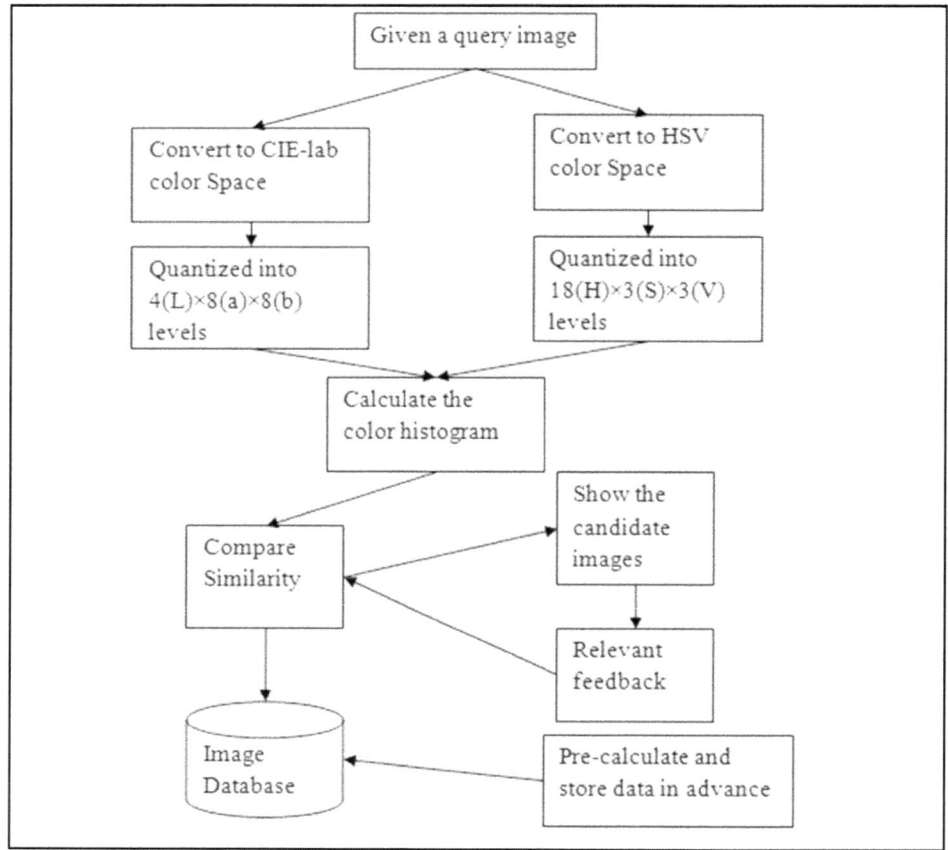

Figure 5. Relevance feedback using EMD [30].

A plan for reducing the gap between the image semantics and it's low level features with the utilization of cubic splines models [33, 34] based on neural system standards have been introduced. The similarity metric used to compare the feature vector of query image and database image is defined as:

$$S(I, q) = \cos(\overrightarrow{v_I}, \overrightarrow{v_q}) = \frac{\overrightarrow{v_I} . \overrightarrow{v_q}}{\|\overrightarrow{v_I}\|\|\overrightarrow{v_q}\|} \tag{21}$$

where $\overrightarrow{v_I}$ and $\overrightarrow{v_q}$ are metric vectors for the database image and query image respectively. When contrasted with other image retrieval strategies, the results obtained are of high accuracy and better effectiveness.

An adaptive image retrieval framework [35] utilizing relevance feedback has been proposed. At user input, the utilization of more than once representing sub schemes can learn and update their comparison criteria with the help of relevance feedback. The generalized similarity measure has been defined as:

$$r_j\left(\underline{q}\right) = s\left(\underline{q}, \underline{x}_j\right) = \Phi^T(\underline{x}_j)\hat{\underline{q}} = \Phi^T(\underline{x}_j)A_j\Phi\left(\underline{q}\right) \tag{22}$$

where $j \in [1, N]$, $\Phi\left(\underline{q}\right)$ is the set of scalar function of query image $\underline{q}$ and for database image $\underline{x}_j$. If compared to standard generalized Euclidean distance measure, it offers a more general similarity function.

The image retrieval error can be reduced to zero percent with the adaptive way of framework. The tests were performed on database of images taken under water and results demonstrated that the framework is fit for learning through the user query and learns the criteria effectively to proceed for further image retrievals.

Adapting in the user's interests from log information [36] and decreasing the relevance feedback time has been analyzed. Log information can be effectively used to understand the user's intentions and can be utilized for further image retrieval process. A similar approach is taking in the framework from log information rather than the user's input. The regularizer selection approach was based on:

$$g(A) = \|A\|_F = \sqrt{\sum_{i,j=1}^{m} a_{i,j}^2} \tag{23}$$

Using Eq. (23), a new Laplacian regularizer has been formulated as:

$$g(A) = \frac{1}{2}\sum_{i,j=1}^{n}\left\|U^T X_i - U^T X_j\right\|^2 W_{ij} \tag{24}$$

where U^T is unlabeled data information with weight matrix W. To calculate distance metric, a laplacian regularized metric learning proposed as:

$$min_{A \geq 0} tr(XLX^T A) + \gamma_s \sum_{(x_i, x_j) \in S}\left\|X_i - X_j\right\|_A^2 - \gamma_d \sum_{(x_i, x_j) \in D}\left\|X_i - X_j\right\|_A^2 \tag{25}$$

Results are good with little and trained data sets yet are not productive for substantial and untrained data sets.

An approach for performing content based query in light of gathering of 3D model databases [37] is exhibited. The plan utilizes 3-level ordering model in light of neural systems for fruitful retrieval. The total number of spin images at the three levels has been formulated as:

$$N_{db} = \sum_{i=1}^{N_{obj}} N_{spin_{images}}(obj_i); \quad \text{at first level}$$

$$N_{db} = dN_{obj}; \quad \text{at second level}$$

$$N_{db} = cN_{obj}; \quad \text{at third level where } d \text{ is the number of nodes in the}$$

self-organizing map and c is the number of clusters produced by the k-means algorithm.

The outcomes demonstrated that the framework performs better on atomic information and can be utilized as a part of any 3-D information retrieval application with productive retrieval.

Inspired from text retrieval techniques, image retrieval technique was implemented by utilizing features of relevance feedback [38]. It combined the two techniques: query point movement and query expansion. Then, the images were classified into clusters using k nearest neighbors classifier, for which k has been selected as:

$$k_i = \min(|C_j|, j = 1:c) \tag{26}$$

where C denotes the cluster number while c is a fixed maximum value randomly selected. The query point is then formulated as:

$$\vec{q}_i = \frac{\sum_{j=1}^{m} \vec{R}_j}{m} - \frac{\sum_{j=1}^{n} \vec{I}_j}{n} \tag{27}$$

where I and R are used for relevant and irrelevant examples respectively.

Experiments performed showed that the combination of above two techniques produced better results as compared to when any technique used alone.

The automatic weighting of images for relevance feedback-based image retrieval system [39] imposes the learning of weight specification. The weight updating for reinforcement learning is carried out as:

$$x(t) = 1: \qquad P_j(t+1) = \begin{cases} (1-G)P_j(t), \forall j \neq i \\ P_j(t) + G\left(1 - P_j(t)\right), j = i \end{cases}$$

$$x(t) = 0: \qquad P_j(t+1) = \begin{cases} \frac{B}{K-1} + (1-B)P_j(t), \forall j \neq i \\ (1-B)P_j(t), j = i \end{cases} \tag{28}$$

where G is the parameter of gain for positive reward while B is the parameter of gain when reward is 0.

Along with standard precision and recall properties, performance of the system was measured on error rate defined as:

$$Error\ Rate = \frac{No.\ non - relevant\ images\ retrieved}{Total\ No.\ images\ retrieved}$$

It is more reliable where user interaction is least required and can be approximated by reinforcement learning of the framework. The users do not need to explicitly mention the weights.

Another two-stage methodology [40] has been proposed in which initial step is to extract features utilizing low level components (color, shape and texture) while Support Vector Machine (SVM) classifier is used as a part of the final step to handle the noisy positive cases. Therefore, a proficient calculation of image retrieval in view of color-correlogram for color element extraction, wavelet transformation for separating shape elements and Gabor wavelet for texture element extraction is presented.

Further, numerous elements and diverse distance measurements are joined to get image comparability utilizing an SVM classifier. Results of this approach are found empowering with respect to color, shape and texture image classification exactness.

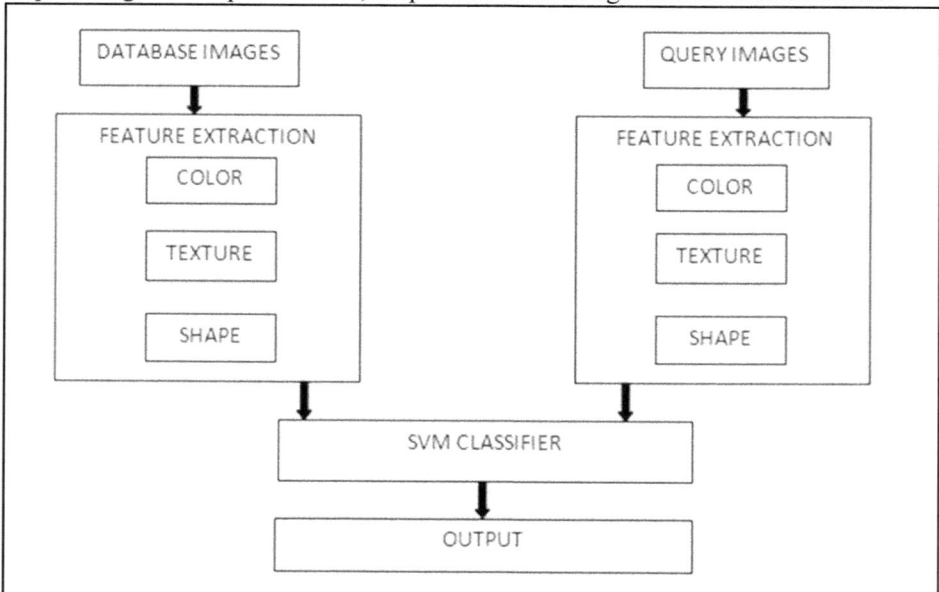

Figure 6. The architecture of the CBIR system using SVM [40].

The low stage features can be utilized as a part of CBIR especially those focused on Scale Invariant Feature Transform (SIFT) descriptors [41]. To remember troublesome emotional belief system, also color and texture components and one global scene descriptor: Gist has been considered with the assumption that the selected elements could verifiably encrypt the high-level information about feelings in light of their exactness in the distinctive CBIR applications. The proposed methodology has been experimented on two different databases.

Table 1. Comparison of different CBIR techniques

S.No. #	Application	Advantages	Limitations	Results
1	Agent-based interleaved image retrieval [9]	Reduced search space results in the faster retrieval.	Management overhead is created due to synchronization of interleaved agents.	Performance can be increased by improved synchronization technique.
2	Online image retrieval system [10]	Implemented on web and tested thoroughly.	The scheme is complex due to multiple query manipulation.	From a user's perspective, system with tested results is always better than systems with less testing.
3	Dynamic updation of similarity matching algorithm [11]	Matching technique is based on search criteria.	Search attributes are not validated.	Since human are interacting to system, makes the retrieval process slow and a non-automated system.
4	Adaptive learning of similarity matching attributes [12]	Matching algorithm may change at run time to provide better relevance.	The system may undergo an invalid matching state if retrieval criteria are invalid.	Practical approach is needed for improving performance.
5	Increased feature space for image retrieval [13]	More relevant can be retrieved efficiently.	-	For better results, it is good to search for specific features in increased features space.
6	Multiple organ of interest based image retrieval [14]	Multiple organs of interest and retrieval.	Images of all organs of humans can vary in shape in different time; thus, the scheme is very complex to implement.	Overall it is a good system but very complex.
7	Simultaneous query modification for image retrieval [15]	Multi-processing gives efficiency.	Dependencies must be removed before initializing multi -tasking.	Performance can be improved by multi-tasking but it also introduces an overhead.
8	Dynamic incorporation of user search criterion [17]	Intelligent user interface reduces human involvement time.	-	System can be automated if user feedback is not involved. Makes the approach more efficient.
9	Usage of self-organized neural networks for	Improved efficiency.	-	Self-organizing neural networks have shown great efficiency in

	image retrieval [18] [19]			image retrieval applications.
10	Suitable weighting with relevance feedback [21]	Increased precision.	-	User's satisfaction as well as improved results is achieved with better precision.
11	Semantic tree for image retrieval [22]	Performance is improved with logical distribution.	Generation of semantic tree can take more time.	A good approach for efficient retrieval if increased number of retrieval tasks.
12	Probabilistic conceptualization for image retrieval [23]	Image categorization allows removing the irrelevant images from result set.	Classifying images is quite difficult by incorporating user experience.	A potential concept for results improvement.
13	Relevance feedback scheme with noise removal log [24]	Log file is filtered to remove noise.	Processing of log file can be slow if the file size is too large.	Removing noise is a new concept for improving image retrieval process.
14	Measuring performance of relevance feedback [25]	Overall performance of the system can be measured by relevance feedback performance.	No other components result in performance parameters.	Relevance feedback is the only significant component.
15	Neural network applied over relevance feedback to improve image retrieval performance [26]	Using neural networks will allow classifying next retrieval according to user experience.	Increased complexity.	Learning from user interest results in improved performance.
16	Overview of relevance feedback methods [27]	Overall advantages of relevance feedback techniques are shown.	Does not provide detailed specifications of algorithms.	Collection of different relevance feedback techniques.
17	Art Image Retrieval [28]	Images that are high aesthetic semantic-based can be easily retrieved.	Human involvement is required for input of linguistic variable.	Art images can be retrieved.
18	Image classification and retrieval system [29]	Reduced search space gives more relevant as well as efficient results.	Time for image classification may increase if dataset size is huge.	Narrowed search set for retrieving an image makes the system to act logically smart.
19	Hybrid image retrieval [30]	-	-	It is a typical hybrid framework for image retrieval.
20	Local general error method for image retrieval [31]	Performance can be improved by labeling only significant data.	-	A fair scheme for image retrieval.
21	Neural network	Performance	Lack of details	Suitable for

	based image retrieval using Symlet transforms [32]	increase.	about algorithm.	modern CBIR systems.
22	Cubic splines based image retrieval [33] [34]	Accuracy with better performance.	-	System can be used as a good technique for image retrieval.
23	Multiple representing schemes for image retrieval [35]	The error for retrieval has been reduced to zero percent.	Multiple mapping can increase time every time an update is made to the database.	With consistent database state the system performs comparatively better.
24	Using log data for relevance feedback based image retrieval [36]	Limits user's input and increased learning.	Problem lies in untrained and large datasets.	Good approach for databases that are small and medium sized.
25	Image retrieval technique for 3D model collection [37]	3D model image retrieval.	3D data is very difficult to handle.	Good approach for working with 3D model images.
26	Combined relevance feedback with query expansion for image retrieval [38]	Technique used from the text retrieval domain. Works fine with image retrieval also.	-	Results in better outcome with implementation.
27	Automated image weighting for image retrieval [39]	User involvement is not mandatory.	Time is consumed in learning.	Practical and logical scheme for dealing with the real life image retrieval scenarios.

3. Sketch Based Image Retrieval

A lot of research has been done in CBIR systems, but in all these systems, the input query required is a digital image with well defined features such as shape, color and texture. Sometimes, the user might not have a clear image of his query but may draw a sketch and search for similar images from database. Such a need requires a new image retrieval system, i.e. Sketch Based Image Retrieval (SBIR). Few researchers have tried to bring the topic in light and have carried out remarkable research in the field. Few of them are described below.

A large number of stable features can be used for transforming image data [42] into scale-invariant co-ordinates. A set of reference features is stored in a database and the query sketch/image features are compared to find the matching by Euclidean distance between them. The keypoint descriptors used here give a good probability match. Cascade filtering approach is used to detect keypoints. To distinguish among the false and correct ones, keypoint subsets are formed on the basis of rotation, scale and orientation. The scale space of an image is given by:

$$L(x, y, \sigma) = G(x, y, \sigma) * I(x, y) \tag{29}$$

where I is the input image and G is defined as Gaussian parameter:

$$G(x, y, \sigma) = \frac{1}{2\pi\sigma^2} e^{-(x^2+y^2)/2\sigma^2}$$

The local self similarity descriptor [43] which allows differentiating between internal geometric layout within images or videos has been implemented. It is based on color, edges and complex textures in a unified way. Textures are compared on the basis of spatial layout. It calculates the sum of square differences (SSD), providing in output the correlation surface as:

$$S_q(x, y) = \exp\left(-\frac{SSD_q(x,y)}{\max(var_{noise}, var_{auto}(q))}\right) \tag{30}$$

where var_{noise} denotes the changes in color, illumination and $var_{auto}(q)$ is the maximum variance among all patches.

The general benchmark [44] for assessing the execution of any SBIR framework has been characterized. For coordinating pictures SBIR framework utilizes the data contained in the outlined 3-D shape. They presented the Spark feature for specific SBIR in a Bag of Visual Words (BoVW) system; Gradient Field - Histogram of Oriented Gradients (GF-HOG) is an image descriptor reasonable for SBIR. It regards sketch's edges as a collection of points, as opposed to depicting image patches; describe lines and their connections to pick out image from dataset. The normalized histograms were created using:

$$H_{ij} = \frac{1}{\sum_k h_{ij}(k)} h_{ij} \tag{31}$$

Further, to compare the two normalized histograms, distance is calculated as:

$$d_{ij} = \sum_k |H_{ij}(k) - \tilde{H}_{ij}(k)| \tag{32}$$

It is much slower patch relationship based approach of Self-Similarity.

The framework that can powerfully create shadows [45] generated or extracted from huge database of images has been proposed. This framework retrieves related images continuously in view of inadequate sketches provided by the user. The gradients are normalized to remove the variations and then binned in groups according to position, orientation and its length. The normalized gradients $\hat{g}_p$, is computed as:

$$\hat{g}_p = \frac{g_p}{\max(\bar{g}_p, \epsilon)} \tag{33}$$

where g_p is the original gradient and $\bar{g}_p$ is the average gradient. Then, for binning a new coordinate for each image pixel is defined as:

$$\begin{bmatrix} x'_p \\ y'_p \end{bmatrix} = R(\theta_p) \begin{bmatrix} x_p \\ y_p \end{bmatrix} \tag{34}$$

where $R(\theta_p)$ is the 2D rotation matrix.

To encode the presence of edges, the normalized gradient histograms are then binarized.

Changing descriptors [46, 47] before clustering may boost benchmark retrieval technique and can deliver results utilizing visual words. It explicitly evaluates the matching quality of the indexed components in the convergence sets by safeguarding difference between those sets. In this feature level comparison, images are combined from different sets of indexed components, in this way; it decreases the effect of vocabulary relationship. The cost function [46] was thus formulated to minimize the effect as:

$$f(\lambda, W) = \sum_{x,y \in P} \mathcal{L}(b_1 - d_W(x, y)) + \sum_{x,y \in nnN} \mathcal{L}(d_W(x, y) - b_1) + \sum_{x,y \in ranN} \mathcal{L}(d_W(x, y) - b_2) + \frac{\lambda}{2} \|W\|^2 \tag{35}$$

where $\mathcal{L}(z) = \log(1 + \exp(-z))$ denotes the logistic loss, d_W denotes the standard Euclidean distance, λ is the controlling parameter, W is the projection function's parameters and b_1 and b_2 are the margin biases for left-hand and right-hand respectively.

Another way is to calculate the conditional probability [47] and using Bayes' theorem to find the merging of the feature vectors. The conditional probability for determining the likelihood of two different feature vectors is as:

$$w(x, y) = p(y \in T_x | y \in A \cap B) \tag{36}$$

where T_x is the set of feature vectors which are common to local set as well as global set. Then the Bayes' theorem can be formulated as:

$$p(T_x | A \cap B) = \left(1 + \frac{p(A \cap B | F_x)}{p(A \cap B | T_x)} \cdot \frac{p(F_x)}{p(T_x)}\right)^{-1} \tag{37}$$

Here F_x is the set of the feature vectors which does not fall in T_x either because they are only global or local features.

The problem of fast, large scale database searching [48] for over one million images have resulted in development of SBIR to ease the user's understanding. Existing image retrieval frameworks does not allow supervising the steps involved in searching. Two techniques are proposed and on performing experiments, it was found that they significantly outperform existing approaches. The descriptors are constructed in such a way that the sketch as well as color image have to undergo the same preprocessing level. To analyze gradient orientations and directions, images with similar structure are found. The histograms are constructed using Eq. (31) for HOG. While for tensor descriptor, unlike HOG, it is portrayed as maximization problem to find a single vector for each cell, which is defined as:

$$x = argmax_{\|x\|=1} \sum_{(u,v) \in C_{i,j}} (x^T g_{uv})^2 \tag{38}$$

such that

$$\sum_{(u,v) \in C_{i,j}} (x^T g_{uv})^2 = \sum_{(u,v) \in C_{i,j}} (x^T g_{uv} g_{uv}^T x) = x^T \left(\sum_{(u,v) \in C_{i,j}} g_{uv} g_{uv}^T\right) x = x^T G_{ij} x$$

where G_{ij} is the sum of products of gradients. Then, best matching images are clustered based on dominant color distributions, to offset the lack of color-based decision at the time of initial search.

A bag-of-regions [49] has been presented to construct a SBIR framework. This framework encodes the notable shapes at different levels of points of interest as enclosed contours of locales. They proposed BoW system that depends on GF-HOG, SIFT and Structural Similarity Index (SSIM) descriptor to restrict the sketched object inside the retrieved image. Frequency histograms H^I and H^Q are first constructed for database image I and the query sketch Q respectively, which are then compared to find the ranking of regions as:

$$d(H^Q, H^I) = \sum_{i=1}^{k} \sum_{j=1}^{k} \left(\omega_{ij} \min(H^Q(i), H^I(j))\right) \tag{39}$$

$$\omega_{ij} = 1 - |\mathcal{H}^Q(i) - \mathcal{H}^I(j)|$$

where H^I is the ith bin of histogram, $\mathcal{H}(i)$ is the normalized visual word corresponding to i^{th} bin. Then the matching score $\Phi(\delta_{R_k}, \delta_{R_s})$ between region of query image R_s and mapped region R_k with bounding box B_s and B_k is computed as:

$$\Phi(\delta_{R_k}, \delta_{R_s}) = e^{-\frac{1}{N} \sum_{\{p_i, p_j\} \in P_c} \left\|\delta_{R_s(p_i)} - \delta_{R_k(p_j)}\right\|^2} \tag{40}$$

where N is the cardinality of the correspondence set.

The problem of fast, large scale sketch-based image retrieval, [50] searching in a database of over one million images was addressed. According to this paper, current retrieval methods do not scale well towards large databases in the context of interactively supervised search and propose two different approaches for which objectively evaluation is carried out that they significantly outperform existing approaches. The proposed descriptors are constructed such that both the full color image and the sketch undergo exactly the same preprocessing steps. First searching is done for an image with similar structure, analyzing gradient orientations. Then, best matching images are clustered based on dominant color distributions, to offset the lack of color-based decision during the initial search. When images have been retrieved from the system, there is need to rank them on the basis of similarity measures. The Kendall's rank correlation coefficient τ is computed as:

$$\tau = \frac{n_c - n_d}{n(n-1)/2} \tag{41}$$

where n_c and n_d are number of concordant and discordant pairs respectively.

In case of large databases, it might happen that same coefficient value is generated for two different images in the database, thus creating ties. Thus, in case of multiple images at same ranking score, the ranking coefficient as defined in Eq. (41) is modified as follows:

$$\tau_b = \frac{n_c - n_d}{[(N-U)-(N-V)]^2} \tag{42}$$

where $N = n(n - 1)/2$ (number of possible pairs in a set of n distinct elements),
$U = \frac{1}{2}\sum_{i=1}^{t} t_i(t_i - 1)/2$ (number of ties in first list),
$V = \frac{1}{2}\sum_{i=1}^{u} u_i(u_i - 1)/2$ (number of ties in second list).

Indexing structure [51] and raw shape-based coordinating algorithm [52] to compute similarities amongst natural and sketch images query, and make SBIR adaptable to different types of images was presented. The similarity from image $\mathcal{D}$ to $\mathcal{Q}$ is calculated as:

$$Sim_{\mathcal{D} \to \mathcal{Q}} = \frac{1}{|\mathcal{D}|} \sum_{p \in \mathcal{D}} H \, it_{\mathcal{Q}}(p) \tag{43}$$

where p is an edged pixel. Using Eq. (43), the Structure-consistent Sketch Matching (SSM) [51] has been defined as:

$$Sim_{\mathcal{Q}, \mathcal{D}}^{SSM} = \left(\prod_{i=1}^{N_{\mathcal{Q}}} Sim_{\mathcal{Q}_i \to \mathcal{D}}\right)^{\frac{1}{2N_{\mathcal{Q}}}} \cdot \left(\prod_{j=1}^{N_{\mathcal{D}}} Sim_{\mathcal{D}_j \to \mathcal{Q}}\right)^{\frac{1}{2N_{\mathcal{D}}}} \tag{44}$$

A visual word is portrayed utilizing a triple (x, y, θ) of the position x and y and angle θ. It empowers a very effective inverted index structure and makes possible to assemble a real-time huge-scale sketch based image search framework. It additionally endures local irregularities in user's sketch query and introduced a modified version of Eq. (44) with Oriented Chamfer Matching (OCM) as follows:

$$D_{A,B}^{OCM} = \frac{1}{2}(\bar{u}_B^T \bar{v}_A + \bar{v}_B^T \bar{u}_A) \tag{45}$$

Researchers compensate the absence of position-invariant matching, as in a large-scale search framework.

A sketch based algorithm [53] for large scale image retrieval and a framework is created to query output from database of millions of images was proposed. Two candidate areas are utilized for components extraction, firstly orientation elements are extracted and after that these elements are composed hierarchically to produce global to local components. The contour saliency map S is as:

$$S = \sum_{j=1}^{N} D_{O_j} \tag{46}$$

such that

$$D_{H_iO_j} = \max_q \left\{ D_{H_iO_jC_q} \right\}, \qquad D_{O_j} = \sum_{i=1}^{M} \left[D_{H_iO_j} \right]_{m \times n}$$

where H_i denotes the ith level image resolution, O_j is the jth orientation, C_q is the qth color component and D is the difference image. After forming the contour saliency map, refined orientation is estimated as:

$$DR_{O_1} = \left\lfloor D_{O_1} - D_{O_3} \right\rfloor_T, \qquad DR_{O_3} = \left\lfloor D_{O_3} - D_{O_1} \right\rfloor_T$$
$$DR_{O_2} = \left\lfloor D_{O_2} - D_{O_4} \right\rfloor_T, \qquad DR_{O_4} = \left\lfloor D_{O_4} - D_{O_2} \right\rfloor_T$$

where $\lfloor . \rfloor_T$ is the truncation function. With contour saliency map, candidate region estimation is carried out which will then allow performing extraction of features. Features are defined as:

$$F_{O_j}^k(t) = \sum \left[DR_{O_j} \right]_{X^k(t)} . G^k(t) \tag{47}$$
$$F^k = \left\{ F_{O_j}^k(t) \right\}, F = \{F^k\}$$

where $G^k(t)$ is the Gaussian kernel.

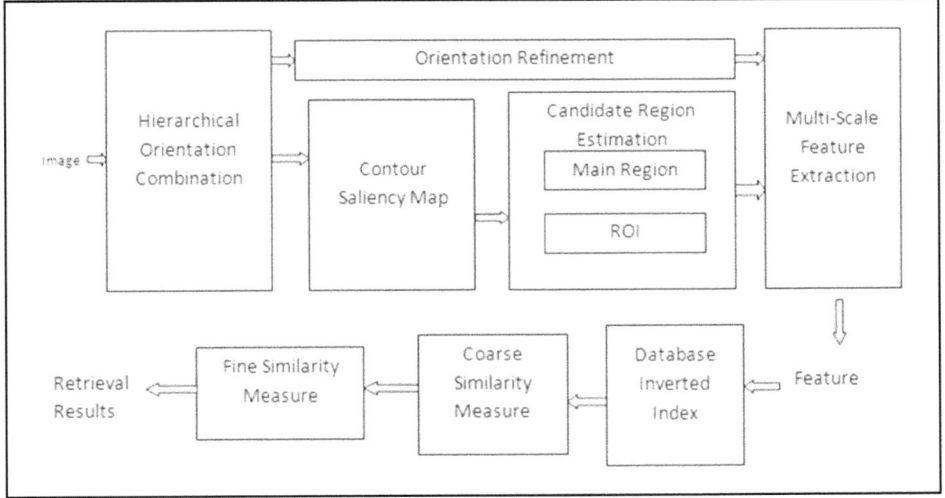

Figure 7. Framework of the SBIR System [53].

Accordingly, various leveled database list is organized and after that image can be retrieved from large-scale image database on the web. This framework shifts through a substantial number of irrelevant images rapidly.

To recognize similarities [54] between a hand drawn sketch and the natural images in a database is an important process. They utilized the voting procedure to distinguish duplicate shape and structure patches. Local Sensitive Hashing procedure is appropriate for evaluating the likeness between sets. The similarity between two sets has been defined as:

$$sim(D_1, D_2) = \frac{|D_1 \cap D_2|}{|D_1 \cup D_2|} \in [0,1] \tag{48}$$

In this framework, effect of noisy edges in the image degrades the retrieval performance.

A tensor-based image descriptor [55, 56] for huge scale SBIR was built-up. It locates a single vector utilizing tensor-based picture descriptor, which is nearest to the majority of parallel edges course direction in a neighborhood area. Though, Sousa et al. utilized topological data to retrieve vector drawings and geometric data is utilized for coordinating shapes. The final effect of trial result is little furthermore there is need of change in geometric sifting.

An image retrieval system for the interactive search [57] of photo collections using free-hand sketches depicting shape has been developed. Described Gradient Field HOG (GF-HOG); an adapted form of the HOG descriptor suitable for SBIR. Also incorporated GF-HOG into a Bag of Visual Words (BoVW) retrieval framework, and demonstrate how this combination may be harnessed both for robust SBIR, and for localizing sketched objects within an image. The similarity comparison for two sets of tags of images is computed as:

$$\frac{\sum_{m=1}^{M} max_n\{p(C_n^1|C_m^2)\}}{N} + \frac{\sum_{n=1}^{N} max_m\{p(C_n^1|C_m^2)\}}{M} \tag{49}$$

with $p(C_n^1|C_m^2)$ is computed as:

$$P(w_i|w_j) = \frac{|w_i \cap w_j|}{|w_j|}$$

where w_i is the set of keywords for image tags while N and M are the total number of tag elements in sets C^1 and C^2 respectively.

Evaluation has been done over a large Flickr sourced dataset comprising 33 shape categories, using queries from 10 non-expert sketchers. GF-HOG is compared against state-of-the-art descriptors with common distance measures and language models for image retrieval, and explore how affine deformation of the sketch impacts search performance.

Bag-of-features [58] model to develop feature set for sketches can be utilized. In this large dataset of sketches gathered to assess human recognition. Certain restrictions with this framework are of importance for specific components that may be dependent on context with the sketch, very predictable for specific sorts of sketches as it contains transient data about sketch. Hand-drawn sketch in light of stroke components are presented for keeping up basic data of visual words codebook is maintained in a hierarchical tree. The corners are detected using:

$$E(x,y) = \sum_{u,v} w(u,v)[I(x+u, y+v) - I(x,y)]^2 \tag{50}$$

where $w(u,v)$ is the Gaussian kernel. Later, to compare similarity between sketches were computed using χ^2 kernel as:

$$D(h_q, h_r) = \frac{1}{2}\sum_{i=1}^{n} \frac{[h_q(i)-h_r(i)]^2}{h_q(i)+h_r(i)} \tag{51}$$

where h_q and h_r are descriptors for given sketch pairs. And then, rank retrievals are followed as:

$$rank(k) = \underset{1,\ldots,k}{argmin} \, D_\wedge$$

where $D_\wedge$ is the distance matrix.

A strategy to lessen the appearance gap [59] in SBIR was proposed. In this paper, sketches and extracted edges are dealt with as set of line sections, establishing the framework for better portray edge depiction and noise effect decrease from another point. Object boundary selection algorithm is utilized to lessen the effect of noisy edges. In this paper, spatial and coherent constraints are proposed to channel the false matches that corrupt the retrieval throughput.

Using convolutional neural networks [60], from 2-D human sketches, 3-D models can be retrieved. Since majority of models are upright, therefore number of views per object for dataset has been reduced to two. The model is based on Siamese Convolution Neural Networks to capture different properties in different domains. Also, an 'align' function has been defined to compare features of query sketch and 3-D models. The function has been defined as:

$$L(s_1, s_2, y) = (1 - y)\alpha D_w^2 + y\beta e^{\gamma D_w} \tag{52}$$

where s_1 and s_2 are two samples, y is the binary similarity label, D_w is the distance between two samples. In each domain, samples are mapped to some feature vectors. The cross domain matching is successful if features from each domain are 'aligned' correctly.

A step of sketch generation on real images is used to obtain a better edgemap [61] for each image. A novel multi label graph cut algorithm is used to group edges according to two key Gestalt principles, i.e., continuity and proximity. Perceptual edge grouping framework produces better edge groups which can be used to improve a variety of higher level tasks. Edge grouping performed should minimize the overall energy function defined by:

$$E(v_L) = \sum_{v_i \in V} D(v_i, v_L) + \sum_{\{v_i, v_j\} \in N} S(v_i, v_j) \tag{53}$$

where

$$D(v_i, v_L) = sigmoid(F(x))^{-1} = sigmoid(\omega^T x(v_i, v_L))^{-1}$$
$$S(v_i, v_L) = d(v_i, v_j)^{-1}$$

where v_L is a set of edges, $D(v_i, v_L)$ is the measure of fitness between edge v_i and assigned cluster v_L.

Sketch-based image retrieval (SBIR) is a challenging task due to the ambiguity inherent in sketches when compared with photos. A novel convolutional neural network [62] based on Siamese network for SBIR has been implemented. The main idea is to pull output feature vectors closer for input sketch-image pairs that are labeled as similar, and push them away if irrelevant. Therefore, the similarity metric is defined as:

$$M_W(S, I) = \|F_W(S) - F_W(I)\| \tag{54}$$

where S is the sketch and I is the database image edgemap. A loss function is then defined on parameter W as:

$$L(W) = \sum_{i=1}^{N} l(W, (S, I, Y)^i) \tag{55}$$
$$l(W, (S, I, Y)^i) = (1 - Y)L_P(M_W(S, I)^i) + YL_N(M_W(S, I)^i)$$

where $(S, I, Y)^i$ is the ith training sample, L_P is the loss function for positive pair while L_N is the loss function for negative pair. This is achieved by jointly tuning two convolutional neural networks which linked by one loss function.

Table 2. Comparison results for various SBIR techniques

Methods	Vocabulary Size	MAP
Siamese CNN [62]	-	0.1954
3DShape [60]	-	0.1831
PerceptualEdge [61]	non-BoW	0.1513
GF-HOG [57]	3500	0.1222

HOG [65]	3000	0.1093
SIFT [42]	1000	0.0911
SSIM [66]	500	0.0957
ShapeContext [16]	3500	0.0814
StructureTensor [48]	500	0.0798
StructureTensor [48]	non-BoW	0.0735

Several results included in the above table shows the Mean Average Precision (MAP) obtained for different techniques. SBIR have been mostly implemented on Flickr dataset of sketch-image pairs which consists of 33 categories of sketches. The MAP is calculated on the overall database by considering each of the sketch as query sketch.

4. Conclusion

The purpose of book chapter is to provide a comparative study between different image retrieval techniques. With the increase in demand of multimedia applications, image retrieval has gained much importance nowadays. This book chapter includes the content based and sketch based image retrieval with the utilization of different neural network and relevance feedback techniques. Different techniques discussed have their own pros and cons and specific applications. Results achieved from different techniques have shown that there is still need of improvement in most of the areas, mainly in sketch based image retrieval.

Several other techniques which have not been yet implemented in SBIR can be considered such as soft computing techniques, optimization techniques and different feature descriptors for sketches as well. Also, similar frameworks can also be applied to different biometric systems in security as well.

References

[1]   N. Vázquez, M. Nakano & H. P. Meana, "Automatic System for Localization and Recognition of Vehicle Plate Numbers", Journal of Applied Research and Technology, pp. 63-77, 2002.
[2]   L. F. Pulido, O. Startostenko, D. F. Quéchol, J. I. R. Flores, I. Kirchning & J. A. C. Aragón, "Content-Based Image Retrieval Using Wavelets", 2nd WSEAS International Conference on Computer Engineering and Applications, pp. 40-45, 2008.
[3]   S. Wang & H. Qin, "A Study of Order-based Block Color Feature Image Retrieval Compared with Cumulative Color Histogram Method", 6th International Conference on Fuzzy Systems and Knowledge Discovery, Vol. 1, pp. 81-84, 2009.
[4]   H. Tamura, S. Mori & T. Yamawaki, "Textural Features Corresponding to Visual Perception", IEEE Transactions on Systems, Man and Cybernetics, Vol. 8, No. 6, pp. 460-473, 1978.
[5]   S. K. Saha, A. K. Das & B. Chanda, "CBIR Using Perception Based Texture And Colour measures", Proceedings of the 17th International Conference on Pattern Recognition, Vol. 2, pp. 985-988, 2004.
[6]   J. Canny, "A computational approach to edge detection", IEEE Transactions on Pattern Analysis and Machine Intelligence, Vol. PAMI-8, No. 6, pp. 679-698, 1986.

[7] S.Nandagopalan, Dr. B.S. Adiga, & N. Deepak, "A Universal Model for Content-Based Image Retrieval", International Journal of Computer, Electrical, Automation, Control and Information Engineering, Vol. 2, No. 10, pp. 3436-3439, 2008.

[8] M. Flickner, H. Sawhney, W. Niblack, J. Ashley, Q. Huang, B. Dom, M. Gorkani, J. Hafher, D. Lee, D. Petkovic, D. Steele & P. Yanker, "Query By Image and Video Content: The QBIC System", Computer, Vol. 28, No. 9, 1995.

[9] P. Charlton, B. Huet & G. Justog, "Modelling Agents in C++CL for Content-Based Image Retrieval", Proceedings of the 4th Euromicro Workshop on Parallel and Distributed Processing, pp. 59-66, 1996.

[10] B. Verma, P. Sharma, S. Kulkarni & H. Selvaraj, "An Intelligent On-line System for Content Based Image Retrieval", 3rd International Conference on Computational Intelligence and Multimedia Applications, pp. 273-277, 1999.

[11] H. K. Lee & S. I. Yoo., "A neural network-based image retrieval using nonlinear combination of heterogeneous features", Proceedings of the 2000 Congress on Evolutionary Computation, Vol. 1, pp. 667-674, 2000.

[12] J. H. Lim, W. J. Kang, S. Singh & D. Narasimhalu, "Learning Similarity Matching in Multimedia Content-Based Retrieval", IEEE Transactions on Knowledge and Data Engineering, Vol. 13, No. 5, pp. 846-850, 2001.

[13] X. L. Li, "Content-based image retrieval system with new low-level features, new similarity metric, and novel feedback learning", International Conference on Machine Learning and Cybernetics, Vol. 2, pp. 1126-1132, 2002.

[14] P. M. Willy & K. H. Kufer. "Content-based Medical Image Retrieval (CBMIR): An Intelligent Retrieval System for Handling Multiple Organs of Interest", 17th IEEE Symposium on Computer-Based Medical Systems, pp. 103-108, 2004.

[15] B. Li & S. Yuan, "A novel relevance feedback method in content-based image retrieval", International Conference on Information Technology: Coding and Computing, Vol. 2, pp. 120-123, 2004.

[16] G. Mori, S. Belongie & J. Malik, "Efficient shape matching using shape contexts", IEEE Transactions on Pattern Analysis and Machine Intelligence, Vol. 27, No. 11, pp. 1832-1837, 2005.

[17] R. Vermilyer, "Intelligent User Interface Agents in Content-Based Image Retrieval", Proceedings of the IEEE SoutheastCon., pp. 136-142, 2006.

[18] S. Wu, M. K. M. Rahman & T. W. S. Chow, "Content-based image retrieval using growing hierarchical self-organizing quad tree map", Pattern Recognition, Vol. 38, No. 5, pp. 707-722, 2005.

[19] C. Theoharatos, N. Laskaris, G. Economou, S. Fotopoulos, "Combining self-organizing neural nets with multivariate statistics for efficient color image retrieval", Computer Vision & Image Understanding, Vol. 102, No. 3, pp. 250-258, 2006.

[20] S. C. Chuang, Y. Y. Xu, H. C. Fu & H. C. Huang, "Multiple-Instance Neural Networks based Image Content Retrieval System", 1st International Conference on Innovative Computing, Information and Control, Vol. 2, pp. 412-415, 2006.

[21] A. J. M. Traina, J. Marques & C. Traina, "Fighting the Semantic Gap on CBIR Systems through New Relevance Feedback Techniques", 19th IEEE International Symposium on Computer-Based Medical Systems, pp. 881-886, 2006.

[22] X. X. Xie, Y. Zhao & Z. F. Zhu, "An Anamnestic Semantic Tree-Based Relevance Feedback Method in CBIR System", 1st International Conference on Innovative Computing, Information and Control, Vol. 3, pp. 91-94, 2006.

[23] M. L. Kherfi & D. Ziou, "Relevance feedback for CBIR: a new approach based on probabilistic feature weighting with positive and negative examples", IEEE Transactions on Image Processing, Vol. 15, No. 4, pp. 1017-1030, 2006.

[24] S. C. H. Hoi, M. R. Lyu, & R. Jin, "A unified log-based relevance feedback scheme for image retrieval", IEEE Transactions on Knowledge and Data Engineering, Vol. 18, No. 4, pp. 509-524, 2006.

[25] P. S. Karthik & C. V. Jawahar, "Analysis of Relevance Feedback in Content Based Image Retrieval", 9th International Conference on Control, Automation, Robotics and Vision, pp. 1-6, 2006.

[26] B. Wang, X. Zhang & N. Li, "Relevance Feedback Technique for Content-Based Image Retrieval using Neural Network Learning", International Conference on Machine Learning and Cybernetics, pp. 3692-396, 2006.

[27] G. Das & S. Ray, "A Comparison of Relevance Feedback Strategies in CBIR", 6th IEEE/ACIS International Conference on Computer and Information Science, pp. 100-105, 2007.

[28] Q. Li, S. Luo & Z. Shi, "Semantics-Based Art Image Retrieval Using Linguistic Variable", 4th International Conference on Fuzzy Systems and Knowledge Discovery, Vol. 2, pp. 406-410, 2007.

[29] Y. Zhu, X. Liu & W. Mio, "Content-Based Image Categorization and Retrieval using Neural Networks", IEEE International Conference on Multimedia and Expo, pp. 528-531, 2007.

[30] X. Wu & D. Fu, "Apply hybrid method of relevance feedback and EMD algorithm in a color feature extraction CBIR system", International Conference on Audio, Language and Image Processing , pp. 163-166, 2008.

[31] T. Zhu, W. W. Y. Ng, J. W. T. Lee, B. B. Sun, J. Wang & D. S. Yeung, "L-gem based co-training for CBIR with relevance feedback", International Conference on Wavelet Analysis and Pattern Recognition, Vol. 2, pp. 873-879, 2008.

[32] H. S. Cruz & E. Bribiesca, "Polygonal Approximation of Contour Shapes using Corner Detectors", Journal of Applied Research and Technology, Vol. 7, No. 3, pp. 275-291, 2009.

[33] S. Sadek, A. A. Hamadi, B. Michaelis & U. Sayed, "Cubic-splines neural network based system for image retrieval", 16th IEEE International Conference on Image Processing, pp. 273-276, 2009.

[34] S. Sadek, A. A. Hamadi, B. Michaelis & U. Sayed, "Cubic-splines neural network based system for image retrieval", 16th IEEE International Conference on Image Processing, pp. 273-276, 2009.

[35] M. R. A. Sadjadi, J. Salazar & Srinivasan, "An Adaptable Image Retrieval System With Relevance Feedback Using Kernel Machines and Selective Sampling", IEEE Transactions on Image Processing, Vol. 18, No. 7, pp. 1645-1659, 2009.

[36] W. Liu & W. Li, "A Novel Semi-Supervised Learning for Collaborative Image Retrieval", International Conference on Computational Intelligence and Software Engineering (CISE), pp. 1-4, 2009.

[37] P. A. de Alarcón, A. D. P. Montano & J. M. Carazo, "Spin Images and Neural Networks for Efficient Content-Based Retrieval in 3D Object Databases", International Conference on Image and Video Retrieval, pp. 225-234, 2002.

[38] N. V. Nguyen, A. Boucher, J. M. Ogier & S. Tabbone, "Clusters-Based Relevance Feedback for CBIR: A Combination of Query Movement and Query Expansion", IEEE RIVF International Conference on Computing and Communication Technologies, Research, Innovation, and Vision for the Future, pp. 1-6, 2010.

[39] Z. Shoaie & S. Jini, "Semantic image retrieval using relevance feedback and reinforcement learning algorithm", 5th International Symposium on I/V Communications and Mobile Network, pp. 1-4, 2010.

[40] K. Sugamya, S. Pabboju & A. V. Babu, "A CBIR Classification Using Support Vector Machines", International Conference on Advances in Human Machine Interaction, pp. 1-6, 2016.

[41] S. Gbèhounou, F. Lecellier & C. F. Maloigne, "Evaluation of local and global descriptors for emotional impact recognition", Journal of Visual Communication and Image Representation, Vol. 38, pp. 276-283, 2016.

[42] D. G. Lowe, "Distinctive Image Features from Scale-Invariant Keypoints", International Journal of Computer Vision, Vol. 60, No. 2, pp. 91-110, 2004.

[43] E. Shechtman & M. Irani, "Matching Local Self-Similarities across Images and Videos", IEEE Conference on Computer Vision and Pattern Recognition, pp. 1-8, 2007.

[44] M. Eitz, K. Hildebrand, T. Boubekeur & M. Alexa, "A descriptor for large scale image retrieval based on sketched feature lines", Proceedings of the 6th Eurographics Symposium on Sketch-Based Interfaces and Modeling, pp. 29-36, 2009.

[45] C. L. Zitnick, "Binary coherent edge descriptors", Proceedings of the 11th European Conference on Computer Vision: Part II, pp. 170-182, 2010.

[46] J. Philbin, M. Isard, J. Sivic & A. Zisserman, "Descriptor learning for efficient retrieval", Proceedings of the 11th European Conference on Computer Vision conference on computer vision: Part III, pp. 677-691, 2010.

[47] L. Zheng, S. Wang, W. Zhou & Q. Tian, "Bayes merging of multiple vocabularies for scalable image retrieval", IEEE Conference on Computer Vision and Pattern Recognition, pp. 1963-1970, 2014.

[48] M. Eitz, K. Hildebrand, T. Boubekeur & M. Alexa, "An evaluation of descriptors for large-scale image retrieval from sketched feature lines", Computers and Graphics, Vol. 34, No. 5, pp. 482-498, 2010.

[49] R. Hu, T. Wang & J. Collomosse, "A bag-of-regions approach to sketch-based image retrieval", 18th IEEE International Conference on Image Processing, pp. 3661-3664, 2011.

[50] M. Eitz, K. Hildebrand, T. Boubekeur & M. Alexa, "Sketch Based Image Retrieval: Benchmark and Bag-Of-Features Descriptors", IEEE Transactions on Visualization and Computer Graphics, Vol. 17, No. 11, pp. 1624-1636, 2011.

[51] Y. Cao, C. Wang, L. Zhang & L. Zhang, "Edgel index for large-scale sketch-based image search", IEEE Conference on Computer Vision and Pattern Recognition, pp. 761-768, 2011.

[52] X. Sun, C. Wang, C. Xu & L. Zhang, "Indexing billions of images for sketch-based retrieval", Proceedings of the 21st ACM International Conference on Multimedia, pp. 233-242, 2013.

[53] R. Zhou, L. Chen & L. Zhang, "Sketch-based image retrieval on a large scale database", Proceedings of the 20th ACM International Conference on Multimedia, pp. 973-976, 2012.

[54] K. Bozas & E. Izquierdo, "Large scale sketch based image retrieval using patch hashing", Advances in Visual Computing, pp. 210-219, 2012.

[55] M. Eitz, J. Hays & M. Alexa, "How do humans sketch objects", ACM Transactions on Graphics, Vol. 31, No. 4, 2012.

[56] P. Sousa & M. J. Fonseca, "Sketch-based retrieval of drawings using spatial proximity", Journal of Visual Languages and Computing, Vol. 21, No. 2, pp. 69-80, 2010.

[57] R. Hua & J Collomosse, "A Performance Evaluation of Gradient Field HOG Descriptor for Sketch Based Image Retrieval", Journal of Computer Vision and Image Understanding, Vol. 117, No. 7, pp. 790-806, 2013.

[58] C. Ma, X. Yang, C. Zhang, X. Ruan & M.-H. Yang, "Sketch retrieval via dense stroke features", Image and Vision Computing, Vol. 46, pp. 64-73, 2016.

[59] S. Wang, J. Zhang, T. X. Han & Z. Miao, "Sketch-Based Image Retrieval Through Hypothesis-Driven Object Boundary Selection With HLR Descriptor", IEEE Transactions on Multimedia, Vol. 17, No. 7, pp. 1045-1057, 2015.

[60] F. Wang, L. Kang & Y. Li, "Sketch-based 3d shape retrieval using convolutional neural networks", IEEE Conference on Computer Vision and Pattern Recognition, pp. 1875-1883, 2015.

[61] Y. Qi, Y. Z. Song, T. Xiang, H. Zhang, T. Hospedales, Y. Li & J. Guo, "Making better use of edges via perceptual grouping", IEEE Conference on Computer Vision and Pattern Recognition, pp. 1856-1865, 2015.

[62] Y. Qi, Y. Z. Song, H. Zhang & J. Liu, "Sketch-Based Image Retrieval via Siamese Convolutional Neural Network", IEEE International Conference on Image Processing, pp. 2460-2464, 2016.

[63] K. Porkaew, M. Ortega & S. Mehrota, "Query reformulation for content based multimedia retrieval in MARS", Vol. 2, pp. 747-751, 1999.

[64] G. Das, S. Ray & C. Wilson, "Feature re-weighting in content-based image retrieval", International Conference on Image and Video Retrieval, pp. 193-200, 2006.

[65] N. Dalal & B. Triggs, "Histograms of oriented gradients for human detection", IEEE Computer Society Conference on Computer Vision and Pattern Recognition, Vol. 1, pp. 886-893, 2005.

[66] E. Shechtman & M. Irani, "Matching local self similarities across images and videos", IEEE Conference on Computer Vision and Pattern Recognition, pp. 1-8, 2007.

Deep Learning for Image Processing Applications
D.J. Hemanth and V.V. Estrela (Eds.)
IOS Press, 2017
© 2017 The authors and IOS Press. All rights reserved.
doi:10.3233/978-1-61499-822-8-94

Advanced Stevia Disease Detection Using Deep Learning

S.Lakshmi[a] and R.Sivakumar[b]
[a] Jeppiaar SRR Engineering College, Chennai,India.
lakshmi1503@gmail.com
[b] Dcs, Chennai, India.
sivaa21@yahoo.com

Abstract. Almost all of us are tempted to take sweets due to its pleasant nature. When it is overused, it will affect our body entirely. Diabetic is a disease that occurs when the blood glucose level is high. According to the study of World Health Organization (WHO), the prevalence percentage of diabetic persons is doubled in the last 10 years. Life style, working environment, nature of the work, food habits and hereditary are few reasons for diabetic. Diabetic leads to various health problems like heart disease, stroke, kidney problems, nerves damage, eye and dental problems over time. Stevia is a sugar substitute which is available all over the world and it is proved to give more safety for diabetic patients. Stevia contains proteins, vitamins and minerals. Stevia plant may be affected by various diseases such as root rot, charcoal rot, wilt, leaf spot disease and so on. This chapter demonstrates the deep learning approach to enable the disease detection through image recognition. A deep convolutional neural network is trained to classify the disease affected leaves, achieving the accuracy of over 99%.

Keywords. Automatic disease detection, deep learning convolutional neural network, stevia, SoftMax function, radial basis function, feature detection

1. Introduction

Stevia is extracted from the herb Stevia rebaudiana which is widely used as a sugar substitute for diabetics. More than thirty million people have been diagnosed with diabetic in India. In rural areas, the prevalence is approximately three percent of the total population. The Impaired Glucose Tolerance (IGT) is also a big health issue in India. The design of a software-integrated tool using deep learning and image processing can greatly improve the Stevia production and maintain the quality of the product. Deep learning comprises artificial neural networks and machine learning algorithms. Models can be created for representing large scale data in image processing applications using deep learning algorithms. Generally deep learning algorithms show good performance results in recognition and mining applications.

CNNs have been successfully used in several domains for mapping between an input vector (such as a diseased vegetal picture) to an output e.g. a crop disease feature vector. The nodes in a neural network implement mathematical functions that take numerical inputs from the incoming edges, and deliver numerical outputs. Deep neural networks just map the input layer to the output layer through a series of stacked (or hidden) layers of nodes. The main challenge is to design the structure of the network as well as the functions (nodes) and edge weights that correctly map the input to the output. CNNs can be trained by tuning the network parameters so that the mapping progresses during the training process, which is computationally demanding.

This chapter examines CNNs applied to plant disease analysis and it is structured as follows. Section 2 portrays the problem. Section 3 discusses the application of computational intelligence in agricultural pest control. Section 4 presents the proposed methodology in detail. Section 5 describes the results and discussions and Section 6 provides the intended future work. Finally, Section 7gives the concluding remarks.

2. Problem Characterization

Stevia is a gift of God to the Diabetic patients and the botanical name is Stevia Rebaudiana Bertoni. It may also be called "sweet leaf","sugar leaf" or"honey leaf". It belongs to Asteraceae (sunflower) family and it contains a glycoside in its leaves. Carbohydrates and fat contents are very less in stevia. It grows in the warmest areas of the United States, Paraguay and Brazil. It was originally used in Paraguay to sweeten the tea. It has been cultivated in many of the Indian states like Rajasthan, Maharashtra, Kerala and Orissa recently.

Among the 150 species of stevua, S.rebaudiana is the sweetest and has been described as a 'wonder plant' or the sweetness of the future owing to its calorie-free natural sweetness. It has been reported to have various nutritional and medicinal properties, such as antimicrobial, antiviral, antifungal, antihypertensive, anti-hyperglycaemic and antitumor effects [5][8]. The stevia leaves are shown in Figure.1.The leaves of a stevia plants contain

- gulcoside 0.3%
- rebaudioside C 0.6%
- rebaudioside A 3.8% and
- Stevioside 9.1%.

Stevia contains proteins, vitamins and minerals. It is also used in folk medicine to treat hypertension and diabetes.Generally, doctors are used to give suggestions for taking more fiber and protein contents for diabetic patients. It is also used to prevent the tooth decay and helps to rejuvenate the pancreatic gland.

The farmers in India turn their attention towards stevia due to the following reasons:

- Its increasing demands for natural sweetness.
- It can act as an alternate to sugarcane.
- It can be added in soft drinks and bakery items to avoid the usage of sugar in long run.
- No tax for stevia production
- No risk in production
- The production of stevia comes early when we compare with other crops.
- It can grow at home garden.
- High potential of return as compared to traditional crop.

Stevia used as sweet substitute in food products such as seafood, soft drinks and candies in Japan and Korea. Initially stevia was banned by US government later on it is approved as food additive in 2008.

Figure.1: Sample Stevia leaves

The extracted dried white powder from stevia leaves are the sweeter than other forms of stevia which is available as teabags in supermarkets. The sweetness of stevia powder depends on the refinement process. Stevia plant may be affected by various diseases such as root rot, charcoal rot, wilt, leaf spot disease and so onwhich can cause significant economic, social and environment loss globally.It is highly difficult to monitor continuously and detect the disease at the earliest stage.

2.1. Stevia Cultivation

The growing field is very important for any plant. The basic requirements for stevia cultivation is listed below:
1. Bed size - 120cm
2. Distance between the plants – 30cm
3. Height - 25cm
4. Width – 50 to 60 cm
5. Rainfall – 150cm
6. Temperature – 30°C to 32°C
7. pH range – between 6.5 and 7.5
8. Soil - red and sandy loam soil

The plant spreads over by seeds, tissue culture or stem cuttings. Seed type cultivation is not an advisable one since it takes forty days to sixty days before transplanting to the field. Tissue culture is expensive. Hence stem cutting is the cheaper and the easier one which will take less time when compare with other technologies. A sample rectangular green house of stevia plant is shown in Figure.2.

Fertilization:

Generally, fertilization played a major role for raising the production in agriculture. Organic and inorganic fertilizers are used for stevia plant growth. The processed chicken manure used as basal and side dressing fertilizers.

Figure 2. Green house of stevia

Weed Control:

The proper procedure for planting stevia is very important to control the growth of weeds in the field. Manual weeding method is used to control the weeds nevertheless costly, time consuming one. The side dressing fertilizers are used to boost up the energy to grow stevia and also to control the weeds in the fields. Biodegradable mulches such as leaves, grass clippings help to control the growth of weed.

Water Management:

The supply of water should be consistent while growing the stevia. It is advisable to use sprinkler irrigation system for producing stevia. [20]

Harvesting:

The harvesting could be done, when the flower buds start to grow the vegetative growth will stop. The consistent intervals between the harvesting are normally 30 to 35 days. The yield will be 20 to 50 grams per plant. [11] [20]

After harvesting the plant should be dried. Drying should be done properly. In case, any delay in the drying process which will definitely affect the quality of the stevia. The steviosides content is reduced by 33% when the drying process is delayed for minimum three days. The moisture content should be less than 10% to store stevia. Normally stevia plants used to produce good yield up to five years then that will be replaced with new one. According to the financial giant Rabobank, Stevia sales are predicted to reach about 700 million dollars in the next few years.

2.2 Pest and Disease Control

Stevia plants are affected by stem rot diseases. Since stevia acts as a sugar substitute and animals like sweet, there is no chance of controlling the pests in the field. Nevertheless whiteflies, aphids and thrips are the problems in green houses. There are several pathologies like fungal, bacteria and virus that affects the stevia plants in different parts like roots, seedling, stem, leaves and fruits [13] [14]. Some of them are listed here with detailed explanation.

i.Alternaria alternata

It is a fugus which is the source of causing leaf spot. It can enter through the stomata or penetrate directly from the top of the leaf using the aspersorium and it is shown in the Figure.3. It is very common in medicinal plants cultivated in various districts of West Bengal, India. Symptoms of leaf spot disease initially appear as small brown colour circular spots and then it may develop to dark brown in irregular shapes. Infections are spreading from small circles to large necrotic areas. These concentric dark brown spots are commonly at the tips of the leaves.

Figure.3:Alternaria alternata

ii. Sclerotinia sclerotiorum

The stevia plants can also be affected by white mould disease due to pathogenic fungus which is shown in in Figure.4. It is also called as cottony rot or watery soft rot. It leads heavy loss when it is identified in the field. It is always advisable to detect this disease earlier so that necessary steps can be taken to avoid the loses.

(iii)Sclerotium rolfsii

It is identified and detected in India by [7] in Figure.5. It is an omnivorus, soil borne fungal pathogen causes diseases on a wide range. It attacks stems, roots, leaves and fruit. It affects the leaves first and the leaf colour is faded or becomes yellow then the stems are bleached or whitened. The affected stems and this fungal attach is visible early in the morning. Mycelium is accompanied by the formation of brown sclerotia 0.5-2mm in diameter.

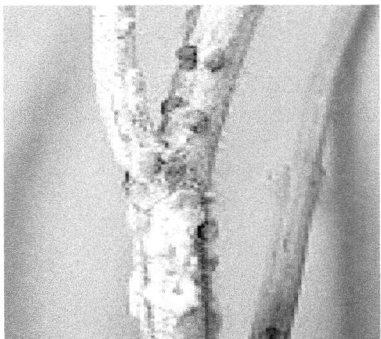

Figure.4 Sclerotinia sclerotiorum

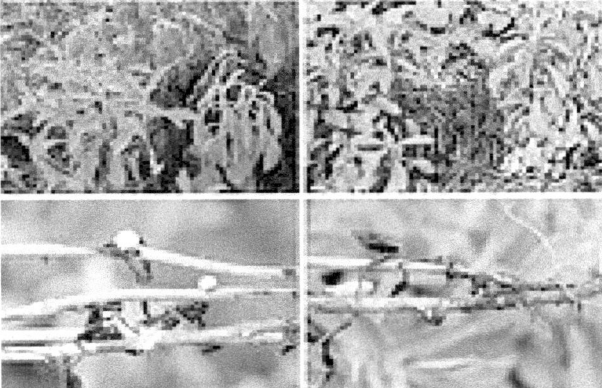

Figure 5. Sclerotium rolfsii

(iv)Septoria steviae

Mostly this disease affects the plant in warm weather. It affects the leaves by light brown colour. When the stevia is affected by this disease, first light brown colour spots are identified and then slowly extended to yellow colour haloes in outer leaves which is shown in Figure.6. Then the colour of the leave turns into gray in the middle portion of the leaf. When the severity rises the leaves may die. The disease may be transmitted through seeds.

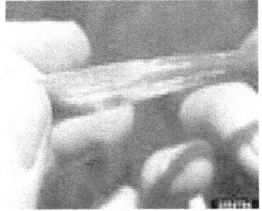

Figure.6 Septoria steviae

(v)Rhizoctonia sp.

Sunken reddish spots, gradually expand to kill the plants which is shown in Figure.7. The early stage of plants is affected and the colour is changed to reddish brown which prevent the regular growth of plants.

Figure.7. Rhizoctonia sp

(vi) Red spider mites

It is a small insect with lean month through which it sucks out the fluids in the plant which is shown in Figure.8. It is very hard to differentiate with other insects. It is always better to detect this as early as possible to reduce the loses.

Figure.8 Red spider mites

(vii) Whiteflyis

Mostly, this is found in the bottom of the leaves which could damage the plants by sucking the liquids and changing the colour of the leaf to yellow. It leads to reduce the yield by making the plants to weak and create an environment to spend the diseases easily. The Whitefly image is shown in the Figure.9.

Figure.9 Whiteflyis

3. Application of Computational Intelligence in Agricultural Pest Control

In India, the main part of our income depends on agriculture. Unexpected diseases reduce the growth of plants which will leads us in heavy loss. Recent developments in technology will act as an aid to identify the diseases earlier so that we can reduce the losses to some extent through which we can raise the production. Hence, it is really useful to our society to have an automated tool to detect the diseases earlier for raising our profit.

It is easy to monitor the entire field if we have an automated tool. This enables machine vision to provide automatic inspection which is more accurate than the visual inspection of fields.

Hence, a number of approaches in machine learning techniques to develop an automated system for plant disease detection at the earlier stages. Most of the techniques will follow the procedure given in Figure.10[1][2][12]. Image acquisition is the starting point of disease identification and recognition. Images are captured using various devices such as web camera, mobile phone, videos etc. The pre-processing steps involves noise reduction, image enhancement and feature extraction. The image classification involves recognition and classification by using various soft computing approaches.

The unwanted noisy details are removed by using various filtering techniques then the images are enhanced to maintain the fine details of the images. The image segmentation techniques are applied to extract the boundaries of the leaves. Finally, the classification techniques are used to identify and recognize the plant diseases. There are various algorithms are used such as neural network, support vector machine and rule based classification. Color is used to identify the following diseases in [1]:
1. Cottony mold
2. Late scorch
3. Scorch
4. Ashen mold and
5. Tiny whiteness

The details of the texture are calculated by using the co-occurrence matrix and they are fed into the neural network to detect the diseases.

Mohan et al., [9] introduced a new system to classify different diseases from paddy leaf images by using scale invariant feature transform(SIFT) feature and then they are classified by using KNN and SVM.

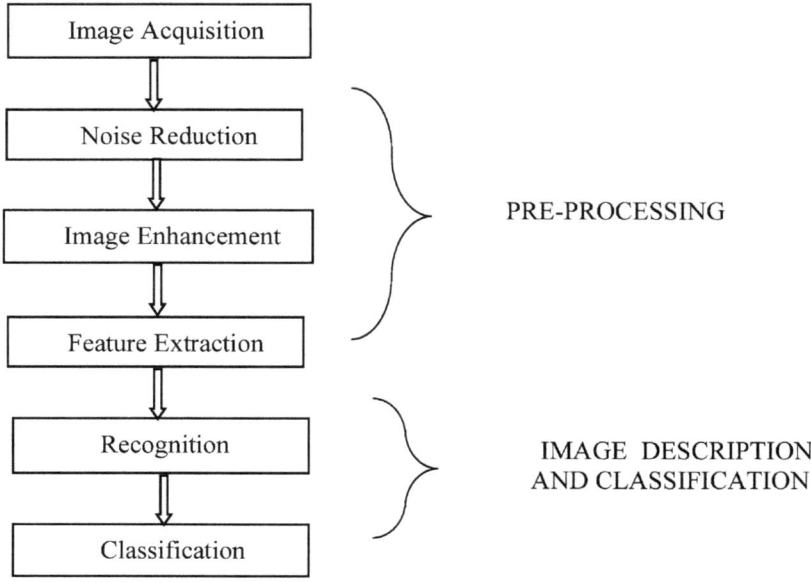

Figure.10 **Common** method for Disease detection

In general, diseases can be identified easily by the experts easily using naked eyes. Farmers are unaware of certain diseases. However, consulting experts is too expensive and time consuming one [1]. As an example, the grapefruit peel maybe infected by several diseases [3]and it can be identified using the squared distance technique [1]. Using high-resolution multispectral and stereo images leaf diseases are classified automatically [17].

Image segmentation techniques can be used to extract the disease affected part of the plants. An ideal threshold value can be calculated using parson window for segmenting the images [21]. Hence, in this work we will use the convolution neural network (CNN) for disease detection.

4.Proposed Method

We present a deep learning approach to identify the disease affected stevia leaves. Figure.11 depicts the architecture of the proposed work. It consists of two important steps:

(i)   Image preprocessing and
(ii) Deep learning-based classification.

We will discuss these two steps in detail.

4.1 Image Pre-processing

Using web camera stevia plant images are captured from the field regularly. The acquired images are stored for analyzing the growth details. Each image is represented by using RGB combinations. The size of the images is altered for making the further process easier. It can be down in MATLAB by using the immersive () function. Each image is resized and stored in a database for testing.

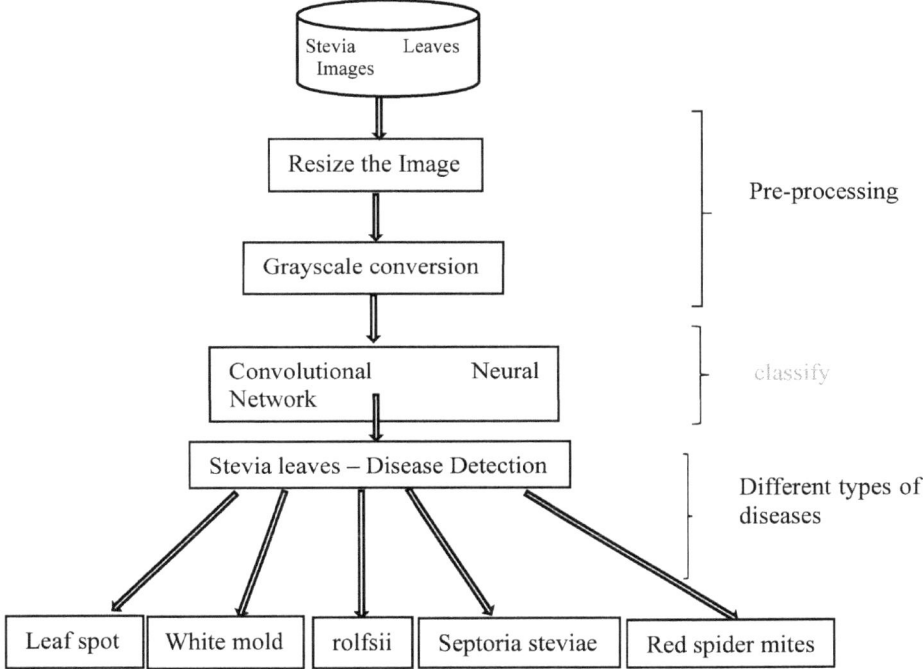

Figure.11 Proposed method

The acquired images are brought to the MATLAB environment by imread() function. The syntax of

    I = imread('filename');

    where the variable I can store the image file values in matrix format.

The image set is generated by capturing the stevia field directly. It may contain the images of healthy as well as unhealthy leaves. When we are dealing with real world images, definitely some percentage of noisy information i.e. unwanted information is added by the time of capturing the images. It is necessary to remove the unwanted information before processing the image so that we can get accurate results. In the literature, we have many filtering techniques such as mean filter, median filter, adaptive mean filter, weighted mean filter, wiener filter and so on. We have applied various filters and analyzed the results then we apply median filter for removing the noise from stevia plant images. The syntax for median filter is

$$J = medfilt2(I);$$

where I is the noisy image and J is the filtered image i.e., denoised image.

Even though color played a major role for disease identification, we have applied our CNN method in gray scale images too for evaluating the results. The color images are converted to gray scale by using the function rgb2gray ( ). Then, the diseases are identified and classified with the help of convolutional neural network.

4.2 Convolutional Neural Network(CNN) Classification

Convolutional neural networks are based on the biological processes. Its uses are not at all a limited one. Some of the application areas of this CNN is listed below:

- Image processing
- Video processing
- Pattern recognition
- Recommender systems and
- Natural language processing

Artificial Neural Networks (ANN) has proved very successful in various machine learning environment. Recent developments in neural network based deep learning architectures have demonstrated promising results in solving image classification problems efficiently.

LeCum proposed CNN which is the combination of neural network with three key concepts and designs where the adjacent layer neuron connections are enforced [15] [16] [22]. The CNN network architecture consists of the following layers:

1. Convolutional layer
2. Sub-sampling layer and
3. An output layers

Convolutional layer:

It is a basic layer in the CNN architecture. Here, neurons are arranged in a two-dimensional array. A feature map is extracted from this 2D array. The output of a plane is called a feature map. A connection is based on the convolution mask which is a matrix of adjustable entries. Bias term is a scalar which is added with the convolutional output. Finally, an activation function is applied on the result to obtain the plane's output.

Convolution map:

The main idea of this convolution map is to extract the features from the given denoised images. It has some set of learnable filters. Each filter is applied to the raw pixel values of the image taking into account the red, green and blue color channels in a sliding window fashion, computing the dot product between the filter pixel and the input pixel. The dot product of the filter and the input pixel is calculated by applying the sliding window procedure for getting the feature map which is activation map of the filter. The features of the given input images such as edges and curves through the learning process. In the training process, the CNN itself learns the values of the filters. The convolving operation can be done by using the following equation:

$$Mi = bi + \sum_j Wij \star Xj \qquad (1)$$

Here,
Mi – feature map
$\star$–operator of convolution
Xj – the jth input channel
Wij – sub kernel of the channel
bi– bias

The convolution layer organization is based on the number of convolution maps and the size of the filters. Hence, the feature map is constructed by adding the bias with the sum of the product of different two-dimensional convolution features. In the feature map, nonlinearity is introduced by using the rectified nonlinear activation function which is named as ReLU. This Rectified activation function is defined as follows:

$$f(x) = \max (0, x) \qquad (2)$$

where x is the input to a neuron.
The LeNet architecture is shown in Figure.12 where the convolution layer and the maximum pooling are played a major role.

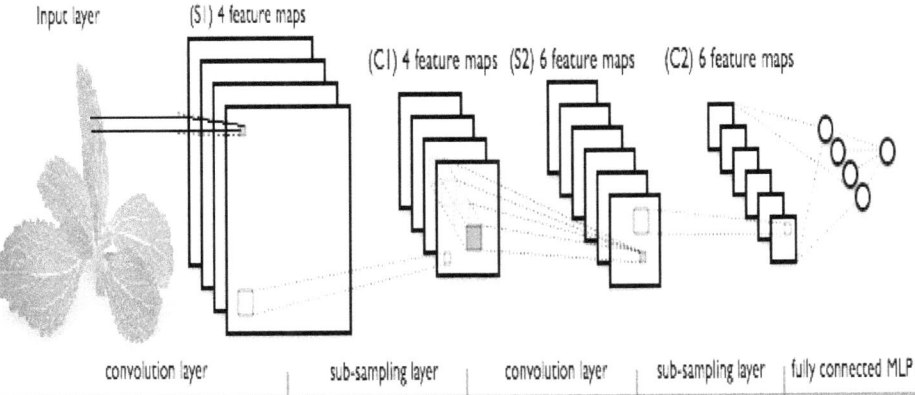

Figure.12. LeNet Architecture

Max-pooling map:

In the CNN architecture, the sub-sampling layers are used not only reducing the size of the convolution maps but also introducing the rotational and translational invariance.

The maximum activation function value is declared as an output of the feature map. The usage of the max-pooling operation is listed as follows:

- Non-maximal values are eliminated for reducing the computation of upper layers.
- Introduce rotational and translational invariance. Normally a pixel has eight directions for translation. In the convolutional layer three results out of eight directions produce the same output.

The number of planes in the sub-sampling layer follows the convolution layer and the sub-sampling layer divides the input into 2 x 2 pixels of non-overlapping blocks. The sum is calculated in each block then multiplied with an adjustable weight and then the bias value is added at the end. The output value is taken by activation functions to produce the result. Hence the sub-sampling layer reduces the input size with dimension. The scalar output is produced in the last convolution layer. In CNN, the output layer is designed by using the sigmoidal function or the radial basis function and the architecture of the radial basis function is shown in Figure.13. This radial bias network is based on the approximation theory.

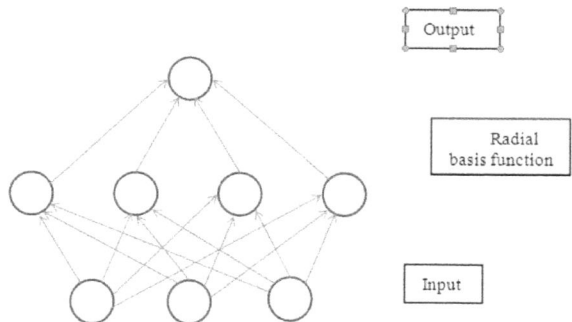

Figure.13. RBN Architecture

The newrb(P,T) function is used for creating the radial basis network in MATLAB where P is the input and T is the output vector. The hidden nodes are used to implement the radial basis function. In real time applications, the output shows the category of the given image. It gives very fast and correct results.

Classification model

In the convolution neural network classification, each neuron offers connection to feature maps from the previous layer. The features are extracted from the input image by the convolution and pooling layers automatically from the input image. The dimensionality of the features is reduced by the pooling layer. The SoftMax activation function is used in the connected layers for computing the various category information. Here the input for the SoftMax activation function is a feature vector of the learning process and the output is the probability of the given image belongs to a given category. The Figure.14. depicts the proposed convolution neural network architecture. The SoftMax activation function takes input in K-dimensional vector z and outputs a K-dimensional vector y of real values between 0 and 1. This function is also called as normalized exponential function and its mathematical representation is as follows:

$$\sigma(\mathbf{z})_j = \frac{e^{z_j}}{\sum_{k=1}^{K} e^{z_k}} \text{ for } j = 1, \ldots, K. \tag{3}$$

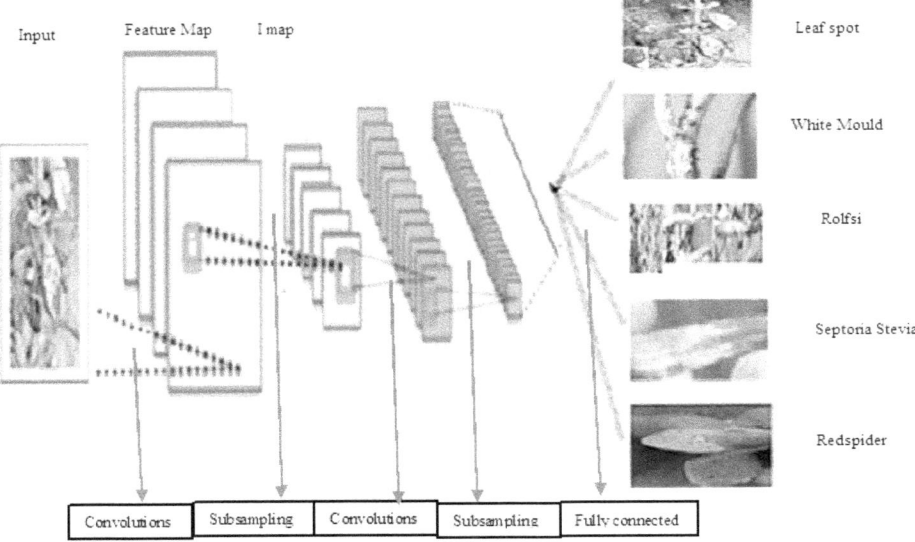

Figure 14. Proposed CNN architecture for Disease detection

CNN Library Usage

To design a CNN involves the following tasks.

i)   Creation of network
ii)   Initializing the network weights and biases
iii) Computation of network output
iv)   Training the network

Some of the functions in CNN library are

cnn_new -> to create a new network
cnn_init -> to initialize a network
cnn_cm-> to create a connection matrix for a network layer
cnn_sim -> compute network output
cnn_train -> to train a network
cnn.train.gd -> to train a CNN using Gradient descent method

5. Results and Discussion

The confusion matrix table is used to measure the performance of the classification model. The accuracy, precision and recall are calculated using thefollowing parameters.

True positive (TP)   -Correctly identified diseased images
True Negative (TN)   - Correctly identified healthy leaves ie., unaffected images
False positive (FP)   -Number of unaffected images are detected wrongly as diseased images
False Negative (FN) -Number of disease affected images are detected wrongly as unaffected images.

Accuracy: This is a ratio of correctly forecasted observation and the total observations.

$$Accuracy = TP+TN/TP+FP+TN+FN \qquad (4)$$

Precision: It is the ratio of correctly forecasted positive observations to the total predicted positive observations.

$$Precision = TP/TP+FP \qquad (5)$$

Recall: It is the ratio of correctly forecasted positive observations to the all observations.

$$Recall = TP/TP+FN \qquad (6)$$

The proposed method is implemented in a set of real data which was acquired by using mobile camera and digital camera for validation. The dataset contains nearly thousand images of healthy and various disease affected stevia leaves. These images are taken with different sizes, different poses, orientation and background. We have tested the different range of training set and testing set to compare our proposed algorithm. The training dataset varies from 80%, 60% and 40%.

Table-1. Accuracy, Precision and Recall of proposed method using CNN

Training(percentage)	Testing(percentage)	Accuracy	Precision	Recall
Color Images				
20	80	0.986	0.985	0.986
40	60	0.986	0.986	0.985
50	50	0.996	0.997	0.997
60	40	0.967	0.969	0.968
80	20	0.922	0.932	0.926
Gray scale images				
20	80	0.933	0.943	0.931
40	60	0.973	0.955	0.912
50	50	0.922	0.913	0.925
60	40	0.912	0.913	0.915
80	20	0.901	0.912	0.902

The stochastic gradient descent algorithm is used in our proposed work to learn the best set of weights and biases of the neural network to minimize the loss function. By using accuracy, precision and recall, we can evaluate the efficiency of the proposed work using color and gray scale images and the values are tabulated in Tabel-1.

The results were obtained using the deep learning model for identifying the stevia disease affected images. Our proposed work was able to find good results to classify the diseases of stevia leaves. Hence, the green color refers the healthy stevia leaves and the leaves with black, brown and yellow color may be considered as disease affected leaves.

6.Future Work

We got better results in the proposed work of disease detection in stevia plant. It can be used as a decision support tool for identifying the disease affected leaves easily. In future, this work can be extended to analyze and estimate the severity of the diseases automatically which will help the farmers for taking the decision easily and effectively at right time.

7. Conclusion

Plant diseases reduce the production and the quality of the end product severely. Automated tools can act as an aid to recognize the problem at the earliest stage so that the production and the quality can be maintained. In this paper, we presented a method based on convolutional neural network to identify and classify the diseases in stevia. It can act as a decision support tool for identifying diseases in stevia. Our main contribution is to apply deep neural networks to detect different types of diseases in stevia field.

References

1) Al-Hiary, H.; Bani-Ahmad, S.; Reyalat, M.; Braik, M.; ALRahamneh, Z.: Fast and accurate detection and classification of plant diseases. International Journal of Computer Applications, 17(1):0975–8887, 2011

2) Cui, Di; Zhang, Qin; Li, Minzan; Hartman, Glen L.; Zhao, Youfu: Image processing methods for quantitatively detecting soybean rust from multispectral images. Biosystems Engineering, 107(3):186–193, 2010.

3) Dheeb Al Bashish, Malik Braik, and Sulieman Bani-Ahmad , (2010)A Framework for Detection and Classification of Plant Leaf and Stem Diseases, International Conference on Signal and Image Procssing pp 113-118.

4) Elaksher A.F. "Multi-Image Matching Using Neural networks and Photogrammetric Conditions", The International Archives of the Photogrammetry, Remote Sensing and Spatial Information Sciences. Vol. XXXVII. Part I,, B3a. Beijing 2008.

5) *Goyal, S.K., Samsher and Goyal, R.K. (2010). Stevia (Stevia rebaudiana) a bio-sweetener: A review.* International Journal of Food Sciences and Nutrition, *61, 1, 1-10.*

6) Junna Cheng, Guangrong Ji, Chen Feng, Haiyong Zheng Application of Connected Morphological Operators to Image Smoothing and Edge Detection of Algae. International Conference on Information Technology and Computer Science. 2009, pp. 73-76.

7) *Kobylewski, S. and Eckhert, C.D. (2008). Toxicology of rabaudioside A: A review. Retrieved July 20, 2011.*

8) Mohammed T.S, Al-Taie, "Artificial Neural Networks as Decision-Makers for Stereo Matching", GSTF International Journal on Computing, Vol.1, No. 3, August- 2012.

9) Mohan, K. Jagan; Balasubramanian, M.; Palanivel, S.: Detection and Recognition of Diseases from Paddy Plant Leaf Images. International Journal of Computer Applications, 144(12):34–41, 2016.]

10) Muhammad Ghawas, M., Wan Zaki W.M, Zawayi M, Mansor M, Muhammad Azhar A,B(2009), Penanaman dan pengeluaran tanaman stevia , Bull Teknol,Tanaman Bil.6

11) Patil, Sagar; Chandavale, Anjali: A Survey on Methods of Plant Disease Detection. International Journal of Science and Research (IJSR), 6(14), 2013.

12) R.A.AI-Yahjao and D.Lupton, Leavy Medicinal herbs:Botany, Chemistry, Postharvest Technology and Uses

13) Ramanathan Parimalavalli and S.Radhai Sri Periyar university , salem, PSG college of Arts and Science, Coimbatore

14) S. L. Phung and A. Bouzerdoum, "A pyramidal neural network for visual pattern recognition," IEEE Transactions on Neural Networks, vol. 27, no. 1, pp. 329–343, 2007.

15) S. L. Phung and A. Bouzerdoum, "MATLAB library for convolutional neural network," Technical Report, ICT Research Institute, Visual and Audio Signal Processing Laboratory, University of Wollongong. Available at: http://www.uow.edu.au/~phung.

16) Sabine D. Bauer, Filip Korc, Wolfgang Forstner, The Potential of Automatic Methods of Classification to identify Leaf diseases from Multispectral images, Published online: 26 January 2011, Springer Science+Business Media, LLC 2011., Precision Agric (2011 12:361–377, DOI 10.1007/s11119-011-921

17) Sandesh B. K., Shalini C., B.R. Brinda, M.A. Kumar. Digital image processing—an alternate tool for monitoring of pigment levels in cultured cells with special reference to green alga Haematococcus pluvialis, Biosensors and Bioelectronics. 2005, 21: 768–773.25

18) Soejarto DD, Douglas K, Farnsworth NR. 1982. Potential sweetening agents of plant origin-III. Organoleptic evaluation of Stevia leaf herbarium samples for sweetness. J Nat Prod 45(5):590-599

19) Tan S. L, Wan Zaki W.M., Muhamad Ghawas, M.Mansor, Zawawi M (2010), "Stevia (Stevia rebaudiana Bertoni), In Teknologi Penananaman dan Pemprosesan Primer Tumbuhan Ubatan (Musa Y, Mansor P, Yahaya H, Wan Zaki editor)]

20) Wang Jue, Wang shitong, Image Thresholding Using Parzen Window Estimation. Jurnal of applied sciences 8(5):772-779, 2008, ISSN 18125654, Asian Network for Scientif Information, 2008].

21) Y. LeCun, L. Bottou, Y. Bengio, and P. Haffner, "Gradient-based learning applied to document recognition," Proceedings of the IEEE, vol. 86, no. 11, pp. 2278–2324, 1998

Deep Learning for Image Processing Applications
D.J. Hemanth and V.V. Estrela (Eds.)
IOS Press, 2017
doi:10.3233/978-1-61499-822-8-111

Analysis of Tuberculosis Images Using Differential Evolutionary Extreme Learning Machines (DE-ELM)

E. Priya[a,1] and S. Srinivasan[b]

[a]*Department of Electronics and Communication Engineering, Sri Sairam Engineering College, West Tambaram, Chennai, India*
[b]*Department of Instrumentation Engineering, MIT Campus, Anna University, Chennai, India*

Abstract. In this work, an attempt has been made to demarcate Tuberculosis (TB) sputum smear positive and negative images using statistical method based on Gray Level Co-occurrence Matrix (GLCM). The sputum smear images (N=100) recorded under standard image acquisition protocol are considered for this work. Haralick descriptor based statistical features are calculated from the sputum smear images. The most relevant features are ranked by principal component analysis. It is observed that the first five principal components contribute more than 96% of the variance for the chosen significant features. These features are further utilized to demarcate the positive from negative smear images using Support Vector Machines (SVM) and Differential Evolution based Extreme Learning Machines (DE-ELM). Results demonstrate that DE-ELM performs better than SVM in terms of performance estimators such as sensitivity, specificity and accuracy. It is also observed that the generalization learning capacity of DE-ELM is better in terms of number of hidden neurons utilized than the number of support vectors used by SVM. Thus it appears that this method could be useful for mass discrimination of positive and negative TB sputum smear images.

Keywords. tuberculosis, sputum smear images, gray level co-occurrence matrix, principal component analysis, support vector machine, differential evolution extreme learning machines

1. Introduction

1.1. Brief introduction on tuberculosis

Tuberculosis (TB) is the only disease ever declared a global emergency by the World Health Organization (WHO). TB is an infectious disease caused by the bacillus *Mycobacterium tuberculosis*. It is an airborne infectious disease that spreads easily in densely populated areas with poor sanitation. TB spreads when people infected with

---

[1] Corresponding Author, E. Priya, Assistant Professor, Department of Electronics and Communication Engineering, Sri Sairam Engineering College, West Tambaram, Chennai, India; E-mail: priya.ece@sairam.edu.in

[2] S. Srinivasan, Associate Professor, Department of Instrumentation Engineering, MIT Campus, Anna University, Chennai, India; E-mail: srini@mitindia.edu

pulmonary TB expel bacteria into air by coughing. It typically affects the lungs (pulmonary TB) but can also affect other organs or tissues such as the brain, kidneys, bone and skin (extra-pulmonary TB) [1, 2].

TB has existed for millennia and remains a major global health problem. Six countries account for 60% of the global TB burden by WHO which includes India, Indonesia, China, Nigeria, Pakistan and South Africa. This is despite the fact that with a timely diagnosis and correct treatment, most people who develop TB disease can be cured [1].

1.2. TB diagnosis

The diagnostic techniques for TB include both invasive and non-invasive methods. Invasive techniques, such as QuantiFERON and T-SPOT blood tests, promise to be more precise and reliable than other commonly used non-invasive methods. However, according to WHO, the invasive methods are too expensive for poor resource countries [3]. The non-invasive diagnostic techniques include smear microscopy, chest radiography and culture test. Repeated examinations of the infected person are needed for early detection of the disease. Conclusive result for culture test takes as much as 2 months because the disease causing agent, the tubercle bacilli take 5 to 20 hours to duplicate. Chest radiography tests work adequately only when there is a high level of infection and so this procedure cannot be used for TB diagnosis in early stages [4-6].

The WHO developed Directly Observed Treatment, Short course (DOTS) strategy for TB control which has been adopted by many national tuberculosis programmes. The DOTS strategy recommends smear microscopy as the most effective tool for the diagnosis of TB and for monitoring patient response to treatment [7, 8]. The low and middle-income countries mainly rely on the smear microscopy for TB screening as it is the backbone of TB screening and cost effective too. Sputum smear microscopy is capable of detecting majority of infectious TB cases thereby reducing TB prevalence and incidence [9].

The widely used two microscopic diagnostic techniques for TB screening are the fluorescence and conventional microscopy. The conventional microscopy uses a conventional artificial light source. The sample smears are stained with carbolfuchsin solution according to Ziehl-Neelsen (ZN) or Kinyoun acid-fast stains which cause the TB bacilli to appear magenta against a light blue background. The bacilli may also take different colours varying from light fuchsia to dark purple. These bacilli are called acid-fast bacilli as they retain the dye even after washing with acid and alcohol [10, 11].

Conventional microscopy is inexpensive, rapid, and highly specific but has poor sensitivity, particularly in patients co-infected with human immune deficiency virus. In addition, examination of ZN-stained smears takes more time than fluorochrome-stained smears. Also the bacilli are not clearly separated from the background in the image obtained by a conventional light microscope [5, 8, 12].

Fluorescence Microscopy (FM) renders improved sensitivity in the diagnosis of pulmonary TB. The technique uses an acid-fast fluorochrome dye such as auramine O or auramine-rhodamine and high intense light source such as a halogen or high pressure mercury vapor lamp. The bacilli appears in different colours such as reddish yellow, reddish golden yellow or bright orange yellow fluorescence in a dark background depending on the staining procedures. The bacilli when stained with auramine O and excited by blue light (450–480 nm) emits in the green-reddish yellow range (500–600 nm) [11, 13].

1.2.1. Manual diagnosis in sputum smear microscopy

The most common method for diagnosing patients with TB is by visually screening for rod-shaped objects (tubercle bacilli) in the stained smears prepared from sputum under the microscopic view fields [10]. In manual screening the specialist analyse between 20 and 100 fields in the microscopic image to achieve correct diagnosis. The positivity of smears depends on the number of tubercle bacilli present in a field or image. Visual evaluation of fluorescence microscopy images are quite often tedious because of inter and intra observer variability. This procedure makes the diagnosis a time consuming, inaccurate and inefficient process that requires between 40 minutes and 3 hours of analysis depending on the patient's level of infection [3, 14, 15].

The manual procedure is labour intensive with high false-negative results that questions the sensitivity of the procedure. Also fatigue and visual strain limits the number of slides administered per day [3, 16, 17]. Hence an automated TB diagnosis is required to handle large number of cases with enhanced accuracy to speed up the screening process, minimize its reliance on technicians, enhance quantitative classification and reduce errors.

1.2.2. Automation of sputum smear microscopy

Attempts have already been made to digitize image captured by a camera attached to the microscope to overcome the manual procedure. Thus the aim of automation in the context of TB screening is to speed up the screening process and to reduce its reliance on technicians and pathologists. The demands on technicians in high-prevalence countries lead to overload and fatigue, which diminish the quality of microscopy [18]. Automation may also improve the low sensitivity of conventional TB screening by microscopy and reduce human variability in diagnosing a slide. Image processing and pattern recognition methods are the suitable approaches for automatic assessment of sputum smears [19, 20].

1.3. Image processing techniques in TB diagnosis

1.3.1. Fluorescence microscopy

Several image processing algorithms have been developed for automatic TB bacilli detection in the captured images. Pattern recognition approaches for the identification of TB were first resolved for auramine-stained sputum smears. Veropoulos et al. (1998) investigated the sputum images using edge pixel linkage and morphological closing operation to separate the bacilli from the background in fluorescence microscopy images [21]. Fourier descriptors have been proposed by the authors to describe the segmented objects and used a feedforward neural network with four hidden units for classification of TB objects [22]. Their method required additional usage of morphological operations because of the adopted gradient based segmentation algorithm. Forero et al. (2004) segmented bacillus in sputum samples by combining color and shape information [23]. In another attempt, Forero et al. (2006) modelled the edited bacillus data set using Gaussian mixture model. Segmented TB objects were described by Hu's moments and a minimum error Bayesian classifier was attempted to classify the objects [20].

Santiago-Mozos et al. (2008) developed pixel classification to identify bacilli in images of auramine-stained sputum and described each pixel by a square patch of neighbouring pixels. They implemented principal component analysis to reduce the number of pixels which was given as input to a support vector machine classifier. Increase in specificity was reported which is due to the edited bacillus data set [24]. Tapley et al. (2013) reported that their proposed CellScope is a novel digital FM, in comparison to conventional Light Emitting Diode (LED) FM. They achieved sensitivity and specificity for their portable digital FM within 15% of those attained by experienced technicians using conventional LED FM [9].

1.3.2. Bright field microscopy

Many research articles focussed on identification of TB bacilli in ZN-stained sputum smears because of its low cost device and maintenance. Lenseigne et al. (2007) implemented support vector machine classifier as an image segmentation method at pixel level in confocal microscopy images [25]. Sadaphal et al. (2008) demonstrated color-based Bayesian segmentation and used prior knowledge to identify the TB objects followed by shape/size analysis to refine detection [16]. Raof et al. (2008) conducted multi-level thresholding on color values in images of ZN sputum slides [26]. Costa et al. (2008) employed Red minus Green (R-G) images from RGB color format for automatic identification of tuberculosis bacilli in conventional light microscopy images [5]. Sotaquira et al. (2009) proposed combining YCbCr and Lab color spaces for segmentation of sputum smear samples prepared by ZN technique [3]. Khutlang et al. (2010) segmented the candidate bacillus using a combination of pixel classifier and object classifier based on the extracted geometric transformation invariant features [19].

Zhai et al. (2010) implemented an automatic system for TB identification which consists of a microscope, an image-based autofocus and identification algorithm [27]. Rulaningtyas et al. (2015) improved image contrast and eliminated background color to identify TB bacilli boundary by sobel edge detection method. They used neural network with backpropagation algorithm for classification to assist clinicians in diagnosing sputum microscopically [28]. Costa Filho et al. (2015) proposed a new rule-based filter in Kinyoun acid-fast stained images. Their method characterizes the sputum smear images that examine the H component of HSI color space of the image's pixels [29]. Panicker et al. (2016) provided a comprehensive and accessible overview of methods that could be useful to researchers and practitioners especially working in the field of TB automation [30].

The literature review on the image processing techniques proposed for ZN-stained sputum smears illustrate that pixel classifiers have the skill to utilize the color differences between bacilli and background in these images. Also the color space models aid in identification of bacilli in ZN-stained sputum smears. The spatial information based identification is considerably preferred in auramine-stained images. The basic segmentation methods and shape based features were particularly used in these images. Most of the authors have used heuristic knowledge about the most frequent bacilli shapes for identification. Apart from these issues if the images have a very complex background due to debris present in the sputum samples then automatic identification will be a challenging task.

1.4. Texture analysis

During the past decade, outcomes from many published articles have revealed the capability of texture analysis algorithms to infer diagnostically significant information from medical images [31]. Texture is a characteristic that is present in almost all images, and is considered to be one of the most important properties used in the identification or classification of image objects or regions [32]. Since the textural properties of images appear to carry useful information for discrimination purposes, it is important to develop features from textural information [33]. Texture or structural features represents the spatial distribution of gray values. Texture features are a rich source of visual information and are key components in image analysis and understanding [34]. Texture features are, in fact, mathematical parameters computed from the distribution of pixels, which characterize the texture type and thus the underlying structure of the objects present in the image [35].

A large body of literature exists for texture analysis of ultrasound, Magnetic Resonance (MR) imaging, Computed Tomography (CT), fluorescence microscopy, light microscopy and other digital images. Optical imaging modalities such as fluorescence microscopy images of colonic tissue sections and light microscopy images of the chromatin structure in advanced prostate cancer have utilized texture analysis [36, 37].

Haralick proposed the utility of Gray Level Co-occurrence Matrices (GLCM) which has become one of the most well-known and widely used texture features in medical image analysis. GLCM also called as gray tone spatial dependency matrix is a tabulation of the frequencies or describes a combination of pixel brightness values in an image [33].

Texture features derived from the co-occurrence matrix have been successfully employed to develop criteria for the categorization of normal and cancerous colonic mucosa, regardless of grade. Haralick's texture features have also been implemented to obtain methods for numerical description, objective representation and successive categorization of cellular protein localization patterns in FM images [36].

Application of texture features include but not limited to identification of masses in digital mammograms, content based image retrieval system for human brain indexing, texture based segmentation and prostate cancer characterization on MR images [38-41]. Literatures have suggested using image texture in combination with color features to diagnose leukemic malignancy in samples of stained blood cells. In combination with color, the texture features significantly improved the correct classification rate of blood cell types compared to using only color features. Various first-order statistics (such as mean gray level in a region) as well as second-order statistics (such as gray level co-occurrence matrices) are derived to differentiate different types of white blood cells [42].

Studies comparing the performance of GLCM features with other texture analysis techniques show that GLCM is one of the most powerful methods for general texture classification. GLCM features perform better than fractal; Markov random field and Gabor filter features in classifying a wide range of texture images including synthetic and natural images [32].

If measures are not taken to reduce the number of features before classification, then it may reflect the noise or random error of the underlying data [43]. This will most certainly result in over training as it gives too many degrees of freedom for the classifier. To get good generalization properties of the classifier, it is desirable to keep the number of features as low as possible. To perform the selection of features in an automatic fashion, a method to judge the quality of the resultant classifier is needed [14].

1.5. Feature selection

Feature selection plays an important role in classification by removing insignificant features from the data set to provide better diagnosis, which is an important requirement in medical applications. When a large number of features are input to a classifier, some may be irrelevant while others will be redundant. This might increase the complexity of the task and at worst hinder the classification by increasing the inter-class variability [44].

The use of superfluous features often leads to inferior performance in pattern recognition. A general practical observation is that it is worth decreasing the dimensionality of the feature space while ensuring that the overall structure of the data points remains intact. A simple way to do this is by means of a transformation that linearly maps the initial feature space to a new one with fewer dimensions. The most popular technique, Principal Component Analysis (PCA) chooses the basis vectors of the transformed space as those directions of the original space to show large variance among the significant data [45].

In the traditional eigenspace methods such as PCA, the feature space is transformed to a set of independent and orthogonal axes. This can be ranked by the extent of variation given by the associated eigenvalues. However, while these eigenspace methods are optimal and effective, they still require the computation of all the features for the given data [44].

1.6. Machine learning techniques

Classifiers are widely used in discriminating pathological condition from the normal. The classification process involves grouping of data into pre-defined classes or finding the class to which a data belongs. This process plays an important role in medical image automation, which is a part of decision making in medical image analysis. Machine learning based classification techniques provide support for many areas of health care, including prognosis, diagnosis and screening [46].

Support Vector Machine (SVM) is a machine learning technique which is based on statistical theory to characterize data and to recognize patterns. It is a supervised learning method. The training principal behind SVM is that it seeks for an optimal separating hyperplane so that the expected classification error for unseen test samples is minimized. The foremost and notable feature of this approach is that the solution is based only on the data points, which are at the extremity called support vectors [47].

Some of the benefits of SVM include handling of continuous and binary classes, with reasonable speed of classification and accuracy. But SVM takes longer time for training dataset and do not tackle discrete attributes. It finds application in classification of brain MR images using genetic algorithm with SVM and is able to classify brain tissue into normal, benign or malignant tumor [48]. SVMs have been used for lung nodule detection from chest CT images, to classify digital mammography images and in combination with multiscale local binary patterns to classify saliency-based folded images [49-51].

Differential Evolutionary Extreme Learning Machine (DE-ELM) takes advantages of both ELM and Differential Evolution (DE) and removes redundancy among hidden nodes and achieves satisfactory performance with more compact and high speed neural networks. The DE procedure is a global search optimization method that adjusts the input weights and hidden layer biases whereas the output weights are determined by the generalized inverse procedure. DE-ELM has been prolifically used in the field of medical diagnosis because of its compact architecture and speed [52-54].

In this work, GLCM matrix based Haralick descriptors are extracted from the digital TB sputum smear images. The most significant GLCM features are selected by PCA and are further classified by supervised learning machines such as SVM and DE-ELM for demarcating the TB positive from the negative images.

1.7. Organization of chapter

The chapter is organized as follows. Section 2 gives a brief description on the methods adopted in this chapter. Section 2.1 presents the details of image acquisition protocol. The remaining topics in section 2 describes the GLCM based texture analysis, PCA based feature selection technique and the machine learning methods such as SVM and hybrid DE-ELM classifiers. Section 3 discusses on the results of the above mentioned methods and section 4 deals with significant conclusions.

2. Methodology

2.1. Image acquisition

The sputum smear slides used were prepared by smearing the sputum specimen on a clean slide. The air dried smears were then fixed to the slide by passing the slides through a low flame two to three times. The slides were flooded with Auramine O stain to bind the cell wall of the acid fast bacilli and left for 10 minutes. Then the slides were decolorized with acid alcohol and washed with running water. To get a contrast background the slides were counter stained with potassium permanganate. Then the slides were rinsed with water and air dried before viewing under the microscope. The fluorescence-stained slides were prepared at the South African National Health Laboratory Services, Groote Schuur Hospital in Cape Town.

The images (N=100) were captured using a camera in monochrome binning mode attached to a 20x objective fluorescence microscope of 0.5 numerical aperture. The camera (AxioCam HR) has a resolution of 4164 x 3120 with a pixel size 6.45 μm (h) x 6.45 μm (v). The images of size 256 x 256 are considered for the analysis with positive and negative sputum smear images of 50 each. The acquired images suffer from non-uniform illumination, and hence these images are pre-processed by non-uniform illumination correction technique [55]. The pipeline stages presented in Figure 1 gives the overview of the work carried out. In the first stage, statistical texture analysis is performed for the pre-processed images based on Gray-Level Co-occurrence Matrix (GLCM) method.

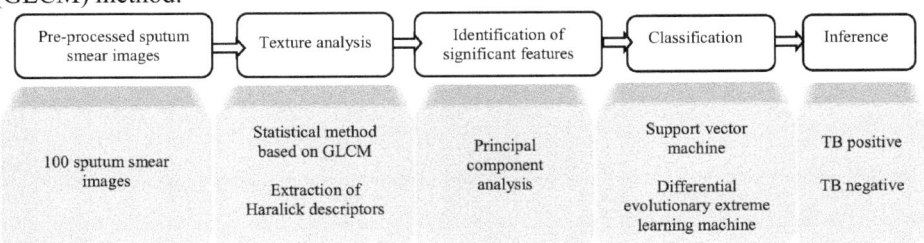

Figure 1. Pipeline stages of the system

2.2. GLCM based texture analysis

Literature reveals that there are four groups of texture analysis methods, such as statistical, geometrical, model-based and signal processing. Each and every method has its own characteristics based on their capabilities and application in which it has been implemented. Among them, the statistical method based on GLCM is reported to be the most commonly and predominantly used [56]. It has been shown that the second-order statistical-based co-occurrence matrix produces better classification accuracy over the other texture analysis methods [57, 58].

Geometrical method-based structural analysis is well suited for the synthesis of an image than its analysis, whereas estimation of model-based parameters is computationally complex. The statistical method of defining texture describes the spatial relationship of pixels in the GLCM. This approach represents the texture of an image by calculating how often pixel pairs with specific values and in a specified spatial relationship occur in an image. These methods normally achieve higher discrimination indexes than the geometrical method based structural or transform methods. In transform methods, the texture properties of the image are analyzed in the frequency or scale space [36].

The GLCM matrices are constructed by computing pixel intensity value co-occurrences at a distance of $d = 1$, representing one pixel distance and for direction θ given as $0°$, $45°$, $90°$ and $135°$. Since single direction might not give enough and reliable texture information, four directions are used to extract the texture information. The four directional GLCM's are averaged to furnish a non-directional matrix from which the textural features are evaluated. The GLCM features obtained from this matrix are rotation invariant, being averaged across $0°$, $45°$, $90°$ and $135°$ intervals [36].

The diagonal of GLCM matrix will have values if an image contains no image texture. The off diagonal values of the GLCM become larger as the image texture increases. The number of rows and columns in GLCM is determined by the number of gray scale intensity values in the image [59].

2.2.1. Haralick descriptors

The Haralick features computed from the GLCM are autocorrelation, contrast, correlation, cluster prominence, cluster shade, dissimilarity, energy, entropy, homogeneity, maximum probability, sum of squares (variance), sum average, sum variance, difference variance, difference entropy, information measure of correlation I and II, normalized and moment normalized inverse difference. Among these, five significant GLCM features chosen by PCA are considered further. The considered features are cluster shade, dissimilarity, entropy, difference entropy and information measure of correlation II. Mathematical formulations of these features are given in Table 1 [33, 36, 60-63].

Table 1. Mathematical formulations of texture feature

Features	Formula
Cluster shade	$\sum_{i=0}^{N_g-1}\sum_{j=0}^{N_g-1}\{i+j-\mu_x-\mu_y\}^3 P(i,j)$
Dissimilarity	$\sum_{i=0}^{N_g-1}\sum_{j=0}^{N_g-1}P(i,j)\lvert i-j\rvert$
Entropy	$-\sum_{i=0}^{N_g-1}\sum_{j=0}^{N_g-1}P(i,j)\log\{P(i,j)\}$
Difference entropy	$-\sum_{i=0}^{N_g-1}P_{x-y}(i)\log\{P_{x-y}(i)\}$
Information measure of correlation II	$(1-\exp[-2.0(HXY2-HXY)])^{1/2}$

where μ_x and μ_y are defined as,

$$\mu_x = \sum_{i=0}^{N_g-1} i \sum_{j=0}^{N_g-1} P(i,j) \tag{1}$$

$$\mu_y = \sum_{i=0}^{N_g-1}\sum_{j=0}^{N_g-1} jP(i,j) \tag{2}$$

HXY , $HXY1$ and $HXY2$ are expressed as,

$$HXY = -\sum_{i=0}^{N_g-1}\sum_{j=0}^{N_g-1}P(i,j)\log\{P(i,j)\} \tag{3}$$

$$HXY1 = -\sum_{i=0}^{N_g-1}\sum_{j=0}^{N_g-1}P(i,j)\log\{P_x(i)P_y(j)\} \tag{4}$$

$$HXY2 = -\sum_{i=0}^{N_g-1}\sum_{j=0}^{N_g-1} P_x(i)P_y(j)\log\{P_x(i)P_y(j)\} \tag{5}$$

$P(i,j)$ is the $(i,j)^{th}$ entry in the normalized gray level co-occurrence matrix representing the probability density and N_g is the number of gray levels in the image. The probability of co-occurrence matrix coordinates of difference $x - y$ is referred as $P_{x-y}(k)$ for $i + j = k$ where

$$P_{x-y}(k) = \sum_{i=0}^{N_g-1}\sum_{j=0}^{N_g-1} P(i,j), \qquad k = 0,1,..., N_g - 1 \tag{6}$$

Cluster shade is a measure of skewness of the co-occurrence matrix, in other words it signifies the lack of symmetry thereby characterizes the content of the image. High values of cluster shade implicate the co-occurrence matrix not to be symmetry [64, 65]. Dissimilarity is a measure of total variation present in each of the image objects. Its value is significant if the image objects contain larger variation [66]. Higher value of dissimilarity is observed when the local region has a high contrast. It therefore represents heterogeneity of gray levels in an image. It is almost similar to GLCM contrast feature, but its value increases linearly as $i - j$ increases [62, 67].

Entropy is a measure of information content. It measures the randomness of intensity distribution in an image which characterizes texture non-uniformity. The value of entropy is large for an image with the elements of co-occurrence matrix being evenly distributed [36]. Also the texturally inconsistent image has very low values for many of the co-occurrence matrix elements which entails that the entropy is very large. This is because the homogeneous image has lower entropy than inhomogeneous image. The image which exhibits high entropy has high contrast too from one pixel to its neighbor [67-70].

Similar to the entropy feature, difference entropy feature measures the randomness or the degree of organization of gray levels in the image. The difference among these entropy features lie in the summation over different combinations of the GLCM elements. The difference entropy is obtained by summing combined GLCM elements along a line parallel to the diagonal or the main diagonal, while the entropy is obtained by summing over single GLCM elements. Hence, the difference entropy is more sensitive than the entropy to the arrangement of the non-zero GLCM elements clustered around the main diagonal [71].

Information measure of correlation II is the linear dependencies of gray level values in an image. The linear dependence between gray levels will increase as the images become more homogenous [72]. Of the textural features defined, the entropy, the difference entropy and the information measure of correlation are invariant under monotonic gray level transformations [36, 73].

2.3. Principal component analysis

PCA is mathematically defined as an orthogonal linear transformation such that the greatest variance of the data lie on the first coordinate called the first principal component, the second greatest variance on the second coordinate, and the rest of the variances lie on the consecutive coordinates. It reveals the combinations of original variables which portray principal patterns and main trends in data. This is done through eigenvector decomposition of covariance matrix of the original variables. The extracted latent variables are orthogonal and they are sorted according to their eigenvalues. The high dimensional space described by matrix X with PCA is represented as

$$X = SP^T + E \tag{7}$$

where S is the score matrix comprising of the principal components, P the loadings comprising of eigenvectors of covariance matrix and E the residual matrix representing the variance. PCA basically rotates the data about their mean in order to line up with the principal components. This procedure combines as much of the variance as possible into the first few dimensions using an orthogonal transformation. The values in the remaining dimensions, therefore, tend to be negligible and may be removed with minimal loss of information [74, 75]. The most significant features chosen by PCA in the second stage are used as input feature vectors to the machine learning algorithms such as SVM and DE-ELM classifiers in the third stage.

2.4. Support vector machines

The support vector machine is a linear machine of one output, formed by the non-linear mapping of the N-dimensional input vector x into a K-dimensional feature space $(K > N)$ through the use of non-linear function. SVM constructs a hyperplane or set of hyperplanes in a high-or infinite-dimensional space, which can be used for classification, regression, or other tasks. Intuitively, a good separation is achieved by the hyperplane that has the largest distance to the nearest training data points of any class (so-called functional margin), since in general the larger the margin the lower the generalization error of the classifier.

The classification of a test sample is determined by a signum function which is defined by the parameters of the hyperplane. The instances closest to the hyperplane are called support vectors and are vital for training. A set of training vectors belonging to two different classes is represented as,

$$D = \left\{ \left(x^1, y^1 \right), \ldots\ldots, \left(x^n, y^n \right) \right\}, x \in \Re^n, y \in \{1, -1\} \tag{8}$$

is separated optimally with a hyperplane

$$\langle w, x \rangle + b = 0 \tag{9}$$

where, w is the vector of hyperplane coefficients, b is a bias term so that the periphery between the hyperplane and the nearest point is maximized. The parameter $\dfrac{b}{\|w\|}$ determines the offset of the hyperplane from the origin along the normal vector w [76, 77]. SVM finds the maximum-margin hyperplane that divides the points having $y_i = 1$ from those having $y_i = -1$. Maximum-margin hyperplane and margins for an SVM trained with samples from two classes. Samples on the margin are called the support vectors. Without loss of generality it is appropriate to consider a canonical hyperplane, where the parameters w, b are constrained by

$$\min_i \left| \langle w, x^i \rangle + b \right| = 1 \tag{10}$$

Different kernel functions such as linear, quadratic, Radial Basis Function (RBF) and polynomial are used to process the data in higher dimensional space. Polynomial mapping is a popular method for non-linear modeling, with a kernel function

$$K(x, x') = \langle x, x' \rangle^d \tag{11}$$

where d is the order of the polynomial kernel. In this analysis, d is varied from three to ten to identify the optimal order for classification based on its performance measures. The optimal order of the polynomial kernel and optimal width of the RBF kernel implemented in SVM classifier is chosen for securing maximum values of performance estimators.

2.5. Extreme learning machine

The Extreme Learning Machine (ELM) is a neural network algorithm proposed as an efficient learning algorithm for Single hidden Layer Feedforward Neural network (SLFN). In ELM, the input weights and the hidden layer biases are chosen randomly, and the output weights (linking the hidden layer to the output layer) are analytically determined by using Moore Penrose (MP) generalized inverse. MP increases the learning speed by randomly generating weights and biases of hidden nodes rather than iteratively adjusting network parameters which are commonly adopted by gradient-based methods. It also avoids many difficulties faced by gradient-based learning methods such as stopping criteria, learning rate, learning epochs, and local minima. However, ELM usually needs higher number of hidden neurons due to the random determination of the input weights and hidden biases [78].

2.6. Differential evolutionary extreme learning machines

The DE procedure is a comprehensive searching optimization method implemented to tune the input weights and hidden layer biases where the output weights are determined by the generalized inverse procedure. Thus to overcome the drawback of ELM, Differential Evolutionary Extreme Learning Machine (DE-ELM) has been adopted. It takes advantages of both ELM and Differential Evolution (DE) and removes redundancy among hidden nodes and achieves satisfactory performance with more compact and high speed neural networks.

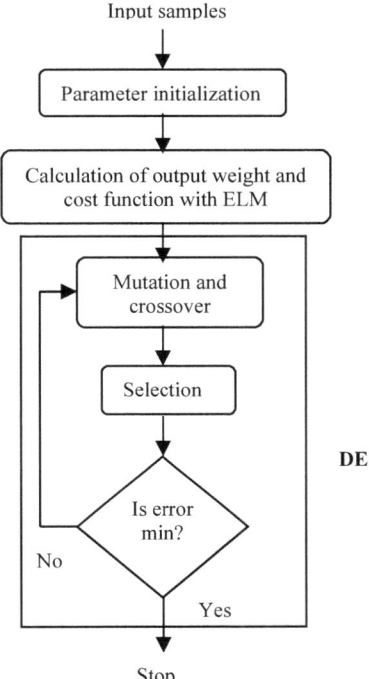

Figure 2. Flow chart for training of ELM based on differential evolutionary process

The SLFN is considered as a linear system after the hidden nodes parameters are randomly initialized. The activation function for the hidden neurons attempted in this work includes sigmoid, sine, hard limit, triangular and radial basis. These functions are considered as there are infinitely differentiable. In this work, the input data are normalized between 0 and 1 while the weights and biases are initialized between -1 and +1. The outputs (targets) are normalized into [-1, 1]. The network has a better generalization performance because of the smaller training error since the norm of weights is small. The training process of ELM based on differential evolutionary process is presented in Figure 2.

In the DE process, the population vector consisting of input weights and hidden layer biases are defined as a vector

$$\theta = \left\{ w_1^T, w_2^T, ..., w_N^T, b_1, b_2, ..., b_N \right\} \qquad (12)$$

of size NP, where NP is the population size. The training process consists of mutation, crossover and selection process. The individuals with better fitness values are retained to the next generation which finally determines the optimal input weights and hidden layer biases. A constant factor F is used to control the amplification of the differential variation in the mutation process. The crossover probability is maintained by a constant CR in the crossover process. The three steps of the DE process are repeated for each of the generated population until the goal is met or the number of maximum learning epochs is reached. The output weights are determined for each of the individuals from the hidden layer output matrix H by Moore Penrose generalized inverse. The structure of ELM resembles the architecture of a single hidden layer feedforward neural network. The main goal of the training process is to determine the network (input and output) weights

$$w_i = [w_{1i}, w_{2i},..., w_{mi}],$$ (13)

$$\beta_i = [\beta_{i1}, \beta_{i2},..., \beta_{im}]^T$$ (14)

and b_i the hidden layer biases. This is to minimize the error function represented by

$$\sum_{j=1}^{N} \|o_j - t_j\|$$ (15)

where

$$o_j = [o_{j1}, o_{j2},..., o_{jn}]^T$$ (16)

represents the network output and

$$t_j = [t_{j1}, t_{j2},..., t_{jn}]^T$$ (17)

is its corresponding target.

The network model of ELM is mathematically modeled as

$$\sum_{i=1}^{M} \beta_i g(w_i \cdot x_i + b_i) = o_j, \qquad j = 1,2,..., N$$ (18)

where $g(\cdot)$ is the activation function. More compactly the equation can be written as $H\beta = T$ from which the output weights are estimated as $\hat{\beta} = H^{\dagger}T$ where $H^{\dagger}$ is the pseudo-inverse of H [79].

2.7. Performance measures of classifier

The performance of the classifier is tested using the following estimators such as sensitivity, specificity and accuracy. Sensitivity and specificity provides information about false negatives and false positives. Accuracy integrates both the above indices and indicates the number of images correctly classified. These measures are computed from the values of True Positive (TP), True Negative (TN), False Positive (FP) and False Negative (FN).

$$Sensitivity = \frac{TP}{(TP + FN)} \qquad (19)$$

$$Specificity = \frac{TN}{(TN + FP)} \qquad (20)$$

$$Accuracy = \frac{(TP + TN)}{(TP + FN + TN + FP)} \qquad (21)$$

Positive Predictive Value (PPV) describes the proportion of positive tests that are TP and represent the presence of disease. Negative Predictive Value (NPV) describes the proportion of negative tests that are TN and represent the absence of disease.

$$PPV = \frac{TP}{(TP + FP)} \qquad (22)$$

$$NPV = \frac{TN}{(TN + FN)} \qquad (23)$$

F - measure is defined as the harmonic mean of precision (P) and recall (R) and is given by

$$F = 2 \times \frac{P \times R}{P + R} \qquad (24)$$

3. Results and discussion

Typical representative of TB positive and negative smear images are shown in Figure 3 (a) and (b) respectively. In general, the objects present in sputum smear images are called as bacilli and non-bacilli. The TB positive image shows the presence of rod-shaped bright foreground objects (bacilli) on a dark background. The negative images show scanty or absence of bacilli. The non-bacilli objects are categorized into outliers and overlapping bacilli. The outliers present can be due to poor or non-specific staining of the smear slides or due to overlapping bacilli. The overlapping bacilli exist when there is a conglomeration of bacilli in the image. The outliers present in the sputum smear images do not have uniform morphology and the only objects that have uniform morphology are the disease causative agent called TB bacilli.

Thus in a sputum smear image distinguishing bacilli from outliers cannot be effectively done by manual intervention. Hence automated procedures aid in demarcation of TB positive from negative smear images. The GLCM based analysis attempted in this work serve as an automated procedure which captures the repetitive patterns in the image, as the TB causing bacilli has a uniform rod shape.

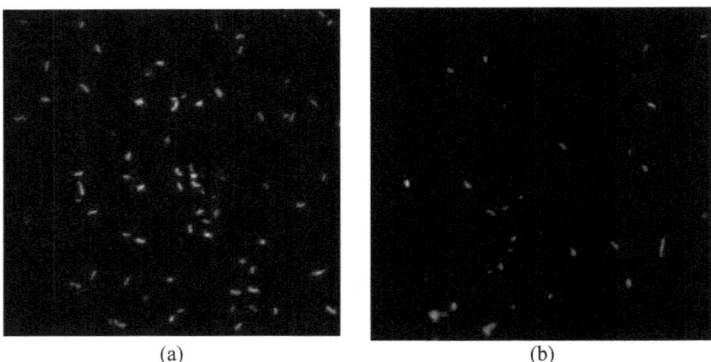

(a)   (b)

Figure 3. Typical TB (a) positive and (b) negative sputum smear image

Among the GLCM based Haralick features, five most significant features are selected using PCA. The selection of the features was based on the highest magnitude of eigenvalues in the first principal component.

Table 2. Contribution of the principal components for TB positive and negative images

Principal components	% variance	
	TB positive	TB negative
PC1	87.31	75.27
PC2	10.00	19.41
PC3	2.09	0.78
PC4	0.13	0.53
PC5	0.02	0.11

The percentage variances of various principal components are shown in Table 2. It is observed that the first five principal components contribute more than 96% of the variance. Since the first principal component PC1 alone contributes to maximum of the variance, the significant features are selected from PC1 based on their magnitude.

Table 3. Variation in eigenvector component magnitudes with the loadings of principal component 1

Features contributing to PC1	Magnitude	
	TB positive	TB negative
Cluster shade	0.15	0.47
Dissimilarity	0.46	0.21
Entropy	0.42	0.42
Difference entropy	0.45	0.26
Information measure of correlation II	0.22	0.39

Table 3 lists the component magnitudes for the eigenvector corresponding to the PC1 which has the largest eigenvalue. The magnitudes of the five component magnitudes corresponding to PC1 are examined. The component dissimilarity has the largest magnitude, followed by, difference entropy, entropy, information measure of correlation II, and cluster shade for TB positive and the component cluster shade have the largest magnitude followed by entropy, information measure of correlation II, difference entropy and dissimilarity for TB negative images.

The higher magnitude denotes the similarity in direction of PC1 with basis vector of original feature space. Thus this feature is the most sensitive feature followed by others. As a result, the presented selection scheme was able to rank the five features. Thus PCA approach is applied to select the most representative features extracted from the original feature set to improve the effectiveness of classification.

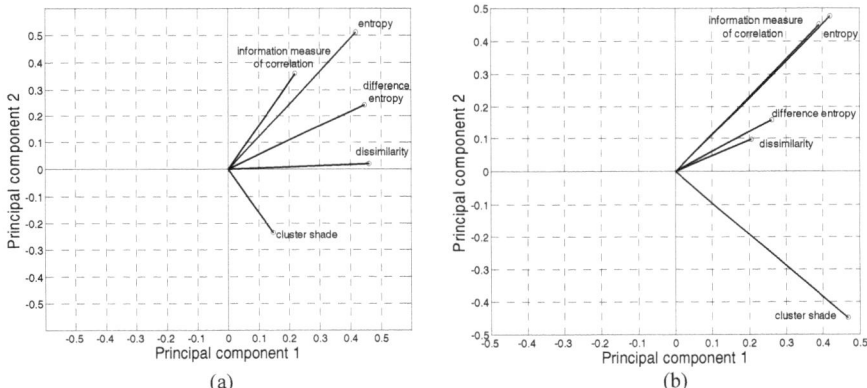

Figure 4. Variation in component magnitudes of selected GLCM features with the first five principal components for TB (a) positive and (b) negative images

The contributions of most significant GLCM features to the magnitudes of first two principal components for TB positive and negative images are shown in Figures 4 (a) and (b) respectively. It is observed that, the magnitude of the vectors greatly differ among the positive and negative images except entropy. The pixel intensity distribution represents the information content for the positive and negative images considered and hence exhibits a similar variance than other features.

The difference in magnitude among the features of positive and negative images is higher for cluster shade and dissimilarity. The highest magnitude of the feature cluster shade in negative images represents the absence of symmetry in spatial arrangement which could be due to the debris and spots exhibiting non-uniform morphology. The number of objects present in TB positive reflects in large amount of variation present in these images hence the variance of dissimilarity is more.

It is observed that the angles between the cluster shade and the other features are larger compared to the angles between them. This shows the independent nature of the feature cluster shade. The angle between the other features is less which shows that the interdependency among the entropy, difference entropy and the information measure of correlation II features.

The orientation of dissimilarity and information measure of correlation II differs greatly among the positive and negative images and they represent the in-homogeneity in them.

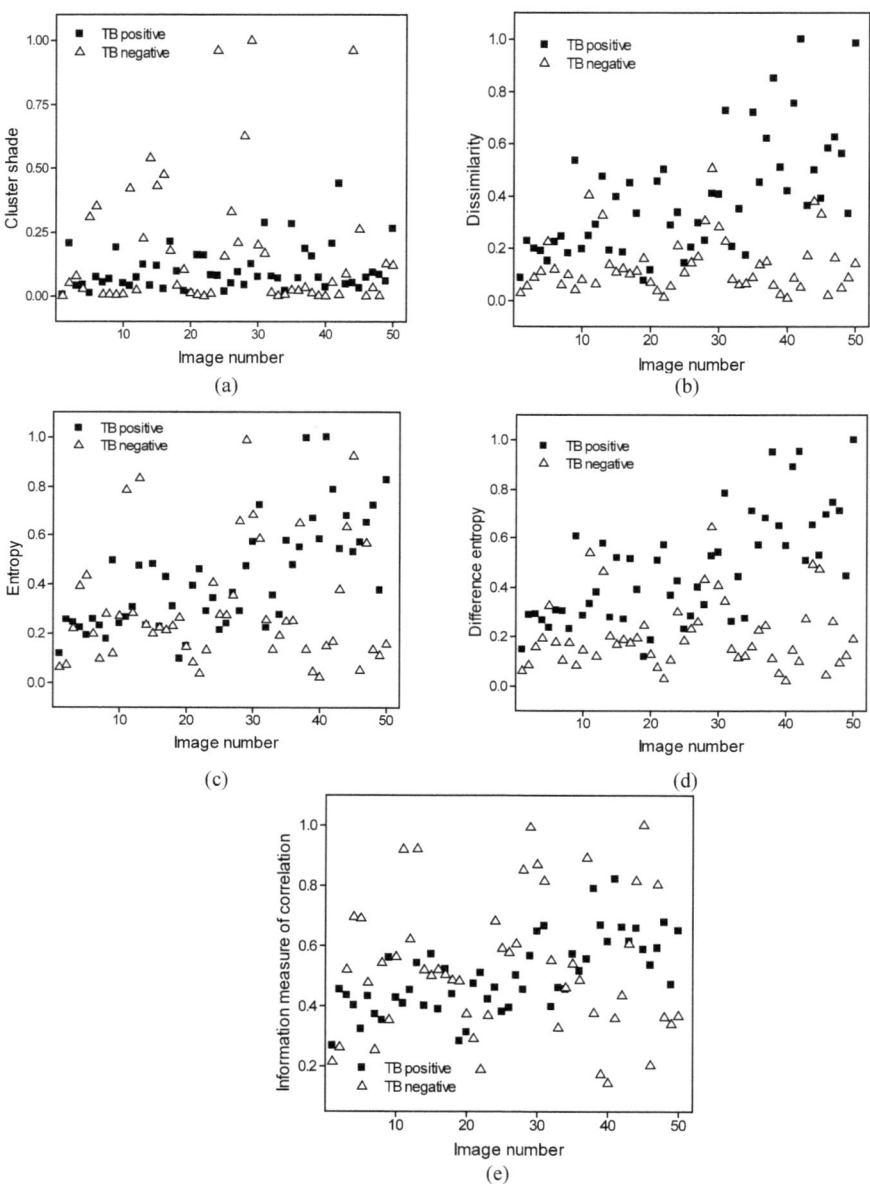

(a)

(b)

(c)

(d)

(e)

Figure 5. Variation in normalized (a) cluster shade (b) dissimilarity (c) entropy (d) difference entropy (e) information measure of correlation II for different images

The GLCM analysis on sputum smear images is further analyzed by scattergram shown in Figure 5 representing the normalized feature values. It is observed from the scattergrams that the TB positive and negative images are indistinguishable as the data points overlap. Similar pattern of variation is observed for TB negative images between dissimilarity and difference entropy but not in TB positive images. Distinct variation is observed for the feature dissimilarity and difference entropy. The presence of tiny rod shaped bacilli influences the magnitude of the dissimilarity feature to be high in positive than negative images. The organization of gray levels influences the magnitude of the difference entropy to be higher in TB positive than negative images.

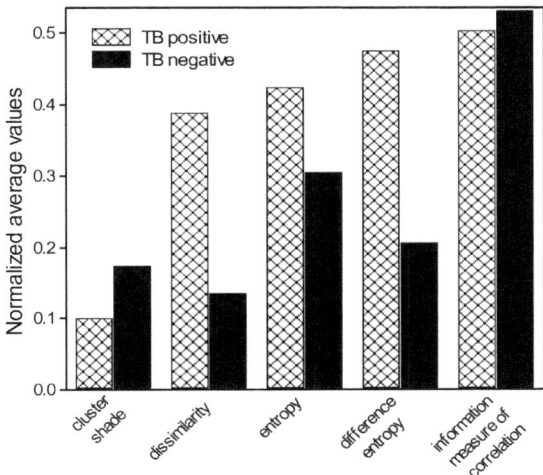

Figure 6. Comparison of variation in the normalized average values

of GLCM features in TB positive and negative images

The variation of normalized average values (computed separately for TB positive and negative images) for the PCA reduced GLCM features are shown in Figure 6. Distinct variation is present between the positive and negative smear images for all the five features. The normalized average values are high for TB positive than negative images except for cluster shade and information measure of correlation II. The variation is high for features dissimilarity and difference entropy than others.

Lack or absence of symmetry in spatial arrangement of the TB negative image is due to the presence of debris and spots which exhibits irregular morphology. Hence cluster shade is high for TB negative images than positive. Since the gray level range in TB positive is more than the negative images the average dissimilarity is more in positive than negative images. Due to the presence of number of objects in TB positive images, there is a large amount of variation present in these images hence dissimilarity is more than negative images.

Entropy, the randomness measure is higher in TB positive images than negative images due to the presence of bacilli in TB positive images. TB negative images considered are homogeneous than positive images and thus exhibits a lower entropy value. The difference entropy is more sensitive than the entropy feature. Since the degree of arrangement of gray levels in the TB positive is more complex this feature exhibits a higher value than negative images. The pixels present in the negative image are mostly uncorrelated; hence the information measure of correlation is more for TB negative images than positive.

The five most significant GLCM features are given as input to SVM and DE-ELM classifier. Among the acquired TB images, 60% of them are chosen for training and remaining 40% for testing. Table 4 shows the results of SVM classification based on the parameter selection. Though the specificity measure is same for all the kernel types, it is observed that the polynomial kernel of order three shows better performance in terms of sensitivity and accuracy. Accuracy is observed to be 92.5% for polynomial kernel with less number of support vectors.

Table 4. Performance analysis of SVM classifier

Performance	Kernel types			
measures	Linear	Quadratic	RBF	Polynomial
*NSV	22	24	55	18
Sensitivity (Recall)	85	70	60	90
Specificity	95	95	95	95
Accuracy	90	83	78	92.5
PPV (Precision)	94	93	92	94.74
NPV	86.36	76	70	90.48
F - measure	89.27	80	73	92.31

*NSV - Number of Support Vectors

Other useful and more informative measures are the PPV, NPV and F-measure. These measures also demonstrate that the SVM classifier performs better for polynomial kernel.

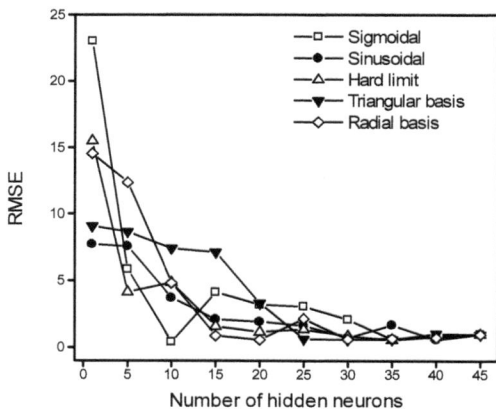

Figure 7. Error plot for varying number of hidden neurons and activation function

The five most significant GLCM features are given as input to the hybrid DE-ELM classifier to achieve better performance than SVM. The performance of DE-ELM classifier is evaluated using RMSE by varying the number of hidden neurons as shown in Figure 7. The evaluation is performed for different activation function such as sigmoidal, sinusoidal, hard limit, triangular and radial basis. Results demonstrate that the generalization performance of the hybrid classifier is stable on a wide range (number) of hidden neurons. It is observed that sigmoidal activation function performs with lower value of RMSE (0.409) for ten numbers of hidden neurons. Hence performance of DE-ELM classifier is further analyzed for this activation function. The slope of the sigmoidal activation function is chosen as 0.2 which is approximately equal to inverse of the number of most significant features or number of input neurons.

Table 5. Confusion matrix of DE-ELM classifier

Confusion matrix		Identified class	
		Positive	Negative
Actual class	Positive	20	0
	Negative	1	19

Table 5 shows the confusion matrix presenting the actual and predicted class of the classifier. Since all the positive images subjected to the classifier are identified correctly, sensitivity is observed to be 100%. Except one of the 40% test data remaining are correctly identified and thus the accuracy is observed to be 97.5%.

Table 6. Performance analysis of DE-ELM classifier

Performance measures(%)	
#NHN	10
Sensitivity (Recall)	100
Specificity	95
Accuracy	97.5
PPV (Precision)	95.24
NPV	100
F - measure	97.56

#NHN – Number of Hidden Neurons

The performance measures of DE-ELM classifier for sigmoidal activation function is presented in Table 6. Results demonstrate that DE-ELM performs better than SVM in terms of performance estimators such as sensitivity, specificity and accuracy. It is also observed that the generalization learning capacity of DE-ELM is better in terms of number of hidden neurons utilized than the number of support vectors used by SVM.

4. Conclusion

Early diagnosis and effective treatment are the essential long-term strategies for controlling TB epidemic. The first component of the WHO post-2015 strategy is early diagnosis of TB [80]. Although many diagnostic methods have been developed, acid fast bacilli smear microscopy is still considered as the gold standard to identify highly contagious patients [81]. Thus performing automated analysis is essential for mass screening of this epidemic.

In this work, an attempt has been made to automate the analysis of digital TB images using statistical method based on GLCM approach. Haralick descriptor based features are extracted from the sputum smear images. The most significant of them are selected based on PCA. Further, these features are subjected to classification using SVM and DE-ELM classifier and the performance analysis is studied.

Results demonstrate that the statistical features based on GLCM are able to differentiate TB negative from the positive images. This would be possible as the GLCM features characterize the pixel intensity distribution in the image. It was observed that SVM classifier with polynomial kernel presented relatively higher sensitivity, specificity and accuracy.

Compared to SVM the hybrid DE-ELM classifier reported a higher sensitivity, specificity and accuracy in classifying the images into positive and negative. The performance measures of the DE-ELM classifier is better because of its improved evolutionary based learning algorithm which identifies more number of true positives and true negatives when compared to SVM. The increase in sensitivity is observed because of the uniform morphology exhibited by the bacilli present in TB positive images. As this automated analysis is important in diagnosing and monitoring of pulmonary tuberculosis, this study seems to be relevant for better clinical interventions.

Acknowledgement

The authors acknowledge Dr. Tania S. Douglas and Mr. Sriram Krishnan of Medical Imaging Research Unit, University of Cape Town, South Africa for the thought worthy discussions during acquisition of sputum smear images.

References

[1] Global Tuberculosis report 2016.
[2] M. Forero, G. Cristobal and J. Alvarez-Borrego, Automatic identification techniques of tuberculosis bacteria. In Optical Science and Technology, SPIE's 48th Annual Meeting, International Society for Optics and Photonics (2003), 71-81.
[3] M. Sotaquirá, L. Rueda and R. Narvaez, Detection and quantification of bacilli and clusters present in sputum smear samples: a novel algorithm for pulmonary tuberculosis diagnosis. In IEEE International Conference on Digital Image Processing, (2009), 117-121.
[4] M. Crnčević-Urek, A. Stipić-Marković, I. Kardum-Skelin, J. Stipić, V. Crnek-Kunstelj and R. Urek, Induced Sputum: A Method for Cytologic Analysis of Bronchial Specimens. *Acta Clinica Croatica* **41**(2), (2002), 89-93.
[5] M.G. Costa, C.F. Costa Filho, J.F. Sena, J. Salem and M.O. de Lima, Automatic identification of mycobacterium tuberculosis with conventional light microscopy. In 30th Annual IEEE International Conference on Engineering in Medicine and Biology Society, (2008), 382-385.
[6] K.V. Ramana and S.K. Basha, Neural image recognition system with application to tuberculosis detection. In International Conference on Information Technology: Coding and Computing, Vol. 2, (2004), 694-698.
[7] R. Lumb, A. Van Deun, I. Bastian, and M. Fitz-Gerald, Laboratory diagnosis of tuberculosis by sputum microscopy: The Handbook, (2013).
[8] K.R. Steingart, M. Henry, V. Ng, P.C. Hopewell, A. Ramsay, J. Cunningham, R. Urbanczik, M. Perkins, M.A. Aziz and M. Pai, Fluorescence versus conventional sputum smear microscopy for tuberculosis: a systematic review. *The Lancet infectious diseases*, **6**(9), (2006), 570-581.
[9] A. Tapley, N. Switz, C. Reber, J.L. Davis, C. Miller, J.B. Matovu, W. Worodria, L. Huang, D.A. Fletcher and A. Cattamanchi, Mobile digital fluorescence microscopy for diagnosis of tuberculosis. *Journal of clinical microbiology*, **51**(6), (2013), 1774-1778.
[10] J. Chang, P. Arbeláez, N. Switz, C. Reber, A. Tapley, J. Davis, A. Cattamanchi, D. Fletcher and J. Malik, Automated tuberculosis diagnosis using fluorescence images from a mobile microscope. *Medical Image Computing and Computer-Assisted Intervention*, (2012), **15**(Pt 3), 345-352.

[11] C.F. Costa Filho and M.G. Costa, Sputum smear microscopy for tuberculosis: Evaluation of autofocus functions and automatic identification of tuberculosis mycobacterium, Understanding Tuberculosis - Global Experiences and Innovative Approaches to the Diagnosis, Dr. Pere-Joan Cardona (Ed.), INTECH Open Access Publisher, (2012).

[12] A. Cattamanchi, J.L. Davis, W. Worodria, S. den Boon, S. Yoo, J. Matovu, J. Kiidha, F. Nankya, R. Kyeyune, P. Byanyima and A. Andama, M. Joloba, D.H. Osmond, P.C. Hopewell and L. Huang, Sensitivity and specificity of fluorescence microscopy for diagnosing pulmonary tuberculosis in a high HIV prevalence setting. *The International Journal of Tuberculosis and Lung Disease*, **13**(9), (2009), 1130-1136.

[13] B.J. Marais, W. Brittle, K. Painczyk, A.C. Hesseling, N. Beyers, E. Wasserman, D. van Soolingen and R.M. Warren, Use of light-emitting diode fluorescence microscopy to detect acid-fast bacilli in sputum. *Clinical Infectious Diseases*, **47**(2), (2008), 203-207.

[14] C. Wählby, J. Lindblad, M. Vondrus, E. Bengtsson and L. Björkesten, Algorithms for cytoplasm segmentation of fluorescence labelled cells. *Analytical Cellular Pathology*, **24**(2, 3), (2002), 101-111.

[15] T.M. Daniel, Toman's tuberculosis. Case detection, treatment and monitoring: questions and answers, (2004), p.351.

[16] P. Sadaphal, J. Rao, G.W. Comstock and M.F. Beg, Image processing techniques for identifying mycobacterium tuberculosis in Ziehl-Neelsen stains [Short Communication]. *The International Journal of Tuberculosis and Lung Disease*, **12**(5), (2008), 579-582.

[17] R.A.A. Raof, M.Y. Mashor, R.B. Ahmad and S.S.M. Noor, Image Segmentation of Ziehl-Neelsen Sputum Slide Images for Tubercle Bacilli Detection, Image Segmentation, Dr. Pei-Gee Ho (Ed.), INTECH Open Access Publisher, (2011).

[18] A. Van Deun, A.H. Salim, E. Cooreman, M.A. Hossain, A. Rema, N. Chambugonj, M.A. Hye, A. Kawria and E. Declercq, Optimal tuberculosis case detection by direct sputum smear microscopy: how much better is more? *The International Journal of Tuberculosis and Lung Disease*, **6**(3), (2002), 222-230.

[19] R. Khutlang, S. Krishnan, R. Dendere, A. Whitelaw, K. Veropoulos, G. Learmonth and T.S. Douglas, Classification of Mycobacterium tuberculosis in images of ZN-stained sputum smears. *IEEE Transactions on Information Technology in Biomedicine*, **14**(4), (2010), 949-957.

[20] M.G. Forero, G. Cristóbal and M. Desco, Automatic identification of Mycobacterium tuberculosis by Gaussian mixture models. *Journal of microscopy*, **223**(2), (2006), 120-132.

[21] K. Veropoulos, C. Campbell, G. Learmonth, B. Knight and J. Simpson, The automated identification of tubercle bacilli using image processing and neural computing techniques. In 8th International Conference on Artificial Neural Networks, Perspectives in Neural Computing. Springer, London, L. Niklasson, M. Bodén, T. Ziemke, (Eds.), (1998), 797-802.

[22] K. Veropoulos, G. Learmonth, C. Campbell, B. Knight and J. Simpson, Automated identification of tubercle bacilli in sputum: a preliminary investigation. *Analytical and quantitative cytology and histology*, **21**, (1999), 277-282.

[23] M.G. Forero, F. Sroubek and G. Cristóbal, Identification of tuberculosis bacteria based on shape and color. *Real-time imaging*, **10**(4), (2004), 251-262.

[24] R. Santiago-Mozos, R. Fernández-Lorenzana, F. Perez-Cruz and A. Artes-Rodriguez, On the uncertainty in sequential hypothesis testing. In 5th IEEE International Symposium on Biomedical Imaging: From Nano to Macro, Paris, France, (2008), 1223-1226.

[25] B. Lenseigne, P. Brodin, H.K. Jeon, T. Christophe, and A. Genovesio, Support vector machines for automatic detection of tuberculosis bacteria in confocal microscopy images. In 4th IEEE International Symposium on Biomedical Imaging: From Nano to Macro, Arlington, VA, USA, (2007), 85-88.

[26] R.A.A. Raof, Z. Salleh, S.I. Sahidan, M.Y. Mashor, S.M. Noor, F.M. Idris and H. Hasan, Color thresholding method for image segmentation algorithm of Ziehl-Neelsen sputum slide images. In 5th IEEE International Conference on Electrical Engineering, Computing Science and Automatic Control, Mexico City, Mexico, (2008), 212-217.

[27] Y. Zhai, Y. Liu, D. Zhou and S. Liu, Automatic identification of mycobacterium tuberculosis from ZN-stained sputum smear: Algorithm and system design. In IEEE International Conference on Robotics and Biomimetics,Tianjin, China, (2010), 41-46.

[28] R. Rulaningtyas, A.B. Suksmono, T.L. Mengko and P. Saptawati, Identification of mycobacterium tuberculosis in sputum smear slide using automatic scanning microscope. In S. Viridi, K. Basar, F. Iskandar, W. Srigutomo, B. E. Gunara (Eds.), AIP Conference Proceedings, 1656(1), (2015), p. 060011.

[29] C.F.F. Costa Filho, P.C. Levy, C.D.M. Xavier, L.B.M. Fujimoto and M.G.F. Costa, Automatic identification of tuberculosis mycobacterium. *Research on Biomedical Engineering*, **31**(1), (2015), 33-43.

[30] R.O. Panicker, B. Soman, G. Saini and J. Rajan, A review of automatic methods based on image processing techniques for tuberculosis detection from microscopic sputum smear images. *Journal of medical systems*, **40**(1), (2016), 17.

[31] R. Lopes and N. Betrouni, Fractal and multifractal analysis: a review. *Medical image analysis*, **13**(4), (2009), 634-649.

[32] R.F. Walker, Adaptive multi-scale texture analysis: with application to automated cytology, PhD Thesis, School of Computer Science and Electrical Engineering, The University of Queensland, (1997).

[33] R.M. Haralick and K. Shanmugam, Textural features for image classification. *IEEE Transactions on systems, man, and cybernetics*, **3**(6), (1973), 610-621.

[34] A. Madabhushi and D.N. Metaxas, Advances in computerized image analysis methods on breast ultrasound. In Medical Imaging Systems Technology, Cornelius T. Leondes (Eds.), Analysis and Computational Methods, 1, (2005), 119-150.

[35] G. Castellano, L. Bonilha, L.M. Li, and F. Cendes, Texture analysis of medical images. *Clinical radiology*, **59**(12), (2004), 1061-1069.

[36] V. Atlamazoglou, D. Yova, N. Kavantzas, and S.Loukas, Texture analysis of fluorescence microscopic images of colonic tissue sections. *Medical and Biological Engineering and Computing*, **39**(2), (2001), 145-151.

[37] K.W. Gossage, T.S. Tkaczyk, J.J. Rodriguez, and J.K. Barton, Texture analysis of optical coherence tomography images: feasibility for tissue classification. *Journal of biomedical optics*, **8**(3), (2003), 570-575.

[38] A.M. Khuzi, R. Besar, W.W. Zaki, and N.N. Ahmad, Identification of masses in digital mammogram using gray level co-occurrence matrices. *Biomedical imaging and intervention journal*, **5**(3), (2009).

[39] J.E.E. de Oliveira, A. de Albuquerque Araújo, and T.M. Deserno, Content-based image retrieval applied to BI-RADS tissue classification in screening mammography. *World journal of radiology*, **3**(1), (2011), 24.

[40] H.B. Kekre, and S. Gharge, Texture based segmentation using statistical properties for mammographic images. *Entropy*, **1**, (2010), p.2.

[41] R. Lopes, A. Ayache, N. Makni, P. Puech, A. Villers, S. Mordon, and Betrouni, Prostate cancer characterization on MR images using fractal features. *Medical physics*, **38**(1), (2011), 83-95.

[42] M. Tuceryan, and A.K. Jain, Texture analysis. Handbook of pattern recognition and computer vision, World Scientific Publishing Co., Inc. River Edge, NJ, USA, 2, (1993), 235-276.

[43] A. Kassner and R.E. Thornhill, Texture analysis: a review of neurologic MR imaging applications. *American Journal of Neuroradiology*, **31**(5), (2010), 809-816.

[44] C.C. Reyes-Aldasoro and A. Bhalerao, Volumetric texture description and discriminant feature selection for MRI. In Biennial International Conference on Information Processing in Medical Imaging, C. Taylor, J.A. Noble, (Eds.), Lecture Notes in Computer Science, Springer, Berlin, Heidelberg, 2732, (2003), 282-293.

[45] F. Wang, J. Wang, C. Zhang and J. Kwok, Face recognition using spectral features. *Pattern Recognition*, **40**(10), (2007), 2786-2797.

[46] P. Luukka, Feature selection using fuzzy entropy measures with similarity classifier. *Expert Systems with Applications*, **38**(4), (2011), 4600-4607.

[47] J.A. Suykens, I. Horvath, S. Basu, C. Micchelli and J. Vandewalle (Eds.), Advances in learning theory: methods, models, and applications, 190, (2003), IOS Press.

[48] S.A. Lashari and R. Ibrahim, A framework for medical images classification using soft set. *Procedia Technology*, **11**, (2013), 548-556.

[49] M. Bergtholdt, R. Wiemker and T. Klinder, Pulmonary nodule detection using a cascaded SVM classifier. In SPIE International Society for Optics and Photonics, 9785, Medical Imaging 2016: Computer-Aided Diagnosis, (2016), 978513.

[50] Y. Jiang, Z. Li, L. Zhang and P. Sun, An improved SVM classifier for medical image classification. In International Conference on Rough Sets and Intelligent Systems Paradigms, M. Kryszkiewicz, J.F. Peters, H. Rybinski, A. Skowron, (Eds.), Lecture Notes in Computer Science, Springer, Berlin, Heidelberg, 4585, (2007), 764-773.

[51] Z. Camlica, H.R. Tizhoosh and F. Khalvati, Medical image classification via SVM using LBP features from saliency-based folded data. In IEEE 14th International Conference on Machine Learning and Applications, Miami, Florida, USA, (2015), 128-132.

[52] H.T. Huynh, and Y. Won, Hematocrit estimation from compact single hidden layer feedforward neural networks trained by evolutionary algorithm. In IEEE World Congress on Computational Intelligence, Hong Kong, China, (2008), 2962-2966.

[53] I.A. Yusoff, N.A.M. Isa, N.H. Othman, S.N. Sulaiman, and Y. Jusman, Performance of neural network architectures: Cascaded MLP versus extreme learning machine on cervical cell image classification. In

IEEE 10th International Conference on Information Sciences Signal Processing and their Applications, Kuala Lumpur, Malaysia, (2010), 308-311.

[54] J. Sánchez-Monedero, P.A. Gutiérrez, F. Fernández-Navarro and C. Hervás-Martínez, Weighting efficient accuracy and minimum sensitivity for evolving multi-class classifiers. *Neural Processing Letters*, **34**(2), 2011), 101-116.

[55] E. Priya, S. Srinivasan and S. Ramakrishnan, Retrospective Non-Uniform Illumination Correction Techniques in Images of Tuberculosis. *Microscopy and Microanalysis*, **20**(05), (2014), 1382-1391.

[56] Y. Zeng, J. Zhang, J.L. Van Genderen, and Y. Zhang, Image fusion for land cover change detection. *International Journal of Image and Data Fusion*, **1**(2), (2010), 193-215.

[57] R. Susomboon, D. Raicu, J. Furst, and T.B. Johnson, A co-occurrence texture semi-invariance to direction, distance, and patient size. In SPIE 6914, International Society for Optics and Photonics, Medical Imaging 2008: Image Processing, (2008), 69141Y.

[58] C.E. Honeycutt and R. Plotnick, Image analysis techniques and gray-level co-occurrence matrices (GLCM) for calculating bioturbation indices and characterizing biogenic sedimentary structures. *Computers & Geosciences*, **34**(11), (2008), 1461-1472.

[59] Z. Cai, X. Yan and Y. Liu, Advances in Computation and Intelligence. L. Kang (Ed.), (2008), Springer.

[60] C.H. Wei, C.T. Li and R. Wilson, A general framework for content-based medical image retrieval with its application to mammograms. In Medical Imaging, International Society for Optics and Photonics, (2005), 134-143.

[61] F. Albregtsen, Statistical texture measures computed from gray level coocurrence matrices. Image processing laboratory, department of informatics, University of Oslo, 5, (2008).

[62] I. Ozdemir, D.A. Norton, U.Y. Ozkan, A. Mert and O. Senturk, Estimation of tree size diversity using object oriented texture analysis and aster imagery. *Sensors*, **8**(8), (2008), 4709-4724.

[63] C.H. Wei, C.T. Li and R. Wilson, A general framework for content-based medical image retrieval with its application to mammograms. In Medical Imaging 2005: PACS and Imaging Informatics, International Society for Optics and Photonics, (2005), 134-143.

[64] B.S. Anami and V.C. Burkpalli, Texture based identification and classification of bulk sugary food objects. *ICGST-GVIP Journal*, **9**(4), (2009), 9-14.

[65] A.L. Ion, Methods for Knowledge Discovery in Images. Information Technology and Control, **38**(1), (2009).

[66] A. Kuzmin, L. Korhonen, T. Manninen and M. Maltamo, Automatic Segment-Level Tree Species Recognition Using High Resolution Aerial Winter Imagery. *European Journal of Remote Sensing*, **49**(1), (2016), 239-259.

[67] D. Patra, and J. Mridula, Featured based segmentation of color textured images using glcm and markov random field model. *World Academy of Science, Engineering and Technology*, **53**(5), (2011), 108-113.

[68] S.D. Newsam and C. Kamath, Comparing shape and texture features for pattern recognition in simulation data. In International Society for Optics and Photonics/SPIE's Annual Symposium on Electronic Imaging, (2005), 106-117.

[69] E.M. van Rikxoort and E.L. van den Broek, Texture analysis. Graduate Research Proposal in AI, 15, (2004).

[70] H. H. Hassan and S. Goussev, Texture Analysis of High Resolution Aeromagnetic Data to Identify Geological Features in the Horn River Basin, NE British Columbia, (2011).

[71] K. Dong, Y. Feng, K.M. Jacobs, J.Q. Lu, R.S. Brock, L.V. Yang, F.E. Bertrand, M.A. Farwell and X.H. Hu, Label-free classification of cultured cells through diffraction imaging. *Biomedical optics express*, **2**(6), (2011), 1717-1726.

[72] C.C. Fagan, C.J. Du, C.P. O'Donnell, M. Castillo, C.D. Everard, D.J. O'Callaghan and F.A. Payne, Application of Image Texture Analysis for Online Determination of Curd Moisture and Whey Solids in a Laboratory Scale Stirred Cheese Vat. *Journal of food science*, **73**(6), (2008), E250-E258.

[73] D. Gadkari, Image quality analysis using GLCM, (2004).

[74] I. Jolliffe, Principal component analysis. John Wiley & Sons, Ltd, (2002).

[75] D. Aguado, T. Montoya, L. Borras, A. Seco and & J. Ferrer, Using SOM and PCA for analysing and interpreting data from a P-removal SBR. *Engineering Applications of Artificial Intelligence*, **21**(6), (2008), 919-930.

[76] V.N. Vapnik, The nature of statistical learning theory. Springer Verlag, New York, (1995).

[77] C.J. Burges, A tutorial on support vector machines for pattern recognition. *Data mining and knowledge discovery*, **2**(2), (1998), 121-167.

[78] N. Liu and H. Wang, Ensemble based extreme learning machine. *IEEE Signal Processing Letters*, **17**(8), (2010), 754-757.

[79] H.T. Huynh and Y. Won, Evolutionary algorithm for training compact single hidden layer feedforward neural networks. In IEEE International Joint Conference on Neural Networks, (IEEE World Congress on Computational Intelligence), Hong Kong, China, (2008), 3028-3033.

[80] C.H. Chen, Y.M. Chen, C.W. Lee, Y.J. Chang, C.Y. Cheng, and J.K Hung, Early diagnosis of spinal tuberculosis. *Journal of the Formosan Medical Association*, **115**(10), (2016), 825-836.
[81] J.C. Palomino, S.C Leão, and V. Ritacco, Tuberculosis 2007; from basic science to patient care (2007).

Deep Learning for Image Processing Applications
D.J. Hemanth and V.V. Estrela (Eds.)
IOS Press, 2017
doi:10.3233/978-1-61499-822-8-137

Object Retrieval with Deep Convolutional Features

Eva Mohedano [a], Amaia Salvador [b], Kevin McGuinness [a], Xavier Giró-i-Nieto [b],
Noel E. O'Connor [a] and Ferran Marqués [b]

[a] *Insight Center for Data Analytics, Dublin City University*
[b] *Image Processing Group, Universitat Politècnica de Catalunya*

Abstract. Image representations extracted from convolutional neural networks (CNNs) outdo hand-crafted features in several computer vision tasks, such as visual image retrieval. This chapter recommends a simple pipeline for encoding the local activations of a convolutional layer of a pretrained CNN utilizing the well-known Bag of Words (BoW) aggregation scheme and called bag of local convolutional features (BLCF). Matching each local array of activations in a convolutional layer to a visual word results in an *assignment map*, which is a compact representation relating regions of an image with a visual word. We use the assignment map for fast spatial reranking, finding object localizations that are used for query expansion. We show the suitability of the BoW representation based on local CNN features for image retrieval, attaining state-of-the-art performance on the Oxford and Paris buildings benchmarks. We demonstrate that the BLCF system outperforms the latest procedures using sum pooling for a subgroup of the challenging TRECVid INS benchmark according to the mean Average Precision (mAP) metric.

Keywords. Information Storage and Retrieval, Content Analysis and Indexing, Image Processing and Computer Vision, Feature Representation, Convolutional Neural Networks, Deep Learning, Bag of Words

1. Introduction

Visual image retrieval aims at organizing and structuring image databases based on their visual content. The proliferation of ubiquitous cameras in the last decade has motivated researchers in the field to push the limits of visual search systems with scalable yet effective solutions.

Representations based on convolutional neural networks (CNNs) have been demonstrated to outperform the state-of-the-art in many computer vision tasks. CNNs trained on large amounts of labeled data produce global representations that effectively capture the semantics in images. Features from these networks have been successfully used in various image retrieval benchmarks with very promising results [1,2,3,4,5,6], improving upon the state-of-the-art compact image representations for image retrieval.

Despite CNN-based descriptors performing remarkably well in instance search benchmarks like the Oxford and Paris Buildings datasets, state-of-the-art an-

Figure 1. Examples of the top-ranked images and localizations based on local CNN features encoded with BoW. Top row: The Christ Church from the Oxford Buildings dataset; middle row: The Sacre Coeur from Paris Buildings; bottom row: query 9098 (a parking sign) from TRECVid INS 2013.

swers for more challenging datasets such as TRECVid Instance Search (INS) have not yet adopted pipelines that depend solely on CNN features. Many INS systems [7,8,9,10] are still based on aggregating local handcrafted features (like SIFT) using the Bag of Words encoding [11] to produce very high-dimensional sparse image representations. Such high-dimensional sparse representations have several benefits over their dense counterparts. High dimensionality means they are more probable to be linearly separable while presenting relatively few non-zero elements, which makes them efficient equally in terms of storage (only nonzero components need to be stored), and computation (only non-zero elements need to be visited). Sparse representations can handle varying information content and are less likely to interfere with one another when pooled. From an information retrieval perspective, sparse representations can be stored in inverted indices, which facilitates efficient selection of images that share features with a query. Furthermore, there is considerable evidence that biological systems make extensive use of sparse representations for sensory information [12,13]. Empirically, sparse representations have repeatedly demonstrated to be effective in a wide range of vision and machine learning tasks.

Many efficient image retrieval engines combine an initial highly scalable ranking mechanism on the full image database with a more computationally expensive yet higher-precision reranking scheme applied to the top retrieved items. This reranking mechanism often takes the form of geometric verification and spatial analysis [14,15,16,8], after which the best matching results can be used for query expansion (pseudo-relevance feedback) [17,18].

In this chapter, inspired by advances in CNN-based descriptors for image retrieval, yet still focusing on instance search, we revisit the Bag of Words encoding scheme using local features from convolutional layers of a CNN. This work presents the following contributions:

- We conduct a comprehensive state-of-the-art review analyzing contemporary approaches using CNN models for the task of image retrieval.
- We propose a sparse visual descriptor based on a bag of local convolutional features (BLCF), which permits fast image retrieval via an inverted index.
- We present the assignment map as a novel compact representation of the image, which maps image pixels ito their corresponding visual words. The assignment map allows fast creation of a BoW descriptor for any region of the image.
- We take advantage of the scalability properties of the assignment map to achieve a local analysis of multiple regions of the image for reranking, followed by a query expansion stage using the obtained object localizations.

Using this approach, we present an image retrieval system that achieves state-of-the-art performance comparing with other non-fine tuned models in content-based image retrieval (CBIR) benchmarks and outperforms current state-of-the-art CNN based descriptors at the task of instance search. Figure 1 illustrates some of the rankings produced by our system on three different datasets.

The remainder of the chapter is structured as follows. Section 2 contains an extensive overview of related work. Section3 presents different retrieval benchmarks. Section 4 introduces the proposed framework for BoW encoding of CNN local features. Section 5 explains the details of our retrieval system, including the local reranking and query expansion stages. Section 6 presents experimental results on three image retrieval benchmarks (Oxford Buildings, Paris Buildings, and a subset of TRECVid INS 2013), as well as a comparison to five other state-of-the-art approaches. Section 7 summarizes the most significant results and outlines future work.

2. Related Work

2.1. First CNN Approaches for Retrieval

Several other authors have proposed CNN-based representations for image retrieval. The first applications focused on replacing traditionally handcrafted descriptors with features from a pre-trained CNN for image classification. Activations from the last fully connected layers from the Alexnet network proposed by Krizhevsky were the first ones to be used as a generic image representation with potential applications for image retrieval [19,20,21]. Similar images generate similar activation vectors in the Euclidean space. This finding motivated early works in studying the capability of CNN models for retrieval, mostly focused on the analysis of fully connected layers extracted from pre-trained CNN classification model Alexnet [2,3,22]. In this context, Babenko et al. [2] showed how such features could reach similar performance to handcrafted features encoded with Fisher vectors for image retrieval. Razavian et al. [3] later outperformed the state-of-the-art of CNN representations for retrieval using several image sub-patches as input to a pre-trained CNN to extract features at different locations of the image. Similarly, Liu et al. [23] used features from fully connected layers evaluated on image sub patches to encode images using Bag of Words.

2.2. Convolutional Features for Retrieval

While descriptors from fully connected layers of a pre-trained CNN in ImageNet achieve competitive performance, local characteristics of objects at instance level are not well preserved at those layers, since information contained is biased towards the final classification task (too semantic) and spatial information is completely lost (each neuron in a fully connected layer is connected to all neurons of the previous layer).

A second generation of works reported significant gains in performance when switching from fully connected to convolutional layers. Razavian et al. [4] performed spatial max pooling on the feature maps of a convolutional layer of a pre-trained CNN to produce a descriptor of the same dimension as the number of filters of the layer. Babenko and Lempitsky [1] proposed sum-pooled convolutional features (SPoc), a compact descriptor based on sum pooling of convolutional feature maps preprocessed with a Gaussian center prior. Tolias et al. [5] introduced a feature representation based on the integral image to quickly max pool features from local patches of the image and encode them in a compact representation. The work by Kalantidis et al. [24] proposed Cross-dimensional weighting and pooling(CroW), a non-parametric spatial and channel-wise weighting schemes applied directly to the convolutional features before sum pooling. Our work shares similarities with all the former in that we use convolutional features extracted from a pre-trained CNN. Unlike these approaches, however, we propose a sparse, high-dimensional encoding that better represents local image features, particularly in difficult instance search scenarios where the target object is not the primary focus of the image.

Several authors have tried to exploit local information in images by passing multiple image sub patches through a CNN to obtain local features from either fully connected [3,23] or convolutional [22] layers, which are in turn aggregated using techniques like average pooling [3], BoW [23], or Vector of Locally Aggregated Descriptors (VLAD) [22]. Although many of these methods perform well in retrieval benchmarks, they are significantly more computationally costly since they require CNN feature extraction from many image patches, which slows down indexing and feature extraction at retrieval time.

An alternative approach is to extract convolutional features for the full image and treat the activations of the different neuron arrays across all feature maps as local features. This way, a single forward pass of the entire image through the CNN is enough to obtain the activations of its local patches. Following this approach, Ng et al. [25] proposed to use VLAD [26] encoding of features from convolutional layers to produce a single image descriptor. Arandjelović et al. [27] chose to adapt a CNN with a layer especially trained to learn the VLAD parameters. Our approach is similar to the ones in [25,27] in that we also treat the features in a convolutional layer as local features extracted at different locations in an image. We, however, use BoW encoding instead of VLAD to take advantage of sparse representations for fast retrieval in large-scale databases.

Several of the cited approaches propose systems that are based or partially based on a spatial search over multiple regions of the image. Razavian et al. [4] achieve a remarkable increase in performance by applying a spatial search strategy over an arbitrary grid of windows at different scales. Although they report high

accuracy in several retrieval benchmarks, their proposed approach is very computationally costly and does not scale well to larger datasets and real-time search
scenarios. Tolias et al. [5] introduce a local analysis of multiple image patches,
which is only applied to the top elements of an initial ranking. They propose an
efficient workaround for sub patch feature pooling based on integral images, which
allows them to quickly evaluate many image windows. Their approach improves
their baseline ranking and provides approximate object localizations. They apply
query expansion using images from the top of the ranking after the reranking stage,
although they do not use the obtained object locations in any way to improve
retrieval performance. In this direction, our work proposes using the assignment
map to quickly build the BoW representation of any image patch, which allows us
to apply a spatial search for reranking. We apply weak spatial verification to each
target window using a spatial pyramid matching strategy. Unlike [5], we use the
object localizations obtained with spatial search to mask out the activations of
the background and perform query expansion using the detected object location.

Another method to improve the representativeness of the convolutional features
is weighting them with some sort of attention map. Jimenez *et al.* [28] have
proposed a technique that can be seen as a combination of the ideas introduced in
CroW [24] and R-MAC [5]. They propose using Class Activation Maps (CAMs) [29],
which is technique that can be applied to most of the the state-of-the-art CNN
networks for classification to create a spatial map highlighting the contribution of
the areas within an image that are more relevant for the network to classify an
image as one particular class. This way, several weighting schemes can be generated
for each of the classes for which the original pre-trained network was trained
(typically the 1000 classes of ImageNet [30]). Each of the weighting schemes can
be used in the same way as in CroW to generate different vectors per class. All the
obtained class-vectors are then sum-pooled to get a final compact representation.
BLCFs can also be enriched with a weighting scheme, as proposed in [31]. In this
case, instead of weighting them with a class-activation map, the attention map
was computed with a prediction of the gaze fixation over egocentric images. In this,
case, a visual saliency map was estimated with SalNet [32], a deep convolutional
network trained for that purpose.

Focused on exploring the advantage of processing different regions of the
image independently, Salvador *et al.* [33] propose to use a fine-tuned version of an
object detection network. In particular, they use the Faster R-CNN [34] which is
a network composed of a base module, which is a fully convolutional CNN (i.e
VGG16 architecture), and a top module composed of two branches: one branch
is a Region Proposal Network that learns a set of window locations, and the
second one is a classifier (composed by three fully connected layers) that learns
to label each window as one of the classes in the training set. Object proposals
can be understood as a way of focusing in specific areas of the image so they
are equivalent to a weighting scheme if their features are pooled. In this sense,
BLCF may also benefit some these type of tools at the expense of an additional
computation time and indexing resources.

2.3. End-to-End Learning

Deep learning has been proven as a mechanism to successfully learn useful semantic representations from data. However, most of the discussed work use off-the-shelf CNN representations for the task of retrieval, where representations have been implicitly learned as part of a classification task on ImageNet dataset. This approach presents two main drawbacks: the first one comes from the *source dataset* ImageNet from where features have been learned. While Imagenet is a large-scale dataset for classification, covering diverse 1000 classes (from airplanes, landmarks, general objects) and allowing models to learn good generic features, it has been explicitly designed to contain high intra-class invariance which is not a desirable property to retrieval. The second, consists in the used *loss function*: Categorical cross entropy evaluates the classification prediction without trying to discriminate between instances from the same class, which may be desirable in several retrieval scenarios.

One simple but yet effective solution to improve the capacity of the CNN features consists in learning representations that are more suitable to the test retrieval dataset by *fine-tuning* the CNN network to perform classification in a new domain. This approach was followed by Babenko [2], where the Alexnet architecture was trained to perform classification in a Landmark[1] dataset, more semantically similar to the target retrieval domain. Despite improving performance, the final metric and the layers utilized were different to the ones actually optimized during learning.

State-of-the art CNN retrieval networks have been tuned optimizing a similarity loss function [35,4,26]. For that, the whole fine-tuning process of a CNN is casted as a metric learning problem, where the CNN represents an embedding function that maps the input image into a space where relative image similarities are preserved. *Siamese* and *Triplet* networks are commonly used for that task.

2.3.1. Siamese Networks

Siamese networks [36,37,38] are architectures composed by two branches (composed by convolutional, ReLu, Maxpooling layers) that share exactly the same weights across each layer. It is trained on paired data consisting in an image pair (i, j) where $Y(i, j) \in \{0, 1\}$ represents the binary label indicating if the images belong to the same category or not. The network optimizes the contrastive loss function defined for each pair as

$$\mathcal{L}(i, j) = \frac{1}{2} \left(Y(i, j) D(i, j) + (1 - Y(i, j)) \max(0, \alpha - D(i, j)) \right), \tag{1}$$

where $D(i, j)$ represents the Euclidean Distance between a pair of images $D(i, j) = \|\mathbf{f}(i) - \mathbf{f}(j)\|_2$ and $\mathbf{f}$ the embedding function (CNN network) that maps an image to a point in an Euclidean space. When a pair of images belong to the same category, the loss function tries to directly reduce the distance in the feature space, whereas when images are different the loss is composed by a hinge

---

[1]http://sites.skoltech.ru/compvision/projects/neuralcodes/

function that maximizes those distances, which are too small as they do not reach a minimum margin α.

First introduced in 1994 for signature verification [39], Siamese networks have been applied for dimensionality reduction [37], learning image descriptors [40,41,42] or face verification [36,38].

2.3.2. Triplet Networks

Triplet networks are an extension of the Siamese networks where the loss function minimizes relative similarities. Each training triplet is composed by an *anchor* or reference image, a positive example of the same class as the anchor, and a negative example of a different class to the anchor. The loss function is defined by the hinge loss as

$$\mathcal{L}(a, p, n) = \max(0, D(a, p) - D(a, n) + \alpha), \tag{2}$$

where $D(a, p)$ is the Euclidean distance between the anchor and a positive example, $D(a, n)$ is the Euclidean distance between the anchor and a negative example and α a margin. The loss ensures that given an anchor image, the distance between the anchor and a negative image is larger than the distance between the anchor and a positive image by a certain margin α.

The main difference between triplet and Siamese architectures is that the former one optimizes relative distances with a reference image or anchor, whereas the later optimizes separately positive and negative pairs; which usually leads to models with better performance [43,44].

2.3.3. Training Data for Similarity Learning

Generating training data for similarity learning is not a trivial task. A usual procedure of collecting a new image dataset is mainly divided into two steps:

- **Web crawling**: Given pre-defined text queries depicting different categories, querying them in some of the popular image search engines (Google Image Search, Bing, Flick) to download a set of noisy labeled images.
- **Data cleaning**: Images retrieved by available search engines usually contain noisy results such as near-duplicates or unrelated images, high intraclass image variations such interior or exterior images of a particular building or high diversity in the image resolution. Two approaches are followed after the web crawling:

  * Manual data cleaning: Which can be based on manual processing, exhaustively inspecting all images for a dataset of moderate or small sizes [1,45,46] or by making use of a crowdsourcing mechanism such as Amazon Mechanical Turk for large scale datasets [30,47,48].
  * Automatic data cleaning: In this approach, metadata associated with the images is exploited as an additional filtering step such as geo-tagged datasets [49,27] and/or the usage of image representations to estimate similarity and geometry consistence between images, a process that usually rely in handcrafted invariant features [50,35,51].

2.3.4. Hard Negative Mining

During learning, networks are optimized via mini-batch Stochastic Gradient Descent (SGD). Sampling pairs or triplets at random is an inefficient strategy because many of them can already accomplish the margin criteria of equations 1 and 2. That means that no error is generated and no gradients are backpropagated, so the weights of the CNN model are not updated and no learning is performed.

To sample positive pairs, a common procedure consists of sampling images that belong to the same class [35], 3D point or cluster [41,51]. Some approaches select positive pairs with minimal distance within the initial embedding space [26]. In order to avoid sampling very similar images, Radenović *et al* [51] make use of the strong matching pipeline with 3D reconstruction to select only positives that share the minimum amount of local matches, so matching images depict the same object but also ensuring variability of viewpoints.

For the negative pairs, a common procedure consists in iterating over non-matching images that are "hard" negatives, those being close in the descriptor space and that incur a high loss. For that, the loss is computed over a set of negative pairs and only a subset with higher losses is selected for training. This procedure is repeated every N iterations of SGD, so hard examples are picked during all the network learning [41,35]. Variability in the sampling is ensured in [51] by selecting the negative pairs from different clusters or 3D points. Selecting negative pairs based on the loss generally leads to multiple and very similar instances of the same object.

More sophisticated approaches take advantage of the training batches. For instance, Song *et al.* [52] propose a loss function that integrates all positive and negative samples to form a lifted structured embedding. A smart mining represents crucial step for succeeding in training SML models and is an active research area.

2.4. Retrieval CNN Architectures

Recent end-to-end networks proposed for retrieval are based on state-of-the-art architectures for image classification (Alexnet, VGG16, ResNet50). Final retrieval representations are built from convolutional layers. Architectures mainly differ in the top layers designed to aggregate the local convolutional features, as illustrated in Figure 2.

Some of the approaches directly fine-tune the original classification network [48, 50,53], using fully connected layers as image representations. For instance, the full Alexnet architecture is used in [48], where authors explore a multitask learning by optimizing the model for similarity learning along with a classification loss for product identification and search. To switch between classification and similarity comparison, the "softmax" operation at the end of the network is replaced with an inner product layer with a L_2-normalized vector. The full architecture Alexnet is also used in [50], in this case, two additional channels containing a shallow CNN are considered to process two low-resolution versions of the original image. With that, the final descriptor includes multi-scale information to alleviate the limitations of working with fully connected layers. Similarly, Wan *et al* [53] perform the fine-tuning of Alexnet directly on the Oxford and Paris datasets. The three approaches, however, heavily rely on manually annotated data [53,48] or

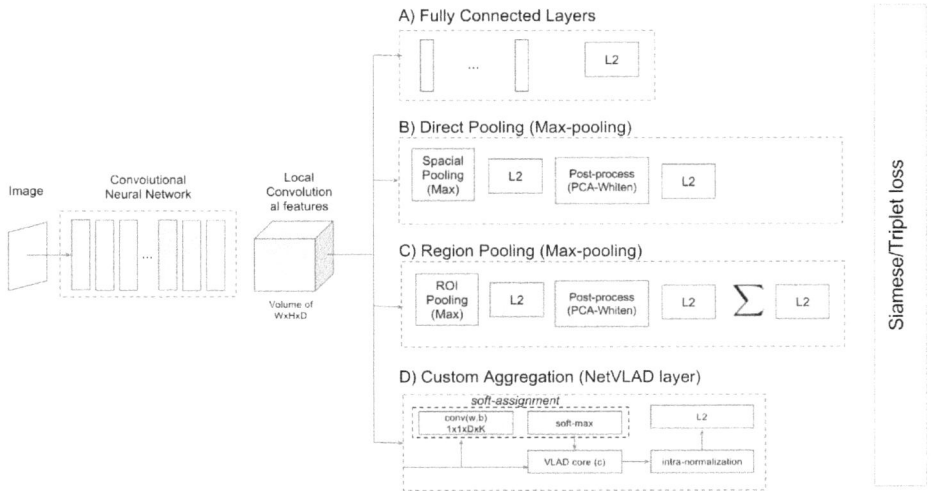

Figure 2. Architectures for similarity learning. The baseline network is initialized with the weights of a state-of-the-art CNN for classification. The top layer can be seen as the aggregation step base in: A) fully connected layers [53]. Approaches dominated by direct pooling: B) direct pooling sum/max-pooling followed by feature post processing [51] and C) Region pooling followed by feature post processing [35] and D) custom aggregation model such as VLAD [27].

a combination of human annotations with a relevance score for image based in handcrafted descriptors [50].

Recent works based their architectures in VGG16 exploiting the capabilities of convolutional layers [51,35,27]. Gordo*et al* *et al* [35] proposed a fine-tuned version of Regional Maximum Activation of Convolutions (R-MAC) [5], where a Region Proposal Network (RPN) [34] is learned as a replacement of the fixed grid originally proposed in [5]. PCA is modeled with a shifting and a fully connected layer that are tuned during the optimization process for similarity learning. Randenović [51] follows the same architecture as in [35] but directly pooling all descriptors generated by the convolutional layer (MAC), without learning an RPN. PCA transformation is learned via linear discriminant projections proposed by Mikolajczyk and Matas [54] using the annotated training data. Arangjelović [27] propose a more sophisticated encoding by implementing a VLAD layer on top of the convolutional features using soft-assignments to be able to tune the parameters via backpropagation. Similarly, Fisher-Vector layer has been proposed in [55] to aggregate deep convolutional descriptors. Although those approaches follow automatic cleaning process (exploiting the GPS associated to with the images [27] or annotating the images based on strong handcrafted baselines [35,51]), image domain is restricted to landmarks and it is uncertain how models perform in more challenging retrieval scenarios.

Table 1 contains the performance of the discussed CNN approaches. Fine-tuned models for retrieval clearly generate better descriptors than those generated by off-the-shelf networks. However, generating a suitable training dataset for retrieval relies in human annotations and computational expensive annotation pro-

Table 1. Summary discussed CNN approaches in different retrieval benchmarks. The table does not include approaches with spatial verification and re-ranking pipelines.

	Method	Dim	Oxford5k	Oxford105k	Paris6k	Paris106k	Holidays
Off-the-shelf Fully connected	Neural Codes [2]	128	0.433	0.386			
	CNNastounding [3]	4-15k	0.68		0.79		
	MOP [22]	2048					0.802
Off-the-shelf Convolutional	SPoC [1]	256	0.589	0.578			0.802
	Ng et al [25]	128	0.593		0.590		0.816
	Razavian [4]	32k	0.843		0.879		0.896
	R-MAC [5]	512	0.669	0.616	0.830	0.757	0.852
	CroW [24]	512	0.682	0.633	0.797	0.710	0.849
End-to-End Training	Neural Codes [2]	128	0.557	0.523			
	Wan [53]	4096	0.783		0.947		
	NetVLAD [27]	256	0.635		0.735		0.843
	R-MAC [35]	512	0.831	0.786	0.871	0.797	0.891
	MAC [51]	512	0.800	0.751	0.829	0.753	0.795

cedures that limits the generalization of the methods, usually related to landmarks scenarios.

Despite the rapid advances of CNNs for image retrieval, many state-of-the-art instance search systems are still based on Bag of Words encoding of local handcrafted features such as SIFT [56]. The Bag of Words model has been enhanced with sophisticated technique such as query foreground/background weighting [57], asymmetric distances [58], or larger vocabularies [45,10]. The most substantial improvements, however, are those involving spatial reranking stages. Zhou et al. [9] propose a fast spatial verification technique which benefits from the BoW encoding to choose tentative matching feature pairs between the query and the target image. Zhang et al. [8] introduce an elastic spatial verification step based on triangulated graph model. Nguyen et al. [7] propose a solution based on deformable parts models (DPMs) [59] to rerank a BoW-based baseline. They train a neural network on several query features to learn the weights to fuse the DPM and BoW scores. In our work, we revisit the Bag of Words encoding strategy and demonstrate its suitability to aggregate CNN features of an off-the-shelf network, instead of using handcrafted ones such as SIFT. Our method is unsupervised and does not require of any additional training data, and it is not restricted to any particular domain. We also propose a simple and efficient spatial reranking strategy to allow query expansion with local features. Although we do not use many of the well-known improvements to the BoW pipeline for image search [57,45,58], we propose a baseline system in which they could be easily integrated.

3. Image Retrieval Benchmarks

Publicly available image retrieval benchmarks such as the Oxford Buildings [45], Paris dataset [46], Sculptures [60], INRIA Holidays [61] or Kentucky [62] are relatively small size datasets used in the image retrieval community to test and to compare different approaches for CBIR systems (see Table 2). Results are reported in terms of mean Average Precision (mAP) of the list of images retrieved from the dataset per query. Metrics such as memory or time required to conduct the search are also important factors to take into account for most real-world problems or when dealing with video, due to the large quantity of images in the dataset. Some recent works reported excellent results using CNNs as image representations [4,35,51,53].

Table 2. Datasets for image retrieval benchmarking. The table shows the total number of images and queries of each dataset as well as the domain of search.

Dataset	Images	Queries	Domain
Oxford	5062	55	Buildings
Paris	6412	55	Buildings
Sculptures	6340	70	Sculptures
INRIA Holidays	1491	500	Scenes/Objects
Kentucky benchmark	10200	2550	Objects

Figure 3. Samples from some retrieval benchmarks. First row, Sculptures; second row Paris; third and fourth rows Kentucky.

However, the kind of queries for these datasets (see Figure 3 for some examples) can be considered simpler than the queries in a generic instance search. In those datasets, the objects are usually the main part of the image and topics to retrieve are usually restricted to a particular domain.

3.1. TRECVid Instance Search

A generic instance search system should be able to find objects of an unknown category that may appear at any position within the images. TRECVID [63] is an international benchmarking activity that encourages research in video information retrieval by providing a large data collection and a uniform scoring procedure for evaluation. The Instance Search task in TRECVID consists of finding 30 particular instances within 464 hours of video (a total of 224 video files, 300GB). For each query, 4 image examples are provided. A common procedure to deal with videos is to perform key frame extraction. For example, in our 2014 participation [64], the image dataset contained 647,628 image frames (66GB) by extracting 0.25 frames/second of the videos (which can be considered a low rate for a key frame extraction).

Figure 4. Query examples for TRECVID Instance search task [63]. Instance queries are divers: they can be logos, objects, buildings or people. Location and scale of the instances is also diverse.

There is no ground truth for the query images within the dataset and the number of examples per query is limited to 4 frames. Figure 4 shows an example of some of the 2014 TRECVid Instance Search queries.

Although promising results have shown the power of CNN representation on different retrieval benchmarks, results have mainly been reported for relatively small datasets, which are not sufficiently representative in terms of generalization or complexity of the queries for real world problem such as instance search in videos. Approaches that work well in small datasets may not work well in larger and more realistic datasets, such as TRECVID

4. Bag of Words Framework

The proposed pipeline for feature extraction uses the activations at different locations of a convolutional layer in a pre-trained CNN as local features. A CNN trained for a classification task is typically composed of a series of convolutional layers, followed by some fully connected layers, connected to a softmax layer that produces the inferred class probabilities. To obtain a fixed-sized output, the input image to a CNN is usually resized to be square. However, several authors using CNNs for retrieval [5,24] have reported performance gains by retaining the aspect ratio of the original images. We therefore discard the softmax and fully connected layers of the architecture and extract CNN features maintaining the original image aspect ratio.

Each convolutional layer in the network has D different $N \times M$ feature maps, which can be viewed as $N \times M$ descriptors of dimension D. Each of these descriptors contains the activations of all neurons in the convolutional layer sharing the same receptive field. This way, these D-dimensional features can be seen as local descriptors computed over the region corresponding to the receptive field of an array of neurons. With this interpretation, we can treat the CNN as a local feature extractor and use any existing aggregation technique to build a single image representation.

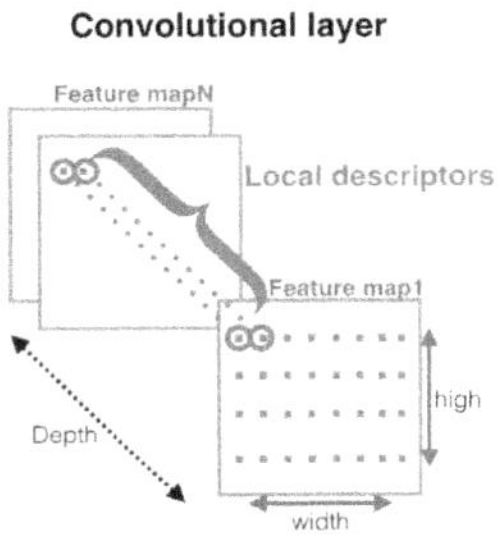

Figure 5. Re-interpretation of activation tensor into local descriptors

We propose to use the BoW model to encode the local convolutional features of an image into a single vector. Although more elaborate aggregation strategies have been shown to outperform BoW-based approaches for some tasks in the literature [26,65], BoW encodings produce sparse high-dimensional codes that can be stored in inverted indices, which are beneficial for fast retrieval. Moreover, BoW-based representations are faster to compute, easier to interpret, more compact, and provide all the benefits of sparse high-dimensional representations previously mentioned in Section 1.

BoW models require constructing a visual codebook to map vectors to their nearest centroid. We use k-means on local CNN features to fit this codebook. Each local CNN feature in the convolutional layer is then assigned its closest visual word in the learned codebook. This procedure generates the *assignment map*, i.e. a 2D array of size $N \times M$ that relates each local CNN feature with a visual word. The assignment map is, therefore, a compact representation of the image, which relates each pixel of the original image with its visual word with a precision of $\left(\frac{W}{N}, \frac{H}{M}\right)$ pixels, where W and H are the width and height of the original image. This property allows us to quickly generate the BoW vectors of not only the full image, but also its parts. We describe the use of this property in our work in Section 5.

Figure 6 shows the pipeline of the proposed approach. The described bag of local convolutional features (BLCF) encodes the image into a sparse high dimensional descriptor, which will be used as the image representation for retrieval.

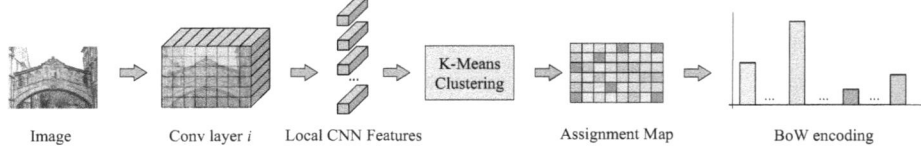

Figure 6. The Bag of Local Convolutional Features pipeline (BLCF).

5. Image Retrieval

This section describes the image retrieval pipeline, which consists of an initial ranking stage, followed by a spatial reranking, and query expansion.

(a) **Initial search:** The initial ranking is computed using the cosine similarity between the BoW vector of the query image and the BoW vectors of the full images in the database. We use a sparse matrix based inverted index and GPU-based sparse matrix multiplications to allow fast retrieval. The image list is then sorted based on the cosine similarity of its elements to the query. We use two types of image search based on the query information that is used:

- Global search (GS): The BoW vector of the query is built with the visual words of all the local CNN features in the convolutional layer extracted for the query image.
- Local search (LS): The BoW vector of the query contains only the visual words of the local CNN features that fall inside the query bounding box.

(b) **Local reranking (R):** After the initial search, the top T images in the ranking are locally analyzed and reranked based on a localization score. We choose windows of all possible combinations of width $w \in \{W, \frac{W}{2}, \frac{W}{4}\}$ and height $h \in \{H, \frac{H}{2}, \frac{H}{4}\}$, where W and H are the width and height of the assignment map. We use a sliding window strategy directly on the assignment map with 50% of overlap in both directions.

We additionally perform a simple filtering strategy to discard those windows whose aspect ratio is too different to the aspect ratio of the query. Let the aspect ratio of the query bounding box be $AR_q = \frac{W_q}{H_q}$ and $AR_w = \frac{W_w}{H_w}$ be the aspect ratio of the window. The score for window w is defined as $score_w = \frac{min(AR_w, AR_q)}{max(AR_w, AR_q)}$. All windows with a score lower than a threshold th are discarded.

For each of the remaining windows, we construct the BoW vector representation and compare it with the query representation using cosine similarity. The window with the highest cosine similarity is taken as the new score for the image (score max pooling).

We also enhance the BoW window representation with spatial pyramid matching [66] with $L = 2$ resolution levels (i.e. the full window and its 4 sub regions). We construct the BoW representation of all sub regions at the 2 levels, and weight their contribution to the similarity score with inverse proportion to the resolution level of the region. The cosine similarity of a sub region r to the corresponding query sub region is therefore weighted by $w_r = \frac{1}{2^{(L-l_r)}}$, where l_r is the resolution level of the region r. Figure 7 depicts the described approach.

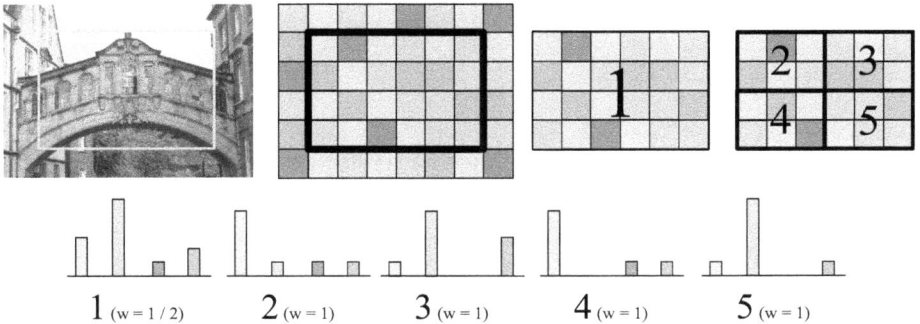

Figure 7. Spatial pyramid matching on window locations.

With this procedure, the top T elements of the ranking are sorted based on the cosine similarity of their regions to the query's, and also provides the region with the highest score as a rough localization of the object.

(c) **Query expansion:** We investigate two query expansion strategies based on global and local BoW descriptors:

- Global query expansion (GQE): The BoW vectors of the N images at the top of the ranking are averaged together with the BoW of the query to form the new representation for the query. GQE can be applied either before or after the local reranking stage.
- Local query expansion (LQE): Locations obtained in the local reranking step are used to mask out the background and build the BoW descriptor of only the region of interest of the N images at the top of the ranking. These BoW vectors are averaged together with the BoW of the query bounding box. The resulting BoW vector is used to perform a second search.

6. Experiments

6.1. Datasets

We use the following datasets to evaluate the performance of our approach:

Oxford Buildings [45] contains 5,063 still images, including 55 query images of 11 different buildings in Oxford. A bounding box surrounding the target object is provided for query images. An additional set of 100,000 distractor images is also available for the dataset. We refer to the original and extended versions of the dataset as Oxford 5k and Oxford 105k, respectively.

Paris Buildings [46] contains 6,412 still images collected from Flickr including query images of 12 different Paris landmarks with associated bounding box annotations. A set of 100,000 images is added to the original dataset (Paris 6k) to form its extended version (Paris 106k).

TRECVid Instance Search 2013 [63] contains 244 video files (464 hours in total), each containing a week's worth of BBC EastEnders programs. Each video is divided in different shots of short duration (between 5 seconds and 2 minutes). We perform uniform key frame extraction at 1/4 fps. The dataset also includes

Figure 8. Query examples from the three different datasets. Top: Paris buildings (1-3) and Oxford buildings (4-6); bottom: TRECVid INS 2013.

30 queries and provides 4 still images for each of them (including a binary mask of the object location). In our experiments, we use a subset of this dataset that contains only those key frames that are positively annotated for at least one of the queries. The dataset, which we will refer to as the TRECVid INS subset, is composed of 23,614 key frames.

Figure 8 includes three examples of query objects from the three datasets.

6.2. Preliminary experiments

Feature extraction was performed using *Caffe* [67] and the VGG16 pre-trained network [68]. We extracted features from the last three convolutional layers (conv5_1, conv5_2 and conv5_3) and compared their performance on the Oxford 5k dataset. We experimented with different image input sizes: 1/3 and 2/3 of the original image. Following several other authors [1,24], we L_2-normalize all local features, followed by PCA, whitening, and a second round of L_2-normalization. The PCA models were fit on the same dataset as the test data in all cases.

Unless stated otherwise, all experiments used a visual codebook of 25,000 centroids fit using the (L_2-PCA-L_2 transformed) local CNN features of all images in the same dataset (1.7M and 2.15M for Oxford 5k and Paris 6k, respectively). We tested three different codebook sizes (25,000; 50,000 and 100,000) on the Oxford 5k dataset, and chose the 25,000 centroids one because of its higher performance.

Table 3 shows the mean average precision on Oxford 5k for the three different layers and image sizes. We also consider the effect of applying bilinear interpolation of the feature maps prior to the BoW construction, as a fast alternative to using a larger input to the CNN. Our experiments show that all layers benefit from feature map interpolation. Our best result was achieved using conv5_2 with full-size images as input. However, we discarded this configuration due to its memory requirements: on a Nvidia GeForce GTX 970, we found that feature extraction on images rescaled with a factor of 1/3 images was 25 times faster than on images

Table 3. Mean average precision (mAP) on Oxford 5k using different convolutional layers of VGG16, comparing the performance of different feature map resolutions (both raw and interpolated). The size of the codebook is 25,000 in all experiments.

	conv5_1	conv5_2	conv5_3
$N \times M$ raw	0.641	0.626	0.498
$2N \times 2M$ interpolated	0.653	0.638	0.536
$2N \times 2M$ raw	0.620	**0.660**	0.540

twice that size. For this reason, we resize all images to 1/3 of their original size and use conv5_1 interpolated feature maps.

6.2.1. Center Prior Weighting

Inspired by the boost in performance of the Gaussian center prior in sum-pooled convolutional (SPoC) feature descriptors [1], we apply a weighting scheme on the visual words of an image to provide more importance to those belonging to the central part of the image. The weighting scheme $w(i, j)$ is described as:

$$w(i, j) = \frac{1}{\sqrt{(i - c_1)^2 + (j - c_2)^2}}, \tag{3}$$

where (i, j) represents the position of a visual word within the assignment map and (c_1, c_2) correspond to the center coordinated of the assignment map. $w(i, j)$ min-max normalized to provide scores between 0 and 1. Table 3 shows the mean average precision on Oxford 5k for the three different layers and image sizes. All results are obtained using this weighting criteria; for conv5_1 in Oxford 5k, increases mAP from 0.626 to 0.653.

6.2.2. Layer Combination

We explore combining different layers in Oxford dataset. For that, layers were reshaped to have the same spatial dimensions by using bilinear interpolation. For instance, the last convolutional layer from VGG16, generates feature maps of dimensions $(512, 11, 8)$ for an input size of $(336, 256)$. When combining with a lower layer such as conv5_1, pool5 maps have to be reshaped to double its dimensions $(21, 16)$ in order to be able to concatenate all the local features on a single volume of $(1024, 21, 16)$. PCA-whitening reduces the dimensionality of the new local descriptors to $512D$. Table 4 shows the effect in performance when combining different layers to conv5_1. We found that layer combination is potentially beneficial for our final representation (as found when combining con5_1 with pool5). Although since improvements found were marginally beneficial we discarded this approach in our pipeline.

6.3. Query augmentation

Previous works [17,69] have demonstrated how simple data augmentation strategies can improve the performance of an instance search system. Some of these apply augmentation strategies at the database side, which can be prohibitively costly

Table 4. Experiments layer combination

conv5_1	conv5_2	conv5_3	pool5	mAP
X				0.653
X	X			0.640
X	X	X		0.645
X			X	0.671

Table 5. mAP on Oxford 5k for the two different types of query augmentation: the flip and the zoomed central crop (ZCC). 2× interpolated conv5_1 features are used in all cases.

	Query	+ Flip	+ ZCC	+ Flip + ZCC
GS	0.653	0.662	0.695	0.697
WS	0.706	0.717	0.735	0.743
LS	0.738	0.746	0.758	0.758

Original   Flip   ZCC   Flip + ZCC

Figure 9. The four query images after augmentation.

for large datasets. For this reason, we use data augmentation on the query side only. We explore two different strategies to enrich the query before visual search: a horizontal flip (or mirroring) and a zoomed central crop (ZCC) on an image enlarged by 50%.

Figure 9 shows an example of the transformations, which give rise to 4 different versions of the query image. The feature vectors they produce are added together to form a single BoW descriptor. Table 5 shows the impact of incrementally augmenting the query with each one of these transformations.

We find that all the studied types of query augmentation consistently improve the results, for both global and local search. ZCC provides a higher gain in performance compared to flipping alone. ZCC generates an image of the same resolution as the original, which contains the center crop at a higher resolution. Objects from the Oxford dataset tend to be centered, which explains the performance gain when applying ZCC.

6.4. Reranking and query expansion

We apply the local reranking (R) stage on the top-100 images in the initial ranking, using the sliding window approach described in Section 5. The presented aspect

Table 6. mAP on Oxford 5k and Paris 5k for the different stages in the pipeline introduced in Section 5. The Q_{aug} additional columns indicate the results when the query is augmented with the transformations introduced in Section 6.3.

	Oxford 5k		Paris 6k	
		$+Q_{aug}$		$+Q_{aug}$
GS	0.653	0.697	0.699	0.754
LS	0.738	0.758	0.820	0.832
GS + R	0.701	0.713	0.719	0.752
LS + R	0.734	0.760	0.815	0.828
GS + GQE	0.702	0.730	0.774	0.792
LS + GQE	0.773	0.780	0.814	0.832
GS + R + GQE	0.771	0.772	0.801	0.798
LS + R + GQE	0.769	**0.793**	0.807	0.828
GS + R + LQE	0.782	0.757	0.835	0.795
LS + R + LQE	**0.788**	0.786	**0.848**	**0.833**

ratio filtering is applied with a threshold $th = 0.4$, which was chosen based on a visual inspection of results on a subset of Oxford 5k. Query expansion is later applied considering the top-10 images of the resulting ranking. This section evaluates the impact in the performance of both reranking and query expansion stages. Table 6 contains the results for the different stages in the pipeline for both simple and augmented queries (referred to as Q_{aug} in the table).

The results indicate that the local reranking is only beneficial when applied to a ranking obtained from a search using the global BoW descriptor of the query image (GS). This is consistent with the work by Tolias et al. [5], who also apply a spatial reranking followed by query expansion to a ranking obtained with a search using descriptors of full images. They achieve a mAP of 0.66 in Oxford 5k, which is increased to 0.77 after spatial reranking and query expansion, while we reach similar results (e.g. from 0.652 to 0.769). However, our results indicate that a ranking originating from a local search (LS) does not benefit from local reranking. Since the BoW representation allows us to effectively perform a local search (LS) in a database of fully indexed images, we find the local reranking stage applied to LS to be redundant in terms of the achieved quality of the ranking. However, the local reranking stage does provide with a rough localization of the object in the images of the ranking, as depicted in Figure 1. We use this information to perform query expansion based on local features (LQE).

Results indicate that query expansion stages greatly improve performance in Oxford 5k. We do not observe significant gains after reranking and QE in the Paris 6k dataset, although we achieve our best result with LS + R + LQE.

In the case of augmented queries ($+Q_{aug}$), we find that this query expansion is less helpful in all cases, which suggests that the information gained with query augmentation and the one obtained by means of query expansion strategies are not complementary.

Table 7. Comparison to state-of-the-art CNN representations (mAP). Results in the lower section consider reranking and/or query expansion.

	Oxford		Paris	
	5k	105k	6k	106k
Ng *et al.* [25]	0.649	-	0.694	-
Razavian *et al.* [4]	**0.844**	-	**0.853**	-
SPoC [1]	0.657	0.642	-	-
R-MAC [5]	0.668	0.616	0.830	**0.757**
CroW [24]	0.682	**0.632**	0.796	0.710
uCroW [24]	0.666	0.629	0.767	0.695
GS	0.652	0.510	0.698	0.421
LS	0.739	0.593	0.820	0.648
LS + Q_{aug}	0.758	0.622	0.832	0.673
CroW + GQE [24]	0.722	0.678	0.855	0.797
R-MAC + R + GQE [5]	0.770	**0.726**	**0.877**	**0.817**
LS + GQE	0.773	0.602	0.814	0.632
LS + R + LQE	0.788	0.651	0.848	0.641
LS + R + GQE + Q_{aug}	**0.793**	0.666	0.828	0.683

6.5. Comparison with the State-of-the-art

We compare our approach with other CNN-based representations that make use of features from convolutional layers on the Oxford and Paris datasets. Table 7 includes the best result for each approach in the literature. Our performance using global search (GS) is comparable to that of Ng et al. [25], which is the one that most resembles our approach. However, they achieve this result using raw Vector of Locally Aggregated Descriptors (VLAD) features, which are more expensive to compute and, being a dense high-dimensional representation, do not scale as well to larger datasets. Similarly, Razavian et al. [4] achieve the highest performance of all approaches in both the Oxford and Paris benchmarks by applying a spatial search at different scales for all images in the database. Such approach is prohibitively costly when dealing with larger datasets, especially for real-time search scenarios. Our BoW-based representation is highly sparse, allowing for fast retrieval in large datasets using inverted indices, and achieves consistently high mAP in all tested datasets.

We find the usage of the query bounding box to be extremely beneficial in our case for both datasets. The authors of SPoC [1] are the only ones who report results using the query bounding box for search, finding a decrease in performance from 0.589 to 0.531 using raw SPoC features (without center prior). This suggests that sum pooled CNN features are less suitable for instance level search in datasets where images are represented with global descriptors.

We also compare our local reranking and query expansion results with similar approaches in the state-of-the-art. The authors of R-MAC [5] apply a spatial search for reranking, followed by a query expansion stage, while the authors of CroW [24] only apply query expansion after the initial search. Our proposed approach also achieves competitive results in this section, achieving the best result for Oxford 5k.

6.6. Experiments on TRECVid INS

In this section, we compare the BLCF with the sum pooled convolutional features proposed in several works in the literature. We use our own implementation of the *uCroW* descriptor from [24] and compare it with BLCF for the TRECVid INS subset. For the sake of comparison, we test our implementation of sum pooling using both our chosen CNN layer and input size (conv5_1 and 1/3 image size), and the ones reported in [24] (pool5 and full image resolution). For the BoW representation, we train a visual codebook of 25,000 centroids using 3M local CNN features chosen randomly from the INS subset. Since the nature of the TRECVid INS dataset significantly differs from that of the other ones used so far (see Figure 8), we do not apply center prior to the features in any case, to avoid down weighting local features from image areas where the objects might appear. Table 8 compares sum pooling with BoW in Oxford, Paris, and TRECVid subset datasets. As stated in earlier sections, sum pooling and BoW have similar performance in Oxford and Paris datasets. For the TRECVid INS subset, however, Bag of Words significantly outperforms sum pooling, which demonstrates its suitability for challenging instance search datasets, in which queries are not centered and have variable size and appearance. We also observe a different behavior when using the provided query object locations (LS) to search, which was highly beneficial in Oxford and Paris datasets, but does not provide any gain in TRECVid INS. We hypothesize that the fact that the size of the instances is much smaller in TRECVid than in Paris and Oxford datasets causes this drop in performance. Global search (GS) achieves better results on TRECVid INS, which suggests that query instances are in many cases correctly retrieved due to their context. Figure 12 shows the mean average precision of the different stages of the pipeline for all TRECVid queries separately. The global search significantly outperforms local search for most queries in the database. Figure 11 shows examples of the queries for which the local search outperforms the global search. Interestingly, we find these particular objects to appear in different contexts in the database. In these cases, the usage of the local information is crucial to find the query instance in unseen environments. For this reason, we compute the distance map of the binary mask of the query, and assign a weight to each position of the assignment map with inverse proportion to its value in the distance map. This way, higher weights are assigned to the visual words of local CNN features near the object. We find this scheme, referred to as weighted search (WS), to be beneficial for most of the queries, suggesting that, although context is necessary, emphasizing the object information in the BoW descriptor is beneficial.

We finally apply the local reranking and query expansion stages introduced in Section 5 to the baseline rankings obtained for the TRECVid INS subset. Since we are dealing with objects whose appearance can significantly change in different keyframes, we decided not to filter out windows based on aspect ratio similarity. Additionally, we do not apply the spatial pyramid matching, since some of the query instances are too small to be divided in sub regions. After reranking, we apply the distance map weighting scheme to the locations obtained for the top 10 images of the ranking and use them to do weighted query expansion (WQE).

Results are consistent with those obtained in the experiments in Oxford and Paris datasets: although the local reranking does not provide significant

Figure 10. Appearances of the same object in different frames of TRECVid Instance Search.

Figure 11. Top 5 rankings for queries 9072 (top) and 9081 (bottom) of the TRECVid INS 2013 dataset.

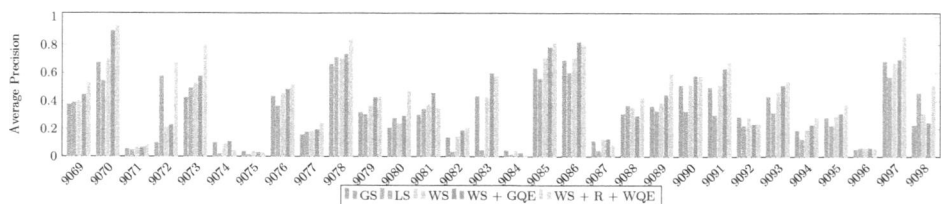

Figure 12. Average precision of TRECVid INS queries.

improvements (WS: 0.350, WS + R: 0.348 mAP), the query expansion stage is beneficial when applied after WS (WS + GQE: 0.391 mAP), and provides significant gains in performance after local reranking (WS + R + GQE: 0.442 mAP) and after local reranking using the obtained localizations (WS + R + WQE: 0.452 mAP).

Table 8. mAP of sum pooling and BoW aggregation techniques in Oxford, Paris and TRECVid INS subset.

		Oxford 5k	Paris 6k	INS 23k
BoW	GS	0.650	0.698	0.323
	WS	0.693	0.742	**0.350**
	LS	**0.739**	**0.819**	0.295
Sum pooling (as ours)	GS	0.606	0.712	0.156
	WS	0.638	0.745	0.150
	LS	0.583	0.742	0.097
Sum pooling (as in [24])	GS	0.672	0.774	0.139
	WS	0.707	0.789	0.146
	LS	0.683	0.763	0.120

7. Conclusion

We proposed an aggregation strategy based on Bag of Words to encode features from convolutional neural networks into sparse representations for instance search. We demonstrated the suitability of these bags of local convolutional features, achieving competitive performance with respect to other CNN-based representations in Oxford and Paris benchmarks, while being more scalable in terms of index size, cost of indexing, and search time. We also compared our BoW encoding scheme with sum pooling of CNN features for instance search in the far more complex and challenging TRECVid instance search task, and demonstrated that our method consistently and significantly performs better. This encouraging result suggests that the BoW encoding, as a virtue of being high dimensional and sparse, is more robust to scenarios where only a small number of features in the target images are relevant to the query. Our method does, however, appear to be more sensitive to large numbers of distractor images than methods based on sum and max pooling (SPoC, R-MAC, and CroW). We speculate that this may be because the distractor images are drawn from a different distribution to the original dataset, and may therefore require a larger codebook to represent the diversity in the visual words better. Future work will investigate this issue.

References

[1] A. Babenko and V. Lempitsky. Aggregating local deep features for image retrieval. In *Proceedings of the IEEE international conference on computer vision*, pages 1269–1277, 2015.

[2] A. Babenko, A. Slesarev, A. Chigorin, and V. Lempitsky. Neural codes for image retrieval. In *Computer Vision–ECCV 2014*, pages 584–599. 2014.

[3] A. Razavian, H. Azizpour, J. Sullivan, and S. Carlsson. CNN features off-the-shelf: an astounding baseline for recognition. In *Computer Vision and Pattern Recognition Workshops*, 2014.

[4] Ali S Razavian, Josephine Sullivan, Stefan Carlsson, and Atsuto Maki. Visual instance retrieval with deep convolutional networks. *ITE Transactions on Media Technology and Applications*, 4(3):251–258, 2016.

[5]   G. Tolias, R. Sicre, and H. Jégou. Particular object retrieval with integral max-pooling of cnn activations. In *International Conference on Learning Representations*, 2016.

[6]   L. Xie, R. Hong, B. Zhang, and Q. Tian. Image classification and retrieval are one. In *Proceedings of the 5th ACM on International Conference on Multimedia Retrieval*, pages 3–10. ACM, 2015.

[7]   V. Nguyen, D. Nguyen, M. Tran, D. Le, D. Duong, and S. Satoh. Query-adaptive late fusion with neural network for instance search. In *International Workshop on Multimedia Signal Processing (MMSP)*, pages 1–6, 2015.

[8]   W. Zhang and C. Ngo. Topological spatial verification for instance search. *IEEE Transactions on Multimedia*, 17(8):1236–1247, 2015.

[9]   X. Zhou, C. Zhu, Q. Zhu, S. Satoh, and Y. Guo. A practical spatial re-ranking method for instance search from videos. In *International Conference on Image Processing (ICIP)*, 2014.

[10] C. Zhu and S. Satoh. Large vocabulary quantization for searching instances from videos. In *International Conference on Multimedia Retrieval (ICMR)*, 2012.

[11] J. Sivic and A. Zisserman. Efficient visual search of videos cast as text retrieval. *IEEE Transactions on Pattern Analysis and Machine Intelligence*, 31(4):591–606, 2009.

[12] P. Lennie. The cost of cortical computation. *Current biology*, 13(6):493–497, 2003.

[13] W. E. Vinje and J. L. Gallant. Sparse coding and decorrelation in primary visual cortex during natural vision. *Science*, 287(5456):1273–1276, 2000.

[14] H. Jégou, M. Douze, and C. Schmid. Improving bag-of-features for large scale image search. *International Journal of Computer Vision*, 87(3):316–336, 2010.

[15] Y. Zhang, Z. Jia, and T. Chen. Image retrieval with geometry-preserving visual phrases. In *Computer Vision and Pattern Recognition (CVPR)*, pages 809–816, 2011.

[16] T. Mei, Y. Rui, S. Li, and Q. Tian. Multimedia search reranking: A literature survey. *ACM Computing Surveys (CSUR)*, 46(3):38, 2014.

[17] R. Arandjelović and A. Zisserman. Three things everyone should know to improve object retrieval. In *2012 IEEE Conference on Computer Vision and Pattern Recognition*, pages 2911–2918, June 2012.

[18] O. Chum, J. Philbin, J. Sivic, M. Isard, and A. Zisserman. Total recall: Automatic query expansion with a generative feature model for object retrieval. In *IEEE International Conference on Computer Vision*, Rio de Janeiro, Brazil, October 2007.

[19] A. Krizhevsky, I. Sutskever, and G. E. Hinton. Imagenet classification with deep convolutional neural networks. In *Advances in neural information processing systems*, pages 1097–1105, 2012.

[20] J. Donahue, Y. Jia, O. Vinyals, J. Hoffman, N. Zhang, E. Tzeng, and T. Darrell. Decaf: A deep convolutional activation feature for generic visual recognition. In *Proceedings of the 31st International Conference on International Conference on Machine Learning - Volume 32*, ICML'14, pages I–647–I–655. JMLR.org, 2014.

[21] J. Yosinski, J. Clune, Y. Bengio, and H. Lipson. How transferable are features in deep neural networks? In *Proceedings of the 27th International Conference on Neural Information Processing Systems*, NIPS'14, pages 3320–3328, Cambridge, MA, USA, 2014. MIT Press.

[22] Yunchao Gong, Liwei Wang, Ruiqi Guo, and Svetlana Lazebnik. Multi-scale orderless pooling of deep convolutional activation features. In *Computer Vision–ECCV 2014*. 2014.

[23] Y. Liu, Y. Guo, S. Wu, and M. Lew. Deepindex for accurate and efficient image retrieval. In *International Conference on Multimedia Retrieval (ICMR)*, 2015.

[24] Y. Kalantidis, C. Mellina, and S. Osindero. Cross-dimensional weighting for aggregated deep convolutional features. In *European Conference on Computer Vision VSM Workshop*, pages 685–701. Springer International Publishing, 2016.

[25] J. Yue-Hei Ng, F. Yang, and L. S. Davis. Exploiting local features from deep networks for image retrieval. In *The IEEE Conference on Computer Vision and Pattern Recognition (CVPR) Workshops*, June 2015.

[26] H. Jégou, M. Douze, C. Schmid, and P. Pérez. Aggregating local descriptors into a compact image representation. In *2010 IEEE Computer Society Conference on Computer Vision and Pattern Recognition*, pages 3304–3311, June 2010.

[27] R. Arandjelović, P. Gronat, A. Torii, T. Pajdla, and J. Sivic. Netvlad: Cnn architecture

for weakly supervised place recognition. In *IEEE Conference on Computer Vision and Pattern Recognition*, 2016.

[28] A. Jimenez, J. M. Alvarez, and X. Giro-i Nieto. Class-weighted convolutional features for visual instance search. In *28th British Machine Vision Conference (BMVC)*, September 2017.

[29] B. Zhou, A. Khosla, A. Lapedriza, A. Oliva, and A. Torralba. Learning deep features for discriminative localization. In *The IEEE Conference on Computer Vision and Pattern Recognition (CVPR)*, June 2016.

[30] J. Deng, W. Dong, R. Socher, L. Li, K. Li, and L. Fei-Fei. Imagenet: A large-scale hierarchical image database. In *Computer Vision and Pattern Recognition, 2009. CVPR 2009. IEEE Conference on*, pages 248–255, June 2009.

[31] C. Reyes, E. Mohedano, K. McGuinness, and X. O'Connor, N.and Giro-i-Nieto. Where is my phone?: personal object retrieval from egocentric images. In *Proceedings of the first Workshop on Lifelogging Tools and Applications*, pages 55–62. ACM, 2016.

[32] J. Pan, E. Sayrol, X. Giro-i Nieto, K. McGuinness, and N. O'Connor. Shallow and deep convolutional networks for saliency prediction. In *Proceedings of the IEEE Conference on Computer Vision and Pattern Recognition*, pages 598–606, 2016.

[33] A. Salvador, X. Giro-i Nieto, F. Marques, and S. Shin'ichi. Faster R-CNN Features for Instance Search. In *The IEEE Conference on Computer Vision and Pattern Recognition (CVPR) Workshops*, June 2016.

[34] S. Ren, K. He, R. Girshick, and J. Sun. Faster r-cnn: Towards real-time object detection with region proposal networks. *IEEE Transactions on Pattern Analysis and Machine Intelligence*, 39(6):1137–1149, June 2017.

[35] A. Gordo, J. Almazán, J. Revaud, and D. Larlus. End-to-end learning of deep visual representations for image retrieval. *International Journal of Computer Vision*, 124(2):237–254, 2017.

[36] S. Chopra, R. Hadsell, and Y. LeCun. Learning a similarity metric discriminatively, with application to face verification. In *2005 IEEE Computer Society Conference on Computer Vision and Pattern Recognition (CVPR'05)*, volume 1, pages 539–546 vol. 1, June 2005.

[37] R. Hadsell, S. Chopra, and Y. LeCun. Dimensionality reduction by learning an invariant mapping. In *2006 IEEE Computer Society Conference on Computer Vision and Pattern Recognition (CVPR'06)*, volume 2, pages 1735–1742, 2006.

[38] Y. Taigman, M. Yang, M. Ranzato, and L. Wolf. Deepface: Closing the gap to human-level performance in face verification. In *Computer Vision and Pattern Recognition (CVPR), 2014 IEEE Conference on*, pages 1701–1708, June 2014.

[39] J. Bromley, I. Guyon, Y. LeCun, E. Säckinger, and R. Shah. Signature verification using a" siamese" time delay neural network. In *Advances in Neural Information Processing Systems*, pages 737–744, 1994.

[40] N. Carlevaris-Bianco and R. M Eustice. Learning visual feature descriptors for dynamic lighting conditions. In *Intelligent Robots and Systems (IROS 2014), 2014 IEEE/RSJ International Conference on*, pages 2769–2776. IEEE, 2014.

[41] E. Simo-Serra, E. Trulls, L. Ferraz, I. Kokkinos, and F. Moreno-Noguer. Fracking deep convolutional image descriptors. *arXiv preprint arXiv:1412.6537*, 2014.

[42] S. Zagoruyko and N. Komodakis. Learning to compare image patches via convolutional neural networks. In *Proceedings of the IEEE Conference on Computer Vision and Pattern Recognition*, pages 4353–4361, 2015.

[43] E. Hoffer and N. Ailon. Deep metric learning using triplet network. In *International Workshop on Similarity-Based Pattern Recognition*, pages 84–92. Springer, 2015.

[44] F. Schroff, D. Kalenichenko, and J. Philbin. Facenet: A unified embedding for face recognition and clustering. In *Proceedings of the IEEE Conference on Computer Vision and Pattern Recognition*, pages 815–823, 2015.

[45] J. Philbin, O. Chum, M. Isard, J. Sivic, and A. Zisserman. Object retrieval with large vocabularies and fast spatial matching. In *2007 IEEE Conference on Computer Vision and Pattern Recognition*, pages 1–8, June 2007.

[46] J. Philbin, O. Chum, M. Isard, J. Sivic, and A. Zisserman. Lost in quantization: Improving particular object retrieval in large scale image databases. In *Proceedings of the IEEE*

Conference on Computer Vision and Pattern Recognition, 2008.

[47] B. Zhou, A. Lapedriza, J. Xiao, A. Torralba, and A. Oliva. Learning deep features for scene recognition using places database. In Z. Ghahramani, M. Welling, C. Cortes, N. D. Lawrence, and K. Q. Weinberger, editors, *Advances in Neural Information Processing Systems 27*, pages 487–495. Curran Associates, Inc., 2014.

[48] S. Bell and K. Bala. Learning visual similarity for product design with convolutional neural networks. *ACM Transactions on Graphics (TOG)*, 34(4):98, 2015.

[49] N. N. Vo and J. Hays. *Localizing and orienting street views using overhead imagery*, pages 494–509. 2016.

[50] J. Wang, Y. Song, T. Leung, C. Rosenberg, J. Wang, J. Philbin, B. Chen, and Y. Wu. Learning fine-grained image similarity with deep ranking. In *Proceedings of the IEEE Conference on Computer Vision and Pattern Recognition*, pages 1386–1393, 2014.

[51] F. Radenović, G. Tolias, and O. Chum. CNN image retrieval learns from BoW: Unsupervised fine-tuning with hard examples. In *European Conference on Computer Vision*, pages 3–20. Springer International Publishing, 2016.

[52] H. Oh Song, Y. Xiang, S. Jegelka, and S. Savarese. Deep metric learning via lifted structured feature embedding. In *Proceedings of the IEEE Conference on Computer Vision and Pattern Recognition*, pages 4004–4012, 2016.

[53] J. Wan, D. Wang, S. C. H. Hoi, P. Wu, J. Zhu, Y. Zhang, and J. Li. Deep learning for content-based image retrieval: A comprehensive study. In *Proceedings of the 22nd ACM international conference on Multimedia*, pages 157–166. ACM, 2014.

[54] K. Mikolajczyk and J. Matas. Improving descriptors for fast tree matching by optimal linear projection. In *2007 IEEE 11th International Conference on Computer Vision*, pages 1–8, Oct 2007.

[55] E. Ong, S. Husain, and M. Bober. Siamese network of deep fisher-vector descriptors for image retrieval. *arXiv preprint arXiv:1702.00338*, 2017.

[56] D. G. Lowe. Distinctive image features from scale-invariant keypoints. *International Journal of Computer Vision*, 60(2):91–110, 2004.

[57] W. Zhang and C. Ngo. Searching visual instances with topology checking and context modeling. In *International Conference on Multimedia Retrieval (ICMR)*, pages 57–64, 2013.

[58] C. Zhu, H. Jégou, and S. Satoh. Query-adaptive asymmetrical dissimilarities for visual object retrieval. In *International Conference on Computer Vision (ICCV)*, pages 1705–1712, 2013.

[59] P. Felzenszwalb, D. McAllester, and D. Ramanan. A discriminatively trained, multiscale, deformable part model. In *Computer Vision and Pattern Recognition (CVPR)*, pages 1–8, 2008.

[60] R. Arandjelović and A. Zisserman. Smooth object retrieval using a bag of boundaries. In *IEEE International Conference on Computer Vision*, 2011.

[61] H. Jégou, M. Douze, and C. Schmid. Hamming embedding and weak geometric consistency for large scale image search. *Computer Vision–ECCV 2008*, pages 304–317, 2008.

[62]

[63] A. F. Smeaton, P. Over, and W. Kraaij. Evaluation campaigns and trecvid. In *International Workshop on Multimedia Information Retrieval (MIR)*, 2006.

[64] K. McGuinness, E. Mohedano, Z. Zhang, F. Hu, R. Albatal, C. Gurrin, N. O'Connor, A. Smeaton, A. Salvador, X. Giró-i Nieto, and C. Ventura. Insight centre for data analytics (DCU) at TRECVid 2014: instance search and semantic indexing tasks. In *2014 TREC Video Retrieval Evaluation Notebook Papers and Slides*, 2014.

[65] F. Perronnin, Y. Liu, J. Snchez, and H. Poirier. Large-scale image retrieval with compressed fisher vectors. In *2010 IEEE Computer Society Conference on Computer Vision and Pattern Recognition*, pages 3384–3391, June 2010.

[66] S. Lazebnik, C. Schmid, and J. Ponce. Beyond bags of features: Spatial pyramid matching for recognizing natural scene categories. In *Computer Vision and Pattern Recognition (CVPR)*, 2006.

[67] Y. Jia, E. Shelhamer, J. Donahue, S. Karayev, J. Long, R. Girshick, S. Guadarrama, and T. Darrell. Caffe: Convolutional architecture for fast feature embedding. In *Proceedings of*

the 22nd ACM international conference on Multimedia, pages 675–678. ACM, 2014.

[68] K. Simonyan and A. Zisserman. Very deep convolutional networks for large-scale image recognition. *arXiv preprint arXiv:1409.1556*, 2014.

[69] P. Turcot and D. Lowe. Better matching with fewer features: The selection of useful features in large database recognition problems. In *ICCV WS-LAVD workshop*, 2009.

164

Deep Learning for Image Processing Applications
D.J. Hemanth and V.V. Estrela (Eds.)
IOS Press, 2017
© 2017 The authors and IOS Press. All rights reserved.
doi:10.3233/978-1-61499-822-8-164

Hierarchical Object Detection with Deep Reinforcement Learning

Miriam Bellver Bueno[a], Xavier Giro-i-Nieto[b], Ferran Marques[b], and
Jordi Torres[a]

[a] Barcelona Supercomputing Center (BSC)
[b] Image Processing Group, Universitat Politècnica de Catalunya

Abstract. This work introduces a model for Hierarchical Object Detection
with Deep Reinforcement Learning (HOD-DRL). The key idea is to focus
on those parts of the image that contain richer information and zoom on
them. We train an intelligent agent that, given an image window, is capable of deciding where to focus the attention on five different predefined
region candidates (smaller windows). This procedure is iterated providing a hierarchical image analysis.We compare two different candidate
proposal strategies to guide the object search: with and without overlap.
Moreover, our work compares two different strategies to extract features
from a convolutional neural network for each region proposal: a first one
that computes new feature maps for each region proposal, and a second
one that computes the feature maps for the whole image to later generate
crops for each region proposal. Experiments indicate better results for
the overlapping candidate proposal strategy and a loss of performance
for the cropped image features due to the loss of spatial resolution. We
argue that, while this loss seems unavoidable when working with a large
number of object candidates, the much more reduced number of region
proposals generated by our reinforcement learning agent allows considering to extract features for each location without sharing convolutional
computation among regions. Source code and models are available at
https://imatge-upc.github.io/detection-2016-nipsws/.

Keywords. Information Storage and Retrieval, Content-based Analysis,
Image Indexing, Feature Representation, Convolutional Neural Networks,
Reinforcement Learning, Hierarchical Object Detection

1. Introduction

When we humans look at an image, we always perform a sequential extraction
of information in order to understand its content. First, we fix our gaze to the
most salient part of the image and, from the extracted information, we guide
our look towards another image point, until we have analyzed all its relevant
information. This is our natural and instinctive behavior to gather information
from our surroundings.

Traditionally in computer vision, images have been analyzed at the local
scale following a sliding window scanning, often at different scales. This approach
analyses the different image parts independently, without relating them. Just by

introducing a hierarchical representation of the image, we can more easily exploit the relationship between regions. We propose to use a top-down scanning which firstly takes a global view of the image to sequentially focus on the local parts that contain the relevant information (e.g. objects or faces).

Our algorithm is based on an intelligent agent trained by reinforcement learning that is capable of making decisions to detect an object in a still image, similarly to [2]. The agent first analyzes the whole image, and decides in which region of the image to focus on a set of predefined ones. Inspired by [13], our agent can top-down explore a set of five different predefined region candidates: four regions representing the four quadrants plus a central region. Two different strategies have been studied: proposing overlapping or non-overlapping candidates. The agent stops its search when it finds an object. Reinforcement learning is useful for our task because there is no single way of completing it. The agent can explore the hierarchical representation in different ways and still achieve its goal. Then, instead of programming every step that the agent should do, we train it so that it makes decisions under uncertainty to reach its target. Notice that the final goal of object detection is to define a bounding box around the object and that, in our work, these bounding boxes are limited to the predefined regions in the hierarchy.

Most state-of-the-art solutions for object detection analyze a large number of region proposals. These algorithms need to leverage the bottleneck of describing all these proposals by reusing convolutional feature maps of the whole image. In our work though, as the reinforcement learning agent and the hierarchy allow us to analyze a very reduced number of regions, we can feed each region visited by the agent through a convolutional network to extract its features. This allows us to work with region representations of higher spatial resolution, which are also more informative than those cropped from a feature map of the whole image. To study this trade-off, we have trained and compared two different models based on each of these two principles: the *Image-Zooms* model, which extracts descriptors at each region, and the *Pool45-Crops* model, which reuses feature maps for different regions of the same image.

This chapter proposes a novel framework following that line of reasoning and adding some improvements, called the Hierarchical Object Detection with Deep Reinforcement Learning (HOD-DRL) model. The first contribution of our work is the introduction of a hierarchical representation to top-down (zoom-in) guide our agent through the image. We explore how the design of the hierarchy affects the detection performance and the number of visited regions. The second contribution is the study of extracting features for each region instead of reusing feature maps for several locations. We show the gain of the region-specific features for our scheme, and argue that the computational overhead is minor thanks to the much-reduced number of regions considered by the agent.

This chapter is structure as follows. Section 2 reviews related background in the field of object detection, with special focus of hierarchical models and those trained with reinforcement learning. Section 3 presents our model for Hierarchical Object Detection with Deep Reinforcement Learning (HOD-DRL) and Section 4 presents the details of its training. Section 5 presents the experiments that estimate the performance of the model and compares the two considered architectures for feature extraction. Finally, Section 6 presents the conclusions of this work and proposes some future research lines.

2. Background

2.1. Reinforcement Learning

Reinforcement learning is a powerful tool that has been used in a wide range of applications. According to [10], reinforcement learning is "a way of programming agents by reward and punishment without needing to specify how the task is to be achieved". This agent is a decision-maker that interacts with the environment and learns through trial-and-error. In the hierarchical object detection task addressed in this chapter, the agent must learn how to find an object in the image by iteratively deciding among different zoom-in alternatives. This agent must learn based on the positive or negative feedback provided during training after all the zoom-in steps are taken.

Reinforcement learning based on deep neural networks gained attention after the impressive results from DeepMind [15], who trained an agent to play Atari 2600 video games by observing only their screen pixels, achieving even superhuman performance. Google Deepmind also trained a computer that won the Go competition to a professional player for the first time [22]. More specifically to traditional computer vision tasks, reinforcement learning has been applied to learn spatial glimpse policies for image classification [14,1], for captioning [26] or for activity recognition [27]. It has also been applied for object detection in images [2], casting a Markov Decision Process (MDP), as our approach does. MDPs are defined in Section 3.1.

2.2. Object Detection

The traditional solutions for object detection are based on region proposals, such as Selective Search [25], CPMC [3] or MCG [17], or other methods based on sliding windows such as EdgeBoxes [29], or hierarchical partitions such as BPTs [20,6]. The extraction of such proposals was independent of the classifier that would score and select which regions compose the final detection. These methods are computationally expensive because rely on a large amount of object proposals. Then the first trends based on Convolutional Neural Networks appeared, such as Fast R-CNN [7], that already studied how to share convolutional computation among locations, as they identified that the extraction of features for the hypothesized objects was the bottleneck for object detection.

More recent proposals such as Faster R-CNN [19,21] and Mask R-CNN [8] have achieved efficient and fast object detection by obtaining cost-free region proposals sharing full-image convolutional features with the detection network. Directly predicting bounding boxes from an image is a difficult task, and for this reason, approaches such as Faster R-CNN rely on a number of reference boxes called anchors, that facilitate the task of predicting accurate bounding boxes by regressing these initial reference boxes. One key of our approach is the refinement of bounding box predictions through the different actions selected by the reinforcement learning agent. Other solutions such as YoLo [18] or MultiBox [4] are also based on anchors. Another research direction is the refinement of predictions as AttentionNet [28], which casts an object detection problem as an iterative classification problem. AttentionNet predicts a number of weak directions pointing to the target object so that a final accurate bounding box is obtained. Similarly, the Single Shot MultiBox Detector (SSD) [12] works with a number of default boxes of different aspect ratios and scales per each feature map location, and adjusts them to better match to the object shape.

Another approach that supports this idea is the Active Object Localization method proposed by [2]. Their method trains an intelligent agent using deep reinforcement learning that is able to deform bounding boxes sequentially until they fit the target-bounding box. Each action that the agent does to the bounding box can change its aspect ratio, scale or position. Our main difference to this approach is that we add a fixed hierarchical representation that forces a top-down search, so that each action zooms onto the predicted region of interest.

A hierarchical path is also adopted in Tree-RL [9] to detect objects with the guidance of an agent trained with reinforcement learning. In their work they allow the agent to decide between zoom-in scaling actions or translations, which become crops at the output of a convolutional layer of a CNN. In our work we allow the agent to zoom in the selected region and show its benefits compared to models that work on crops of lower resolution.

How to benefit from super-resolution has also been studied by other works. In the paper of [13] a model is trained to determine if it is required to further divide the current observed region because there are still small objects on it, and in this case, each sub-region is analyzed independently. Their approach could also be seen as hierarchical, but in this case, they analyze each sub-region when the zoom prediction is positive, whereas we just analyze the sub-region selected by the reinforcement learning agent. On contrast to their proposal, we analyze fewer regions so we can afford the extraction of high-quality descriptors for each of them.

3. Hierarchical Object Detection Model (HODM)

This section presents our Hierarchical Object Detection Model (HODM) trained with reinforcement learning. We formulate the object detection problem as the sequential decision process of a goal-oriented agent interacting with a visual environment that is our image. At each time step, the agent should decide in which region of the image to focus its attention so that it can find objects in a few steps.

3.1. Markov Decision Process (MDP)

We cast the problem as a Markov Decision Process (MDP), that provides a framework to model decision-making when outcomes are partly uncertain. A MDP process is defined as a *state*, a set of possible *actions* and a *reward*.

State: The state is composed by the descriptor of the current region and a memory vector. The type of descriptor defines the two models we compare in our work: the *Image-Zooms* model and the *Pool45-Crops* model. These two variations are explained in detail in Section 3. The memory vector of the state captures the last 4 actions that the agent has already performed in the search for an object. As the agent is learning a refinement of a bounding box, a memory vector that encodes the state of this refinement procedure is useful to stabilize the search trajectories. We encode the past 4 actions in a one-shot vector. As there are 6 different actions presented in the following section, the memory vector has 24 dimensions. This type of memory vector was also used in [2].

Actions: There are two types of possible actions: *movement actions* that imply a change in the current observed region, and the *terminal* action to indicate that the object is found and that the search has ended. One particularity of our system is that each movement action can only transfer the attention top-down between regions from a predefined hierarchy. A hierarchy is built by defining five sub-regions over each observed bounding box: four quarters distributed as 2x2 over the box and a central overlapping region. We have explored two variations of this basic 2x2 scheme: a first one with *non-overlapped* quarters (see Figure 1), and a second one with *overlapped* quarters (see Figure 2), being the size of a sub-region 3/4 of its ancestor. Then, there are five movement actions, each one associated to one of the yellow regions. If, on the other hand, the terminal action is selected, there is no movement and the final region is the one marked with blue.

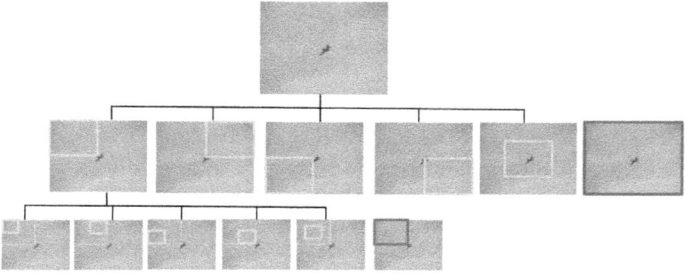

Figure 1. Image hierarchy of three levels with non-overlapped quarters

Reward: The reward functions used are the ones proposed by [2]. The reward function for the movement actions can be seen in Equation 1 and the reward function for the terminal action in Equation 2. Given a certain state s, a reward is given to those actions that move towards a region b' with a greater Intersection Over Union (IoU) with the ground truth g than the region b considered at the previous step. Otherwise, the actions are penalized. For the trigger action, the reward is positive if the Intersection Over Union of the actual region b with the ground truth is greater than a certain threshold τ, and negative otherwise. We consider $\tau = 0.5$, because it is the threshold for which a detection is considered positive, and η is 3, as in [2].

$$R_m(s, s') = sign(IoU(b', g) - IoU(b, g)) \qquad (1)$$

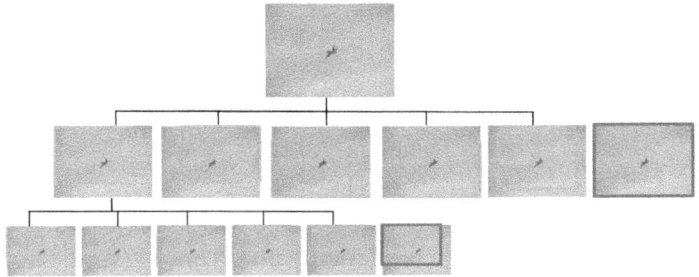

Figure 2. Image hierarchy of three levels with overlapped quarters

$$R_t(s, s') = \begin{cases} +\eta & if \ IoU(b, g) \geq \tau \\ -\eta & otherwise \end{cases} \tag{2}$$

3.2. Q-learning

The reward of the agent depending on the chosen action a at state s is governed by a function $Q(s,a)$, that can be estimated with Q-learning. Based on $Q(s,a)$, the agent will choose the action that is associated to the highest reward. Q-learning iteratively updates the action-selection policy using the Bellman equation 3, where s and a are the current state and action correspondingly, r is the immediate reward and $max_{a'}Q(s', a')$ represents the future reward. Finally, γ represents the discount factor. In our work, we approximate the Q-function by a Deep Q-network trained with Reinforcement Learning [15].

$$Q(s, a) = r + \gamma max_{a'}Q(s', a') \tag{3}$$

3.3. Visual Feature Extraction with Zoom or Crops

We study two variations of our **HOD-DRL** model depending on how the visual features are extracted, referred in the remaining of the chapter as *Image-Zooms* and *Pool45-Crops*. Figure 3 depicts the two variations with the common reinforcement learning network.

We compare two models to extract the visual features that define the state of our agent: the *Image-Zooms* model and the *Pool45-Crops* model. For the *Image-Zooms* model, each region is resized to 224x224 and its visual descriptors correspond to the feature maps from Pool5 layer of VGG-16 [23]. For the *Pool45-Crops* model, the image at full-resolution is forwarded into VGG-16 [23] through Pool5 layer. As [7], we reuse the feature maps extracted from the whole image for all the regions of interest (ROI) by pooling them (ROI pooling). As in SSD [12], we choose which feature map to use depending on the scale of the region of interest. In our case, we only work with the Pool4 and Pool5 layers, that are the two last pooling layers from VGG-16. Once we have a certain region of interest from the hierarchy, we decide which feature map to use by comparing the scale of the ROI and the scale of the feature map. For large objects, the algorithm will select the deeper feature map, whereas for smaller objects a shallower feature map is more adequate.

The two models for feature extraction result into a feature map of 7x7 which is fed to the common block of the architecture. The region descriptor and the memory vector are the input of the Deep Q-network that consists of two fully connected layers of 1024 neurons each. Each fully connected layer is followed by a ReLU [16] activation function and is trained with dropout [24]. Finally, the output layer corresponds to the possible actions of the agent, six in our case.

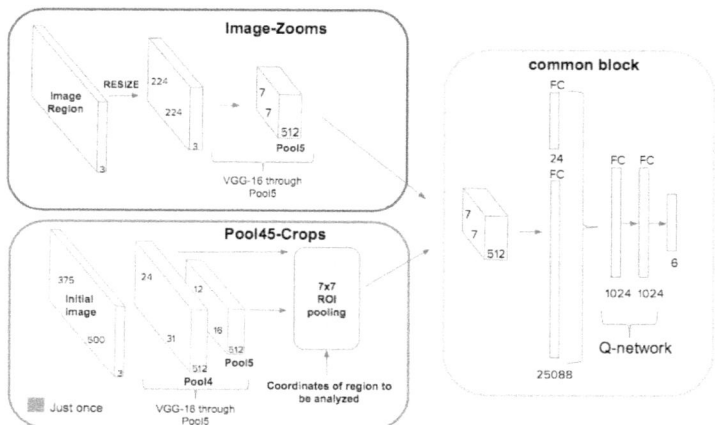

Figure 3. Architecture of our HOD-DRL model in its two varations for feature extraction: Image-Zooms (upper branch) and Pool45-Crops (lower branch).

4. Training the Q-network

This section introduces the training details of the Q-network, which corresponds to the deeper layers of our HOD-DRL model, as shown in Figure 3. This is the only trained part of our model, as convolutional layers are used off-the-shelf from the VGG-16 model.

.

Exploration-Exploitation: To train the deep Q-network with reinforcement learning we use an ϵ-greedy policy, that starts with $\epsilon=1$ and decreases until $\epsilon=0.1$ in steps of 0.1. Then, we start with random actions, and at each epoch the agent takes decisions relying more on the already learnt policy. Actually, in order to help the agent to learn the terminal action, which in random could be difficult to learn, we force it each time the current region has an IoU ¿ 0.5. With this approach, we can accelerate the training. Notice that we always do exploration, so we do not get stuck into a local minimum.

Learning Trajectories: One fact that we detected while training was that we should not impose which object of the image to look first. At each time step, the agent will focus on the object in the current region with the highest overlap with its ground-truth. This way, it is possible then that the target object changes during the top-down exploration.

Training Parameters: The weights for the Deep Q-network were initialized from a normal distribution. For learning, we used Adam optimizer [11] with a learning rate of 1e-6 to avoid that the gradients explode. We trained each model for 50 epochs.

Experience Replay: As we have seen previously, Bellman Equation 3 learns from transitions formed by *(s, a, r, s')*, which can also be called experiences. Consecutive experiences in our algorithm are very correlated and this could lead to inefficient and unstable learning, a traditional problem in Q-learning. One solution to make the algorithm converge is collecting experiences and storing them in a replay memory. Random minibatches from this replay memory are used to train the network. We used an experience replay of 1,000 experiences and a batch size of 100.

Discount Factor: To perform well in the long run, the future rewards should also be taken into account and not only the immediate ones. To do this, we use the discounted reward from Bellman Equation 3 with a value of $\gamma = 0.90$. We set the gamma high because we are interested in balancing the immediate and future rewards.

5. Experiments

Our experiments on object detection have used images and annotations from the PASCAL VOC dataset [5]. We trained our system on the trainval sets of 2007 and 2012, and tested it on the test set of 2007. We performed all the experiments for just one class, the *airplane* category, and only considering pictures with the target class category. This experiment allows us to study the behavior of our agent and estimate the amount of regions that must be analyzed to detect an object.

5.1. Qualitative results

We present some qualitative results in Figure 4 to show how our agent behaves on test images. These results are obtained with the *Image-Zooms* model with overlapped regions, as this is the one that yields best results, as argued in the following sections. We observed that for most images, the model successfully zooms towards the object and completes the task in a few steps. As seen in the second, third and fourth rows, with just two or three steps, the agent selects the bounding box around the object. The agent also performs accurately when there are small instances of objects, as seen in the first and last rows.

5.2. Precision-Recall Curves:

We will analyze the precision and recall curves for different trained models, considering that an object is correctly detected when the Intersection over Union (IoU) of its bounding box compared to the ground truth is over 0.5, as defined by the Pascal VOC challenge [5].

The Precision-Recall curves are generated by ranking all regions analyzed by the agent. The sorting is based on the reward estimated by the sixth neuron of the Q-network, which corresponds to the action of considering the region as terminal.

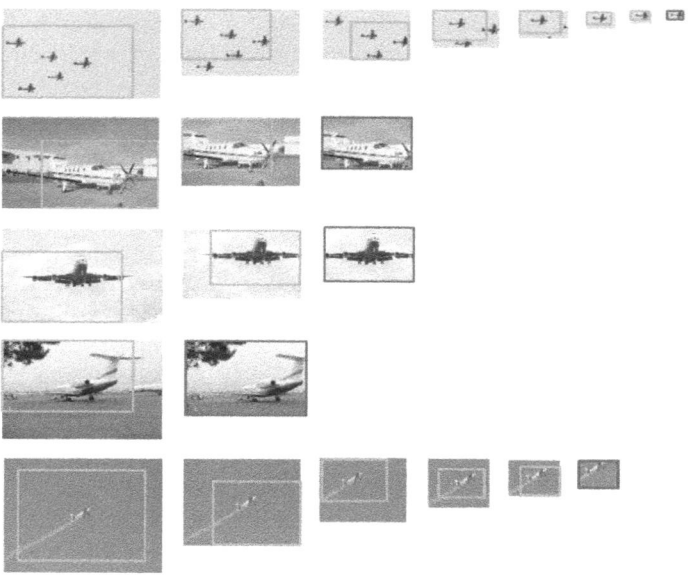

Figure 4. Visualizations of searches for objects

Upper Bound and Random Baselines: Our results firstly include baseline and upper bound references for a better analysis. As a baseline we have programmed an agent that chooses random actions and detection scores at each time step. As an upper bound, we have exploited the ground truth annotations to manually guide our agent towards the region with the greatest IoU. The result of these random baselines and upper bounds for hierarchy type can be seen in Figure 5. It is also important to notice that the best upper-bound option does not even achieve a recall of 0.5. This poor performance is because more than half of the ground truth objects do not fit with the considered region proposals, so they cannot be detected in our framework.

Overlapped and Non-overlapped Regions: The results obtained with the upper bound and baseline methods provide enough information to compare the overlapped and non-overlapped schemes. The overlapped regions scheme is the one that provides higher precision and recall values, both for the upper bound and the random models. This superiority of the overlapped case can be explained by the slower reduction of spatial scale with respect to the non-overlapped model: as bounding box regions are larger due to the overlap, their division in equal-size sub-regions also generate larger sub-regions. This also implies that the agent will require more steps to reach a lower resolution, but this finer top-down exploration is shown as beneficial in our experiments as the chances of missing an object during the descent are also lower.

Model Comparison: The *Image-Zooms* model and the *Pool45-Crops* model are compared in Figure 6. Results clearly indicate that the *Image-Zooms* model performs better than the *Pool45-Crops* model. We hypothesize that this loss of performance is due to the loss of resolution resulting from the ROI-pooling

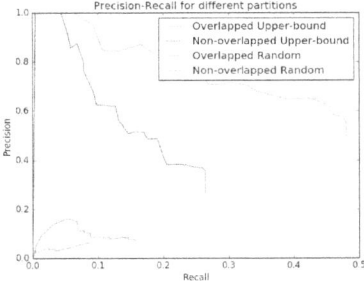

Figure 5. Baselines and upper-bounds

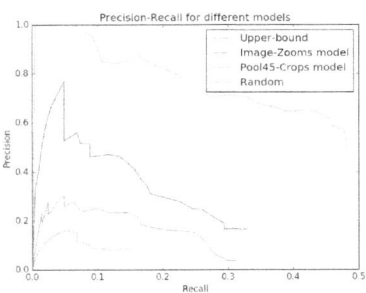

Figure 6. Comparison of the two models

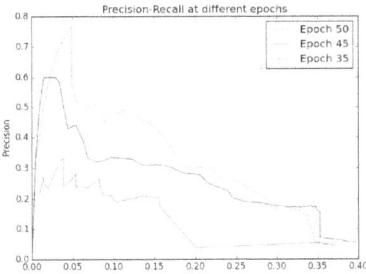

Figure 7. Image-Zooms at different epochs

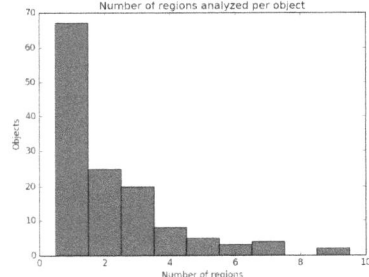

Figure 8. Regions analyzed per object

over Pool4 or Pool5 layers. While in the *Image-Zooms* model the 7x7 feature maps of Pool5 have been computed directly from a zoom over the image, in the *Pool45-Crops* model the region crops over Pool4 or Pool5 could be smaller than 7x7. While these cases would be upsampled to the 7x7x512 input tensor to the deep Q-Net, the source feature maps of the region would be of lower resolution than their counterparts in the *Image-Zoom* model.

Models at Different Epochs: We study the training of our *Image-Zooms* model by plotting the Precision-Recall curves at different epochs in Figure 7. As expected, we observe how the performance of the model improves with the epochs.

5.3. Number of regions analyzed per object

A histogram of the number of regions analyzed by our agent is shown in 8. We observe that the most part of objects are already found with a single step, which means that the object occupies the major part of the image. With less than 3 steps we can almost approximate all objects we can detect.

6. Conclusions

This paper has presented our HOD-DRL model as a deep reinforcement learning solution for object detection. Our solution is characterized by a top-down exploration of a hierarchy of regions guided by an intelligent agent. Adopting a coarse-to-fine analysis of the image provides a scalable approach for an object localization task, by starting from a global view of the image to later focusing in those candidate regions to contain an object. In contrast to most state-of-the art solutions that consider a large amount of object proposals which are filtered in a second stage, we propose to directly generate high quality candidates.

The precomputed hierarchical decomposition of the image reduces the complexity of the agent, as the movement actions can only choose between five zoom-in alternatives. Our experiments indicate that objects can be detected with very few proposals from an appropriate hierarchy, However, this light-weighted approach presents the limitation in terms of recall, as the agent is not free to adapt the boundaries of the available bounding boxes to the image contents. A possible solution to this problem would be refining the approximate detections provided by the agent with a regressor, as in [19].

Finally, our results indicate the limitations of cropping region features from the convolutional layers, especially when considering small objects. We suggest that, given the much smaller amount of region proposals considered by our reinforcement learning agent, feeding each region through the network is a solution that should be also considered.

The presented work is publicly available for reproducibility and extension at https://imatge-upc.github.io/detection-2016-nipsws/.

Acknowledgments

This work has been developed in the framework of the project BigGraph TEC2013-43935-R, funded by the Spanish Ministerio de Economia y Competitividad and the European Regional Development Fund (ERDF). This work has been supported by the grant SEV2015-0493 of the Severo Ochoa Program awarded by Spanish Government, project TIN2015-65316 by the Spanish Ministry of Science and Innovation contracts 2014-SGR-1051 by Generalitat de Catalunya. The Image Processing Group at the UPC is a SGR14 Consolidated Research Group recognized and sponsored by the Catalan Government (Generalitat de Catalunya) through its AGAUR office. We gratefully acknowledge the support of NVIDIA Corporation with the donation of the GeForce GTX Titan Z used in this work and the support of BSC/UPC NVIDIA GPU Center of Excellence. We also want to thank all the members of the X-theses group for their advice.

References

[1]   J. Ba, V. Mnih, and K. Kavukcuoglu. Multiple object recognition with visual attention. *arXiv preprint arXiv:1412.7755*, 2014.
[2]   J. C. Caicedo and S. Lazebnik. Active object localization with deep reinforcement learning. In *Proceedings of the IEEE International Conference on Computer Vision*, pages 2488–2496, 2015.
[3]   J. Carreira and C. Sminchisescu. Cpmc: Automatic object segmentation using constrained parametric min-cuts. *Pattern Analysis and Machine Intelligence, IEEE Transactions on*, 34(7):1312–1328, 2012.

[4]   D. Erhan, C. Szegedy, A. Toshev, and D. Anguelov. Scalable object detection using deep neural networks. In *Proceedings of the IEEE Conference on Computer Vision and Pattern Recognition*, pages 2147–2154, 2014.

[5]   M. Everingham, L. Van Gool, C. K. Williams, J. Winn, and A. Zisserman. The pascal visual object classes (voc) challenge. *International journal of computer vision*, 88(2):303–338, 2010.

[6]   X. Giro and F. Marques. Detection of semantic objects using description graphs. In *Image Processing, 2005. ICIP 2005. IEEE International Conference on*, volume 1, pages I–1201. IEEE, 2005.

[7]   R. Girshick. Fast r-cnn. In *Proceedings of the IEEE International Conference on Computer Vision*, pages 1440–1448, 2015.

[8]   K. He, G. Gkioxari, P. Dollár, and R. Girshick.   Mask r-cnn.   *arXiv preprint arXiv:1703.06870*, 2017.

[9]   Z. Jie, X. Liang, J. Feng, X. Jin, W. Lu, and S. Yan. Tree-structured reinforcement learning for sequential object localization. In *Advances in Neural Information Processing Systems*, pages 127–135, 2016.

[10]   L. P. Kaelbling, M. L. Littman, and A. W. Moore. Reinforcement learning: A survey. *Journal of artificial intelligence research*, 4:237–285, 1996.

[11]   D. Kingma and J. Ba. Adam: A method for stochastic optimization. *arXiv preprint arXiv:1412.6980*, 2014.

[12]   W. Liu, D. Anguelov, D. Erhan, C. Szegedy, S. Reed, C.-Y. Fu, and A. C. Berg. Ssd: Single shot multibox detector. In *European conference on computer vision*, pages 21–37. Springer, 2016.

[13]   Y. Lu, T. Javidi, and S. Lazebnik. Adaptive object detection using adjacency and zoom prediction. In *Proceedings of the IEEE Conference on Computer Vision and Pattern Recognition*, pages 2351–2359, 2016.

[14]   V. Mnih, N. Heess, A. Graves, et al. Recurrent models of visual attention. In *Advances in Neural Information Processing Systems*, pages 2204–2212, 2014.

[15]   V. Mnih, K. Kavukcuoglu, D. Silver, A. A. Rusu, J. Veness, M. G. Bellemare, A. Graves, M. Riedmiller, A. K. Fidjeland, G. Ostrovski, et al. Human-level control through deep reinforcement learning. *Nature*, 518(7540):529–533, 2015.

[16]   V. Nair and G. E. Hinton. Rectified linear units improve restricted boltzmann machines. In *Proceedings of the 27th International Conference on Machine Learning (ICML-10)*, pages 807–814, 2010.

[17]   J. Pont-Tuset, P. Arbeláez, J. T. Barron, F. Marques, and J. Malik. Multiscale combinatorial grouping for image segmentation and object proposal generation. *IEEE Transactions on Pattern Analysis and Machine Intelligence (TPAMI)*, 2016.

[18]   J. Redmon, S. Divvala, R. Girshick, and A. Farhadi. You only look once: Unified, real-time object detection. *arXiv preprint arXiv:1506.02640*, 2015.

[19]   S. Ren, K. He, R. Girshick, and J. Sun. Faster r-cnn: Towards real-time object detection with region proposal networks. In *Advances in neural information processing systems*, pages 91–99, 2015.

[20]   P. Salembier and L. Garrido.   Binary partition tree as an efficient representation for image processing, segmentation, and information retrieval. *IEEE transactions on Image Processing*, 9(4):561–576, 2000.

[21]   A. Salvador, X. Giró-i Nieto, F. Marqués, and S. Satoh. Faster r-cnn features for instance search. In *Proceedings of the IEEE Conference on Computer Vision and Pattern Recognition Workshops*, pages 9–16, 2016.

[22]   D. Silver, A. Huang, C. J. Maddison, A. Guez, L. Sifre, G. Van Den Driessche, J. Schrittwieser, I. Antonoglou, V. Panneershelvam, M. Lanctot, et al. Mastering the game of go with deep neural networks and tree search. *Nature*, 529(7587):484–489, 2016.

[23]   K. Simonyan and A. Zisserman. Very deep convolutional networks for large-scale image recognition. *CoRR*, abs/1409.1556, 2014.

[24]   N. Srivastava, G. E. Hinton, A. Krizhevsky, I. Sutskever, and R. Salakhutdinov. Dropout: a simple way to prevent neural networks from overfitting. *Journal of Machine Learning Research*, 15(1):1929–1958, 2014.

[25]   K. E. Van de Sande, J. R. Uijlings, T. Gevers, and A. W. Smeulders. Segmentation as selective search for object recognition. In *2011 International Conference on Computer Vision*, pages 1879–1886. IEEE, 2011.

[26] K. Xu, J. Ba, R. Kiros, K. Cho, A. Courville, R. Salakhudinov, R. Zemel, and Y. Bengio. Show, attend and tell: Neural image caption generation with visual attention. In *International Conference on Machine Learning*, pages 2048–2057, 2015.

[27] S. Yeung, O. Russakovsky, G. Mori, and L. Fei-Fei. End-to-end learning of action detection from frame glimpses in videos. In *Proceedings of the IEEE Conference on Computer Vision and Pattern Recognition*, pages 2678–2687, 2016.

[28] D. Yoo, S. Park, J.-Y. Lee, A. S. Paek, and I. So Kweon. Attentionnet: Aggregating weak directions for accurate object detection. In *Proceedings of the IEEE International Conference on Computer Vision*, pages 2659–2667, 2015.

[29] C. L. Zitnick and P. Dollár. Edge boxes: Locating object proposals from edges. In *European Conference on Computer Vision*, pages 391–405. Springer, 2014.

Deep Learning for Image Processing Applications
D.J. Hemanth and V.V. Estrela (Eds.)
IOS Press, 2017
doi:10.3233/978-1-61499-822-8-177

Big Data & Deep Data: Minding the Challenges

DR. MADHULIKA BHATIA[a,1] , DR. MAMTA MITTAL [b,2] , MADHURIMA[c,3]

[a] *Manav Rachna International University, Haryana*
[b] *G.B Panth Engineering college, Delhi,*
[c] *Amity University, Noida*

Abstract. Now a day's big data is an important topic in corporate as well as in academics. The root of big data is the ability to study and analyze large sections of information to search for patterns and finding the trends. The root of big data is analytics, After applying the analytics in will lead to many findings that were undiscovered before. Big data simply take existing data and looks into a different way. Deep data on the other hand gathered data on daily basis and lined it with experts of industry. The main role of deep data is to section down the massive amount of data in Exabyte's or perabytes exclude the information that is duplicate or use less. But there are many challenges in switching the current scenario from Big data to Deep data. We have many machine learning approaches that can be applied to Big data. Deep learning is one of those machine learning approaches. But there are many challenges that are to be addressed. The objective is to discuss the various challenges in analyzing Big data as well as Deep data using Deep learning.

Keywords. Deep learning, Big data, challenges, Deep data analytics

1. Introduction

Enormous information in the form of big data has turned into an essential topic for each industry. The capacity to contemplate and dissect substantial areas of data to discover new trends and patterns in medicine, business and everything in the middle of it. Application of analytics in your business can prompt to advancement and revelations that we won't see generally.

Big data is not a new word but it simply takes available data and exploring it in a different way. The traditional business tools are unable to manage and process Big Data' because it refer to a large set of data. On the other hand Deep data is the real tool that we can use to change the data .

2. What is Big Data and Big Data analytics?

Big data is an concoction of all of the data collected by a business. The data can be names of clients, contact information or routine data etc. Predictive analysis can be applied to find out patterns and trends to abstract the useless and redundant information.

---

[1] Corresponding Author.

The massive amount of data is pares down into useful section of information excluding redundant information .It's a collection of massive and complex data sets that when it is difficult to capture, analyze, store and search using traditional data base system. Figure 1 below shows the place of big data in various contexts.

The use of advanced analytic techniques for very large, diverse data sets that include various varieties such as structured or unstructured and different sizes from terabytes to zettabytes. The term Big data coined to show data sets whose size or type is beyond the handling by traditional relational databases to capture, manage, and process the data with low-latency. And it has one or more of the following characteristics – high volume, high velocity, or high variety. Big data comes from data generated in a huge amount from sensors, devices, video/audio, networks, log files, transactional applications, web, and social media generated in real time and in a very large scale.

Analyzing big data allows analysts, researchers, and business users to make better and faster decisions using data that was previously inaccessible or unusable. Using advanced analytics techniques such as text analytics, machine learning, predictive analytics, data mining, statistics, and natural language processing, businesses can analyze previously untapped data sources independent or together with their existing enterprise data to gain new insights resulting in significantly better and faster decisions. Fig 1 shows Big data in various context.

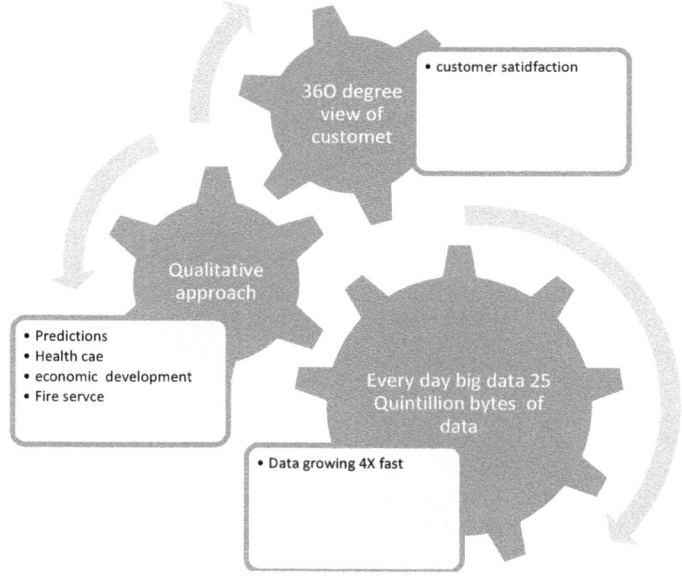

Fig 1: Big data in various context

2.1. What's the Difference--Deep Data?

Big data and deep data are inherently similar both use mass of information that can be collected on daily basis. Industry can pair this with data with analytics and use in prediction to help in prediction of trends or changes. Useful Trends can find out on this mass of data using techniques of big data, but deep data on the other side focus on specific information and predict trends.

For example If we want to predict which clothing style are going to sell the best during the next calendar year. Then we wouldn't necessarily be looking at customer's especially if it's an online selling. Deep data instead, focus on data like sales numbers and information of product to make predictions. This is how deep data works.

If we apply Deep data analysis to medicine and many fields as well. Deep data focus on one particular demographic features such as age, weight, gender or race, can help searching of trail participant in a more streamlined way and accuracy can be increased for treatment or drug trials.

Learning Deep data rapidly popular field that involve in modeling of complex patterns as multilayered networks. The challenges in machine learning and artificial intelligence are best solved by Deep learning. Areas like recognizing images, text analytics, recognizing speech companies like Microsoft and Google use deep learning to find out solutions in such areas. The model constructed by deep learning require sufficient computing power.

3. What is Big Data and Big Data analytics?

Choice of Big data or Deep data for any business need depends upon the kind of business running and what is the type of data we are collecting. Deep data is a best option when you are observant for specific trends or focusing individual pieces of information. Deep data let you allow to eliminate vain or unessential pieces of data while retaining the foremost information that will benefit company.

Big data and deep data are necessity not an option they both are very useful techniques for any type of business.

4. Data Science, Deep Data, Big data, Data analytics: Comparison

Table 1. Table shows the comparison between Data Science , Deep Data , Big data, Data analytics: Comparison on parameters.

	Data science	Deep Data	Big data	Data Analytics
What ?	Comprises of everything related to data, cleansing, preparation, analysis	Deep data takes out massive amount of information into useful sections, excluding redundant information.	Used for analysis and better decision	Understanding of data set with combination of queries and procedures.

Use?	Searching on internet. Advertising digitally Recommendation system Recognition of speech and images Planning of air line routes Gaming Price comparison websites Delivery logistic	For finding individual and specific trends. Semantic indexing Image and video tagging	Financial service Retailing communication Netflix recommendation system Doctor performance Weather	Uncovering hidden patterns Fast and efficient in most business intelligence solution Control of health information Help business increases revenue improve operational efficiency, optimize marketing campaigns and customer service efforts

5. Shift Big to Deep Data: The change

Behavior of today's customers changed a lot as compared to customer of fifteen years back. The thought process is totally different. If they are getting standardized

services and solutions that matched those of their neighbors, but now they expect products and services that best fit their individual needs and interests. For example phone service delivery and application delivery as same service to everyone which fits best in one's lifestyle.

Presence of big data is increasing day by day and each business making themselves more and more equipped to handle abundance of data about their information on customers. There is some value embed in this volume of data, there is need of adding meaning full value to the customer. Here Comes Deep Data. Realization of that particular business value big data move beyond that, things needs change here. Companies move towards a framework called the "Deep Data" framework. It's an approach that says data streams rich in information rich information can retrieve more value then data streams small number of information-rich data.

Shifting of approach from big to deep made business are better able to understand their clients. In many sectors, technology driven by deep data is helping better engaging consumers. There is a need of data centric view at every level of organization. From the organizational perspective, companies must start to internalize and adopt a data-centric view at every level of the organization.

A data company incorporate three important elements business specific knowledge. computational skills and infrastructure. To build models of consumer behavior companies should leverage deep expertise to abstract specific insights related to consumer behavior.

Deep data is impassive to change the way organization engage their customers. Regardless of industry, deep data is poised to disrupt the way organizations engage customers. The companies which are embracing deep data models gain success in sales and customer engagement. Those that were unable to incorporate deep data model are and far away from analytics are fail to meet the customer satisfaction and consumer demand.

6. Here Comes Deep Data: The origin

There are things that need to be changed. From 2015 , companies moved towards framework of deep data that state that data streams that are rich in information can retrieve more value then mass of data. When a company shifts towards deep data big data businesses are able to better understand their customers and offer actionable, scalable and customized insights while crucially enhancing the value of the economic investment in data to their businesses.

In the energy sector, deep data-driven technology is helping utilities better engage consumers and benefit from trusted customer relationships in the face of new energy choices, like solar, microgrids and retail energy providers. As consumers become "prosumers" who create new energy options – often at their own sites, utilities must find new, innovative ways to deliver value to customers who want the most cost-effective, energy efficient options. The below figure 2 shows the origin of Deep Data:

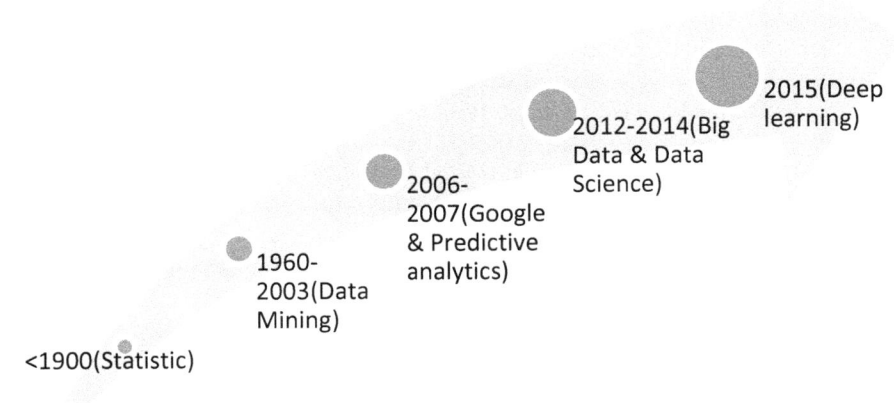

Fig 2: Origin of Deep Data

7. Achieving Data Regularization: Steps to success

There exist a need of data gain access accurately in real time to produce positive returns on our decision-making. Sales people need real time data about customers before their consumer meetings, marketers need real time data to create targeted campaigns, plus our professionals need easily digestible data in order to make business decisions in real time--especially when on the go.

The trend is known as data democratization or regularization allowing access to data to everyone who needs it, for purpose they need it, and in the required form. The result of data democratization is in increase in overall impact of company on difference in the revenue growth, increased retention in customer, and efficiency. If data regularization is done it can be as a key differentiator for your company.

The regularization of data can prove a dramatic change for our company, Below are the steps to achieve that:

1. How is companies data-driven decisions will become SOP for end users and for client processes.

2. Data needs to be abundant throughout your company and use of that data should be simple and automated.

3. The use of tools should prove that how these tools are useful for embedded analytics, mobile view of data and workflow integration and enhanced visualizations for our organization.

4. Data presented should have capability to influence the end user to consume that data effectively. The influence of end user only make effective utilization of tools otherwise it is wastage of money and time of company.

5. Presentation of information extracted from data should be in such a way that the volume feature of data become insignificant.

6. In work flow process only the most abstracted form of information should be distributed.

7. The user significance curve is of great importance. The company should give self-service data preparation, data integration, and data enrichment.

8. Regularization or democratization and Business intelligence tool adoption is improved when we consider profiles of users , about what they expect from their data.

8. Overcoming challenges

Every organization can appreciate the promise of accessing data easily. But the problem is to access the right tool. According to a recent study done, almost seventy percent of the companies failed to use analytics tool properly for data regularization and seventy percent of the companies percent willing to increase their budget for analytics in order to use better analytics tools. Figure 3 shows some open challenges between Big Data and Deep Data.

Fig 3: Challenges between Big Data and Deep Data.

The adoption of advance analytic tools made companies to get much better business intelligence which will in turn increase transparency which aids fast decision making. Below Table 2 mention some of the challenges and solution:

Table 2: challenges and solution

Challenges	Solution
Predictive capabilities for faster decisions	App
Extract, transform, or load for data migration	CRM tool
Data enrichment , data visualization or report creation,	Self-service BI tools.

9. Applications of Deep Learning in Big Data analytics

Algorithms implementing deep learning retrieve abstract representations of raw data through multilevel learning approach. Data is available in large amount and deep learning can be applied to labeled data for learning. Learning can also be done from unsupervised from unlabelled data to retrieve meaningful pattern.

10. Global relationship and data patterns are also retrieved from deep learning

Linear models retrieval can also be obtained from complex data representations and can be successfully applied to text, video etc. Abstraction of raw data can lead to relational and semantic data. Deep learning architecture are more suitable to address the issues and problems of veracity, variety , volume, velocity as shown in Fig below:

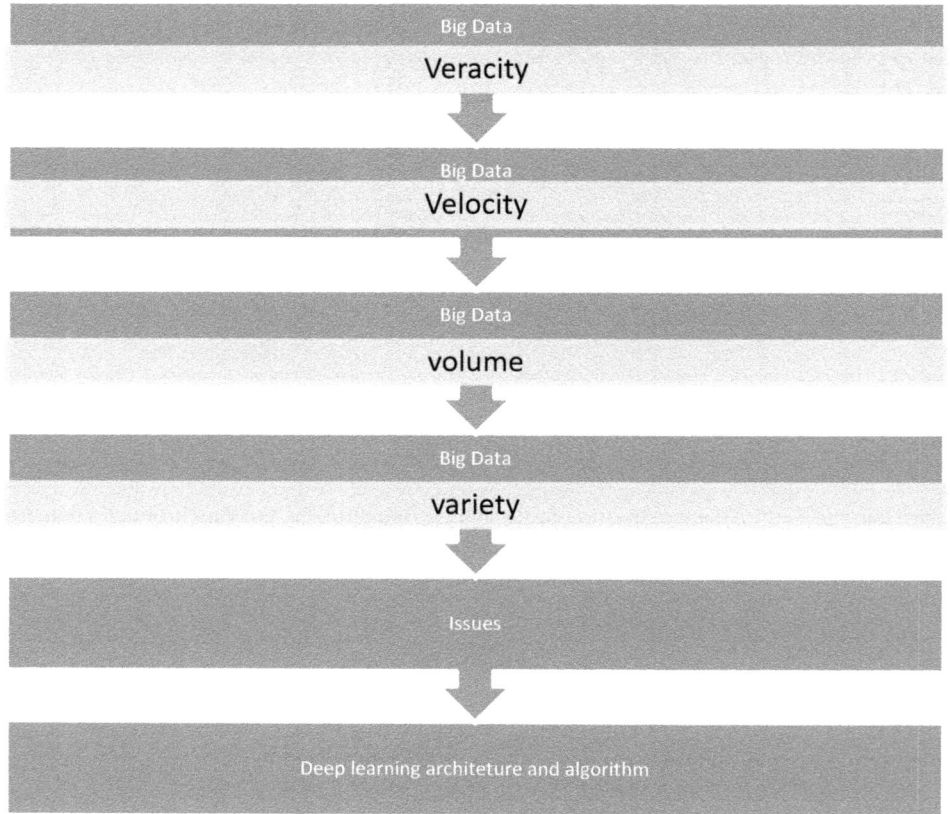

Fig 4 Veracity, Velocity, volume and variety

Some algorithm have shallow learning hierarchies which are not capable of understanding high data patterns complexities. The most important feature of deep learning is to deals with data abstraction and representations so it is best suited for analyzing raw data in different formats and from different sources. While presenting different challenges for more conventional data analysis approaches, Big Data Analytics presents an important opportunity for developing novel algorithms and models to address specific issues related to Big Data.

 Deep Learning concepts provide one such solution venue for data analytics experts and practitioners. For example, the extracted representations by Deep Learning can be considered as a practical source of knowledge for decision-making, semantic indexing, information retrieval, and for other purposes in Big Data Analytics, and in addition, simple linear modeling techniques can be considered for Big Data Analytics when complex data is represented in higher forms of abstraction.

In the remainder of this section, we summarize some important works that have been performed in the field of Deep Learning algorithms and architectures, including semantic indexing, social tagging. Our focus is that by presenting these works in Deep Learning, experts can observe the novel applicability of Deep Learning techniques in Big Data Analytics, particularly since some of the application domains in the works presented involve large scale data. Deep Learning algorithms are applicable to different kinds of input data; however, in this section we focus on its application on image, textual, and audio data.

11. Deep learning and Big Data: Relation & Application

There are lot of enormous amount of domain specific information collected by public and private organizations and these information are used for solving problems in marketing, technology, medical science, national intelligence, fraud detection. The process of data acquire is really complex and crucial because the data is unlabeled, uncategorized and immensely complex in handling and analyzing. But deep learning algorithm is very much use in analysis of such huge volume of data which is unsupervised. Handling of data with deep learning algorithms continuously improve the data and making the tools very much useful for analysis of big data. Deep learning is adapted for handling enormous amounts of data, thus very much capable of addressing the *volume* factor. The deep learning algorithm addresses variety factor by analysis of raw data from variety of formats and sources. Thus it offers unique solutions to complex problems.

12. Semantic Indexing

Face book, twitter and many social media sites, shopping portals, traffic monitoring, security systems, etc. yield information in the form of text, video, audio, and image. These information extracted by many social media sites, shopping portals, traffic monitoring, security systems are not only in high volumes but they also have different formats also. Such data, therefore, can't be stored as data bit strings.

Its deep learning that make storage efficient and data retrieval easily. Before deep learning use of raw data was done for data indexing but now with the emergence of deep data algorithms there is use of high level abstract data representations for semantic indexing. This representation of semantic indexing by deep learning make search engines working quickly and efficiently. The semantic indexing approach of deep learning to represents the data in a way that makes data very much useful source for discovery of knowledge and understanding. Figure 5 shows the process of semantic indexing.

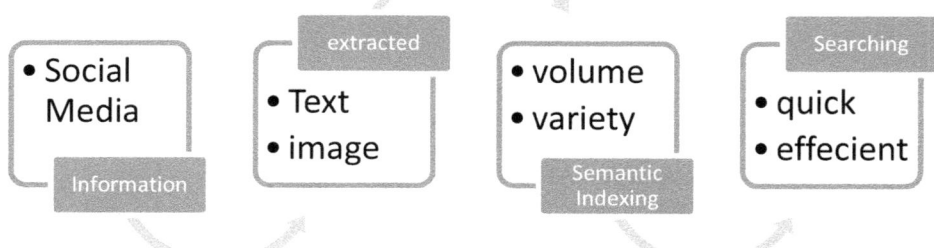

Fig 5: Semantic Indexing

The quick and efficient searching of images, audios, voices is the purpose of big data so as to increase their accessibility in a quicker and more efficient fashion. Extraction of nonlinear features from variety of data is obtained by applying complex deep learning algorithm to big data. Application of non linearity makes deep learning more closer to artificial intelligence.

This way, data analysts benefit from the vast reserves of knowledge in the pool of big data. On the other hand, by enabling the application of simple linear analytics, deep learning offers computational efficiency.

13. Semantic Tagging

There are lot of users daily connected with internet and the rise of digital content has been exponential. There are multiple sources from where images and videos are being uploaded. The repositories of images are massive, For searching of images there should be improvement in image searches, the browsing process and retrieval should be light and fast. There is requirement of tagging of images and videos with automation. With the help of deep learning these images , text, audio, video can be represented in complex form and can take form of high level of abstraction. Then this representation can be used for tagging of images and is much benefited for huge data. Figure 6 below shows the process of semantic tagging.

Fig 6: Semantic tagging

14. Social Targeting

There are capabilities in deep learning that holds the potential to guess the unstated emotions and events in a text. It can identify objects in photos. It can also make knowledgeable predictions about people's likely future behavior. All these features make it a hot property in the fields of intelligence, sales, marketing, and advertising. No wonder then that Face book has set up an internal team to reap the benefits of deep learning in their work.

Social media and many platforms are generating data, Companies are mining those data to extract meaning. With the use of deep learning approach social targeting can be more specific than traditional style.

With deep learning the analysis of target audience is on the basis of pattern collection of followers , instead of doing analysis of some percentage of people, analysis is done on all audience. Deep learning models coming out are more correct as compare to others.

15. Does Deep Learning apply to my business?

When deep learning should be adopted in business organization. Below figure7 shows the situations where deep learning should be adopted:

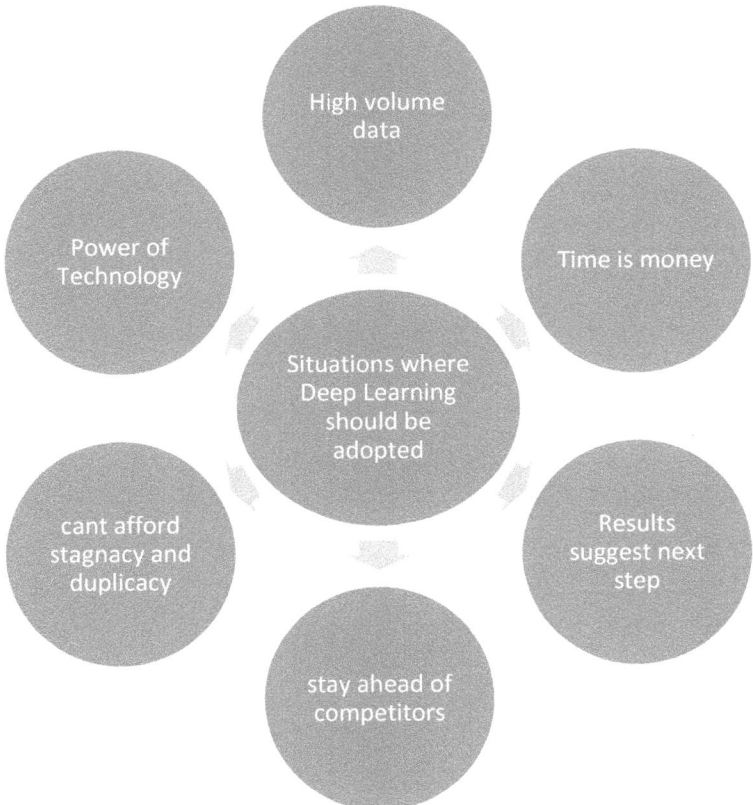

Figure 7. Situations where deep learning should be adopted

16. Tools Insight: Tools for analytics

Table 3: Tool for Big Data & Deep Data

Big Data Tools	
Hadoop	Hadoop is an open-source software for storing large datasets of distributed on . clusters. Scaling up and scaling down of infrastructure is not an issue. Any kind and size of data can be stored with Hadoop with high processing power and Hadoop can virtual task concurrently.
Cloudera	It's an enterprise solution provide better access to data. It also provide security for sensitive data.
MangoDB	It's an alternative to relational database management system. mangoDB is a good option for semi structure, unstructured and dynamic data.
Talend	It's an open source tool. Maintenance of data base is a complex task for companies. It allow you to maintain your own database on Talend.
OpenRefine	It's an open source tool that helps in cleaning of unstructured data.
DataCleaner	Provide data warehouse and data management service. It converts unstructured data to readable form.
Deep Data tools	
multiBamSummary	Its tool used for data integration
PlotProfile	Tools used for data visualization
PlotHeatmap	Tools for data visualization

17. Big Data with Data Science

Now a days there is a need of assessing the information more significantly. Data science helps analyst to assess the information more significantly and helps to take decisions more intelligently. In decision making process big data along with data science provided much stronger platform. The measurement of information now can be done in a massive amount as well with remarkable precision. This helps analyst to find more tuned solution and help full in making decision making process.

The Buzz of Big data is becoming popular in thinking long term, decision making and in beliefs. Big data is used as management tool and gained insight from almost all industry leaders.

The cost of buying computing and organizing data has been decreased from last few years and there is sudden rise in adopting Big Data tools. There are variety of data types and data exist and organization are still in process of thinking how to deal with this change. The advance technology devices yielding enormous amount of data but the data science and Big Data helping them to take our most significant useful information. Below Figure 8 shows concepts related to Big Data and Data science.

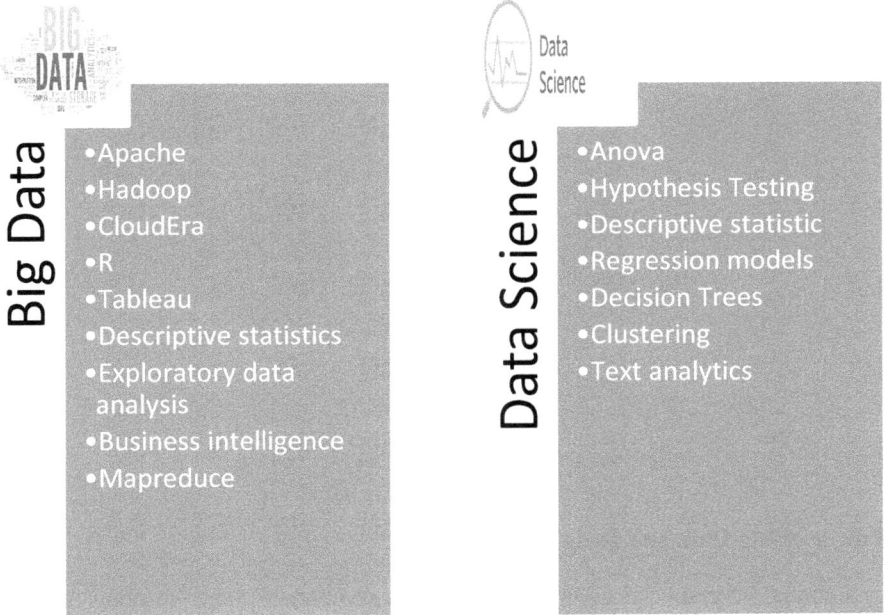

Fig 8: Concepts related to Big Data and Data science

18. Leading towards machine learning

For making a analytical platform a variety of Machine Learning and data mining algorithms are available. There are variety of many algorithms are in existence to handle specifically problems related to business. These algorithm are proved beneficial in reminding patients medicine to Manufacturing of automobiles.

The purpose of various algorithm are unique. The unique use of each algorithms allow manager and analytics to find out more promising solution to complex business problems.

Supervised and unsupervised clustering algorithms have different use in dataset of organization. In the same way clustering algorithm have different application on different data set. Below figure 9 shows various machine learning algorithm used in Big Data.

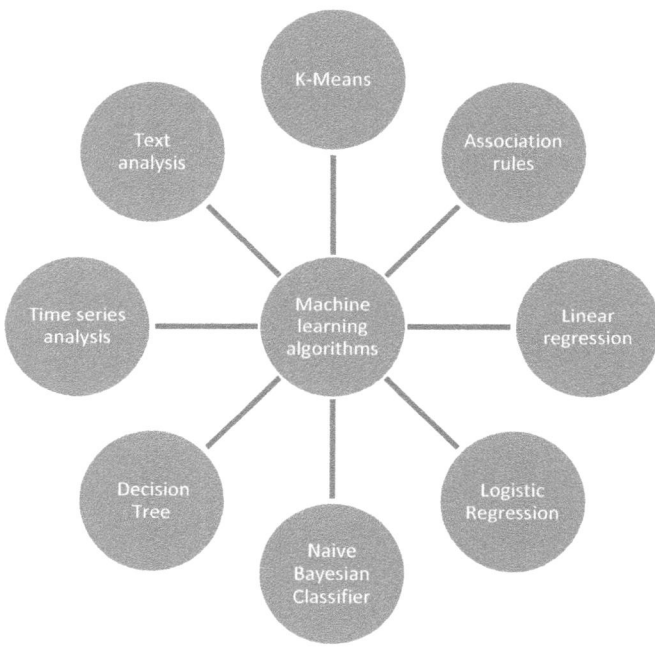

Fig 9: Machine learning algorithm used in Big Data.

19. Power of Big Data and Deep Data

Deep learning have special computing power as compare to other machine learning techniques.

1. Detection of complex features.

2. low-level features can be extracted from raw data.

3. Deep learning can easily work with high class memberships

4. It work beautiful with unlabelled data.

Taken together, these four powers deep learning have strength to generate more correct models than other methods also it reduces time require for model generation.

There are many variety of variables in data set. Deep learning detects relationship between data variables. For example, suppose that a medicine causes negative effects in baby girl infants, but not in kids. A predictive model that incorporates the combined effect of sex and age will perform much better than a model based on sex alone.

Traditional modeling methods can only find out this , with performing hypothesis testing manually. Deep learning have power to detect the interactions automatically and does not depend on analyst.

Deep learning also works best with high-cardinality class memberships. These class membership are a type of values that have immense number of discrete values. For examples word is a type that belong to speech class and picture belongs to a large class of images.

Deep Data is also best suited for handling untagged data. Deep learning also have a power to learn from this untagged data of articles, news, speech, image etc. Deep learning can help in finding out useful patterns from such untagged data. Power of Deep Data is shown in figure 10.

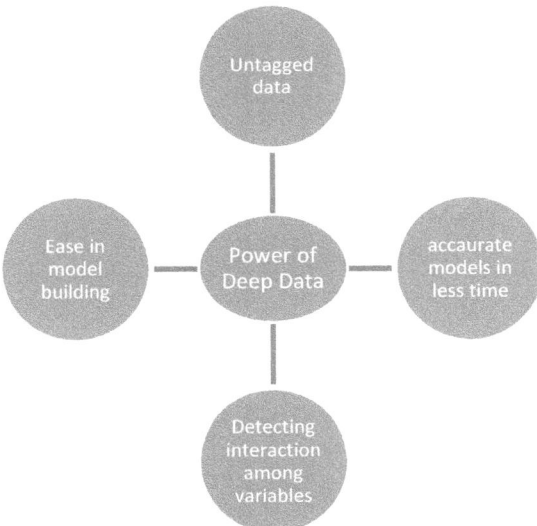

Fig 10: Below shows the power of Deep Data

20. The Limitations: Big Data and Deep Data

The below table explains the limitations of Deep Data and Big Data

Table 4: Limitations Deep Data and Big Data

Deep Data	Big Data
Require thousand of data	leads to change in existing appraoch
Expensive to train in terms of computation	Data flowing in company become constant the periodic
Theoritical foundation missing	Anlysis of real time data leads to privacy issues
Trainig method is not defined	Unresaonable searches cant be handled
Learning is not comprehensive	

References

[1] A. Efrati, *How 'deep learning' works at Apple beyond. Information*, Dec. 2013.
[2] Y. Bengio, "Learning deep architectures for AI", *Found. Trends Mach. Learn.*, vol. 2, no. 1, pp. 1-127, 2009.
[3] H. Larochelle, Y. Bengio, J. Louradour, P. Lamblin, "Exploring strategies for training deep neural networks", *J. Mach. Learn. Res.*, vol. 10, pp. 1-40, Jan. 2009.
[4] Bengio Y, LeCun Y: **Scaling learning algorithms towards, AI.**In *Large Scale Kernel Machines* Edited by: Bottou L, Chapelle O, DeCoste D, Weston J. MIT Press, Cambridge, MA; 2007, 321–360.
[5] Bengio Y, Courville A, Vincent P: **Representation learning: A review and new perspectives.** *Pattern Analysis and Machine Intelligence, IEEE Transactions on* 2013,**35**(8):1798–1828. doi:10.1109/TPAMI.2013.50 doi:10.1109/TPAMI.2013.50 10.1109/TPAMI.2013.50
[6] Bengio Y: **Deep learning of representations: Looking forward.** In *Proceedings of the 1st International Conference on Statistical Language and Speech Processing. SLSP'13.* Springer, Tarragona, Spain; 2013:1–37. http://dx.doi.org/10.1007/978-3-642-39593-2_1 http://dx.doi.org/10.1007/978-3-642-39593-2_1 10.1007/978-3-642-39593-2_1

[7] Chen, Xue-Wen, and Xiaotong Lin. "Big data deep learning: challenges and perspectives." IEEE Access 2 (2014): 514-525.

[8] Manyika, James, et al. "Big data: The next frontier for innovation, competition, and productivity." (2011).

[9] Chen, Xue-Wen, and Xiaotong Lin. "Big data deep learning: challenges and perspectives." *IEEE Access* 2 (2014): 514-525.

[10] Manovich, Lev. "Trending: The promises and the challenges of big social data." *Debates in the digital humanities* 2 (2011): 460-475.

[11] Lohr, Steve. "The age of big data." *New York Times* 11.2012 (2012).

[12] Dawn Nafus, "Deep Data: Notes on the n of 1," in *Quantified:Biosensing Technologies in Everyday Life* , 1, MIT Press, 2016, pp.280-

[13] Najafabadi, Maryam M., et al. "Deep learning applications and challenges in big data analytics." *Journal of Big Data* 2.1 (2015): 1.

[14] Liu, Weibo, et al. "A survey of deep neural network architectures and their applications." *Neurocomputing* 234 (2017): 11-26.

[15] Wang, Lidong. "Machine learning in big data." *International Journal of Advances in Applied Sciences* 4.4 (2016): 117-123.

[16] Najafabadi, Maryam M., et al. "Deep learning applications and challenges in big data analytics." (2015).

[17] Kashyap, Hirak, et al. "Big data analytics in bioinformatics: A machine learning perspective." *arXiv preprint arXiv:1506.05101* (2015).

[18] Wang, Lidong. "Machine learning in big data." *International Journal of Advances in Applied Sciences* 4.4 (2016): 117-123.

[19] Labrinidis, Alexandros, and Hosagrahar V. Jagadish. "Challenges and opportunities with big data." *Proceedings of the VLDB Endowment* 5.12 (2012): 2032-2033.

[20] Marx, Vivien. "Biology: The big challenges of big data." *Nature* 498.7453 (2013): 255-260.

[21] Kaisler, Stephen, et al. "Big data: Issues and challenges moving forward." *System sciences (HICSS), 2013 46th Hawaii international conference on*. IEEE, 2013.

[22] Katal, Avita, Mohammad Wazid, and R. H. Goudar. "Big data: issues, challenges, tools and good practices." *Contemporary Computing (IC3), 2013 Sixth International Conference on*. IEEE, 2013.

[23] Kitchin, Rob. "Big data and human geography: Opportunities, challenges and risks." *Dialogues in human geography* 3.3 (2013): 262-267.

Deep Learning for Image Processing Applications
D.J. Hemanth and V.V. Estrela (Eds.)
IOS Press, 2017
doi:10.3233/978-1-61499-822-8-194

Sparse-Filtered Convolutional Neural Networks with Layer-Skipping (SF-CNNLS) for Intra-Class Variation of Vehicle Type Recognition

Suryanti AWANG[a,1] and Nik Mohamad Aizuddin NIK AZMI[a]

[a] *Soft Computing and Intelligence Systems Research Group (SPINT), Faculty of Computer Systems & Software Engineering (FSKKP, Universiti Malaysia Pahang, Malaysia*

Abstract. Vehicle type recognition has become an important application in Intelligence Transportation Systems (ITSs) to provide a safe and efficient road and transportation infrastructure. There are some challenges in implementing this technology including the complexity of the image that will distract accuracy performance, and how to differentiate intra-class variation of the vehicle, for instance, taxi and car. In this paper, we propose to use a deep learning framework that consists of a Sparse-Filtered Convolutional Neural Network with Layer Skipping (SF-CNNLS) strategy to recognize the vehicle type. We implemented 64 sparse filters in Sparse Filtering to extract discriminative features of the vehicle and 2 hidden layers of CNNLS for further processes. The SF-CNNLS can recognize the different types of vehicles due to the combined advantages of each approach. We have evaluated the SF-CNNLS using various classes of vehicle namely car, taxi, and truck. The implementation of the evaluation is during daylight time with different weather conditions and frontal view of the vehicle. From that evaluation, we able to correctly recognize the classes with almost 91% of average accuracy and successfully recognize the taxi as a different class of car.

Keywords. Vehicle Type Recognition, Classification, Deep Learning, Computational Intelligence, Convolutional Neural Network with Layer Skipping (CNNLS), Sparse Filtering

1. Introduction

Intelligence Transportation Systems (ITSs) are advanced technology that aims to provide an application with Artificial Intelligence (AI) that able to improve safety and efficiency of road transportation. One of the applications is vehicle type recognition which can be applied in various systems including Automatic Toll Collection (ATC), traffic control and forecast, traffic census and many other transportation management systems.

Vehicle type recognition is grouped into two categories namely sensor-based and camera-based. The problem with sensor-based is it will be costly during maintenance.

---

[1] Suryanti Awang, suryanti@ump.edu.my.

Camera-based able to reduce cost because the hardware requirement is not as expensive as a sensor-based system. However, camera-based required intelligence techniques to recognize the vehicle types.

Visually recognizing vehicle types is computationally difficult. On a surveillance camera, a vehicle of the same class can appear in many variations, and some vehicles from different class share the same appearance. The environmental conditions can also change the appearance of a vehicle. Each vehicle can have different body designs, accessories, and painted decorations. These variations make visual recognition difficult. However, when a vehicle class shares similar appearance with other vehicle class, these similarities make the visual recognition more difficult. The surface of a vehicle may contain a variety of environmental reflection and specular lighting patterns. Harsh lighting from sunlight produces hard-edged shadows on the road that can change the shape of a vehicle when appeared on the camera.

More variations and similarities of vehicle classes mean more difficulties to recognize vehicle types. Thus, the main difficulties for visual recognition of vehicles are:

    i. Vehicles from the same class but has a lot of variations (inter-class variation);
    ii. Vehicles from different class but shares similar appearance (intra-class variation); and
    iii. Various environmental conditions such as weather and light illumination.

This chapter discusses techniques to classify vehicles from an image obtained by a surveillance camera. The second section in this chapter is about the various implementation of Convolutional Neural Network (CNN) in vehicle recognition system from the existing related researches. The third section is the detail explanation of the SF-CNNLS methodology in vehicle recognition system. The next section is about how the experiments execution and the discussion on the obtained results. The last section in this chapter is the conclusion of this research.

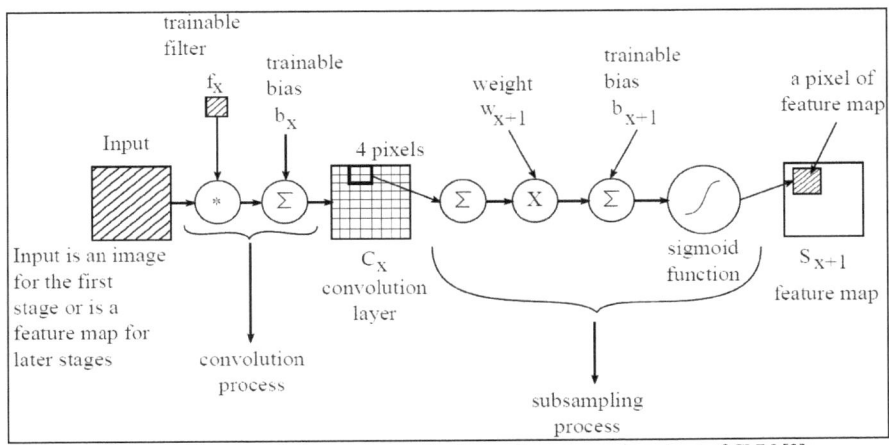

Figure 1. The convolution process and subsampling process in a stage of CNN [2]

2. CNNs in Vehicle Recognition

This section will discuss existing works that used related techniques to classify vehicles from an image obtained by a surveillance camera into the vehicle classes, for instance, car class, van class, truck class, etc. to get accurate results for traffic monitoring, management, and other related applications.

A CNN is a multi-layer feed-forward neural network that is specifically designed to extract features from two-dimensional data such as an image. Usually, the arrangement of the CNN layer is in stages. The CNN is commonly used in image recognition because it can directly process a one channeled image (grayscale image). If an image has three channels, for example, an RGB image, the CNN can process each channel in parallel. A few intelligence applications that use CNN are face detection by Tivive and Bouzerdoum [4], Chen et al. [5], vehicle type recognition by Dong et al. [1, 3], Bautista et al. [6] and document analysis by Simard et al. [7]. The processes of CNN shown in Figure 2.

Based on figure 1, the input is either an image or a feature map depending on which stage is deployed. A stage of CNN usually consists of two processes, which are convolution process and subsampling process. The convolution process is applied to the input to extract features. The outcome of the convolution process is a set of convolved images or feature maps C_x, where x denotes the hidden layer level. Secondly, subsampling process is applied on the C_x. The outcome of the subsampling process is a set of feature maps S_{x+1} which will be used as input for a further stage.

During the convolution process, a trainable filter is required for the convolution operation that denoted by the asterisk symbol, $*$. Some filter techniques that can be deployed, namely, Independent Component Analysis (ICA), Sparse Coding, Sparse Autoencoder and Sparse Filtering. The outcome of the convolution operation is a set of extracted features. The features will be summed with a trainable bias to produce the output, C_x. The trainable bias is obtained through CNN back-propagation training.

During the subsampling process, a small patch of C_x with size 2 by 2 pixels is extracted and applied with subsampling process to produce a pixel of S_{x+1}. The patch extraction including subsampling process is repeated until all patches from C_x are extracted. There are four operations involved during the subsampling process which are summation by its patch to produce a scalar result, multiplied with a scalar weight w_{x+1}, summed with a scalar trainable bias b_{x+1}, and finally the scalar result is applied with sigmoid activation function to produce a pixel of S_{x+1}.

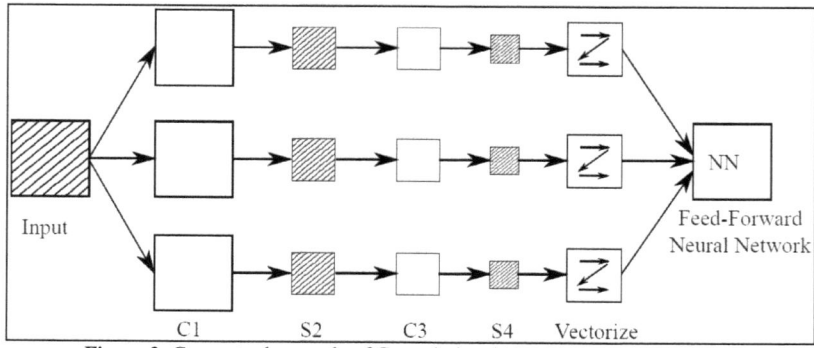

Figure 2. Conceptual example of Convolutional Neural Network (CNN) [2]

Figure 2 shows the conceptual example of a CNN that contains three channel of hidden layers with each channel have four hidden layers and one output layer. The three channels of hidden layers can be performed in parallel. The output layer of the CNN is the implementation of a classifier such as Feed-Forward Neural Network (FFNN), Softmax Regression, Support Vector Machine (SVM), etc [17][18].

The hidden layers of the CNN are designed to extract features and reduce dimensionality of the extracted features to ensure they are robust to geometric variations. The C1 and C3 are the convolved results while the S2 and S4 are the feature maps obtained through processes described in the figure 2. At the end of the hidden layer which is before the extracted features are supplied into the output layer, the extracted features will be vectorized into a one-dimensional vector. The classifier in the output layer will use the vector to train the classifier itself, and after the classifier is trained the vector will be used to perform classification process. The outcome of the output layer is the classification results that described which class that the extracted features represent.

Most of the implemented works are CNNs that typically accepted a grayscale image with fixed size as an input, and the output is the set of sorted images according to the existing categories [12]. Dong et al. [1] introduced a layer-skipping strategy into CNN that enable a CNN to extract both low-level and high-level features of a vehicle. The CNN consists of hidden layer stage 1 and hidden layers stage 2. Each stage of hidden layer consists of five similar components, which are convolution layer, absolute rectification layer, contrast normalization layer, average pooling layer and subsampling layer. The output from the hidden layer stage 1 are forwarded to two different locations, which are the hidden layer stage 2 and the average pooling with subsampling layer. The final layer for both stages is vectorization layer that vectorized two-dimensional data into a fully connected vector. Both vectors will be concatenated into a single vector and then forwarded to Softmax Regression classifier for classification task. Prior the convolution layer at the hidden layer stage 1, they add zero padding into the image with the purpose to make the features of vehicle is consistent. However, this leads to the distraction of the vehicle features that difficult to differentiate the aforementioned second issue. They used the BIT-Vehicle dataset [9] and achieved more than 95% of accuracy based on vehicle class of car, van, truck, and bus. However, taxis were classified as car class.

Rong and Xia [11] also proposed a CNN extending the layer-skipping strategy from Dong et al. using a Sparse Auto Encoder (SAE) as the trainable filter for the convolution layer. This CNN framework consisted of three stages of hidden layers, which are layer one, layer two, and layer three. Each stage of the hidden layer consists of convolutional layer and pooling layer. The output from each stage of hidden layer will be forwarded to Principle Component Analysis (PCA) layer. In the PCA layer, the output from each hidden layer are vectorized and concatenated into a single one-dimensional vector. The vector is compressed with PCA to reduce its dimensionality. Finally, the vector fed to the classifier for classification. The vehicle dataset from Caltech, which has two classes (car and van) and no taxi image was used. They tested the performance using three different classifiers namely Softmax Regression, SVM, and DBN. The Softmax Regression is able to surpass other 2 classifiers with the accuracy of 84%.

Huo et al. [12] proposed a multitask of Region-based CNN (R-CNN) model with one input layer, a convolution stage, and a multi-task stage. There are some components with different matrices inside the convolution stage which are four maximum pooling layers and three convolution layers. Inside the multi-task stage, there are one fully connected layer and three output layers to classify vehicle into sedan, van, bus, and truck. The multitask in this work defined by the labels that they used in the output layers which is to classify the vehicle based on vehicle class, different angle view (front, side, and back) and daylight and nightlight. With their proposed model, 83% accuracy is achieved for the classification purpose. Another recent implementation of CNN in vehicle type classification is done by Wang et al., where the CNN is used to detect vehicle from video image [13]. The vehicle images are trained in two types of learning namely fully connected CNN and Extreme Learning (ELM). Vehicle features known as CNN features are extracted from the fully connected CNN. Additional samples are used to train the ELM in obtaining the features from ELM known as weak labels. These two types of features are classified using adaptive clustering to classify the vehicle into class of compact car, mid-size car (van) and heavy-duty. In this research, they considered taxi as the compact car class. They managed to achieve 85.56% of accuracy based on front and back angle of vehicle images.

Therefore, based on these related works, we can conclude that most of the recent works implemented deep learning method especially CNN in their research. However, none of them classify the vehicle that involves in the intra-class variation issue as different class, for example, taxi as taxi class and not the same class as car.

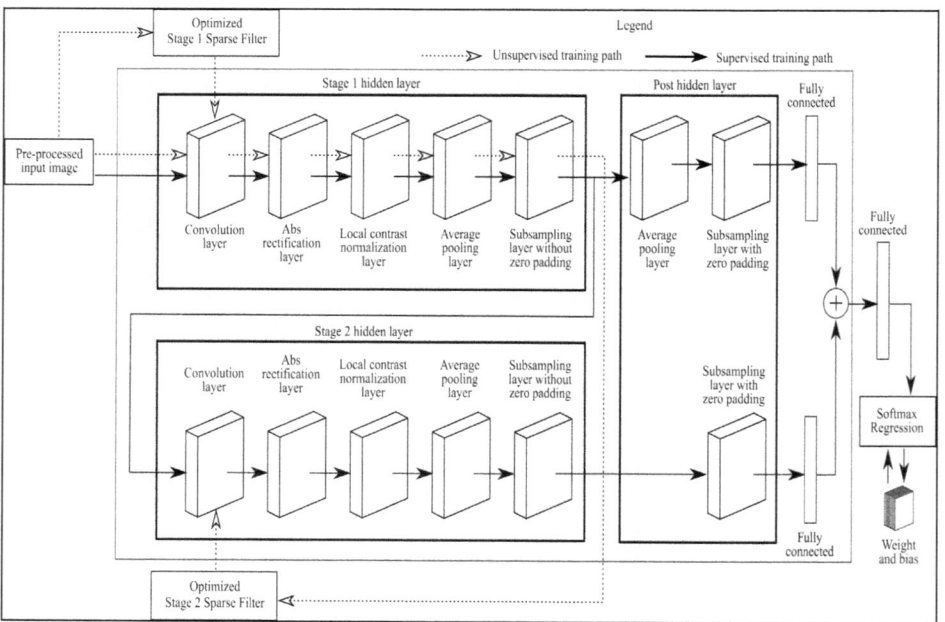

Figure 3. Overall SF-CNNLS Framework

3. The Sparse-Filtered Convolutional Neural Network with Layer Skipping (SF-CNNLS) Strategy

The next subsections describe the stages of the proposed SF-CNNLS system based on the overall SF-CNNLS shown in figure 3.

3.1. Image Acquisition

The vehicles are recorded using a surveillance camera for the BIT dataset and the self-obtained dataset known as SPINT dataset. The recorded video frames containing frontal-view of a vehicle are selected. From each selected video frames, a region containing vehicle is manually cropped to ensure the classification process is focused on the vehicle. The illustration of the cropping procedure shown in figure 4. Size and aspect ratio of a cropped image is varied for every selected video frames, due to variations in vehicle size. The cropped image is stored into training and testing dataset.

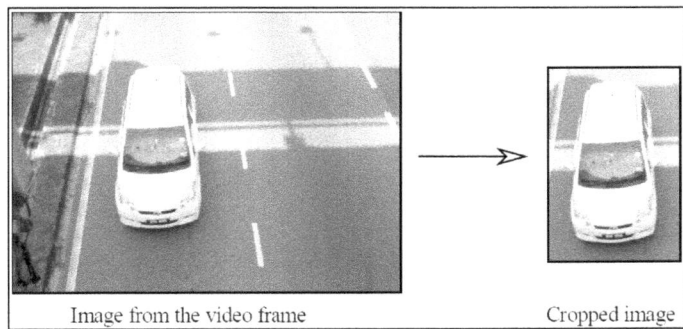

| Image from the video frame | Cropped image |

Figure 4. Example of image from the video frame and the cropped image

3.2. Pre-Processing

There are five steps in the pre-processing procedure that has been used based on a combination of existing works [1][6][15][16], which are resizing with maintained aspect ratio, converting from RGB color space to grayscale, Histogram Equalization (HE), normalizing to zero mean and unit variance, and Local Contrast Normalization (LCN). Flowchart for the pre-processing procedure shown in figure 5. According to that flowchart, the first process is to fetch an input image from either training or testing dataset. The fetched image is resized while maintaining its aspect ratio and then converted from RGB color space to grayscale. HE is then applied to normalize by using OpenCV 2.4 built-in HE function. The purpose of applying HE is to ensure its pixels intensity value will uniformly distributed. The resulting image will be normalized to zero mean and unit variance. LCN is applied as the final process to eliminate unwanted features such as light illumination and shading.

Resize an image while maintaining its aspect ratio is implemented by resizing its longest side to a specified length and then resize its shortest side by dividing the specified length with its aspect ratio. The procedure shown in figure 6. To demonstrate the procedure, supposed an input image with size 220 by 322 pixels is chosen to be resized, for example, to 256 pixels while maintaining its aspect ratio. Based on the size of the input image, the longest side will be its height (322 pixels), and the shortest side will be its width (220 pixels). The longest side will be resized to 256 pixels, whereas the shortest side is to the lower boundary of 256 multiplied by its aspect ratio which results in 174 pixels. Thus, the new size of the image is reduced from 220 by 322 pixels to 174 by 256 pixels without altering its aspect ratio. Maintaining aspect ratio during resizing is to ensure the shape of the vehicle remains consistent as possible.

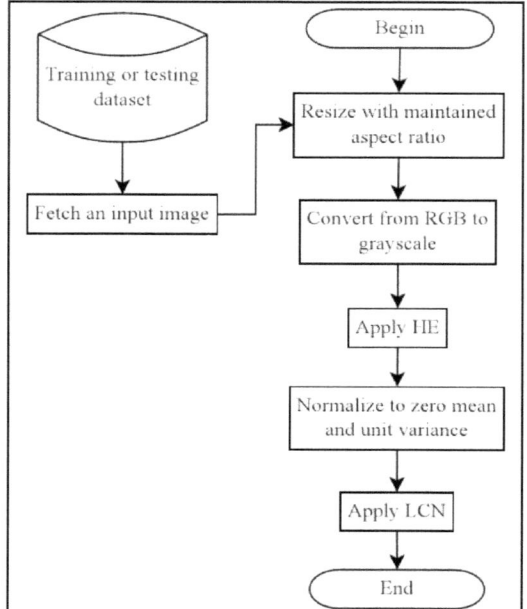

Figure 5. Flowchart for the pre-processing specific to the SF-CNNLS

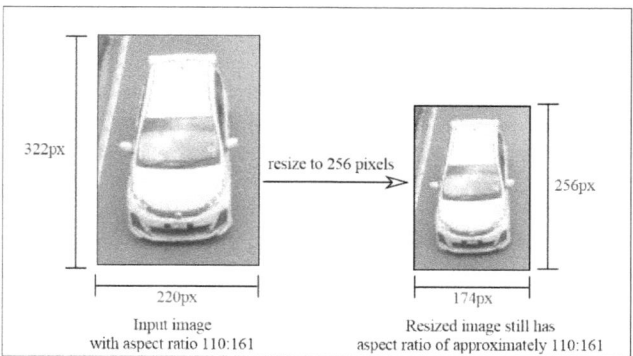

Figure 6. Resizing with maintained aspect ratio

Normalizing the input image to zero mean and unit variance is done by subtracting with its mean and divided by its standard deviation. The first step is to calculate the mean and standard deviation of the input image by using equation (1) and (2) respectively. With the mean and standard deviation obtained from the calculation, the second step is to subtract the input image with mean and then divide it with standard deviation. The resulting image will have zero mean and unit variance. This normalization method used in any machine learning tasks. Without normalization, the training process will be difficult to achieve convergence.

$$\mu = \frac{\sum\limits_{i}^{H}\sum\limits_{j}^{W} x_{i,j}}{n(x)} \tag{1}$$

$$\sigma = \frac{\sqrt{\sum\limits_{i}^{H}\sum\limits_{j}^{W}(x_{i,j-\mu})^2}}{n(x)} \tag{2}$$

where μ is mean, σ is standard deviation, $x_{i,j}$ is pixel value at index i and j of the input image, $n(x)$ is cardinality of input pixels, while H and W is height and width of the input image respectively.

The last step in this pre-processing is applying LCN. The LCN consists of two equations which are subtractive normalization (equation 3) and divisive normalization (equation 4).

$$z_{i,j} = x_{i,j} - \sum\limits_{p=-4}^{4}\sum\limits_{q=-4}^{4} w_{p,q} x_{i+p,j+q} \tag{3}$$

$$y_{i,j} = \frac{z_{i,j}}{\max(M, M(i,j))} \tag{4}$$

$$M(i,j) = \sqrt{\sum\limits_{p=-4}^{4}\sum\limits_{q=-4}^{4} w_{p,q} z^2_{i+p,j+q}} \tag{5}$$

$$M = 1 \tag{6}$$

where x is the input image, $w_{p,q}$ is normalized Gaussian filter with size 9x9 and z is an output of the subtractive normalization. The input image consists of i and j that denote its row and column index respectively. The subtractive normalization (equation 3) firstly applied on the input image. Later, divisive normalization (equation 4) applied on the resulting image. Thus, the final output from this phase is a pre-processed image that will be used to extract the vehicle features.

3.3. Feature Extraction

In this process, the feature from the pre-processed image will be extracted by using trained CNNLS framework. To explain how the the CNNLS framework implemented the feature extraction, suppose that the components of the CNNLS framework will be firstly explained based on figure 4. The CNNLS requires two stages of optimized Sparse Filters to extract local and global features from the pre-processed input image.

The hidden layers stage 1 and stage 2 consist of five components which are convolutional layer, Absolute Value Rectification (AVR) layer, Local Contrast Normalization (LCN) layer, average pooling layer, and subsampling layer without zero padding. The difference between the implementation of both hidden layers is the input. During the hidden layer stage 1 at the convolutional layer, the input will be the pre-processed image, whereas, for the convolutional layer in the hidden layer stage 2, the input replaced with a local feature extracted from the hidden layer stage 1. Here, the extracted local feature is convolved with the optimized stage 2 Sparse Filter to extract global features.

The next hidden layer is post hidden layer. The components in the post hidden layer are different for stage 1 and stage 2 hidden layers. Post hidden layer for stage 1 contains average pooling and subsampling layer with zero padding, while for stage 2, it contains only subsampling layer with zero padding. Please note that the process in each component is similar according to the related components in each layer and the output from each component will be an input into another component.

During convolutional layer in stage 1 hidden layer, the pre-processed image will be convolved with the optimized stage 1 Sparse Filter to extract local features. The convolutional operation demonstrated in figure 7. Equation 7 and 8 used for the convolution operation.

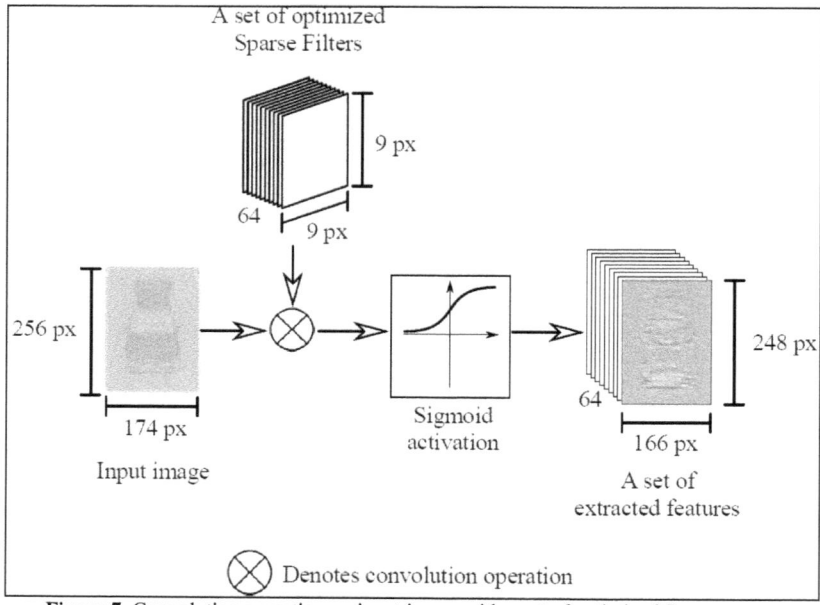

Figure 7. Convolution operation on input image with a set of optimized Sparse Filters

The convolution operation in figure 8 can demonstrated as the pre-processed image with 256 by 174 pixels is convolved with 64 optimized Sparse Filters to produce 64 convolved images. Then, sigmoid activation function is applied to each convolved image. The outcome of this process is 64 extracted local features. Note that the size of each extracted feature is smaller than its input size due to border effects from the convolution operation.

$$y_i = sig(x \otimes s_i) \tag{7}$$

$$sig(x) = \frac{1}{1 + \exp(-x)} \tag{8}$$

where x is an input image from the pre-processed image, s_i is optimized sparse filters, y_i is extracted features and $sig(.)$ is sigmoid activation function.

The next component is absolute value rectification (AVR) layer that applies absolute value operation on the extracted feature by using equation 9. The output will have absolute value elements. It is inspired by a biological system where human eyes do not perceive images in negative values.

$$y_i = |x_i| \tag{9}$$

where x_i and y_i are input and output features respectively.

The output features from AVR layer delivered to the Local Contract Normalization (LCN) layer. The LCN applied during CNNLS hidden layers is slightly different compared to the LCN applied during the pre-processing phase. Both LCNs have similar subtractive, and divisive operations except the differences are the input is a set of extracted features from the convolutional layer, and the maximum value denoted by M. The equation for subtractive normalization and divisive normalization for the LCN layer is shown in equation 10 and 11 respectively. The output from this algorithm is a set of LCN normalized features that used in average pooling layer.

$$z_{i,j,k} = x_{i,j,k} - \sum_{p=-4}^{4} \sum_{q=-4}^{4} \sum_{r=1}^{s3} w_{p,q} z_{i+p,j+q,r}^2 \tag{10}$$

$$y_{i,j,k} = \frac{z_{i,j,k}}{\max(M, M(i,j))} \tag{11}$$

$$M(i,j) = \sqrt{\sum_{p=-4}^{4} \sum_{q=-4}^{4} \sum_{r=1}^{s3} w_{p,q} z_{i+p,j+q,r}^2} \tag{12}$$

$$M = \frac{\sum_{i=1}^{s1} \sum_{j=1}^{s2} M(i,j)}{s1 \times s2} \tag{13}$$

where others symbols are similar to the equation 3,4 and 5 except k is number of features, $s3$ is number of filters and M is the maximum value in that group (4x4x$s3$).

In the average pooling layer, average filtering is convolved on the extracted features to make it less sensitive to variation in angle and size of a vehicle. Figure 9 shows the illustration of average pooling process.

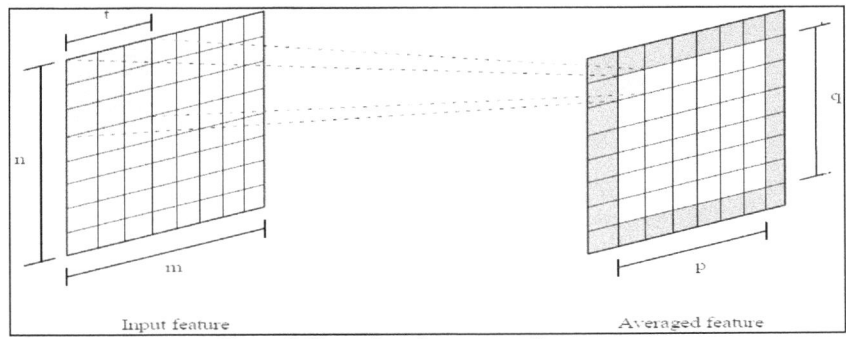

Figure 8. Illustration of average pooling process

Based on figure 8, an extracted feature with size m by n pixels is convolved with an average filter with a kernel size of t by t pixels. The purpose of the convolution is to produce averaged feature with size p by q. The size of the averaged feature is smaller due to the border effect from the convolution operation. Note that the dark gray border pixels in the figure denote the discarded pixels.

The next component is subsampling layer without zero padding where the process in this component is similar to resize the image with maintained aspect ratio as described the pre-processing phase except the input image is the extracted features as illustrated in figure 9. Based on that figure, suppose there is a feature with size 240 by 158 pixels reduced to 64 pixels. The output of this subsampling is a feature that has been resized to 64 by 42 pixels without altering its aspect ratio. It is to ensure the features of vehicle are maintained.

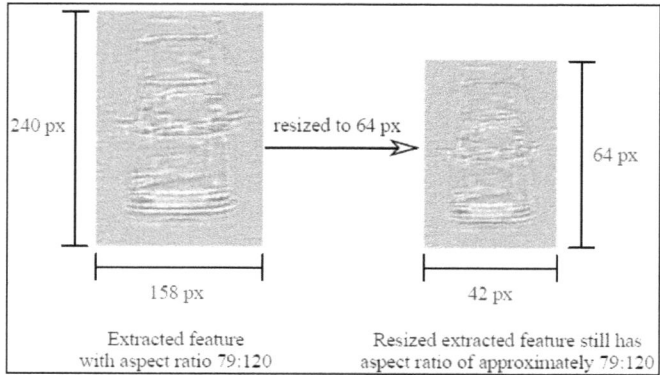

Figure 9. Subsampling without zero padding

Next is the subsampling layer with zero padding is applied on the extracted feature to ensure every feature has the same size and has an aspect ratio of 1:1 prior the classification process by Softmax Regression. The procedure for the subsampling with zero paddin shown in figure 10.

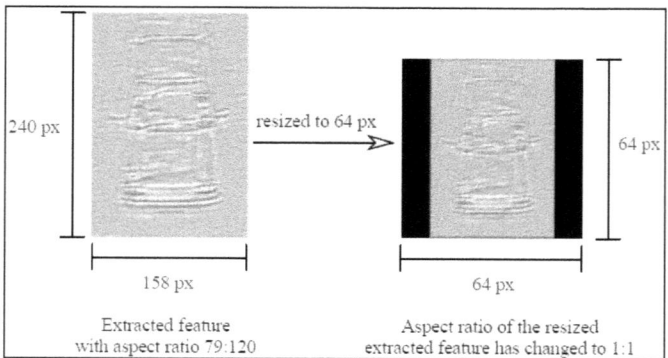

Figure 10. Subsampling with zero padding

To demonstrate the procedure, suppose that an input feature with size 158 by 240 pixels reduced to 64 pixels. Firstly, the input feature resized to 64 pixels with maintained aspect ratio. Secondly, the shortest side of the resized input feature will be padded with zero pixels to ensure the shortest side has the same length with the longest side. Thus, the resized feature will have an aspect ratio of 1:1. It is to avoid inconsistency in the extracted features size which will results in a fatal error during the matrix multiplication with Softmax Regression weight.

The last component is the fully connected where the extracted features from both hidden layers and post hidden layer concatenated into a one-dimensional vector. Figure 11 shows a demonstration on how the fully connected vector formed. Suppose that the feature from hidden layer stage 1 consists of element $\{1,2,3,...,9\}^{3\times3}$ and the feature from stage 2 hidden layer consists of element $\{A,B,C,...,I\}^{3\times3}$. Each feature will be firstly vectorized into a one-dimensional vector and then concatenated to form a single one-dimensional vector.

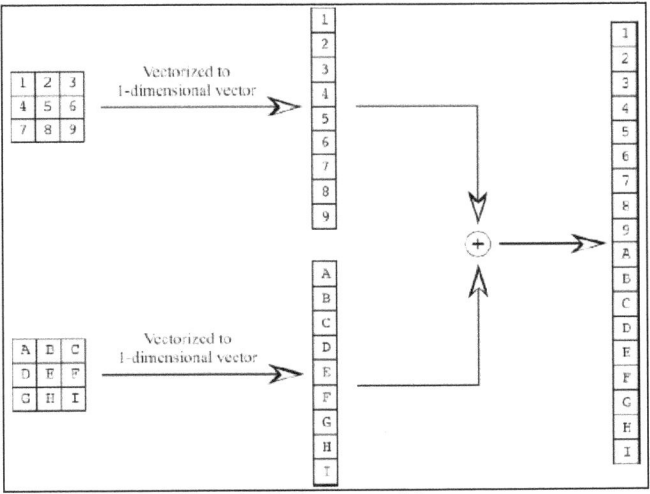

Figure 11. Fully connected features

3.4. Softmax Regression Classifier

In this section, we will describe the Softmax Regression used as the classifier. The classifier is a simple classifier where it is sufficient when the extracted features are discriminant [19]. The vehicle features that extracted from CNNLS will be used by this classifier to classify the vehicle. Classifying vehicles worked by executing Softmax Regression hypothesis, h_θ in equation 14.

$$h_\theta = \begin{bmatrix} \Pr(y=1|x;\theta,b) \\ \Pr(y=2|x;\theta,b) \\ \vdots \\ \Pr(y=K|x;\theta,b) \end{bmatrix} = \frac{1}{\sum\limits_{j=1}^{K} \exp\!\left(\theta_j^T x + b_j\right)} \begin{bmatrix} \exp\!\left(\theta_1^T x + b_1\right) \\ \exp\!\left(\theta_2^T x + b_1\right) \\ \vdots \\ \exp\!\left(\theta_k^T x + b_k\right) \end{bmatrix} \tag{14}$$

where, $h_\theta \in \Re^d$ is a hypothesis for K vehicle classes, K is a number of vehicle classes, $x \in \Re^d$ is the vehicle features extracted from CNNLS, d is a number of elements in the vector x, $\theta_k \in \Re^d, k = 1,2,..,K$ is weight, while $b_k \in \Re^d, k = 1,2,..,K$ is bias, y is the actual result and $\Pr(y = k|x;\theta,b)$ is the probability of $y=k$ when given feature x.

To demonstrate how a Softmax Regression works, suppose that the Softmax Regression is trained to recognize $K = 3$ types of vehicle class which is car, taxi, and truck. Thus, $k = 1$ represents car class, $k = 2$ represents taxi class, and $k = 3$ represents truck class, such that $k = 1,2,..,K$. The feature extracted from CNNLS denoted as one-dimensional vector x with a length of d. Since the Softmax Regression is trained with K classes, it will have K number of trained weights, θ_k and K number of trained bias, b_k.

The vectors of θ_1, θ_2 and θ_3 represent trained weight for car class, taxi class, and truck class respectively, while the vectors of b_1, b_2 and b_3 represent trained bias for the car, taxi, and truck class respectively. Each of θ_k vector and b_k vector is a one-dimensional vector with a length of d. The hypothesis for K vehicle classes, denoted as h_θ is a one-dimensional vector with a length of K. The hypothesis, h_θ, contains a list of K probabilities that show in which vehicle class represents the feature x. The probability of actual result $y=k$ vehicle class which denoted as $\Pr(y = k|x;\theta,b)$ is calculated to find out which k vehicle class that has the highest probability to represent the feature x.

The amount of probability obtained from the calculation is divided by $\sum_{j=1}^{K} \exp(\theta_j^T x + b_j)$ to ensure that the amount of probability is within a range of [0.0-1.0].

Finally, from the list of K probabilities, only one k with the highest probability will be chosen to represent the feature x. For example, whenever the hypothesis calculation gives a result of $h_\theta = \begin{bmatrix} 0.1013 \\ 0.8531 \\ 0.0456 \end{bmatrix}$, thus the feature x will be classified as a taxi due to the second index which represents $k=2$ in the vector h_θ has the highest probability.

3.5. Unsupervised Training

This section describes the unsupervised training that is executed according to that path shown in figure 4. Note that, before this unsupervised training is a part of training methods for the CNNLS. The purpose of the unsupervised training is to generate two stages of optimized sparse filters, while the purpose of supervised training is to generate the trained weight and bias that will be used by the Softmax Regression for vehicle classification task.

The unsupervised training is performed to optimize stage 1 sparse filter and later use the optimized stage 1 sparse filter to train the stage 2 sparse filter. A set of pre-processed input images is first delivered into Sparse Filtering function to generate a set of optimized stage 1 sparse filters. CNN needs trainable filters to extract features that inspired by the visual cortex in the human brain. In this research, we choose to use Sparse Filtering function due to its advantage of the fastest filtering function in unsupervised training. After that, the set of pre-processed input images is delivered into CNNLS stage one hidden layer and convolved with the optimized stage 1 sparse filters. The output from the CNNLS stage one hidden layer is used as input for the Sparse Filtering function to generate a set of optimized stage 2 sparse filters. Thus, the outcome of the unsupervised training is a set of optimized stage 1 sparse filters and a set of optimized stage 2 sparse filters. The components of the Sparse Filtering function shown in figure 12.

Based on figure 12, the Sparse Filtering function has a pre-processing phase before the optimized Sparse Filters are produced. The pre-processing phase has two processes which are splitting a set of input images (or a set of features) into small patches, and then applying zero mean and unit variance normalization on each patch. After pre-processing phase, the optimizing sparse filters function will be executed to initialize a set of unoptimized sparse filter, and then apply optimization on the unoptimized sparse filter to generate a set of optimized sparse filters.

The splitting process in the pre-processing phase illustrated in figure 13, where given a set of t input images (or input features), each input image with size w x h split into m small patches with the size of p x p. The stride size denotes by notation s, is the step size for patch extraction.

The second process in this pre-processing is normalizing input patches using zero mean and unit variance normalization is used for normalizing the input patches. Normalization is done in two steps. The first step is a normalization across the patches and the second step is a locally normalization for each patch. These normalization techniques called as global and local centering.

Next, the process of optimizing sparse filter is executed where this process will optimize a set of the unoptimized sparse filter into a set of the optimized sparse filter. Note that this process has a few steps as shown in the flowchart depicted in figure 14 where optimizing sparse filter require several initialization processes. The processes are initializing sparse filter with random normal distribution number, vectorized input patches into one-dimensional vectors, and configure Broyden-Fletcher-Goldfarb-Shanno (BFGS) optimization algorithm. The BFGS implementation used is based on GNU GSL package [13]. Optimizing Sparse Filter is done by minimizing its objective equation 15 through backpropagation method using BFGS optimization algorithm. The optimization process is executed iteratively on a forward and backward pass for 200 iterations. Usually, Sparse Filtering optimization is achieved at the acceptable convergence of 200 iterations based on our observation. When the 200 iterations reached, we normalized each sparse filter in the range of [-1 – 1] to avoid exponent overflow during the convolution layer in the hidden layer stage 2. This normalization implemented while storing the optimized sparse filters.

$$\sum_{i=1}^{C} \left\| \hat{f}^{(i)} \right\|_1 = \sum_{i=1}^{C} \left\| \frac{\tilde{f}^{(i)}}{\left\| \tilde{f}^{(i)} \right\|_2} \right\|_1 \tag{15}$$

where C is a number of input patches and $\tilde{f}^{(i)}$ obtained from $\dfrac{f^{(i)}}{\left\| f^{(i)} \right\|_2}$ in which $f^{(i)}$ is

soft-absolute activation function based on equation 16.

$$f^{(i)} = \sqrt{\varepsilon + \left(w^T x^{(i)}\right)^2} \tag{16}$$

where ε is 10^{-8}, w is the weight that known as Sparse Filter and x is vectorized input patches.

During forward pass, the Sparse Filtering objective equation 14 calculated. To execute the equation 14 $f^{(i)}$ is firstly calculated using soft-absolute function (equation 15). Then, the $f^{(i)}$ normalized across all examples by its L2-norm, $\tilde{f}_j = \dfrac{f_j}{\left\|f_j\right\|_2}$, where $f_j^{(i)}$ represents the jth feature value (rows) for the ith example (columns). The $\tilde{f}_j$ then normalized per example, $\hat{f}^{(i)} = \dfrac{\tilde{f}^{(i)}}{\left\|\tilde{f}^{(i)}\right\|_2}$. Finally, the absolute value of all entries in $\hat{f}^{(i)}$ is summed up, $\left\|\hat{f}^{(i)}\right\|_1$. During backward pass, the procedure from forward pass is calculated in the backpropagation method, to find the amount of gradient needed to update the w parameter in equation 15.

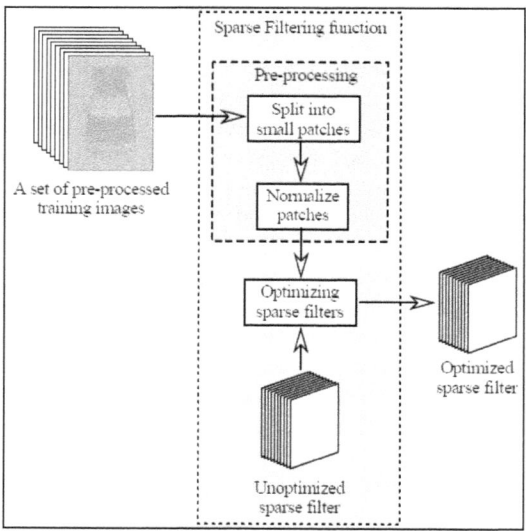

Figure 12. Overview of Sparse Filtering Function

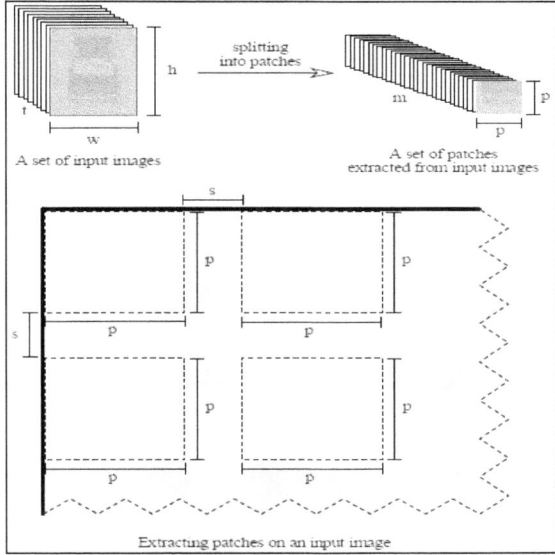

Figure 13. Splitting input image into small patches

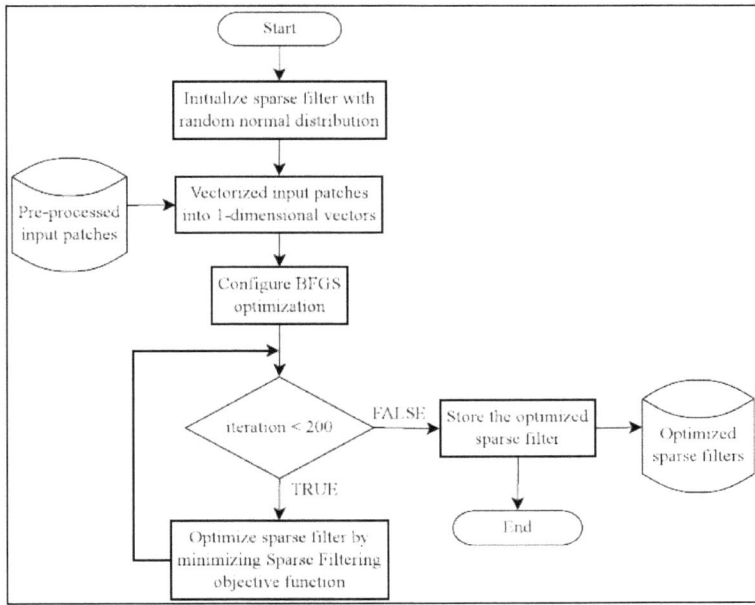

Figure 14. Flowchart of the Optimizing Sparse Filter

Figure 15 shows the optimized sparse filters for stage 1. For this research, the optimized sparse filters that we obtained are 81 with the size of 9x9 each. While figure 16 shows the optimized sparse for stage 2 that convolved from the sparse filters in figure 15. It consists of 9 sparse filters with the size of 9x9 each.

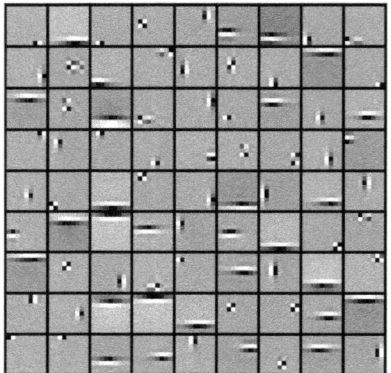

Figure 15. The optimized sparse filters for stage 1

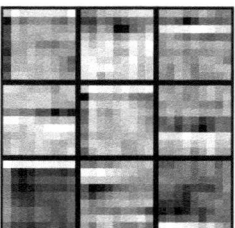

Figure 16. The optimized sparse filters for stage 2

3.6. Supervised Training – Softmax Regression

The path for supervised training shown in figure 3 and all the components that this training executed are explained earlier except the training for Softmax Regression. Here we explain about how the Softmax Regression is implemented in the supervised training. The Softmax Regression will be trained to produce trained weights and biases. The training is done by minimizing both negative log-likelihood equation (equation 17) and Mean Squared Error (MSE) equation (equation 18) by using gradient descent method. Minimizing the negative log-likelihood equation is equivalent to minimizing Kullback–Leibler divergence which is used by Dong et al. [1]. The optimization is executed for 10000 iterations to ensure the weight θ_k and bias b_k achieved convergence. Equation 19 and 20 are derivative equations for updating weight and bias.

$$J(\theta) = -\frac{1}{M}\left[\sum_{i=1}^{M}\sum_{k=1}^{K}1\{y_i = k\}\log \Pr(y_i = k|x_i;\theta,b)\right] + \frac{\lambda}{2}\|\theta\|_2^2 \tag{17}$$

$$MSE = \frac{1}{K \bullet M}\sum_{k=1}^{K}\sum_{i=1}^{M}\left[\Pr(y_i = k|x_i;\theta,b) - 1\{y_i = k\}\right]^2 \tag{18}$$

$$\nabla_{\theta_k} J(\theta) = -\frac{1}{M}\sum_{i=1}^{M}\left[x_i\left(1\{y_i = k\} - \Pr(y_i = k|x_i;\theta,b)\right)\right] + \lambda\theta_k \tag{19}$$

$$\nabla_{b_k} J(\theta) = -\frac{1}{M}\sum_{i=1}^{M}\left[1\{y_i = k\} - \Pr(y_i = k|x_i;\theta,b)\right] \tag{20}$$

$$\Pr\left(y_i = k \middle| x_i; \theta, b\right) = \frac{\exp\left(\theta^{(k)T} x^{(i)} + b^{(k)}\right)}{\sum\limits_{j=1}^{K} \exp\left(\theta^{(j)T} x^{(i)} + b^{(j)}\right)} \tag{21}$$

where K is a number of vehicle classes, M is a number of training features from all K vehicle classes. $x \in \Re^d, k = 1,2,..,K$ is the vehicle features extracted from CNNLS with d is a number of elements in the vector x. $1\{y_i = k\}$ is indicator function where it returns 1 if y_i is equal to k, otherwise returns 0. $\theta_k \in \Re^d, k = 1,2,..,K$ is weight and $b_k \in \Re^d, k = 1,2,..,K$ is bias for all vehicle classes. While y is the actual result and λ is a non-negative regularization parameter.

The derivative of equations 19 and 20 are calculated to minimize the output of the negative log-likelihood (equation 17) for each iteration. The aim is to iteratively update the weight θ_k and bias b_k in the equation 17. The MSE equation is calculated for each end of the iteration to monitor the supervised training progress. Usually, the MSE value after 10000 iterations may achieve an acceptable amount of 0.2% error. Note that the Softmax Regression used in this research contains a non-negative regularization parameter, denoted as λ. The purpose of the regularization parameter is to control the generalization performance of the Softmax Regression. The larger the λ value, the bigger the amount of generalization. The λ value needs to be chosen such that the classification of the Softmax Regression is not too general and not too specific to the training dataset. A small amount of generalization could improve the classification accuracy because the classification will not too dependent on the training dataset. Usually, the value of λ is chosen somewhere between 0:20 to 1:00. Setting λ to zero will disable the regularization.

3.7. Testing

In this section, the procedure for testing the trained CNNLS is discussed. Recall that the purpose of this testing is to evaluate the performance of the CNNLS including the Softmax Regression classifier. According to the testing path in figure 3, the testing flow is exactly similar to the supervised training path, except that the input images fetched from the testing dataset. The trained weights and biases for the Softmax Regression are loaded from the supervised training to the testing, and the hypothesis equation (equation 14) is calculated instead of minimizing the negative log-likelihood equation (equation 17).

The testing procedure can be demonstrated in such suppose that the Softmax Regression is trained to recognize for three types of vehicle class which are car, taxi, and truck. Testing is performed on each vehicle class dataset. The testing results are observed based on true-positive and false-positive. The true-positive is known as accuracy performance whereby the vehicle type correctly recognized in the predicted class. The false-positive is the vehicle type that successfully recognized in unpredicted class. The true-positive and false-positive are calculated using equation 22 and 23 respectively for every vehicle class testing dataset. The recognition result for every vehicle class will be displayed in confusion matrix.

$$TruePositive = \frac{n}{N} \times 100\% \qquad\qquad (22)$$

$$FalsePositive = \frac{u}{N} \times 100\% \qquad\qquad (23)$$

where n is number of recognized in predicted class, u is number of recognized in unpredicted class and N is number of samples in testing dataset.

To implement this research, we use different software for different purpose as listed below:

- FreeBSD 10.3 Operating System; FreeBSD is chosen in this research because it is compatible for any companies that are interested to develop their proprietary operating system with integration to this research work. The OS is free, open source, and BSD licensed which allow users to modify and make it proprietary operating system.
- Clang 3.4.1 compiler; The system in this research iwritten in C++ language. The Clang compiler provide C/C++ compilers to compile the system's source code.
- Boost 1.63 C++ libraries; This set of libraries provide high-level functions to use operating system functionalities such as file searching, serialization, error handling, and multi-threading.
- Qt5 Framework; This framework provides high-level functions to develop Graphical User Interface (GUI) for the system.
- CMake 3.7.2 cross-platform makefile generator; CMake used for building the system source code. It will all required libraries and use the Clang compiler to compile the source code.
- OpenCV 2.4 library including its third party libraries; These libraries provide high-level functions to handle image, matrices and provide image processing functions.
- GNU GSL 1.16 library; This library contains numerical functions such as BFGS optimization.

4. Experimental Results and Discussion

In this section, we test the SF-CNNLS methodology and evaluate its performance. We used a benchmark database from the BIT-Vehicle [1] and a self-obtained database named the SPINT-Vehicle databases. The BIT database has various vehicle types commonly used by people as well as the SPINT-Vehicle. Table 1 below is the distribution of dataset in the training and testing for each vehicle class for each database. Please note that for the training, number of samples for each class is preferable to be balanced to avoid any bias during the training. Thus, we used 40 samples for the dataset as the training dataset for each class, whereas, for the testing set, we used various number of samples for each class in each database. It shown that the taxi class has fewer samples in the BIT-Vehicle dataset, whereas, the truck has fewer samples in the SPINT-Vehicle dataset. For condition of the vehicle images, BIT and SPINT captured images from frontal angle of surveillance camera during daylight and with slight illumination and shadow. In SPINT, we obtained the vehicle data during morning (9am-10.59am), afternoon (11pm-2.59pm) and evening (3pm-6pm) to evaluate if the classification performance reflects to the various of lighting conditions. However, we unable to compare this condition with BIT because that information is not provided. Thus, we decided to compare it based on daylight condition in general. Table 2 shows the samples image for each class in each database. Based on that table, it shown that the vehicle image is almost similar in terms of angle and size of vehicle. It is to ensure the comparison result is valid.

Figure 17 and 18 depict the example of the extracted features for a taxi from the hidden layer stage 1 and the hidden layer stage 2 respectively. Based on figure 17, there are 81 of local and global features of taxi that have been extracted based on the convolution process with the 81 optimized sparse filters previously. Whereas, for figure 18, there are 729 extracted features of local and global where each of the extracted features from the hidden layer stage 1 convolved with 9 sparse filters in stage 2.

Table 1. Training and Testing Samples Distribution

Dataset	Class	Set	
		Training	Testing
BIT	Car	40	67
	Taxi	40	17
	Truck	40	21
SPINT	Car	40	65
	Taxi	40	20
	Truck	40	19

Table 2. Samples Image

Dataset	Class	Set	
		Training	Testing
BIT	Car		
	Taxi		
	Truck		
SPINT	Car		
	Taxi		
	Truck		

Figure 17. Example of the extracted features from stage 1

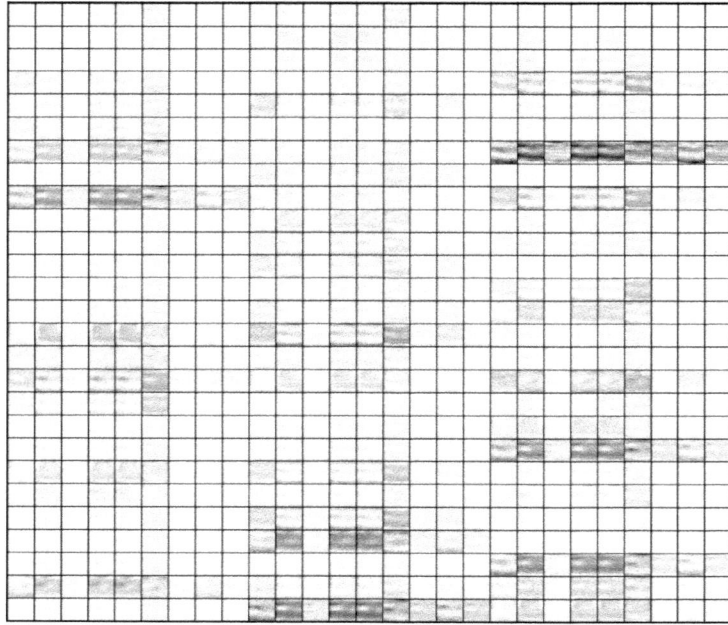

Figure 18. Example of the extracted features from stage 2

Based on that setting, we split our experiments into two main experiments; the first experiment is to obtain the True Positive for each class in each database and the second one is to obtain the False Positive. Thus, for the True Positive, there are 3 experiments and 6 experiments for the later. Table 3 is the True Positive for each class as well as the average performance, while table 4 shows the False Positive that represented in the confusion matrix.

Table 3. True Positive

Class	True-Positive		Average (BIT / SPINT)	
	BIT	SPINT	BIT	SPINT
Car	92.5%	98.5%		
Taxi	89%	75%	90.5%	90.83%
Truck	90%	99%		

Table 4. False Positive in Confusion Matrix

Predicted\Actual	Car		Taxi		Truck	
	BIT	SPINT	BIT	SPINT	BIT	SPINT
Car	92.5%	98.5%	4 %	6%	3.5%	0%
Taxi	11%	19%	89%	75%	0%	0%
Truck	4%	1.05%	6%	0%	90%	99%

Based on the results in table 3 and 4, shown that our method able to classify the vehicle class especially the taxi as different class from car with 89% and 75% of true-positive in respective dataset. However, 11% and 19% of the taxi class misclassified as car in which the highest False Positive compared to other classes. For car, 92.5% is correctly classified with 4% misclassified as taxi class and 3.5% as truck class in BIT dataset, whereas, 98.5% of car is correctly classified with 6% misclassified as taxi class and none of the car is classified as truck in SPINT dataset. Overall, SPINT dataset produced a better result compared to BIT due to the illumination in SPINT dataset is less than BIT dataset. In terms of processing time, our methodology able to recognize the testing samples in 10 minutes for BIT dataset and 10 minutes 15 seconds for SPINT dataset.

The above results obtained when we test with car without sunroof. Thus, Softmax Regression able to differentiate taxi and car as different class. However, when we consider car with sunroof in the car class, the results are significantly dropped although the number of car with sunroof is limited. It is due to the features of sunroof is almost similar to the taxi sign on top of taxi roof. Therefore, Softmax Regression unable to discriminate the features effectively. Table 5 and 6 show the results that we obtained when car with sunroof is considered.

Table 5. True-Positive (Car with sunroof)

Class	True Positive		Average	
	BIT	SPINT	BIT	SPINT
Car	59.70%	79.07%		
Taxi	23.53%	44.44%	46.79%	74.17%
Truck	57.14%	99%		

Table 6. False-Positive in Confusion Matrix (Car with sunroof)

Predicted\Actual	Car		Taxi		Truck	
	BIT	SPINT	BIT	SPINT	BIT	SPINT
Car	59.70%	79.07%	13.43%	20.93%	26.87%	0%
Taxi	41.18%	55.56%	23.53%	44.44%	35.29%	0%
Truck	28.57%	0%	14.28%	0%	57.14%	99%

Based on those tables, despite of decrement in the overall performance, the vehicle classes can be classified despite of low accuracy. For example, 59.70% and 79.07% of testing dataset from BIT and SPINT respectively is correctly recognized as the car class. Taxi shows most significant distraction in this case, where the taxi being misclassified as car class is higher than taxi class with 41.18% and 23.53% in BIT dataset respectively. The situation is similar with SPINT dataset for the taxi class. It is due to the similarity features of intra-class, all of the classes' performances are distracted. Thus, in future, we suggest to extract most discriminant features from each class to be trained in the classifier. For example, using feature selection technique prior the training phase in classifier or add more channel in CNNLS. The reason to add more channels is to ensure CNNLS will extract more features of global and local.

5. Conclusion

Vehicle type recognition consists of sensor-based and camera-based. The vehicle type recognition system that used in this research is a camera-based and requires artificial intelligence technique to classify the vehicle types. CNN, which is one of the deep learning approaches, is chosen for this research to classify the vehicle types. Specifically, we used a modified CNN with Layer Skipping (CNNLS) strategy. Some changes such as in the pre-processing image to maintain the original features. Thus, the low-level and high-level of features of vehicle will be extracted significantly without the distraction of zero padding during the convolution layer. We also modified the subsampling layer with zero padding at the end of the post hidden layer for the hidden layer stage 1 to avoid a matrix multiplication error during the classification process in Softmax Regression. The results show promising performance when we tested our methodology with standard car type, taxi, and truck. We used a benchmark dataset that consists of all the mentioned vehicle classes called BIT. We also have the self-obtained dataset that consists of similar vehicle classes called SPINT. The datasets consist of frontal view of vehicle that obtained from a mounted camera from a surveillance camera in daylight. The difference among these two dataset is SPINT has less illumination condition compared to BIT due to the different period of time that we gather the data. We used 40 samples for each vehicle class in each dataset as the training sample and various number of vehicle class samples for the testing during our experiment. From the experiment, it shows that our methodology is able to correctly classified taxi as different class of car in which all the related researches classify the taxi as the same class of car. It is due to the almost identical features that taxi and car shared. To conclude, vehicle type can be enhanced the accuracy performance if more discriminant features are extracted and trained.

References

[1] Z. Dong, M. Pei, Y. He, T. Liu, Y. Dong and Y. Jia, Vehicle type classification using unsupervised convolutional neural network. *22nd IEEE International Conference on Pattern Recognition (ICPR)* (2014), 172–177.

[2] I. Arel, D.C. Rose and T.P. Karnowski, Deep machine learning - a new frontier in artificial intelligence research. *IEEE Computational Intelligence Magazine*, 5(4) (2010), 13–18.

[3] Z. Dong, Y. Wu, M. Pei and Y. Jia, Vehicle type classification using a semisupervised convolutional neural network. *IEEE Transactions on Intelligent Transportation Systems*, 16(4) (2015). 2247–2256.

[4] F.H.C. Tivive and A. Bouzerdoum, A new class of convolutional neural networks (siconnets) and their application of face detection. *Proceedings of the International Joint Conference on Neural Networks*, vol 3. (2003), 2157–2162.

[5] Y.N. Chen, C.C. Han, C.T. Wang, B.S. Jeng and K.C. Fan, The application of a convolution neural network on face and license plate detection. *18th International Conference on Pattern Recognition (ICPR'06)*, vol 3, (2006), 552–555.

[6] C.M. Bautista, C.A. Dy, M.I. Manalac, R.A. Orbe and M. Cordel, Convolutional neural network for vehicle detection in low resolution traffic videos. *IEEE Region 10 Symposium (TENSYMP)* (2016), 277–281.

[7] P.Y. Simard, D. Steinkraus and J.C. Platt. Best practices for convolutional neural networks applied to visual document analysis. *ICDAR*, vol. 3 (2003), 958–962.

[8] J. Ngiam, Z. Chen, S.A. Bhaskar, P.W. Koh and A.Y. Ng, Sparse filtering, *Advances in neural information processing systems*, (2011), pages 1125–1133.

[9] Z. Dong, Y. Wu, M. Pei and Y. Jia, Vehicle type classification using a semisupervised convolutional neural network, *IEEE Transcations on Intelligent Transportation Systems*, (2015), page in press.

[10] H.T. Phan, A.T. Duong and S. T. Tran, Hierarchical sparse autoencoder using linear regression-based features in clustering for handwritten digit recognition. *8th International Symposium on Image and Signal Processing and Analysis (ISPA)* (2013), pages 183–188.

[11] H. Rong and Y. Xia, A vehicle type recognition method based on sparse auto encoder, *Proceedings of the International Conference on Computer Information Systems and Industrial Applications*, 2015, DOI: 10.2991/cisia-15.2015.88

[12] Z. Huo, Y. Xia and B. Zhang, Vehicle type classification and attribute prediction using multi-task RCNN, *9th International Congress on Image and Signal Processing, BioMedical Engineering and Informatics (CISP-BMEI)* (2016), pp. 564-569.

[13] B. Gough, *GNU Scientific Library Reference Manual - Third Edition*, Network Theory Ltd., 2009.

[14] S. Wang, F. Liu, Z. Gan and Z. Cui, Vehicle type classification via adaptive feature clustering for traffic surveillance video, *8th International Conference on Wireless Communications & Signal Processing (WCSP)* (2016), Yangzhou, pp. 1-5.

[15] N. Pinto, D.D. Cox and J.J. DiCarlo, Why is real-world visual object recognition hard?, *PLOS Computational Biology, 4(1)* (2008), 1-6.

[16] Y. Tang, C. Zhang, R. Gu, P. Li and B. Yang, Vehicle detection and recognition for intelligent traffic surveillance system. *Multimed Tools Appl.*, *243* (2015).

[17] A. Chantakamo and M. Ketcham, The multi vehicle recognition using hybrid blob analysis and feature-based. *Proceedings 7th International Conference on Information Technology and Electrical Engineering: Envisioning the Trend of Computer, Information and Engineering, ICITEE*. Chiang Mai, Thailand; (2015) 453-457.

[18] N. Najva and K.E. Bijoy, SIFT and Tensor Based Object Detection and Classification in Videos Using Deep Neural Networks, *Procedia Computer Science, 6th International Conference On Advances In Computing & Communications, ICACC, 6-8*. vol 93. Cochin, India, (2016) 351-358.

[19] S. Awang, R. Yusof, M. F. Zamzuri and R. Arfa, Feature Level Fusion of Face and Signature Using a Modified Feature Selection Technique, *International Conference on Signal-Image Technology & Internet-Based Systems*, (2013), pp. 706-713.

218

Deep Learning for Image Processing Applications
D.J. Hemanth and V.V. Estrela (Eds.)
IOS Press, 2017
doi:10.3233/978-1-61499-822-8-218

On the Prospects of Using Deep Learning for Surveillance and Security Applications

Shuo Liu [a], Vijay John [b] and Zheng Liu [a]

[a] *School of Engineering, Faculty of Applied Science, University of British Columbia*
(Okanagan), 1137 Alumni Avenue Kelowna, BC V1V 1V7 Canada
[b] *Toyota Technological Institute, Tenpaku-Ku, Nagoya, 468-8511 Japan*

Abstract. Convolutional neural networks have achieved great success in computer vision, significant improving the state of the art in image classification, semantic segmentation, object detection and face recognition. In this chapter, we illustrate the advance made by the convolutional neural network (CNN) in surveillance and security applications using two examples. For the surveillance application, a novel military object detector called Deep Fusion Detector was proposed, which incorporates information fusion techniques and the CNN. Specifically, we fused multi-channel images within a CNN to enhance the significance of deep features, and adapted a state-of-the-art generic object detector for military scenario. For the security application, with inspiration from recent advances in the deep learning community, we presented an effective face recognition system called Deep Residual Face. Where the Inception-ResNet CNN architecture was utilized to extracting deep features and the center loss function was adopted for training the face verification network. The extensive experiments showed the effectiveness of the presented methods.

Keywords. Deep Learning, Automatic Object Detection, Image Fusion, Face Recognition, Surveillance, Security, Deep Multi-Channel Fusion, Deep Face

1. Introduction

Visual surveillance is an important research area in image processing, computer vision, and machine learning, due to its relevance to many real-world applications. Typical surveillance applications rely on providing safety and security in the sensitive areas such as battlefields, banks, shopping malls etc. The main task of surveillance is the detection and identification of suspicious behaviour in these areas. The standard visual surveillance system consists of several components such as target detection, tracking, and recognition. Among these components, detecting and recognizing the object in surveillance videos are challenging tasks due to the variations in object appearance and complex background.

Automatic target detection (ATD) is an important component of the visual surveillance system. Given an image or a frame sampled from the video, ATD is able to automatically localize and recognize targets in it. Traditionally, ATD methods adopt a general pipeline where a "sliding window" is utilized to exhaustively search candidate regions.

Subsequently, engineered feature extraction and classification is performed for each candidate region.

The target locations estimated by the ATD are given as input to subsequent algorithms like object recognition for high-level analysis. Face recognition and face verification, an example of object recognition, is an important component of visual surveillance. In face verification, two face images are compared and verified if they belong to the same person. The general pipeline of the face verification is as follow: face patches are detected and aligned firstly, then high-dimensional over-complete visual features are extracted from each aligned face patches, after which they are fed into the similarity metrics or binary classifiers to obtain the verification result.

In the last few years, deep learning algorithms have received significant attention, especially the Convolutional Neural Networks (CNNs). Many researchers have started to employ the CNN on their ATD and face recognition applications. In this chapter, we present two such CNN-based applications, namely, automatic military target detection and deep face recognition. We illustrate the advances made by deep learning techniques in automatic visual surveillance and security systems. In the first CNN-based application, we present a state-of-the-art military target detector which integrates a novel image fusion method and the CNN. In the second CNN-based application, we present a CNN-based face recognition system, where we incorporate the recent advances in deep learning.

The chapter is organized as follows: Section 2 introduces the proposed application of military automatic target detection in details. Section 3 illustrates the face recognition application. For each application, we describe their background, detailed method, experiments and summary in several subsections. Finally, we conclude both applications in Section 4.

2. Case 1-Military Automatic Target Detection

2.1. Background

Automatic target detection (ATD) is key to automatic military operations and surveillance missions. In a military mission, sensors can be placed on the ground or mounted on unmanned aerial vehicles(UAVs) and unmanned ground vehicles (UGVs) to acquire information. The acquired sensory data will be processed using an ATD algorithm, which aims to find bounding boxes to localize the target. Fast and accurate object detectors can increase the survivability of the weapon platform and soldiers. The automatic identification of the threat in military scenario is of the essence.

In recent years, several ATD algorithms have been proposed. Generally, these algorithms can be classified into two main categories: 1) background modeling approaches, 2) and learning-based approaches.

Background modeling approaches assume that background pixels have a similar color (or intensity) over time in a fixed camera, and the background model is built on this assumption. The background is abstracted from the input image, and the foreground (moving objects) region is determined by marking the pixels in which a significant difference occurs. In [39], the authors modeled the background using a kernel density estimation (KDE) method over a joint domain-range representation of image pixels. Mul-

Figure 1. Left: the appearance of target is undistinguishable from background environment. Right: the scale of target is various dramatically.

tilayer codebook-based background subtraction (MCBS) model was proposed in [16], which can remove most of the non-stationary background and significantly increase the processing efficiency. Reference [6] proposed a motion detection model based on probabilistic neural networks. Above methods are designated for the stationary camera scenario. In the works of[58][20][13], the authors proposed several schemes that address the issues with moving camera. The background modeling based methods are effective for detecting moving objects. On the other hand, the performance of background modeling is limited for still or slowly moving objects.

Another popular category is the learning-based approaches. Traditionally, engineered features like scale-invariant feature transform (SIFT) [24] or histogram of oriented gradient (HOG) [9] are firstly extracted and then fed into a classifier, such as Boosting[32], support vector machine (SVM)[47] and random forest [4]. The typical work in this paradigm is the deformable part models (DPM) [11]. More recently, convolutional neural networks (CNNs) have reported state-of-the-art detection accuracy on many difficult object detection challenges [35] [10] [29]. *Overfeat* [37] firstly utilized CNN models in a sliding window fashion on ATD task successfully. The *Overfeat* has two CNNs, one for classifying if a window contains an object and the other for predicting the bounding box of the object. Another popular CNN-based ATD framework is the R-CNN [15]. The R-CNN uses a pre-trained CNN to extract features from box proposals generated by selective search [52], and then it classifies them with class specific linear SVMs. The significant advantage of this work is derived from replacing hand-engineered features by a CNN feature extractor. Then, the variants of R-CNN were proposed to mainly solve the problem with computational load [14] [19] [34].

Nevertheless, above ATD methods are only applicable to the general natural scene, and many challenges come up from the military scenario. First, the environment of battlefields is extremely complex. As shown in Figure1, the appearance of the object includes color and texture is similar to the background in left example, because soldiers always attempt to camouflage themselves or their vehicles. And due to the vast battlefield, the scale of objects always dramatically changes with their distance to sensors. Thus, those environmental factors will always limit the ability of generic object detection algorithms. Second, military ATD application always runs on the embedded platform whose computational and memory resources are limited. In this case, the ability to run at high frame rates with relatively high accuracy becomes a crucial issue for military ATD.

Several image fusion based methods were proposed to enhance target representation in literature [3] [31] [17] [42]. Multiple images acquired with different range of electromagnetic spectrum were fused into one image by pixel-level image fusion algorithms such as principal components analysis (PCA) based weighted fusion [42]and discrete wavelet transform (DWT) [31], and then fed into an ATD system. However, the traditional fused images are limited in the performance for ATD tasks. To address the serious limitation, we propose a novel image fusion approach to improving detector performance in the military scenario, which exploits the significant advantage of the unsupervised feature learning characteristic of CNNs. Compared with high-level image fusion, the proposed method can achieve a higher accuracy and computational efficiency. In addition, we adopted the state-of-the-art generic object detection framework into the military scenario and used a cross-domain transfer learning techniques to cover the shortage of insufficient data. In this way, the proposed framework achieves promising results on the military sensing information analysis center (SENSIAC) dataset.

2.2. Methods

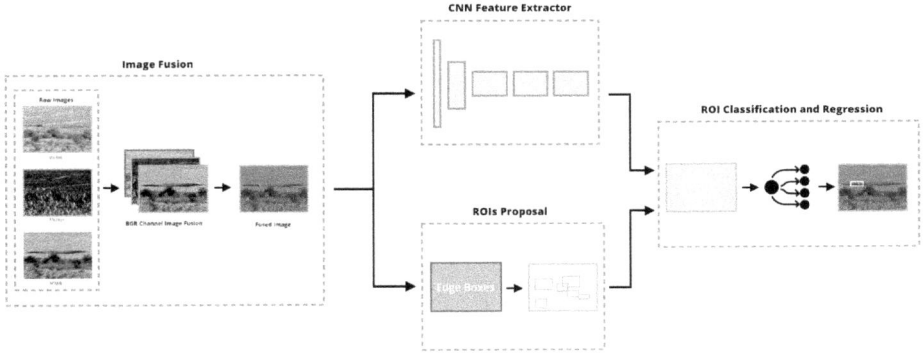

Figure 2. The pipeline of proposed object detector framework, which include four main components:1) image fusion, 2) CNN feature extractor, 3) ROI proposal, and 4) ROI classification and regression

In this section, we will elaborate the overall proposed ATD system. As you can see in the Figure 2, the whole system is composed of four modules: 1) an image fusion module, which can fuse three different type of images into a BGR image; 2) a CNN feature extractor, used for extracting high-level semantic representations from the fused image; 3) a region of interest (ROI) proposal module manipulated on fused image is utilized for generating hundreds or thousands of candidate bounding boxes, for each ROI on feature map produced by feature extractor module; and 4) a ROI classification and regression is performed to obtain fine bounding boxes and corresponding class.

2.2.1. Image Fusion

Image Selection:

Multi-sensor data often provide complementary information for context enhancement, which may further enhance the performance of object detection. In our work, we investigated two type of images from different sensors, mid-wave infrared image (MWIR) and visible image (VI), respectively. In addition to the images acquired from these two sensors, we also incorporate motion image generated from two consecutive visible frames in order to complement sufficient description of objects.

MWIR: Depending on the different range of electromagnetic spectrum, the infrared (IR) spectrum can be divided into different spectral bands. Basically, the IR bands include the active IR band and the passive (thermal) IR band. The main difference between active and passive infrared bands is that the passive IR image can be acquired without any external light source. The passive (thermal) IR band is further divided into the mid-wave infrared (3-5 um) and the long-wave infrared (7-14 um). In general, the mid-wave infrared (MWIR) cameras can sense temperature variations over targets and background at a long distance, and produce thermograms in the form of 2D images. Its ability to present large contrasts between cool and hot surfaces is extremely useful for many computer vision tasks such as image segmentation and object detection. However, the MWIR sensor is not sensitive to cool background. Besides, the texture corresponded to the high frequencies of the objects and they were mostly missed, because of the possible absence of auto-focus lens capabilities and low-resolution sensor arrays.

VI: The range of electromagnetic spectrum of visible image is from 380 nm to 750 nm. This type of image can be easily and conveniently acquired via various kinds of general cameras. In comparison with MWIR image, the VI image is sensitive to illumination changes, preserve high-frequency information and can provide a relatively clear perspective of the environment. In most of the computer vision topics, the VI image has become major focus of interest for many decades. Thus, there are a large number of public VI datasets across many research areas. On the other hand, the significant drawbacks of VI image are that it has poor quality in the harsh environmental conditions with unfavourable lighting and pronounced shadows, and there is no dramatic contrast between background and foreground when the environment is extremely complicated such as the battlefield.

| t | t-5 | motion |

Figure 3. The procedure of motion estimation: where t is the current frame and t-5 is the previous 5th frame, and the motion is what our algorithm estimate.

Motion Image: In general, the moving objects are the targets in the battle fields. Therefore, estimating the motion of objects can provide significant cues to segment those targets. Various motion estimation algorithms have been proposed in recent decades, such as dense optical flow methods, points correspondence methods, and background subtraction. And each of them has shown effectiveness on many computer vision tasks. However, considering the trade-off between accuracy and computational complexity, we do not opt for any of the complicated motion estimation approaches but utilize a straightforward and easier to be implemented method. The method is illustrated in Figure 3, where we estimate the motion map based on two consecutive frames. To be specific, the objective images are sampled at every 5 frames, and then force the current frame to subtract the last frame, the resulting image is the desired motion image. The method can be formulated as follow:

$$M_n(x,y) = |I_n(x,y) - I_{n-5}(x,y)| \tag{1}$$

where $M_n(x,y)$ represents the motion value of frame n at pixel point (x,y) and $I_n(x,y)$ denotes the pixel value of frame n at pixel point (x,y).

In this way, we do not need to consider multiple frames to estimate background, like the background subtraction methods, and only the subtraction operator is employed in this procedure, which is more efficient that other state-of-the-art methods. Even though this method can introduce lots of noise in the motion image, the noisy motion image with complementary information is still useful for subsequent fusion.

Fusion Methodology:

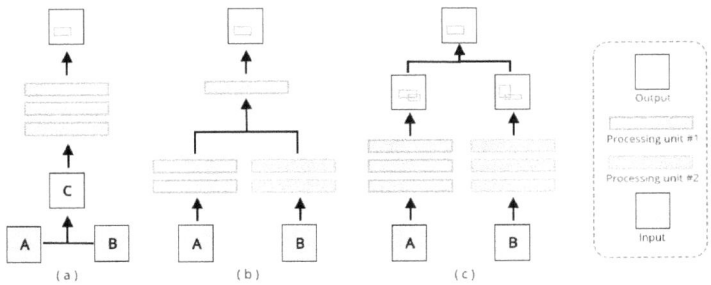

Figure 4. Illustration of different information fusion architectures: (a) pixel-level fusion architecture; (b) feature-level fusion architecture; (c) decision-level fusion architecture.

Here, we formalize the possible configurations of information fusion for object detection into three categories, namely, *pixel-level fusion* architecture, *feature-level fusion* architecture and *decision-level fusion* architecture. An illustration is shown in Figure 4. Having these possibilities in mind will help to highlight the important benefits of our proposed fusion method in terms of efficiency and effectiveness.

Pixel-level Fusion: A typical pixel-level fusion architecture is illustrated in Figure 4-a. Where it deals with the pixels obtained from the sensor directly and tries to improve the visual enhancement. Typically, multiple images from different sources are combined into one single image in a pixel-wise manner, after which it is fed into the object detection system to generate final results. One of the main advantages of the pixel-level fusion methods is the low computational complexity and easy implementation.

Feature-level Fusion: As an higher level fusion system, one might pursue the feature-level fusion shown in Figure 4-b, in which different type of images are simultaneously fed into their independent lower part of the entire object detection system, which is typically called feature extractor. For instance, this lower-level system might be the hand engineered feature extractor for the traditional object detection system and high-level convolution layer for the CNN-based system. After which the concatenated features produced by the various independent lower systems are fed into one upper decision-making system to produce the final results. Although this feature-level fusion is usually robust to the noise, it is computationally expensive to deal with feature fusion procedure in a parallel fashion, especially for the CNN-based methods.

Decision-level Fusion: The decision-level fusion scheme illustrated in Figure 4(c) which operates on the highest level, and refers to fusing discriminate results from different systems designed for various type images. Note that for an object detection system based on learning algorithms, the decision-level fusion does not capture the intrinsic relationship between different images. In addition, this method might also be difficult to implement, apart from being computationally expensive.

In our framework, we propose a novel image fusion approach. As shown in the image fusion module in Figure 2, firstly, the three type of raw images (MWIR, VI and Motion image) are concatenated into a BGR-style three-channel image where MWIR is in the red channel, motion image in green channel and VI in the blue channel. After the fused image is obtained, we fed it into a convolutional neural network (CNN) for training our object detector in an end-to-end manner. Meanwhile, the feature from different source images can be fused together in the last feature maps of the CNN in an unsupervised learning fashion. Therefore, compared with feature-level and decision-level fusion methods, our approach is easier to implement and low computational complexity. And for pixel-level fusion, we employ unsupervised learning style to fuse images from different sources instead of utilizing hand-engineered pixel-level fusion algorithms such as discrete wavelet transform (DWT) pixel-level image fusion methodologies.

2.2.2. Regions of Interest Proposal

As you can see in the ROIs proposal module in Figure 2, given an image, the ROIs proposal algorithms can output a set of class-independent locations that are likely to contain objects. Different from the exhaustive search "sliding window" paradigm which will propose every possible candidate locations and generate around $10^4 - 10^5$ windows per image, ROIs proposal methods try to reach high object recall with considerably fewer windows. In the most popular object detectors such as R-CNN [15] and fast R-CNN [14], they use the selective search [52] method as their ROIs proposal module.

The selective search [52] is a ROIs proposal that combines the intuitions of bottom up segmentation and exhaustive search. The whole algorithm can be simplified as follows. Firstly, [12] algorithm is adopted to create initial regions. Then the similarities between all neighbor regions are calculated and the two most similar regions are grouped together. After that, the new similarities are calculated between the resulting region and its neighbors. In this iterative manner, the process of grouping the most similar regions is repeated until the whole image becomes a single region. Finally, the object location boxes can be extracted from each region. Because of this hierarchical grouping process, the generated locations come from all scales.

2.2.3. Network Architecture

The great success of Convolutional Neural Networks (CNNs) in recent years aroused broader interest in CNNs-based generic object detection among researchers. Typically, a CNN comprises of a stack of convolutional and pooling layers. The convolutional layer can generate feature maps by convolving the input feature maps or image with a set of learnable kernels. And the pooling layer can pool information of a given region on output feature maps in order to achieve down sampling and expansion of the receptive field.

Table 1. Network configuration: The complete network architecture contains two modules, where the first module is called *CNN feature extractor* which includes 5 convolutional layers (conv 1-5), while the second module is the *ROI classification and regression* which has a ROI pooling layer and 4 fully connected layers.

Name	Conv1	Norm1	Pool1	Conv2	Norm2	Pool2	Conv3	Conv4	Conv5	ROI Pooling	FC6	FC7	Cls	Bbox
Input Channels	3	96	96	96	256	256	256	512	512	512	36	4096	1024	1024
Output Channels	96	96	96	256	256	256	512	512	512	36	4096	1024	2	8
Kernel Size	7×7		3×3	5×5			3×3	3×3	3×3	6×6				
Type	conv	LRN	max-pool	conv	LRN	max-pool	conv	conv	conv	ROI-pool	fc	fc	fc	fc
Stride	2		2	2		2	1	1	1					
Pad				1			1	1	1					
Activation function	relu			relu			relu	relu	relu					
Dropout											✓	✓		

An example of a CNNs-based object detector is the R-CNN [15], which utilizes selective search method to generate a set of ROIs proposal from input image and then feed each ROI to a CNN to obtain final results. However, this paradigm is slow, because lots of heavily overlapped ROIs have to go through the CNN separately, resulting in increased computational complexity. SPP-net [19] and fast R-CNN [14] successful solved this problem by proposing a spatial pyramid Pooling (SPP) and ROI pooling, respectively. They suggested the whole image can go through CNN once and the final decision is made at the last feature maps produced by the CNN using their proposed pooling strategies.

As shown in Figure 2, our approach builds on the paradigm of fast R-CNN [14]. Where the fused three channel image is firstly fed into our CNN feature extractor to generate conv feature maps. It should be noted that the final conv feature maps in our project is also the fusing results of the three types of images by unsupervised learning. After which, for each ROIs generated by the ROIs proposal, we conduct an ROI pooling process directly on the conv feature maps instead of input image to extract an fixed length feature vector. The reason why we choose ROI pooling instead of SPP is that the gradients can propagate to the CNN layers in training stage and this can help CNN learn how to fuse the multiple channel-independent image in an unsupervised fashion. Finally,the extracted vector need to be sent to a fully connected neural network which has two output ports where one is for classification and another one is for bounding boxes regression.

The architecture of CNN feature extractor used in our framework is the **VGGM** from [5] , why we chose it is because we take into account the trade-off between accuracy and computational complexity. The VGGM is a shallow version of VGG16 [41] and wider version of AlexNet[25], but faster than VGG16 as well as more accurate than AlexNet. More details about the VGGM configuration can be seen in table 1.

2.2.4. Training Details

Transfer Learning:

Transferring information between different data source for related tasks is an effective technique to help deal with insufficient training data and overfitting in the deep learning community. For instance, training a CNN model on the large ImageNet [35] dataset firstly and then fine-tuning it on the domain-specific dataset. However, these techniques are limited to transferring information between RGB (visible image) models. This limits the utilization of transfer learning to datasets, which include the visible images, IR images, and generated motion maps.

We propose to address this issue and transfer the CNN parameters trained on large-scale public visible image datasets, such as ImageNet [35] to the fused dataset. The VGGM model is pre-trained on the large-scale RGB image dataset, ImageNet, which contains common objects and scenes observed in daily life. These pre-trained weights are then used to initialize the weights of the CNN being trained on the fused dataset. During the fine-tuning process, we initialize the weights of "conv1" to "conv5". Additionally, unlike some prior work, we do not freeze the lower layers of CNN during the fine-tuning. This enables our network to adapt to the data distribution of the fused data.

Loss Functions

As shown in Table 1, the network has two output heads. The first is for classifying each ROI, which will output a discrete probability distribution over two categories(background and target). And the second is for regressing the bounding box offsets of ROI where for each category, it will output a tuple of (t_x, t_y, t_w, t_h), the elements indicate the shift value relative to the central coordinate, height and width of original proposal ROI.

Similar to [14], the following negative log likelihood objective is used for classification:

$$L_{cls}(p, u) = -log(p_u) \qquad (2)$$

where, p represents the predicted probability of one of categories and u is the ground truth class.

For regression, the smooth L_1 loss function is used:

$$L_{bbox}(t^u, v) = \sum_{i \in \{x,y,w,h\}} smooth_{L_1}(t_i^u - v_i) \qquad (3)$$

in which t^u is the bounding box offsets of the u class. And v is the true offsets.

In the training stage, the objective functions are combined as following:

$$L(p, u, t^u, v) = L_{cls}(p, u) + \lambda [u = 1] L_{bbox}(t^u, v) \qquad (4)$$

$u = 1$ means only when the class is target, the bounding box regression can be trained. The λ is used to control balance between classification and regression, we set it as 1 in all experiments.

2.3. Experiments

2.3.1. Dataset

We evaluate our approach on a public released ATR database from the military sensing information analysis center (SENSIAC). This database package contains 207 GB of MWIR imagery and 106 GB of visible imagery along with ground truth data. All imagery was taken using commercial cameras operating in the MWIR and visible bands. The types of targets include people, foreign military vehicles, and civilian vehicles. The datasets were collected during both daytime and night and the distance between cameras and targets varied from 500 to 5000 meters.

In our experiments, we only consider the vehicle objects, and split the 5 types of vehicles into training targets and 3 types of vehicles into testing targets. The details of the split are shown in Figure 5. We selected each type of vehicles with 3 range of distances between the camera and the target (1000, 1500 and 3000 meters). The dataset contains 4573 training images and 2812 testing images corresponding to every 5-th frame sampled from the original dataset. It should be noted that we consider all the types of vehicle as one class, "vehicle". Consequently, the problem becomes a binary (vehicle and background) object detection problem.

Figure 5. Appearance of targets in training data and testing data

2.3.2. Experimental Setup

Our framework is implemented by using Caffe deep learning toolbox [21]. For the training machine, we use a computer with a NVIDIA GeForce GTX 1080 GPU, a Intel Core i7 CPU and 32 GB Memory. For the setup of hyper-parameters, we also follow the fast R-CNN [14], where we train all the networks each for 40000 iterations with initial learning rate 0.001 and 0.0001 for the last 10000 iterations, momentum 0.9 and weight decay 0.0005.

2.3.3. Evaluation

Metrics:

For all of metrics, we consider detections as true or false positives based on whether the area of overlap with ground truth bounding boxes exceed 0.5. The overlap area can be calculated by the below equation:

$$a_o = \frac{area(B_p \cap B_{gt})}{area(B_p \cup B_{gt})} \tag{5}$$

Where a_o denotes the overlap area, B_p and B_{gt} denote the predicted bounding box and ground truth bounding box, respectively.

Mean Average Precision(mAP) is a golden standard metric for evaluating the performance of an object detection algorithm, where it first calculates the average precision (AP) of each class and then averages all the obtained AP values. Because there is only one class (vehicle) in our experiments, we select AP as one of the evaluation metrics. The AP value can be easily obtained by computing the area under the precision-recall curve.

Top1 Precision is a metric that is widely used in classification tasks, where the probability of multiple classes is predicted and the class having the highest score is selected. Subsequently, the top1 precision score is calculated, which corresponds to the number of predicted labels that match the target label, divided by the total number of data. In our case, there is only one target in each image. Thus, we can employ top1 precision metric in experiments to evaluate the performance of our framework in a practical scenario.

Performance Comparison and Analysis:

We perform six incremental experiment designs to examine the effectiveness of our fusion method. We also attempt to see the performance of the detection algorithms on three type of images (Visible, MWIR and Motion) independently. Note that because all of the independent images are single-channel format and the input format requirement of CNN is three-channels image, we generate the desired images by duplicating the single-channel image in three times. After that, we try to fuse visible and MWIR images together and examine whether the fused image without short-temporal information can boost the overall performance or not. To meet the requirements of CNN, we duplicate the visible channel twice. Then, we incorporate the short-temporal information, the motion image, and generate our complete fused 3-channels image. In addition, we also test the decision-level fusion method, where we combine the three outputs of three single networks on three type of independent images.

Figure 6 shows the AP curves of the six incremental experiments. In independent image experiments, we can see that the overall performance of the CNN-based detector is good, especially for the single visible image, which achieved 97.31% average precision and 98.04% top1 accuracy, as shown in Table 2. In case of the visible-MWIR fused image detector, we observe that it achieves a better result than the performance of the single image detector. It should be noted that our 3-channels image achieves both the highest average precision(98.34%) and top1 accuracy (98.90%), with only 16 false positive in the 2812 testing frames. Thus the average precision of the decision fusion method is higher than the best single image method. However, its top1 accuracy is lower than the single visible image approach and it is also computationally expensive taking an average of (3.961s) per frame.

To further verify the effectiveness of our unsupervised image fusion method, we visualize the feature map of the last convolutional layer and the final output of our framework in Fig.7. The feature map is the output of CNN feature extractor in Fig.2, and the fused image, and it corresponds to the fused high-level features. It could be reasoned that if the object in the feature map is segmented clearly, the framework will get a better result. In the examples of Fig 7, we can see that the 3-channels can well fuse the complementary information from the three independent images, enhancing the segmentation in

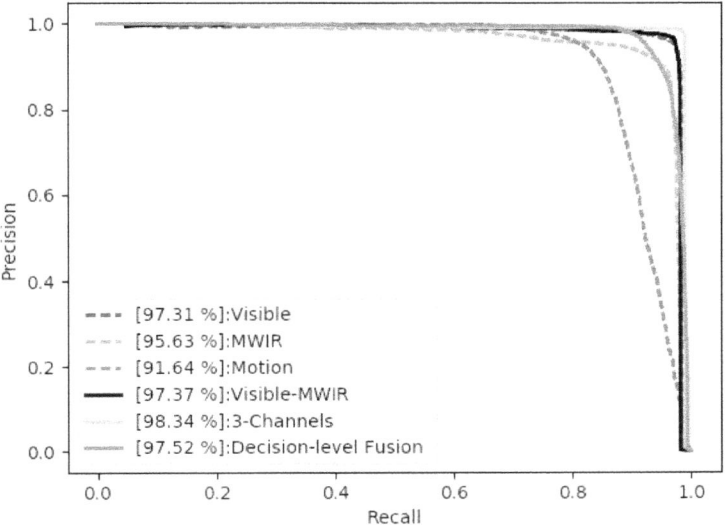

Figure 6. Average precision (AP) comparison between different experimental designs. Independent input of visible, MWIR and Motion image, fusion image of visible and MWIR image (Visible-MWIR), fusion image of visible, MWIR and Motion (3-Channels) and decision-level fusion, respectively

Table 2. Performance comparison on accuracy and time cost of different methods.

Methods	Accuracy (%)		Running Time (s/image)		
	AP	Top1	ROIs Proposal	Networks	Overall
Visible	97.31	98.04	1.378	0.164	1.542
MWIR	95.63	96.91	**1.144**	0.069	1.213
Motion	91.64	92.39	1.167	**0.038**	**1.205**
Visible-MWIR	97.37	98.18	1.505	0.248	1.753
3-Channels	**98.34**	**98.90**	1.272	0.235	1.507
Decision-level Fusion	97.52	97.93	3.690	0.271	3.961

the feature map. The final output also confirms the reasoning that the enhanced feature map can boost the performance.

2.4. Summary

In this work, an unsupervised learning based image fusion method is proposed to integrate the ATD network, which fused visible, MWIR and motion information effectively. We further adopted state-of-the-art generic object detector for the battle field object detection. We also utilized cross-domain transfer learning techniques to deal with the insufficient data by training the model on large-scale visible image dataset firstly and then

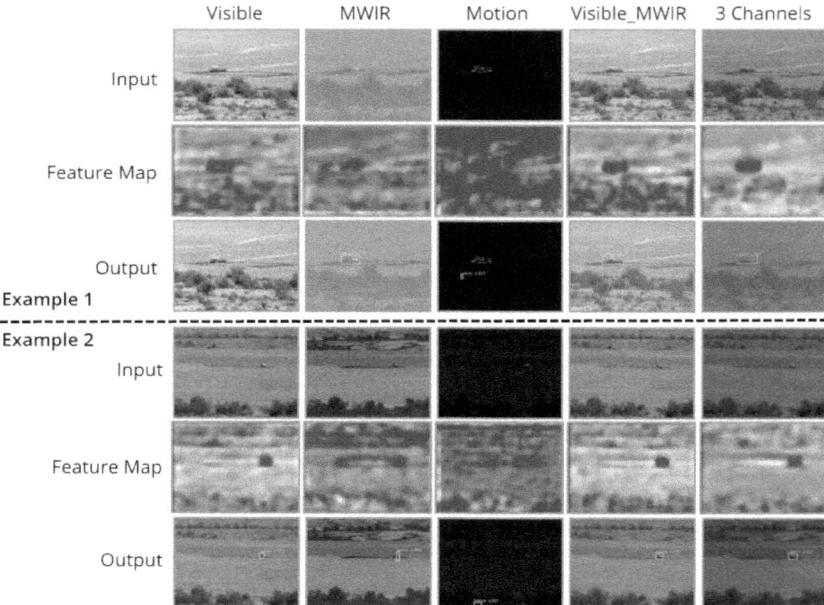

Figure 7. Example of the visualised results of our framework. Example 1 and 2 demonstrate the performance with varied inputs on large and small object detection, respectively. Different columns denote the different types of input image. The raw input image, generated feature map and the final output are showed in consecutive rows. In the final output image, the green bounding box represent the position of object predicted by system.

fine-tuning on the small-scale fused image dataset. The proposed framework was evaluated with the SENSIAC dataset. It achieved 98.34% average precision and 98.90% top1 accuracy. However, the computational times is still high for real-time applications. This remains a topic for our future work.

3. Case2-Face Recognition

3.1. Background

Face recognition in unconstrained images has remained as one of the main research topics in computer vision for decades, due to its numerous practical applications in the area of information security, access control, and surveillance system.

There are two well-known paradigms of face recognition, which are identification and verification. In identification, a set of representations for specific individuals to be recognized is stored in a database. At test time, when a new image with people is presented, the system will check if the test people is present in the stored database. If present, the identity of the test individual is retrieved. However, the task of verification system is to analyze two face images and decide whether they represent the same person or two different people. Generally, neither of the images to be tested are from any training dataset. Because the face verification only need to compare the two presented images, it can yield results more quickly than the identification system. In this chapter, we focus on the face verification tasks.

Some of the challenges in the face recognition systems include variation in the appearance of the same person due to different poses, illuminations, expressions, ages, and occlusions. Therefore, reducing the intra-personal variations while increasing the inter-personal differences is a primary task in face recognition.

Most recently, deep Learning has significantly improved the state-of-the-art in many applications. In the world of face recognition, deep models such as CNNs have been proved effective for extracting high-level visual features. Thus boosting the performance of face recognition significantly [51][45].

In this chapter, we present a unified system for face recognition in unconstrained conditions, which contains a face detection, face alignment and face verification module. The overall system is inspired by the recent advances in deep learning community, such as the Inception-ResNet architecture, center loss, Multi-Task CNNs, etc. In the stage of experiments, we compared the presented method with the state-of-the-art on the widely used Labeled Faces in the Wild (LFW) benchmark and showed its effectiveness.

3.2. Related Works

A face recognition system typically includes three essential cascaded components: 1)face detection, 2) face alignment, 3) and face verification. In below sections, we will review the literature related to these components separately.

3.2.1. Face Detection

Face detection has made significant stride in the recent decades. Viola and Jones[53] first proposed a cascade Adaboost framework using the Haar-like features and performed face detection in real-time. In recent years, many CNN-based face detection methods have been proposed [28][43][22][54]. For example, Li et al.[28] presented a method which integrates a CNN and a 3D face model in an end-to-end multi-task learning framework. [22] applied the Faster R-CNN [34], one of state-of-the-art generic object detector, and achieved promising results. Furthermore, Wan et al.[54] combined Faster R-CNN face detection algorithm with hard negative mining as well as ResNet architecture [18], which achieved significant boosts in detection performance on face detection benchmarks like FDDB. In recent years, the Multi-Task CNNs framework is proposed by [60] and obtained the state-of-the-art performance, which leverages a cascaded CNN architecture to predict face and facial landmarks in a coarse-to-fine manner.

3.2.2. Face Alignment

Generally, almost every face recognition systems used aligned faces as the input. The usual way for face alignment is predicting facial landmarks from the detected facial patches. Early works on facial landmarks prediction includes Active Contours Models [23], and Appearance Models (AAM)[8]. Recently, deep learning based methods [44][61] [59] [38] have shown their advantages for face landmark localization. Sun *et al.* [44] applies a DCNN based method to handle the problem of face landmark detection via three-level cascaded convolutional networks (totally 23 CNNs). Zhang *et all.* [59] uses successive auto-encoder networks for face alignment (CFAN) by multiple convolutional networks. [61] uses the same network structure with [44] for face landmark localization with multitasks which named TCDCN. Shao *et al.* [38] adopts a deep network learning deep representation from coarse to fine for face alignment.

3.2.3. Face Verification

Numerous literature about face verification in unconstrained conditions have been proposed in recent years. In tradition, the high-dimensional over-complete face descriptors were used to represent faces, followed by shallow models. For instance, the method in [2] encoded faces into the learning-based(LE) descriptors in and then calculated the L_2 distance between the LE descriptors after PCA. In [40], the SIFT descriptors were extracted densely and then encoded into Fisher vectors, followed by a learned linear projection for discriminative dimensionality reduction. Recently, CNN-based models have been used for face verification. [7] trained Siamese networks for forcing the similarity metric of same faces to be small and of different faces to be large. [46] incorporated identification signal into the CNNs learning process, which brought identity-related feature to the deep representations. Furthermore, [36] proposed a CNN-based framework with a novel loss function named "triplet loss", which is able to minimize the distance between an anchor and a positive representation while to maximize the distance between an anchor and a negative one. After that, a novel loss function called "center loss" was proposed by Wen *et all.*[55], which allowed them to achieve the state-of-the-art accuracy on several well-known face verification benchmarks.

3.3. Methods

The overview of the proposed framework is illustrated in Figure 8. It consists of two primary modules, the Multi-Task CNN (MTCNN) module to predict face and landmark location simultaneously, and the face verification module to verify whether the given two faces belong to the same person. To be specific, the Multi-Task CNN leverages a cascaded architecture with three stages of lightweight CNNs to conduct face detection and alignment in a coarse-to-fine manner. The face verification module utilizes a deep CNN to extract discriminative representations, and then transform them into embedding feature space where $L2$ distance is calculated between two face embedding and verification, after which the results can be obtained by a thresholding operation. In the later section, each module of our face recognition system will be elaborated.

3.3.1. Face Detection and Alignment

Architecture:

The flowchart and architecture of the MTCNN are illustrated in Figure 2. Initially, given an image, a pyramid with multi-scale images is constructed, which is the input of the following cascaded CNNs.

   P-Net: The first CNN is a fully convolutional network, called proposal network (P-Net). After the multi-scale image pyramid is forwarded through this shallow network, the coarse candidate facial bounding boxes and their regression vectors can be obtained. Then the candidates can be refined by the estimated bounding box regression vectors. At the end of this network, the non-maximum suppression is utilized to merge highly overlapped candidates. The P-Net primarily includes a "trunk" stream and two "head"

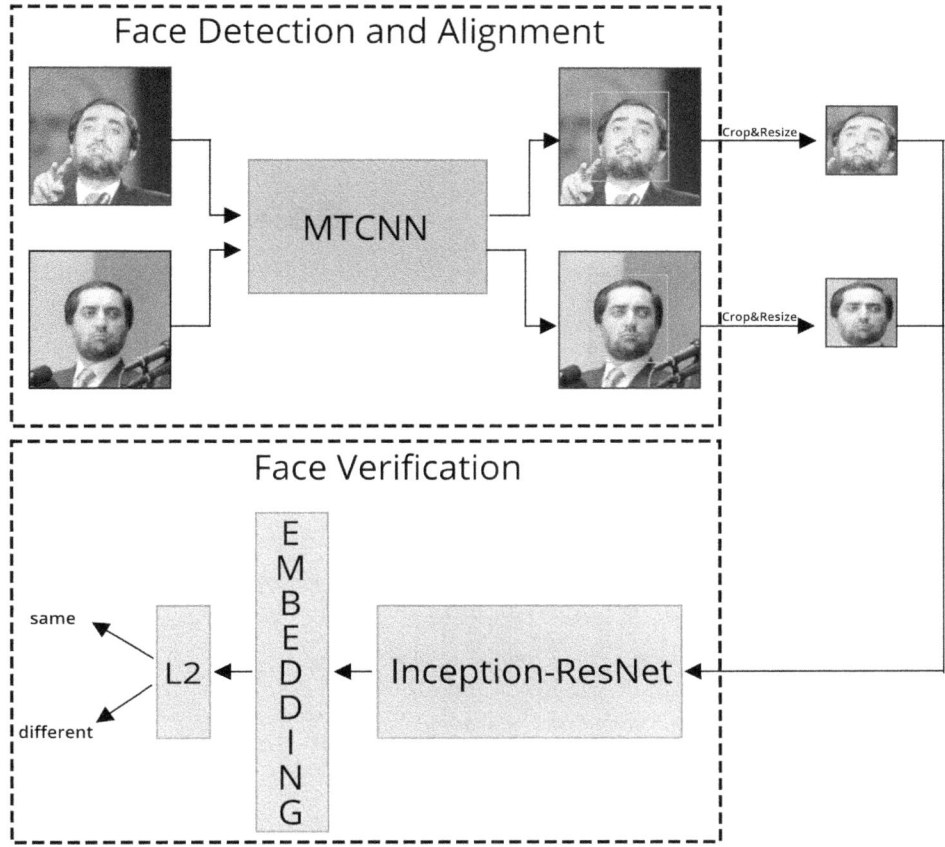

Figure 8. The pipeline of the face recognition system

streams. To be specific, there are three convolutional layers in the trunk steam and with a max pooling layer followed the first convolutional layer. Each convolutional layer has the same receptive field with 3×3 and a different number of filters (10, 16, 32 respectively). In this network, the parametric rectified linear unit (PReLU) is applied as non-linearity activation function after the convolution layers. In the "head" streams, there is a $1 \times 1 \times 2$ convolution for classification,and a $1 \times 1 \times 4$ convolution for estimating the bounding box regression vectors.

R-Net: All the candidates generated by the P-Net are fed to the refine network (R-Net), which further rejects a large number of false candidates. The architecture of R-Net is slightly different than the P-Net. Where it also has three convolutional layers in the "trunk" stream, but there is an additional max pooling layer followed by the second convolutional layer and a size of 128 fully connected layer added at the end of "trunk" stream. For the "head" streams, compared with that in P-Net, they were replaced by two fully connected layers with the size of 2 and 4, respectively. Note that the input of the R-Net requires the size of 24×24.

O-Net: The final network in the cascaded CNNs framework is the output network (O-Net), which aims to identify face regions with more supervision. In particular, the

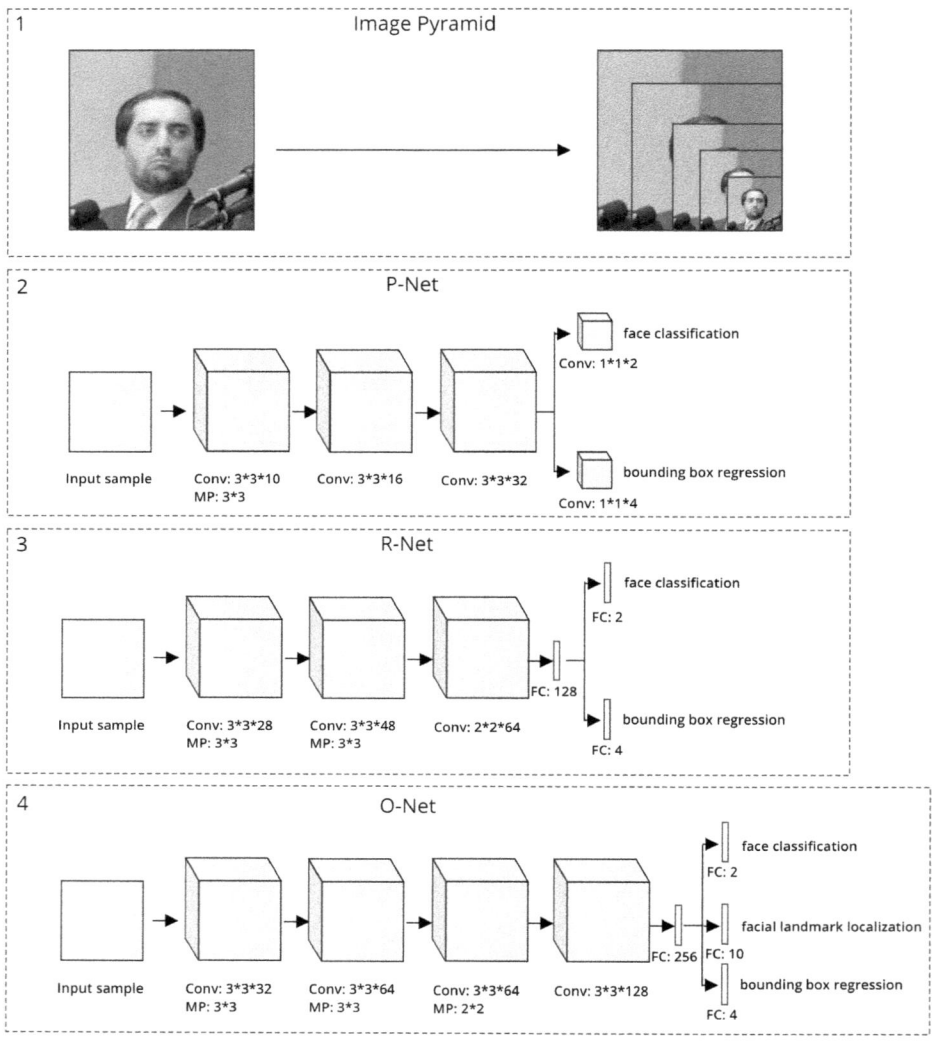

Figure 9. The flowchart and architecture of the Multi-Task CNN

network will output five facial landmarks. In the architecture of the O-Net, there are four different sizes of convolutional layers in the "trunk" stream and followed by a fully-connected layer with the size of 256. In the "head" steams, there are three fully connected layers which are used to classification, bounding box regression and facial landmark localization.

Training:

The three networks (P-Net, R-Net, and O-Net) are trained with multi-task losses: face classification, bounding box regression, and facial landmark localization.

Face Classification: The learning objective is formulated as a two-class classification problem. For each sample x_i, the cross-entropy loss is employed:

$$L_i^{det} = -(y_i^{det} \log(p_i) + (1 - y_i^{det})(1 - \log(p_i)))$$ (6)

where p_i is the probability produced by the network that indicates sample x_i being a face. The notation $y_i^{det} \in \{0, 1\}$ denotes the ground truth label.

Bounding Box Regression: For each candidate bounding box, the offset between it and the nearest ground truth is predicted. The learning objective is formulated as follow:

$$L_i^{box} = \|\hat{y}_i^{box} - y_i^{box}\|_2^2$$ (7)

where $\hat{y}_i^{box}$ is the regression target obtained from the network and y_i^{box} is the ground truth coordinate. There are four coordinates, including left top, height and width.

Facial Landmark Localization: Similar to bounding box regression task, facial landmark detection is formulated as a regression problem:

$$L_i^{landmark} = \|\hat{y}^{landmark} - y_i^{landmark}\|_2^2$$ (8)

where $\hat{y}_i^{landmark}$ is the coordinates of facial landmarks obtained from the network and $y_i^{landmark}$ is the ground truth coordinate for the ith sample.Five facial landmarks are considered :left mouth corner,right mouth corner, nose, left eye, and right eye.

3.3.2. Face Verification

Architecture:

As you can see in the face verification module in the Figure 8, there are three main parts in the proposed face verification module: (1) deep feature extractor, (2) feature space embedding, and (3) feature distance measurement.

Deep Feature Extractor: Given an image x, we strive for a feature extractor $g(x)$ which is able to transform x into a feature space $\mathbb{R}^d$. Inspired by the Inception-ResNet [48], the networks are very deep and wide, in the sense that they comprise a long sequence of Inception modules in a ResNet fashion. Such CNNs have recently achieved state-of-the-art performance in the ImageNet classification challenge. [35]. The large scale structure of the Inception-ResNet architecture is given in Figure 10 and the detailed structure of its components is illustrated in Figures 111213. The structure of Inception-ResNet primarily includes a stem, three Inception clusters and two reduction modules. The stem component is a set of cascaded convolution, which aims to extract low-level features. Moreover, each Inception cluster comprise of several Inception blocks.

All the convolutional layers, including those inside the Inception-ResNet modules, use the rectified linear activation (Relu). The input image's size in our network is 128×128 with RGB color channels and mean subtraction. As shown in Figure. 12, instead of using the original Inception [49], the cheaper but effective Inception blocks is implemented in the Inception-ResNet. It should be noted that the last convolutional layer in each Inception blocks is a 1×1 filter expansion layer, which is designed for increasing the dimensions of the filter bank before the addition to match the depth of the input. However, there is a reduction module followed by the first two Inception clusters, which is used for reducing the dimension of the feature maps.

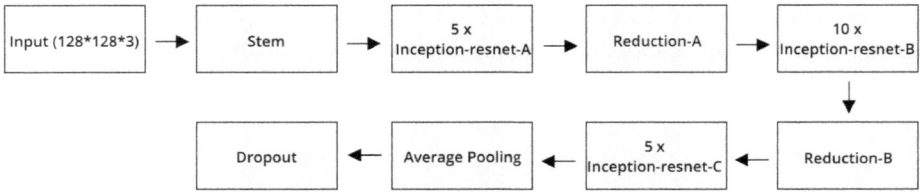

Figure 10. The large scale structure of the Inception-ResNet network.

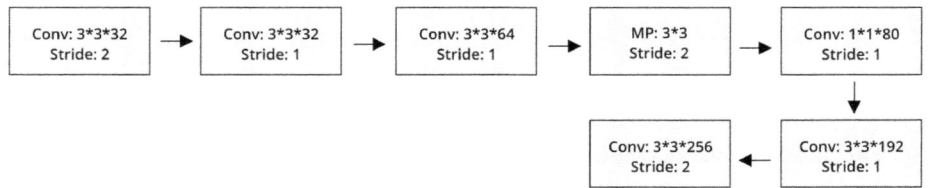

Figure 11. The structure of stem in the Inception-ResNet.

Feature Space Embedding: The output of the stage of the deep feature extractor is a high-dimension feature vector in the space $\mathbb{R}^d$. For face verification task, the deeply learned embedding need to be not only discriminative but also compact. Thus a embedding function $f(x) \in \mathbb{R}^e$ is needed, from a high-dimension feature vector into a compact low-dimension embedding. To end this, we follow the ideas in [36] using a fully connected layer and a $L2$ normalization to directly learn a projection from the feature space $\mathbb{R}^d$ to embedding space $\mathbb{R}^e$ (e is 128 in our experiments).

Feature Distance Measurement: The squared $L2$ distances in the compact embedding space directly corresponds to face similarity: faces of the same person have small distances and faces of distinct people have large distance. In this way, the face verification task becomes straightforward, which simply involves thresholding the distance between the two embeddings.

Training:

Constructing highly efficient loss function for discriminative feature learning in CNNs is non-trivial. In this application, we utilized the "center loss" proposed in [55] to efficiently bring the learned embedding with the discriminative power. Specifically, a class center vector, which has the same dimension as the embedding feature is learned. In the stage of training, the distances between the embedding features and their corresponding center vectors are minimized. Note that the center vectors will be updated at the same time. We train the entire network by the joint supervision of the center loss as well as the softmax loss. And there is a hyperparameter for balancing the two supervision signals. Basically, the center loss efficiently forces the embedding features of the same class to their centers while the softmax loss enable the embedding features of different classes keeping large distances. Under the joint supervision, We can not only enlarge the inter-class features variations , but also decrease the intra-class features differences. The center loss function is formulated as follows:

$$L_c = \frac{1}{2} \sum_{i=1}^{m} \|x_i - c_{y_i}\|_2^2 \tag{9}$$

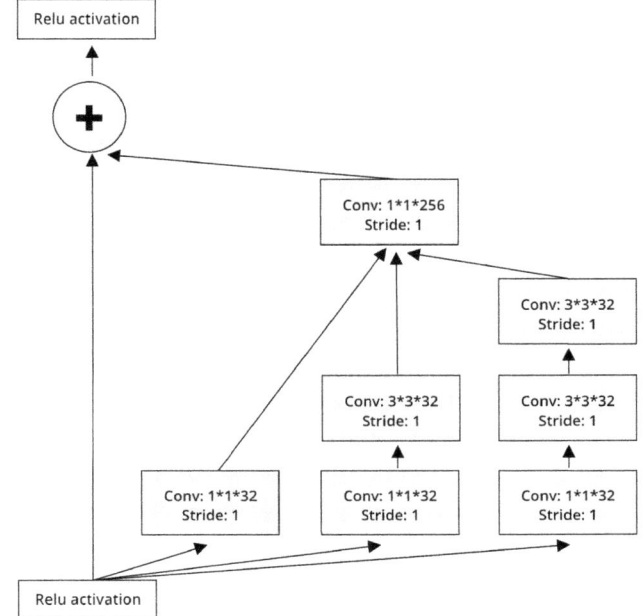

(a) Inception-ResNet-A.

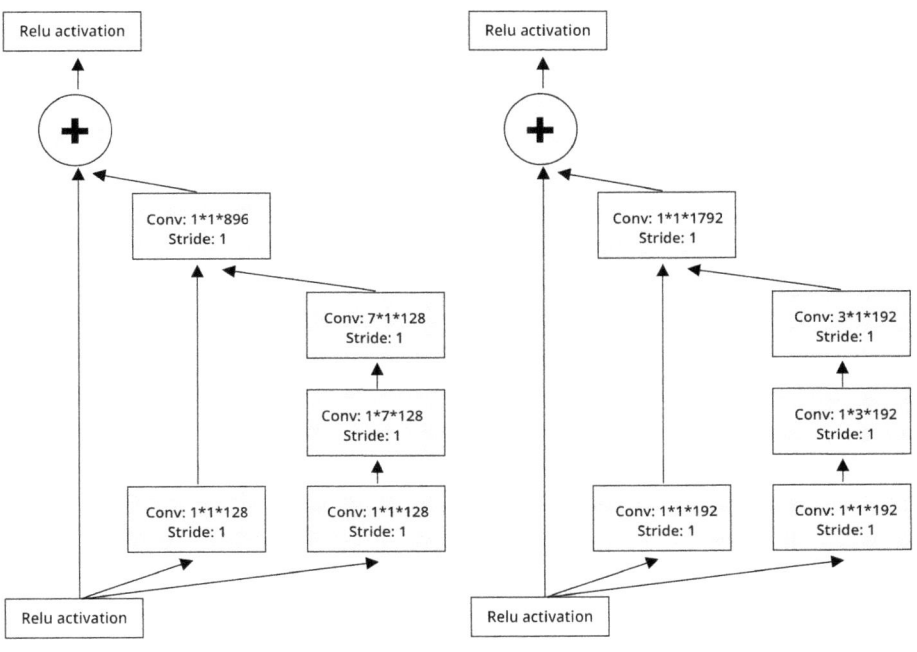

(b) Inception-ResNet-B.

(c) Inception-ResNet-C.

Figure 12. The structure of submodules of Inception-ResNet.

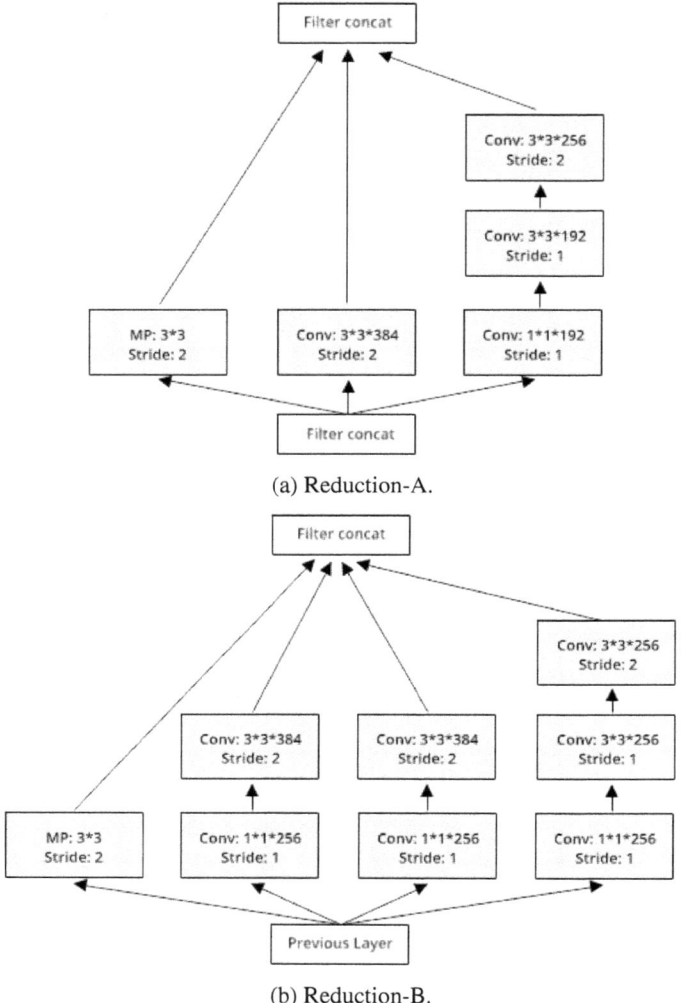

(a) Reduction-A.

(b) Reduction-B.

Figure 13. The structure of reduction modules

The $c_{y_i} \in \mathbb{R}^e$ denotes the y_i th class center of embedding features. The formulation aims to reduce the intra-class variations. Furthermore, the joint center loss and softmax loss is formulated as follows:

$$L = L_s + \lambda L_c = -\sum_{i=1}^{m} \log \frac{e^{W_{y_i}^T x_i + b_{y_i}}}{\sum_{j=1}^{n} e^{W_j^T x_i + b_j}} + \frac{\lambda}{2} \sum_{i=1}^{m} \|x_i - c_{y_i}\|_2^2 \qquad (10)$$

The L_s and L_c indicate the softmax loss and center loss, respectively. And we use the scalar λ for balancing the two loss functions.

3.4. Experiments

3.4.1. Dataset

We use CASIA-Webface [56] as our training set and evaluate on the labeled faces in the wild (LFW)[27] dataset which is the de-facto academic test set for face verification in unconstrained conditions. The CASIA-Webface consists of 494,414 images of 10,575 subjects, and LFW contains 13,233 face images of 5749 identities collected from the Internet. For comparison purposes, algorithms typically report the mean face verification accuracy.

3.4.2. Performance

In Table 3, we compare the performances between our method and other state-of-the-art methods on the LFW face verification benchmark. We follow the standard protocol for unrestricted, labeled outside data. Even thought it is well-known that an ensemble of multiple models can improve the overall performance slightly, we only compare CNN-based single model methods to focus on the power of network design. It is clear that the performance will increases typically with the scale of training dataset. With larger dataset like the FaceNet, we can achieve the best performance in LFW (260M images of 8M subjects). In our experiments, our model is only trained on the public dataset CASIA-Webface. In comparison with the methods[57][56] which were also trained on the CASIA-Webface, our method achieved state-of-the-art performance with 98.80 ± 0.005 accuracy. It should be noted that the human-level performance LFW is 97.5% [26], the presented system is able to surpass it by a large margin.

Table 3. Performance comparison on LFW dataset

Method	# Net	Training Set	Metric	Accuracy $\pm$ Std (%)
DeepID2[45]	1	202,599 images of 10, 177 subjects, private	Joint-Bayes	95.43
DeepFace[51]	1	4.4M images of 4, 030 subjects, private	cosine	95.92 ± 0.29
CASIANet[56]	1	494, 414 images of 10, 575 subjects, public	cosine	96.13 ± 0.30
Littwin and Wolf[30]	1	404, 992 images of 10, 553 subjects, public	Joint-Bayes	98.14 ± 0.19
p-CNN[57]	1	494, 414 images of 10, 575 subjects, public	cosine	98.27 ± 0.64
MultiBatch[50]	1	2.6M images of 12K subjects, private	Euclidean	98.20
VGG-DeepFace[33]	1	2.6M images of 2, 622 subjects, public	Euclidean	98.95
Wen et al.[55]	1	0.7M images of 17, 189 subjects, public	cosine	99.28
FaceNet[36]	1	260M images of 8M subjects, private	L2	99.63 ± 0.09
Ours	1	494, 414 images of 10, 575 subjects, public	L2	98.80 ± 0.005

Besides the performance, another important factor is the time complexity. We evaluated the running time of each module (face detection with alignment, and face verification) as shown in Table 4. The application was implemented by using the tensorflow deep learning tool [1] and running on a machine with an NVIDIA GeForce GTX 1080 GPU, a Intel Core i7 CPU and 32 GB memory. In testing stage, two images with size of 250×250 were feed into the application. As shown in the Table 4, it takes 1.092 second for face detection and alignment, 1.067 second for face verification. So, totally the Deep Residual Face application takes around 2.159 second. To meet the real-time requirement in a real scenario, we need to do more work on improving the speed of our face recognition application in the future.

Table 4. Running time of each module in terms of second

	Face Detection and Alignment	Face Verification	Total
Running Time (s)	1.092	1.067	2.159

3.5. Summary

In this case study, a CNN-based face recognition system is proposed to show the effectiveness of deep learning on security applications. We adopted the state-of-the-art face detector, Multi-Task CNNs, to perform face patch detection and alignment. Furthermore, the recent proposed Inception-ResNet CNN architecture was utilized for deep features extracting. With the help of $L2$ embedding procedure and center loss training tricks, the proposed face recognition achieved a comparative results on the well-known FLW benchmark.

4. Conclusion

In this chapter, two cases, military automatic target detection and face recognition, were presented to show the effectiveness of using deep learning for surveillance and security applications. In the first case, a CNN-based military ATD method using a new deep image fusion technique was proposed, which fused multi-channel images within a CNN to enhance the significance of deep features and achieved promising results on the SENSIAC dataset. In the second case, we also presented a novel face recognition system motivated by the recent advances in the deep learning community, where the Inception-ResNet CNN architecture was utilized to extracting deep features and the center loss function was adopted for training the face verification network. Our novel face recognition system is able to surpass human-level performance on the face verification benchmark LFW.

References

[1]   Martn Abadi, Ashish Agarwal, Paul Barham, Eugene Brevdo, Zhifeng Chen, Craig Citro, Greg S Corrado, Andy Davis, Jeffrey Dean, Matthieu Devin, Sanjay Ghemawat, Ian Goodfellow, Andrew Harp, Geoffrey Irving, Michael Isard, Yangqing Jia, Rafal Jozefowicz, Lukasz Kaiser, Manjunath Kudlur, Josh Levenberg, Dan Mané, Rajat Monga, Sherry Moore, Derek Murray, Chris Olah, Mike Schuster, Jonathon Shlens, Benoit Steiner, Ilya Sutskever, Kunal Talwar, Paul Tucker, Vincent Vanhoucke, Vijay Vasudevan, Fernanda Viégas, Oriol Vinyals, Pete Warden, Martin Wattenberg, Martin Wicke, Yuan Yu, Xiaoqiang Zheng, and Google Research. TensorFlow: Large-Scale Machine Learning on Heterogeneous Distributed Systems.
[2]   Melih S. Aslan, Zeyad Hailat, Tarik K. Alafif, and Xue-Wen Chen. Multi-channel multi-model feature learning for face recognition. *Pattern Recognition Letters*, 85:79–83, 2017.
[3]   Gaurav Bhatnagar and Zheng Liu. A novel image fusion framework for night-vision navigation and surveillance. *Signal, Image and Video Processing*, 2015.
[4]   Leo Breiman. Randomforest2001. pages 1–33, 2001.

[5] Ken Chatfield, Karen Simonyan, Andrea Vedaldi, and Andrew Zisserman. Return of the Devil in the Details: Delving Deep into Convolutional Nets. *arXiv preprint arXiv: . . .*, pages 1–11, 2014.

[6] Bo-hao Chen and Shih-chia Huang. Probabilistic neural networks based moving vehicles extraction algorithm for intelligent traffic surveillance systems. *Information Sciences*, 299:283–295, 2015.

[7] Sumit Chopra Raia Hadsell Yann LeCun. Learning a Similarity Metric Discriminatively, with Application to Face Verification.

[8] Timothy F Cootes, Gareth J Edwards, and Christopher J Taylor. Active Appearance Models.

[9] Navneet Dalal, Bill Triggs, Oriented Gradients, Detection Cordelia, Navneet Dalal, and Bill Triggs. To cite this version : Histograms of Oriented Gradients for Human Detection. pages 886–893, 2010.

[10] Mark Everingham, Luc Van Gool, Christopher K I Williams, John Winn, Andrew Zisserman, M Everingham, L KU Van Gool Leuven, Belgium CKI Williams, J Winn, and A Zisserman. The PASCAL Visual Object Classes (VOC) Challenge. *Int J Comput Vis*, 88:303–338, 2010.

[11] Pedro F Felzenszwalb, Ross B Girshick, David Mcallester, and Deva Ramanan. Object Detection with Discriminatively Trained Part Based Models. *IEEE Transactions on Pattern Analysis and Machine Intelligence*, 32(9):1–20, 2009.

[12] Pedro F Felzenszwalb and Daniel P Huttenlocher. Efficient Graph-Based Image Segmentation. *International Journal of Computer Vision*, 59(2):167–181, 2004.

[13] Francisco, Javier López-Rubio, and Ezequiel López-Rubio. Foreground detection for moving cameras with stochastic approximation. *Pattern Recognition Letters*, 68:161–168, 2015.

[14] Ross Girshick. Fast R-CNN. In *Proceedings of the IEEE International Conference on Computer Vision*, 2016.

[15] Ross Girshick, Jeff Donahue, Trevor Darrell, and Jitendra Malik. Rich feature hierarchies for accurate object detection and semantic segmentation.

[16] Jing-ming Guo, Senior Member, Chih-hsien Hsia, Member Ieee, Yun-fu Liu, and Student Member. Fast Background Subtraction Based on a Multilayer Codebook Model for Moving Object Detection. 23(10):1809–1821, 2013.

[17] Ju Han and Bir Bhanu. Fusion of color and infrared video for moving human detection. *Pattern Recognition*, 40:1771–1784, 2007.

[18] Kaiming He, Xiangyu Zhang, Shaoqing Ren, and Jian Sun. Deep Residual Learning for Image Recognition. *Arxiv.Org*, 7(3):171–180, 2015.

[19] Kaiming He, Xiangyu Zhang, Shaoqing Ren, and Jian Sun. Spatial Pyramid Pooling in Deep Convolutional Networks for Visual Recognition. *IEEE Transactions on Pattern Analysis and Machine Intelligence*, 37(9):1904–1916, 2015.

[20] Wu-Chih Hu, Chao-Ho Chen, Tsong-Yi Chen, Deng-Yuan Huang, and Zong-Che Wu. Moving object detection and tracking from video captured by moving camera. 2015.

[21] Yangqing Jia, Evan Shelhamer, Jeff Donahue, Sergey Karayev, Jonathan Long, Ross Girshick, Sergio Guadarrama, and Trevor Darrell. Caffe: Convolutional Architecture for Fast Feature Embedding *.

[22] Huaizu Jiang and Erik Learned-Miller. Face Detection with the Faster R-CNN.

[23] Michael Kass and Andrew Witkin. Snakes: Active Contour Models. *International Journal of Computer Vision*, pages 321–331, 1988.

[24] Scale-invariant Keypoints and David G Lowe. Distinctive Image Features from. *International Journal of Computer Vision*, 60(2):91–110, 2004.

[25] Alex Krizhevsky, Ilya Sutskever, and Geoffrey E Hinton. ImageNet Classification with Deep Convolutional Neural Networks. *Advances In Neural Information Processing Systems*, pages 1–9, 2012.

[26] Neeraj Kumar, Alexander C Berg, Peter N Belhumeur, and Shree K Nayar. Attribute and Simile Classifiers for Face Verification.

[27] Erik Learned-Miller, Gary Huang, Aruni Roychowdhury, Haoxiang Li, Gang Hua, and Gary B Huang. Labeled Faces in the Wild: A Survey.

[28] Yunzhu Li, Benyuan Sun, Tianfu Wu, and Yizhou Wang. Face Detection with End-to-End Integration of a ConvNet and a 3D Model.

[29] Tsung-Yi Lin, Michael Maire, Serge Belongie, Lubomir Bourdev, Ross Girshick, James Hays, Pietro Perona, Deva Ramanan, C Lawrence Zitnick, and Piotr Dolí. Microsoft COCO: Common Objects in Context.

[30] Etai Littwin and Lior Wolf. The Multiverse Loss for Robust Transfer Learning.

[31] Yifeng Niu, Shengtao Xu, Lizhen Wu, and Weidong Hu. Airborne infrared and visible image fusion for target perception based on target region segmentation and discrete wavelet transform. *Mathematical*

Problems in Engineering, 2012, 2012.

[32]   M Jones P. Viola. Rapid Object Detection Using A Boosted Cascade of Simple Features. *Proceedings of the 2001 IEEE Computer Society Conference on Computer Vision and Pattern Recognition*, (1):511–518, 2001.

[33]   Omkar M Parkhi, Andrea Vedaldi, and Andrew Zisserman. Deep Face Recognition.

[34]   Shaoqing Ren, Kaiming He, Ross Girshick, and Jian Sun. Faster R-CNN: Towards Real-Time Object Detection with Region Proposal Networks.

[35]   Olga Russakovsky, Jia Deng, Hao Su, Jonathan Krause, Sanjeev Satheesh, Sean Ma, Zhiheng Huang, Andrej Karpathy, Aditya Khosla, Michael Bernstein, Alexander C Berg, Li Fei-Fei, O Russakovsky, J Deng, H Su, J Krause, S Satheesh, S Ma, Z Huang, A Karpathy, A Khosla, M Bernstein, A C Berg, and L Fei-Fei. ImageNet Large Scale Visual Recognition Challenge.

[36]   Florian Schroff, Dmitry Kalenichenko, and James Philbin. FaceNet: A Unified Embedding for Face Recognition and Clustering.

[37]   Pierre Sermanet, David Eigen, Xiang Zhang, Michael Mathieu, Rob Fergus, and Yann Lecun. OverFeat: Integrated Recognition, Localization and Detection using Convolutional Networks. 2014.

[38]   Zhiwen Shao, Shouhong Ding, Yiru Zhao, Qinchuan Zhang, and Lizhuang Ma. LEARNING DEEP REPRESENTATION FROM COARSE TO FINE FOR FACE ALIGNMENT. 2016.

[39]   Yaser Sheikh and Mubarak Shah. Bayesian Object Detection in Dynamic Scenes. 2005.

[40]   Karen Simonyan, Omkar M Parkhi, Andrea Vedaldi, and Andrew Zisserman. Fisher Vector Faces in the Wild.

[41]   Karen Simonyan and Andrew Zisserman. VERY DEEP CONVOLUTIONAL NETWORKS FOR LARGE-SCALE IMAGE RECOGNITION. 2015.

[42]   Menno A Smeelen, Piet B W Schwering, Alexander Toet, and Marco Loog. Semi-hidden target recognition in gated viewer images fused with thermal IR images. *Information Fusion*, 18:131–147, 2014.

[43]   Xudong Sun, Pengcheng Wu, and Steven C H Hoi. Face Detection using Deep Learning: An Improved Faster RCNN Approach.

[44]   Yi Sun, Xiaogang Wang, and Xiaoou Tang. Deep Convolutional Network Cascade for Facial Point Detection.

[45]   Yi Sun, Xiaogang Wang, and Xiaoou Tang. Deep Learning Face Representation by Joint Identification-Verification.

[46]   Yi Sun, Xiaogang Wang, and Xiaoou Tang. Deep Learning Face Representation from Predicting 10,000 Classes.

[47]   J A K Suykens and J Vandewalle. Least Squares Support Vector Machine Classifiers. *Neural Processing Letters 9*, pages 293–300, 1999.

[48]   Christian Szegedy, Sergey Ioffe, Vincent Vanhoucke, and Alex Alemi. Inception-v4, Inception-ResNet and the Impact of Residual Connections on Learning.

[49]   Christian Szegedy, Wei Liu, Yangqing Jia, Pierre Sermanet, Scott Reed, Dragomir Anguelov, Dumitru Erhan, Vincent Vanhoucke, and Andrew Rabinovich. Going deeper with convolutions.

[50]   Oren Tadmor, Yonatan Wexler, Tal Rosenwein, Shai Shalev-Shwartz, and Amnon Shashua. Learning a Metric Embedding for Face Recognition using the Multibatch Method.

[51]   Yaniv Taigman, Ming Yang, Marc Aurelio Ranzato, and Lior Wolf. DeepFace: Closing the Gap to Human-Level Performance in Face Verification.

[52]   J R R Uijlings, K E A Van De Sande, T Gevers, and A W M Smeulders. Selective Search for Object Recognition. *Int J Comput Vis*, 104:154–171, 2013.

[53]   Paul Viola and Michael J Jones. Robust Real-Time Face Detection. *International Journal of Computer Vision*, 57(2):137–154, 2004.

[54]   Shaohua Wan, Zhijun Chen, Tao Zhang, Bo Zhang, and Kong-Kat Wong. Bootstrapping Face Detection with Hard Negative Examples. 2016.

[55]   Yandong Wen, Kaipeng Zhang, Zhifeng Li, and Yu Qiao. A Discriminative Feature Learning Approach for Deep Face Recognition.

[56]   Dong Yi, Zhen Lei, Shengcai Liao, and Stan Z Li. Learning Face Representation from Scratch.

[57]   Xi Yin and Xiaoming Liu. Multi-Task Convolutional Neural Network for Face Recognition. 2017.

[58]   Kimin Yun, Jongin Lim, and Jin Young Choi. Scene conditional background update for moving object detection in a moving camera. *Pattern Recognition Letters*, 88:57–63, 2017.

[59]   Jie Zhang, Shiguang Shan, Meina Kan, and Xilin Chen. LNCS 8690 - Coarse-to-Fine Auto-Encoder Networks (CFAN) for Real-Time Face Alignment. 2014.

[60]   Kaipeng Zhang, Zhanpeng Zhang, Zhifeng Li, and Yu Qiao. Joint Face Detection and Alignment using Multi-task Cascaded Convolutional Networks. *IEEE Signal Processing Letters*, PP(99):1499–1503, 2016.

[61]   Zhanpeng Zhang, Ping Luo, Chen Change Loy, and Xiaoou Tang. LNCS 8694 - Facial Landmark Detection by Deep Multi-task Learning. 2014.

Deep Learning for Image Processing Applications
D.J. Hemanth and V.V. Estrela (Eds.)
IOS Press, 2017
doi:10.3233/978-1-61499-822-8-244

Super-Resolution of Long Range Captured Iris Image Using Deep Convolutional Network

Anand DESHPANDE[a], Prashant P. PATAVARDHAN[b]
[a] *Department of Electronics &Communication Engineering, Angadi Institute of Technology and Management, Belgaum, India/Research Scholar, Department of Electronics and Communication Engineering, Gogte Institute of Technology, Belgaum, India.*
E-mail:deshpande.anandb@gmail.com
[b] *Department of Electronics and Communication Engineering, Gogte Institute of Technology, Belgaum, India.*

Abstract This chapter proposes a deep convolutional neural network based super-resolution framework to super-resolve and to recognize the long-range captured iris image sequences. The proposed framework is tested on CASIA V4 iris database by analyzing the peak signal-to-noise ratio (PSNR), structural similarity index matrix (SSIM) and visual information fidelity in pixel domain (VIFP) of the state-of-art algorithms. The performance of the proposed framework is analyzed for the upsampling factors 2 and 4 and achieved PSNRs of 37.42 dB and 34.74 dB respectively. Using this framework, we have achieved an equal error rate (EER) of 0.14%. The results demonstrate that the proposed framework can super-resolve the iris images effectively and achieves better recognition performance.

Keywords: deep learning, convolutional neural network, super resolution, iris recognition, biometrics, image processing, computer vision

1. Introduction

The identification of the people when they use their credit cards, pass through airports or other high-secured areas or when they log into computers, just to name a few situations, is paramount today. User credentials such as username and password are used whereas in other cases personal identification cards are used. The problem with the user name and password is they can be forgotten and whereas, the identity cards can be stolen. The need for improvement in the human identification is required to develop new techniques, which are reliable and more accurate than the traditional ones.

---

[1] Anand Deshpande, Research Scholar, Department of Electronics and Communication Engineering, Gogte Institute of Technology, Belgaum, E-mail: deshpande.anandb@gmail.com

Biometrics is one of the areas that demand more research in the science and technology. Based on individual behavioral and physiological characteristics, biometrics is used for authentication purpose through an automated method. Iris biometrics, which is considered as the most robust and highly accurate method of recognition has popularly been employed in airports for access control, security in general, border vigilance, etc. Many researchers are working towards recognition of iris images captured from a long distance, approximately 3 meters.

Stop and stare is the technique used for most conventional short-distance recognition of the iris. As a result, the participants face inconvenience. A diameter of 200 pixels of the iris is required for recognition, according to the International Standards Organization (ISO). However, this resolution is suitable for a distance up to a few centimeters. The following are the major problems iris recognition systems face for short distances:

a) Closer acquisition distance;
b) Delay in acquisition time, which leads to low throughput; and
c) Standstill of the participants is required during acquisition.

New techniques are focusing more on overcoming these limitations, which can function at a distance. The resolution of the captured iris image plays a vital and troubled role.

Long distances present additional challenges. Illumination causes dilation and contraction of the iris due to a change in the brightness so that the recognition procedure will be degraded, and the images could be unusable due to poor illumination. Other challenging tasks for the iris image acquisition are tracking, deciding and capturing the iris depending on where and when a person is. An iris acquisition system is illustrated in the Figure1.

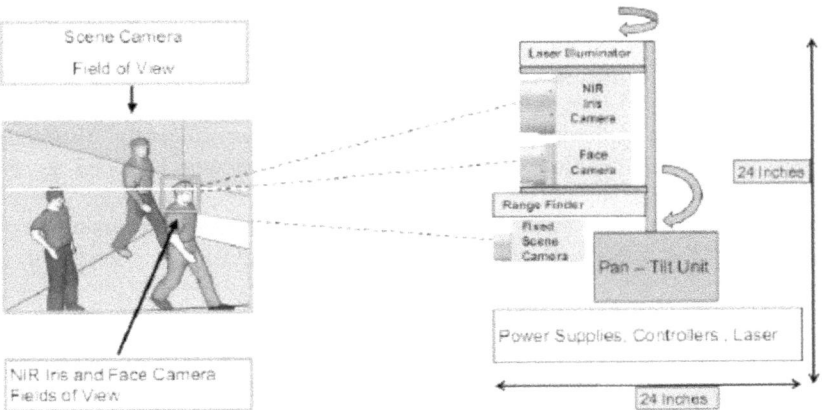

Figure 1. An iris being probed from a distance and on the move recognition system [1]

Most remote iris recognition systems are slight variations of the framework from Figure 1 and have five major components:

• Camera for human detection and tracking from a low-resolution (LR) wide field-of-view (FOV).
• Camera for face detection and tracking from an LR wide FOV.
• Camera for capturing irises from a high-resolution (HR) narrow FOV.

- Pan-tilt head for simultaneous movement of the face and the iris.
- Controllers for illumination.

The first iris recognition system was proposed in [2]. By using infrared camera and telescope, their system could image the iris at a distance between 5 and 10 meters. The illumination was provided with the help of an880nm collimated illuminator. Across a typical iris diameter, the system could acquire iris images with 128-pixel resolution. For recognition purposes, the resolution is good enough. However, the constraints involved with the participants in this system were (i) fixed position of the head, and (ii) staring at the fixed spot. On the other hand, by increasing the vertical range of acquisition and the depth of the field the constraints were tried to relax by the other researchers. Thus, to achieve this resolution the remote iris recognition system should be carefully designed. The images captured at a long range suffer from LR, which leads less information or loss of detail.

The loss of pixel resolution reduces the iris recognition system's performance. To overcome this issue, super-resolution (SR) techniques are used. The analyses of still images and video involve huge amounts of data and rich information, as they are the main carriers of perceived data. The acquisition of image and video has become very convenient due to the development of smart mobile phones. Most visual information has to be acquired and stored in LR because of the limitation of the bandwidth and storage capacity. Based on LR images, an HR version of the scene has to be built to display the scene on an HD screen.

The size and number of the sensors account for the resolution of the captured image. Thanks to constraints on the sensor resolutions and functionalities, an HD image cannot always be available [3]. Due to the generation of the shot noise, the image quality gets degraded. To enhance the spatial resolution, another approach is by increasing the chip size, which as a result leads to increase in capacitance. This method is not considered to be effective since large capacitances complicate the transfer rate of charge [4].

SR can remediate the problems discussed before. However, since it is a quite intensive computational technique, deep neural networks arise as an option to super-resolve and to recognize the long range captured iris images efficiently. This chapter is structured as follows. Section 2 discusses the SR framework applied to the iris recognition. Section 3 suggests a deep neural network implementation for the iris recognition problem when there are long distances. Section 4 discusses the results obtained using the proposed system. Finally, the conclusion is discussed in the Section5.

2. Iris Recognition using Super-Resolution

To overcome the intrinsic limitations of the imaging systems and the sensors, the new approaches in increasing spatial resolution are required. In many commercial applications, the high cost of the precision optics and image sensors play an important factor. A promising approach to constructing an HR image from one or more LR observations is achieved by means of image processing. There is a natural loss of spatial resolution when capturing an image using digital systems caused by optical distortion, lack of adequate focus, motion blur due to limited shutter speed or relative movement between the camera and the object, diffraction limits, aliasing, sensor noise, transmission problems and insufficient sensor density. Aliasing distorts the high-frequency contents of the image when it is sampled at low rates. Improvement in resolution by applying image processing tools has been a topic of great interest. High spatial resolution images can be obtained from one or more LR images with SR. The high-frequency content lost during the image acquisition process has to be recovered by SR techniques. From under-sampled LR observations, the main concern of the super resolution algorithm is to reconstruct HR images. It produces high-quality images from blurred, noisy and degraded images. The characteristics of the technique overcoming the inherent resolution limitation of LR imaging systems underlines and represents the word 'super'. Some of the advantages of SR are: i) low costs, ii) existing LR systems can be used without any additional hardware, and iii) it offers flexibility.

It is necessary to have a detailed understanding of how images are captured and the transformation they undergo in order to apply a SR algorithm. As said before, the HR image goes through a sequence of degradations such as blur, additive noise, and down-sampling during image acquisition. Due to camera motion like zooming, tilting and panning the frames captured using video camera could be rotated and scaled. Thus due to relative motion between the observations, blur may be introduced. Hence, the observed images account to degraded versions of the HR images. A mathematical model that represents the image acquisition process has to be formulated to analyze the SR reconstruction problem.

This model, known as forward model or observation, relates the original HR image to be observed and the LR image(s). The important role in the success of any SR approach is the correct formulation of the observation models. Translation, blur, aliasing, and noise are the standard forward models for SR reconstruction. Fig.2 illustrates the typical SR model.

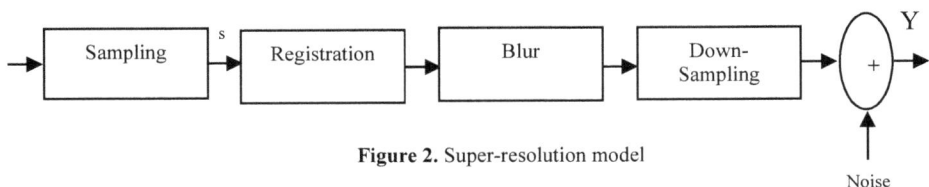

Figure 2. Super-resolution model

Here, X is desired HR image which is band limited and sampled above Nyquist rate, Y_k is the kth observed LR output. Let camera captures k LR images of X, where the LR observations are related with the HR [5] scene X by:

$$Y_k = DB_k M_k X + N_k \qquad \text{with } k = 1, 2, 3, \dots K, \qquad (1)$$

where D is the down-sampling operator, B_k is the blur for the kth LR image, M_k contains the motion data, and N_k is the noise in the kth LR image. Notations used in this equation are as below.
Upper case bold letters X and Y denotes the vector form in lexicographical order for HR and LR images respectively. Lower case k denotes a vector form.

The existing SR algorithms are classified as interpolation, reconstruction, and example learning based methods. Interpolation-based SR methods interpolate the HR image from the LR input using a smooth kernel function [6] [7] [8] [9] [10]. These methods are fast in operation, but fails to recover high-frequency details and responsible to introduce zigzag artifacts. The reconstruction-based methods [11] [12] [13] [14] [15] [16] [17] [18] [19] [20] provides solution for an ill-posed inverse problem of up-sampling, deblurring and denoising for high quality image by using smoothness priors. But these methods produce watercolor-like artifacts and with increase in magnification factor the quality of images gets degraded. Because the richness of images is complicated to capture analytically, researchers are exploring a learning-based approach for super-resolving images [21] [22] [23] [24]. This method consists of two phases:

- Training: Image patches dictionary is created.
- SR: Up-samples the input image patches using the dictionary.

Two types of dictionaries can be created, external and internal dictionary. The external directory, which can be built in advanced using a set of external training images and internal dictionary built without using other images. The internal dictionary uses the property of self-similarity, in which structure of image repeats within and across an image of different scales.

Learning-based SR approach uses function dependent priors to gather the unknown HR image [25] [26] [27] [28] [29] [30] [31] [32] [33] [34] [35]. The input LR image is divided in overlapping or non-overlapping patches. Then the best match is selected from the training database. The output HR image is reconstructed using corresponding HR patches.

Deep learning approaches have been successfully applied for image restoration problems. Various methods have been proposed for image SR based on the deep neural network model. These attained better performance than other models. The author [36] proposed single image SR method based on a deep convolutional neural network method, which studies a continuous mapping between the LR or HR images. The author also showed that the sparse-coding based SR methods could be observed as a deep convolutional network. This structure has a lightweight and processes fast for real-time usage. The author explored numerous structures of network and parameter settings and analyzed the performance and speed. The author also extended this work to manage red, green and blue color channels and showed better performance regarding the reconstruction quality. The author [37] proposed deep learning and gradient transform based single image SR method. The LR images are upsampled by convolutional neural network and gradients of the up-scaled images are calculated and transformed to required gradients by using gradient transformation network which establish the energy function of reconstruction. Finally, the energy function is optimized to estimate the HR image. This approach produces sharp HR image along with ringing artifacts. The author [38] proposed a method for light-field image SR using a deep convolutional neural network. The proposed method analyzed for real-world applications such as refocusing and depth map estimation. The author [39] shows that the sparse coding model can be casted as a neural network and trained in a cascaded structure from end-to-end. The author [40] proposed a novel super resolution method with multi-channel convolutional neural networks. In this method, depending on the positions of pixels output pixels are classified into four groups. These groups are created into 2×2 magnified image. This architecture is independent of the use of Bicubic interpolation method. Using this approach, the average PSNR is higher than 0.39 dB than the conventional SRCNN.

Falmy [41] proposed autoregressive signature model between successive LR based SR method. This approach is not suitable for unconstrained iris recognition approach as this method uses entire eye image for the registration process. To overcome this issue, author Nguyen [42] proposed a pixel-wise SR method for LR iris video sequences. The author used the normalized iris polar image is super resolved, instead of the whole eye image.

The bilinear interpolation method is used to increase the resolution of the normalized iris images. The intensity values of an individual pixel fused using the robust mean algorithm. This method is tested on sequences of 628 NIR video and 8589 NIR images of MBGC NIR portal iris video database. Using this approach 4.1×10^{-2} EER is achieved. The author further worked on a concept proposed in [43] to reduce EER. Nguyen [41] proposed a method to improve performance for variations in lighting, size and occlusion using a focus assessment. The experiments conducted on sequences of 628 NIR video and 8589 NIR images of MBGC NIR portal iris video database. Using this approach 2.1×10^{-2} of EER is achieved. Nguyen et al. [44] suggested a feature-domain based SR method for iris recognition using Eigen features of the iris image. Using this method 0.8% EER is achieved. Nguyen et al. [45] further extend this feature domain work by proposing a feature-domain framework to super resolve the long range captured iris images. He has described a feature domain SR process using nonlinear 2D Gabor phase-quadrant features within the framework. The experiments conducted on sequences of 628 NIR video and 8589 NIR images of MBGC NIR portal iris video database. The author achieved 0.5% of EER. Nadia Othman et al. [46] proposed an image fusion method recognizing the iris captured while a person is moving. The novelty of this approach is the introduction in the fusion scheme, at the pixel level, of a local quality measure depending on a GMM estimation of the allocation of a texture of iris image. The performance of proposed approach is evaluated on MBGC database having facial videos of 129 persons moving through a gateway placed at 3 meters from a NIR camera. The author shows that the proposed method gives improvement of 4.79% EER than GQ based fusion method.

In our previous research works, we have proposed two frameworks for recognition of long range captured iris image sequences [47, 49, 50, 51]. In paper [47] Gaussian Process Regression (GPR) [48] based framework is proposed to super resolute the long range captured iris polar image. The framework uses linear kernel co-variance function in GPR during the process of super resolution of iris image, without external dataset. The new patch selective technique is proposed to reduce the time taken to super resolute the iris polar image patches. In paper [49], enhanced iterated back projection (EIBP) method is proposed to super-resolve the iris polar images. This work modifies existing IBP to get better super-resolved image compared to traditional IBP. In paper [50], a framework is proposed to super-resolve the long range captured iris polar images. In this work, modified diamond search and enhanced total variation algorithms are proposed to super-resolve the long range captured iris polar multi-frame images. The modified diamond search algorithm is proposed to calculate motion vector. In paper [51], the proposed framework to super-resole the long range captured iris image using Gaussian process regression (GPR) and EIBP SR approach. In this framework, modified diamond search algorithm is also proposed to calculate motion vector. The proposed framework super-resolve the iris image in very less time compared to the traditional GPR.

Various iris databases are available to analyze the performance of the developed system. The list of the most relevant existing iris database is as shown in Table 1.

Table 1. Summary of open iris database

Database	Size	Camera	Light Wavelength	Distance
CASIA V1	756	CASIA	NIR	Short
CASIA V2	225	CASIA	NIR	Short
CASIA V3	22051	OKI iris pass-h	NIR	Short
CASIA V4	2576	CASIA	NIR	Long
MMU1	450	LG EOU2200	NIR	Short
MMU2	995	Panasonic BM ET 100 US	NIR	Short
BATH	16000	ISG LW 1.3 S 1394	NIR	Short
WVU	3099	OKI iris pass-h	NIR	Short
MBGC	Video	MBGC-Portal	NIR	Long
ICE1	2900	LG EOU2200	NIR	Short
ICE2	75000	LG EOU2200	NIR	Short
UBIRIS v1	1877	NIKON E5700	Visible	Short
UBIRIS v2	11357	Canon EOS 5D	Visible	Long
UPOL	384	Sony DXC 950P 3CCD with TOPCON TRC501A	Visible	Short
QFIRE05	Video	Dalsa 4M30	NIR	Long
QFIRE07	Video	infrared camera	NIR	Long
QFIRE11	Video	Dalsa 4M30	NIR	Long

The Table 1 shows that the CASIA V4 dataset is more suitable for the proposed research objectives as it contains NIR images captured at a long distance.

3. Proposed System

Most of the SR approaches are work towards remote sensing application. Very less amount of work has been carried out in the field of biometric using SR based on convolution neural network. In this proposed work we have used convolution neural network based SR method to recognize the long-range captured iris image. The proposed system to fuse and to super-resolve the iris image as shown in Figure 3

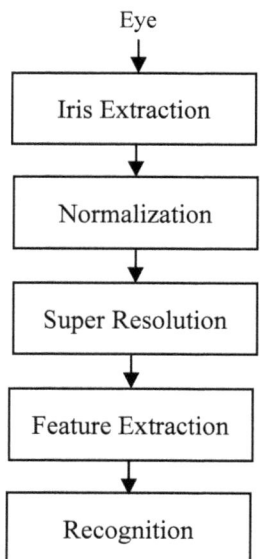

Figure 3. Proposed super-resolution based iris recognition framework

The proposed system contain contains the following blocks:

- Iris extraction: To extract the iris part from a sequence of eye
- Normalization: The extracted circular iris image is converted in to a rectangular shape.
- SR: The LR images are super-resolved using deep neural network to get an HR image
- Feature Extraction: Various features of super-resolved iris polar images are extracted.
- Recognition: Features of the super-resolved image are used to recognize the iris image.

3.1. Iris Extraction and Normalization

In this block, AdaBoost [52] [53] approach is used to extract face and eye by using face and eye-pair classifiers. This method is low complex and gives high detection accuracy at high speed. This is due to the use of Haar features and a cascaded classifier structure, which excludes the image window assumption rapidly. The off-angle and blinked images are detected by correlating the image with averaged image [54]. The correlation coefficient, C, is given by

$$C = \frac{\sum_m \sum_n (x_{mn} - \bar{x})(y_{mn} - \bar{y})}{\sqrt{\sum_m \sum_n (x_{mn} - \bar{x})^2 \sum_m \sum_n (y_{mn} - \bar{y})^2}} \tag{2}$$

where x_{mn}- frame, $\bar{x}$ is mean of x_{mn}, y_{mn} - averaged frame, $\bar{y}$ is mean of y_{mn}.

The specular reflection may affect the segmentation of iris images. This can be minimized or removed as below.

- Find the positions of specular reflections by applying the thresholding.
- Fill the reflected regions by applying in-painting.
- Apply median filter to smooth and to remove the boundary artifacts introduced by inpainting method.

After removing the specular reflection, the iris part is extracted as below.

- Eyebrow and eyelashes are removed via thresholding as these contain low intensity.
- The pupil is obtained by using geometric properties and extracting the connected components having maximum height and width.
- Draw horizontal lines from the center of the pupil towards outside to the sclera region.
- Check the change in intensity and the point where the intensity increases quickly should be the location where those lines hit the boundary, as the sclera emerges brighter than the iris.
- Calculate the meeting point of the vertical bisectors of the lines that pass through the pairs of those points.

The dimension of the iris is not constant due to rotation of the camera or eyes, change in capturing distance, etc. The iris is transformed into polar form [55] to get the same dimension for all the images, such that two images of the same iris captured under various conditions will have characteristic features at the same spatial location.

3.2. Super-Resolution

The single iris polar image is super-resolved using a convolutional neural network as discussed in [36]. The overview of the convolution neural network is as shown in Figure 4.

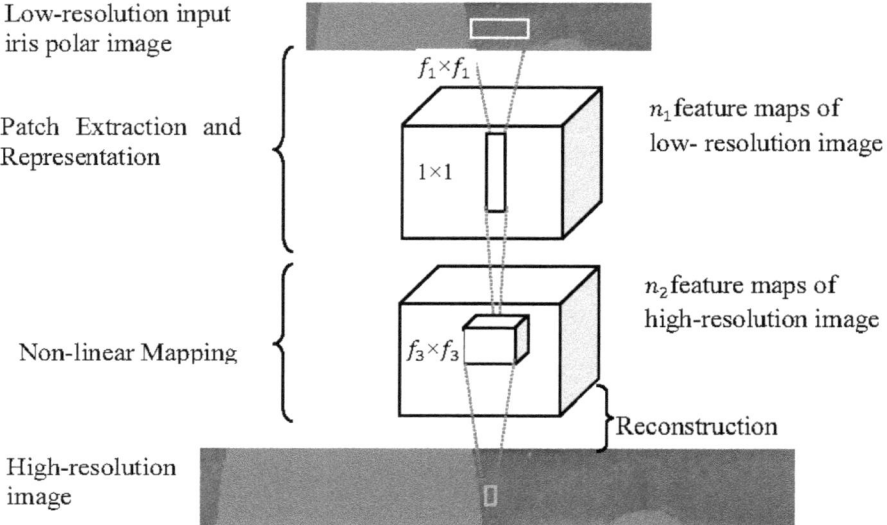

Low-resolution input iris polar image

Patch Extraction and Representation

$f_1 \times f_1$

1×1

n_1 feature maps of low-resolution image

n_2 feature maps of high-resolution image

Non-linear Mapping

$f_3 \times f_3$

Reconstruction

High-resolution image

Figure 4. Overview of convolution neural network

The super resolution of iris polar image is carried out in following steps.

a) First layer: This layer is called as —patch Extraction and representation layer. The popular strategy for image reconstruction is by extracting patches and representing them by set of pre-trained bases. This approach is similar to convolving the image by set of filters, each of which is In this layer, overlapped patches of images are extracted and represented by a set of pre-trained discrete cosine transform bases. Let y be the LR iris polar image. It is up-sampled to required size by using Bicubic interpolation approach to get Y. The goal is to recover from Y and image $F(Y)$ which is as similar as possible to the ground truth high-resolution image Y .This layer is represented as

$$F_1(Y) = max(0, W_1 * Y + B_1) \tag{3}$$

where W_1 is a convolution filter having a size of $m \times f_1 \times f_1 \times n_1$ in which f_1 is spatial size of filter, n_1- number of filters, m is number of channels, and B_1 is a biases. The output is composed of n_1 feature maps. B_1 is an n_1-dimensional vector, whose each element is associated with a filter.

b) Second layer: This layer is called as Non-linear mapping layer. n_1 dimensional feature vectors are mapped onto n_2- dimensional feature vectors. This is achieved by

$$F_2(Y) = max(0, W_2 * F_1(Y) + B_2) \tag{4}$$

The size of W_2 is $n_1 \times 1 \times 1 \times n_2$, B_2 is n_2 dimensional vector and n_2 is the number of feature maps.

c) Third layer: This layer is called as Reconstruction layer. All predicted HR patches are averaged to produce the final HR image. This is achieved by equation (5)

$$F(Y) = W_3 * F_2(Y) + B_3 \tag{5}$$

The size of W_3 is $n_2 \times f_3 \times f_3 \times k$ and B_3 is a l-dimensional vector.

In the training process, network parameters $P = (W_1, W_2, W_3, B_1, B_2, B_3)$ have to be determined to learn end-to-end mapping function F. These network parameters are obtained by reducing the loss between HR image X and the reconstructed images $F(Y, P)$. Let Y_i be the LR image and Y_i be the corresponding HR image. The loss function is calculated as,

$$L(P) = \frac{1}{n}\sum_{i=1}^{n} ||F(Y_i, P) - X_i||^2 \tag{6}$$

The stochastic gradient descent with the standard back propagation [45] is used to minimize the loss.

3.3. Feature Extraction

In the process of iris recognition, feature extraction and feature selection play a major role in enhancing the recognition accuracy. This part proposes a feature extraction method using discrete cosine transform (DCT) domain based no-reference image quality analysis (IQA) model, Gray Level Co-occurrence Matrix (GLCM), Hu seven moments and statistical features. It also proposes fuzzy entropy and interval-valued fuzzy set measure based feature selection method. The block parametric model for DCT domain feature extraction is as shown in Figure 5. The features of iris polar images are extracted in DCT domain using the parameters of the model. The reasons for feature extraction in DCT domain are 1) Variation in DCT coefficients occurs due to degree and type of image distortion 2) Ease of computation. DCTs can be computed efficiently [51] [56][57] by variable-change transforms from computationally efficient fast Fourier transform algorithms. Applying the model-based method to coefficient increases the computational efficiency.

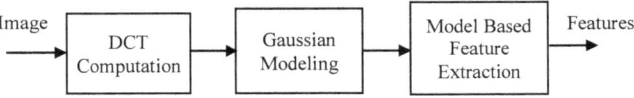

Figure 5. Proposed parametric model for feature extraction

In the first stage, the image is subjected to DCT coefficient computation. In this stage, image is partitioned into $n \times n$ size blocks or patches. DCT coefficients are obtained for all the patches. In the second stage, a generalized Gaussian density model is applied to DCT coefficients of each block. The DC coefficient in a block is ignored as it does not express structural information about the block. The generalized Gaussian model is given by,

$$f(x|\alpha,\beta,\gamma) = \alpha e^{-(\beta|x-\mu)^{\gamma}} \tag{7}$$

where, γ- shape parameter, μ- mean, α and β are the normalizing and scale parameters given by

$$\alpha = \frac{\beta\gamma}{2\Gamma(1/\gamma)} \tag{8}$$

$$\beta = \frac{1}{\sigma}\sqrt{\frac{\Gamma(3/\gamma)}{\Gamma(1/\gamma)}} \tag{9}$$

where, σ is the standard deviation, r denotes gamma function given by,

$$\Gamma(z) = \int_0^{\infty} t^{z-1}e^{-t}dt \tag{10}$$

This family of distribution includes the Gaussian distribution (β=2) and Laplacian distribution (β=1). As $\beta \rightarrow \infty$, the distribution converges to a uniform distribution. Using generalized Gaussian model functions, four features of image are obtained in the third stage. They are as shown below.

• *Shape Parameter*
The shape parameter (γ) model based feature is computed over all blocks in the image. It determines the decay rate of the gamma function.

• *Coefficient of Frequency Variation*
Let X is a random variable representing the histogram of DCT coefficients. The coefficient of frequency variation feature (ξ) is the ratio of the measure of the spread of the DCT coefficient magnitudes ($\sigma_{|X|}$) to measure of the center of the DCT coefficient magnitude distribution($\mu_{|X|}$). The average of coefficient of frequency variation feature is measured.

• *Energy Sub-band Ratio*

This feature measures the energy distribution in lower and higher bands, which can be affected by distortions. Sub band of 5×5 DCT coefficient matrix is divided into three groups, as shown in the Figure 6.

The average energy in frequency band n is given by,

$$E_n = \sigma_n^2. \tag{11}$$

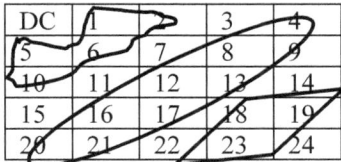

Figure 6. DCT coefficients in 3 bands

where:

Energy sub-band is a ratio of large discrepancy in the frequency energy between a frequency band to the average energy in bands of lower frequencies.

$$R_n = \frac{|E_n - \frac{1}{n-1}\sum_{j<n} E_j|}{E_n + \frac{1}{n-1}\sum_{j<n} E_j} \tag{12}$$

The energy sub-band ratio is large to uniform frequency content in the image patch and is low to a small frequency disparity between the feature band and the average energy in the lower bands. This feature is calculated for all blocks in the image and the mean of the energy band is measured.

- *Orientation Mode*

Here, each block of DCT coefficients is divided into three orientation bands and modeled. The oriented DCT coefficients are represented in three different shades as shown in Figure 7.

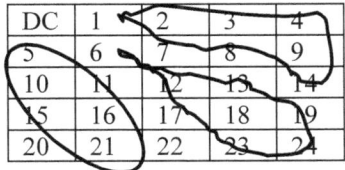

Figure 7. DCT coefficients in three orientations

where:

To each band in a block corresponds a generalized Gaussian model and the coefficient of frequency variation ξ is calculated. The variance and mean of ξ are calculated for each of the three orientations.

Fourteen GLCM features [58], Hu seven moments [59] and a set of statistical features (mean, median, standard deviation, variance, skewness, kurtosis, and entropy) comprise the features of the iris polar images. These features are empirically selected for the proposed work as these methods take less computation time. The GLCM method is an approach of extracting second-order statistical texture features. These describe the image texture by calculating rate of pair of pixels with specific value and rate of specified spatial correlation. The amount of rows and column in this matrix are equal to the number of gray levels G in the image. Various features extracted from the GLCM are as below.

- Contrast

$$Contrast = \sum_{n=0}^{G-1} n^2 \left\{ \sum_{i=1}^{G} \sum_{j=1}^{G} P(i,j) \right\} \tag{13}$$

where $P(i,j)$ is the relative frequency with which two pixels separated by a distance $(\Delta x, \Delta y)$ occur within a given region, with intensity j and i.

- Inverse Difference Moment

$$IDM = \sum_{i=1}^{G-1} \sum_{j=1}^{G-1} \frac{1}{1+(i-j)^2} P(i,j) \tag{14}$$

It gives maximum value when matrix contains same elements. GLCM contrast and homogeneity are inversely proportional to each other.

- Entropy

$$Entropy = -\sum_{i=1}^{G-1} \sum_{j=1}^{G-1} P(i,j) \times log(P(i,j)) \tag{15}$$

It is inversely correlated to energy.

- Correlation

$$Correlation = \sum_{i=1}^{G-1} \sum_{j=1}^{G-1} \frac{(i \times j) \times P(i,j) - (\mu_x \times \mu_y)}{\sigma_x \times \sigma_y} \tag{16}$$

where $\mu_x, \mu_y, \sigma_x, \sigma_y$ are the means and standard deviations of P.

- Sum of Squares (Variance):

$$Variance = \sum_{i=1}^{G-1} \sum_{j=1}^{G-1} (i - \mu)^2 \times P(i,j) \tag{17}$$

- Sum Average

$$Average = \sum_{i=0}^{2G-2} i P_{x+y}(i) \tag{18}$$

- Sum of Entropy

$$Sum\ of\ Entropy = -\sum_{i=0}^{2G-2} P_{x+y}(i) log(P_{x+y}(i)) \tag{19}$$

- Difference of Entropy

$$Difference\ of\ Entropy = -\sum_{i=0}^{G-1} P_{x-y}(i) log(P_{x-y}(i)) \tag{20}$$

- Cluster Shade

$$Shade = \sum_{i=0}^{G-1} \sum_{j=0}^{G-1} \{i + j - \mu_x - \mu_y\}^3 \times P(i,j) \qquad (21)$$

- Cluster Prominence

$$CP = \sum_{i=0}^{G-1} \sum_{j=0}^{G-1} \{i + j - \mu_x - \mu_y\}^4 \times P(i,j) \qquad (22)$$

- Energy or Angular second moment

$$Energy = \sum_{i=0}^{G-1} \sum_{j=0}^{G-1} P(i,j)^2 \qquad (23)$$

- Autocorrelation

$$Autocorrelation = \sum_{i=0}^{G-1} \sum_{j=0}^{G-1} (i,j)P(i,j) \qquad (24)$$

- Dissimilarity

$$Dissimilarity = \sum_{i=0}^{G-1} \sum_{j=0}^{G-1} P(i,j) \times |i - j| \qquad (25)$$

- Inverse difference normalized (INN)

$$INN = \sum_{i=0}^{G-1} \sum_{j=0}^{G-1} \frac{P(i,j)}{1+|i-j|^2/G^2} \qquad (26)$$

3.4. Moment Invariance and Statistical Features

The seven Hu moments and the statistical measures(mean, median, standard deviation, variance, skewness, kurtosis, and entropy)are used as features of images in pattern recognition.

3.5. Feature Selection

The fuzzy entropy and interval-valued feature selection method to select the best feature which increases the recognition performance is proposed. The algorithms for feature selection based on fuzzy entropy and interval-valued are discussed [51] [60] [61]. Entropy measures the amount of disorder or uncertainty of random variables. The major step in using entropy in various cases is the discretization of the constant range of variables. As a result, there will be several observations, which are placed close to the boundaries between two adjacent intervals [62] [63]. This results in an erroneous selection in the discretization process and the performance of the selected feature set decreases. Fuzzy entropy and interval-valued fuzzy sets can be applied to overcome this issue; as an effect, observations close to the boundaries among intervals will be categorized as belonging to both intervals and increase in the information extracted from the chosen features.

Consider A as a fuzzy set identified on an interval of pattern space containing k elements   and X as a collective set with n elements scattered in a pattern space: $X = \{x_1, x_2, x_3 \ldots x_n\}$. $\mu_A(x_i)$ is the mapped membership degree of the element x_i with A. $\{C_1, C_2, C_3 \ldots C_m\}$ are m classes of element n. The number of intervals on each dimension plays a major role in increasing the classification efficiency and learning accuracy. For each feature in the model, decide the best possible number of fuzzy sets to carry out cluster analysis on the feature values, find out the cluster centers and generate the membership functions. To evaluate the information of distribution pattern in an interval, assigning a corresponding membership function to every class is necessary which indicates the degrees of the elements. The center of an interval has the maximum membership value, and as the distance between this element and the consequent interval center increases, the membership value decreases. Two membership functions: An upper and lower membership value describes an interval valued fuzzy number. By using this, feature selection methods can be improved by taking into account the observations close to the boundaries of intervals.

Left most cluster center, C_1

$$A_1^U(x) = \begin{cases} 0.5 + \frac{0.5(x - x_{min})}{c_1 - x_{min}} & if\ x_{min} \leq x \leq c_1 \\ \frac{c_2 - x}{c_2 - c_1} & if\ c_1 \leq x \leq c_2 \\ 0 & otherwise \end{cases} \tag{27}$$

Right most cluster center, C_1

$$A_{kj}^U(x) = \begin{cases} \frac{x - c_{k-1}}{c_k - c_{k-1}} & if\ c_{kj-1} \leq x \leq c_{kj} \\ 0.5 + \frac{0.5(x_{max} - x)}{x_{max} - c_k}, & if\ c_{kj} \leq x \leq x_{max} \\ 0 & otherwise \end{cases} \tag{28}$$

For internal cluster center:

$$c_i : A^U = (c_i, c_i - c_{i-1}, c_{i+1} - c_i) \tag{29}$$

The match degree [64] can be calculated as

$$D_j = \sum_{i=1}^n \frac{1 - max\left(1 - \mu_A^U(x_i), \mu_A^L(x_i)\right)}{1 - min\left(1 - \mu_A^U(x_i), \mu_A^L(x_i)\right)} \tag{30}$$

The fuzzy entropy is calculated as

$$H(A) = \sum_{j=1}^m -D_j log\ D_j \tag{31}$$

The entropy of the feature is calculated with respect to outcome variable, after determining the best possible number of fuzzy numbers for each feature, include that feature in the final feature subset. New features are appended to this set one by one in the succeeding steps of the algorithm. The new optimal feature is determined by calculating the joint entropy of a subset of features as well as the previously chosen features and the one which is not selected yet. The following step describes joint entropy calculation when selecting the selecting the second feature.

$$D_j^{1,h}(s,t) = \sum_{i=1}^{n} \frac{\min\left\{1-\max\left(1-\mu_{A_s}^{U1}(x_i),\mu_{A_s}^{L1}(x_i)\right),1-\max\left(1-\mu_{A_t}^{Uh}(x_i),\mu_{A_t}^{Lh}(x_i)\right)\right\}}{\max\left\{1-\max\left(1-\mu_{A_s}^{U1}(x_i),\mu_{A_s}^{L1}(x_i)\right),1-\max\left(1-\mu_{A_t}^{Uh}(x_i),\mu_{A_t}^{Lh}(x_i)\right)\right\}} \qquad (32)$$

The entropy of pair (A_s^1, A_t^h),

$$H(A_s^1, A_t^h) = \sum_{j=1}^{m} -D_j^{1,h}(s,t) \log D_j^{1,h}(s,t) \qquad (33)$$

The overall entropy is:

$$H(F_1, F_h) = \sum_{s=1}^{k_1} \sum_{t=1}^{k_h} H(A_s^1, A_t^h) \qquad (34)$$

The pair of features having optimal entropy will be selected as the best pair. If the improvement in the gained information is more than a predefined value, then the features are included.

3.6. Recognition

The extracted iris IQA features, GLCM features and Hu moments are feed to a Neural Network (NN) to recognize the iris image. Back propagation is widely applied neural network architecture as the capability of back propagation networks to learn complex multidimensional mapping [51]. This architecture consists of fully interconnected layers or rows of processing units [65]. The features are the input signal for the neural network. Here, $x_1, x_2, x_3 \ldots x_m$ are input feature values and $y_1, y_2, y_3 \ldots y_n$ are the output iris patterns. The NN model for l value is

$$y_l = f_i \left(\sum_{i=1}^{h2} C_{il} \cdot f_i \left(\sum_{j=1}^{h1} D_{ji} \cdot f_j \left(\sum_{k=1}^{h2} W_{kj} \cdot x_k \right) \right) \right) \qquad (35)$$

where f- is the activation function, C_{il} is the weight between output and the second hidden layers, D_{ji} are the weights between hidden layers, W_{kj} are the weights between the input and first hidden layers. $l = 1, 2, 3, \ldots n$. h_1 and h_2 are the number of neurons in the first and the second hidden layers, n is the number of neurons in the output layer, m is the number of neurons in input layer, as shown in Figure8.

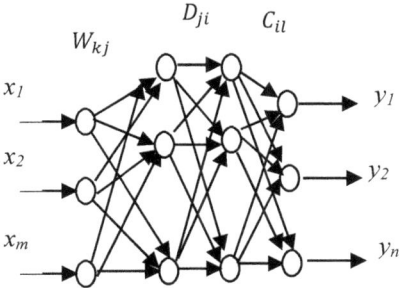

Figure 8. Neural network layers

The training of the parameters of NN starts only after the activation of the neural network and this trained network is used for the iris recognition. In the proposed work, a gradient-based learning algorithm with adaptive learning rate is adopted.

4. Results

The performance analysis of the proposed system is validated by performing the experiments on CASIA long-range iris image database [66]. The proposed algorithms are tested for 500 iris polar images. The algorithms are implemented using Matlab2009a on Intel Core i3 machine with a processor speed of 1.8GHz and RAM size of 4 GB. The original iris images having 2352×1728 pixel resolution are down-sampled to 50% (resolution of 1176×864) and 25% (resolution of 588×432) size of the original images, referred as Set S_1, Set S_2, and Set S_3 respectively. The normalized iris image resolutions are 600×80, 300×40 and 150×20 corresponding to S_1, Set S_2 and Set S_3. The normalized images of Set$_2$ having a resolution of 300×40 are super-resolved to 600×80 using proposed method with up-sampling factor Λ =2 and Set$_3$ having a resolution of 150×20 are super-resolved to 600×80 using proposed method with up-sampling factor (Λ) =4. In the training process, 500 training images are used. These images are subdivided into 32×32 sub-images to get approximately 28,000 images. The size of filters are set in this experiments are $f_1 = 9$ and $f_3 = 5$. The feature maps $n_1 = 64$ and $n_2 = 32$. The size of the input iris polar images is 300×40, and up-sampling factor (magnification factor) is 2. The iris polar image resolution after SR is 600 × 80 as shown in Figure 9.

Original Image	Super-Resolved Image

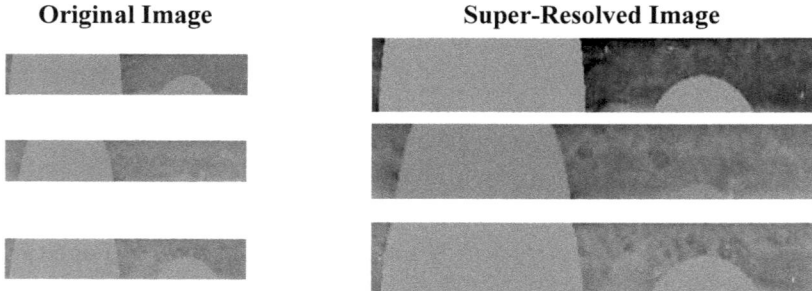

Figure 9. Sample images of LR and corresponding super-resolved iris images using the proposed approach

The performance of the proposed system is evaluated by quality measures [67] [68] [69] [70] such as SSIM, VIFP, PSNR.

The structural similarity (SSIM) is a measure for assessment of quality, motivated by the information that the human visual system is sensitive to distortions of the structural components. This measure assesses the changes in structural components occurred between two images. The SSIM between two images is computed as below.

Divide the original image and the super-revolved image into a number of patches. Let x and y are the image patches selected from the same positions of two images. The similarity $S(x, y)$ can be calculated as,

$$S(x, y) = \left(\frac{2\mu_x\mu_y + K_1}{\mu_x^2 + \mu_y^2 + K_1}\right) \left(\frac{2\sigma_x\sigma_y + K_2}{\sigma_x^2 + \sigma_y^2 + K_2}\right) \left(\frac{2\sigma_{xy} + K_3}{\sigma_x\sigma_y + K_3}\right) \tag{36}$$

where, μ_x and μ_y are means of patches x and y. σ_x and σ_y are standard deviations of patches x and y. K_1, K_2 and K_3 are positive constants to prevent the statistical unsteadiness that may take place when division with denominators. σ_{xy} is the cross correlation of x and y.

$$\sigma_{xy} = \frac{1}{T-1}\sum_{i=1}^{T}(x_i - \mu_x)(y_i - \mu_y) \tag{37}$$

where x_i and y_i are pixel intensities in image patches x and y and T is total number of pixels in x and y patches.

The SSIM score of the image is obtained by taking the average value of SSIM of the patches in the image. The range of SSIM value is between 0 to 1, where better image quality corresponds to high structural similarity value.

Peak Signal-to-Noise Ratio (PSNR)

PSNR is the ratio between the highest possible pixel value in the image and the noise power. It is expressed in terms of the logarithmic decibel (dB), is given by

$$PSNR_{dB} = 10\,log_{10}\frac{(2^n-1)^2}{MSE} \tag{38}$$

where $(2^n - 1)^2$ is the square of the highest intensity value in the image, and n is the number of bits per image sample.

The mean square Error (MSE) is expressed as

$$MSE = \frac{1}{M\times N}\sum_{i=0}^{M-1}\sum_{j=0}^{N-1}(C_{ij} - R_{ij})^2 \tag{39}$$

where M is the height and N is the width of the image. C_{ij} is the original image and R_{ij}j is the distorted image.

The proposed system is analyzed by comparing its output with the results of the state-of-the-art algorithms from Nguyen [43] and Anand [51] for iris polar images as shown in Figure 10.

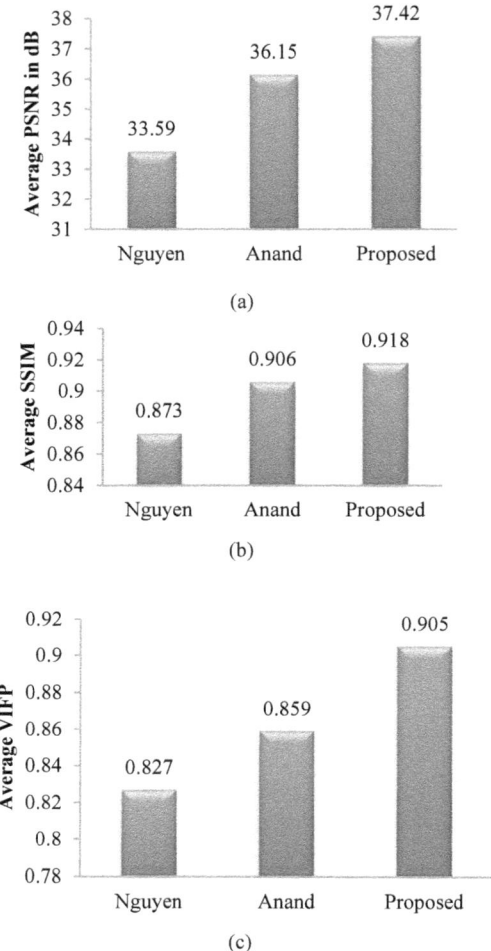

Figure 10. Performance analysis of proposed method for upsampling factors 2
(a) average PSNR (b) average SSIM (c) average VIFP

From the Figure 10, it can be seen that the proposed system gives better image quality compared to the state-of-the-art methods. The proposed system is analyzed for up-sampling factors 2 and 4 on Set₃. The obtained resolution for up-sampling factors 2 and 4 is 300×40 and 600×80 respectively. The graphical representation of the average PSNR, average SSIM and average VIFP for up-sampling factors 2 and 4 are as shown in Figure 11 and 12 respectively.

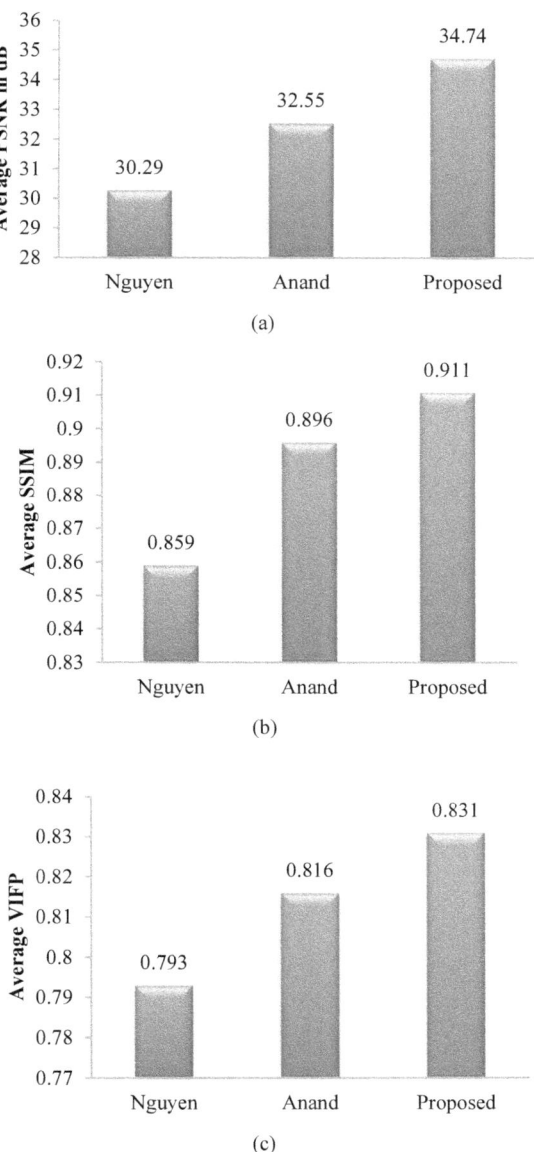

(a)

(b)

(c)

Figure 11. Performance analysis of proposed method for up-sampling factors = 2 of   Set₃ images (a) average PSNR (b) average SSIM (c) average VIFP

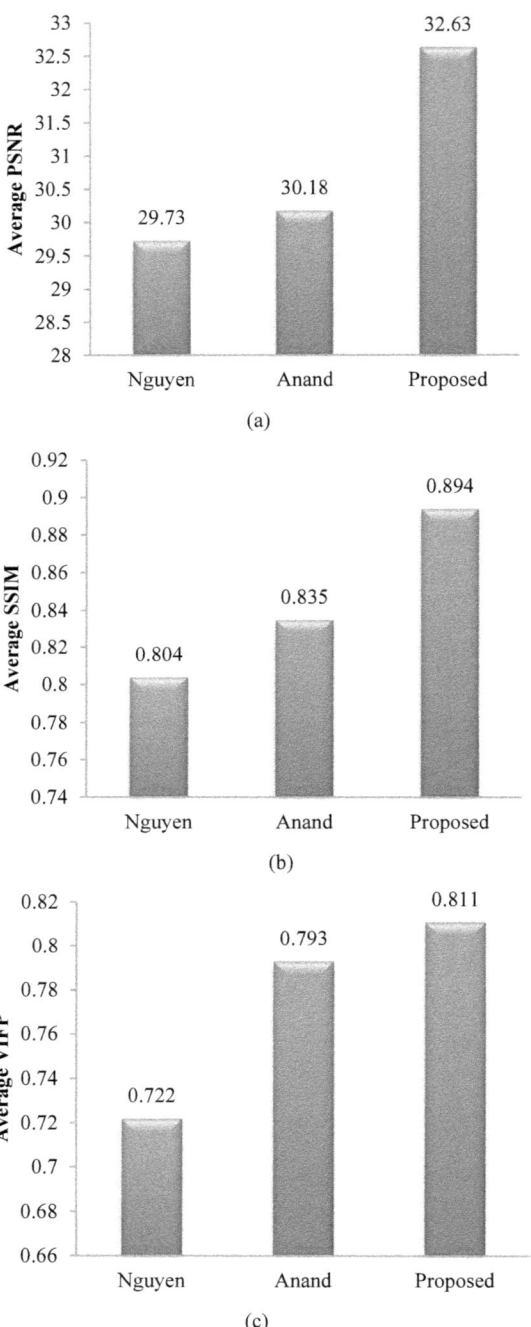

Figure 12. Performance analysis of proposed method for upsampling factors = 4 Set$_3$ images (a) average PSNR (b) average SSIM (c) average VIFP

The Figure 11 and 12 show that, as the upsampling factor increases the average PSNR, average SSIM and average VIFP of proposed method reduces, but compared to state-of-the-art methods proposed method gives a good quality image.

The robustness of proposed method is analyzed for salt-and-pepper noise condition. The algorithm is analyzed by adding salt-and-pepper noise by varying the % of noise addition from 0 to 25.

The graphical representation of average analysis of image quality for salt-and-pepper noise is shown in Figure13.

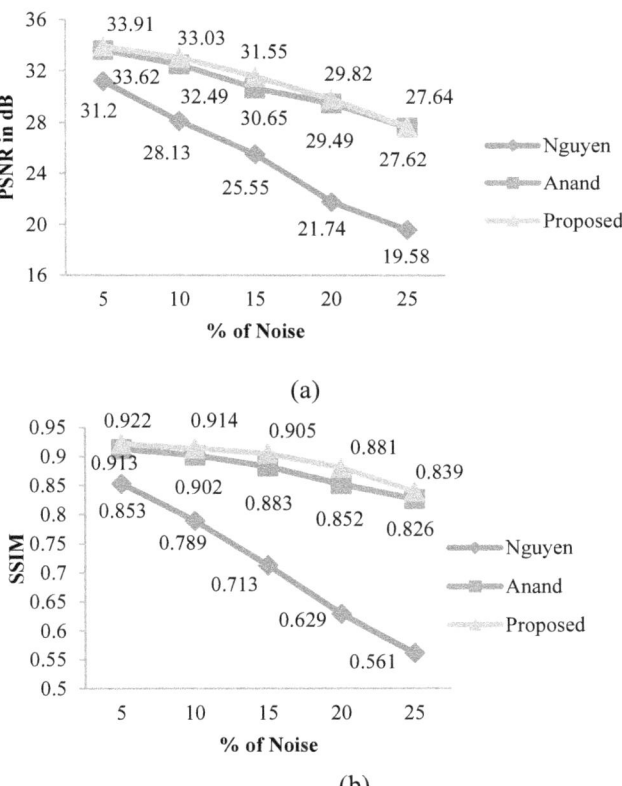

(a)

(b)

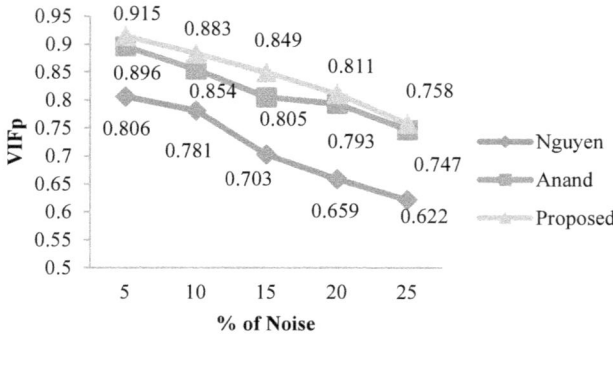

(c)

Figure 13. Image analysis under Salt-and –Pepper noise condition (a) % of Noise vs. PSNR (b) % of Noise vs. SSIM (c) % of Noise vs. VIFP

From Figure 13, it can be seen that the proposed method performance better reconstructions in noisy environment than other algorithms.

In this experiment, 100 different persons and 5 images of each person have been used to train the NN classifier. To test the performance of the proposed system, we have used two sets of data   1) 50 known persons and each person with 2 unknown person images 2) 20 unknown individuals and each person with 5 images. The performance of the proposed system is improved by fusing a proper number of images. The Comparison of Receiver Operating Characteristic (ROC) curves for the proposed system and state-of-the-art-algorithms using images from Set_2 and Set_3 are as shown in Figure 14, 15 and 16.

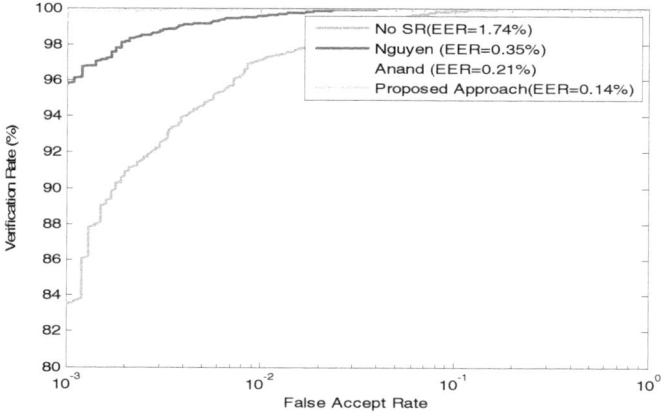

Figure 14. Comparison of the ROC curves of the proposed system with state-of-the-art-algorithms for Set_2 images

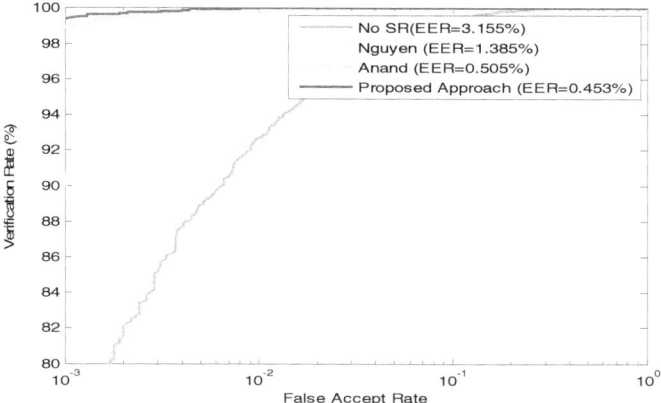

Figure 15. Comparison of the ROC curves of the proposed system with state-of-the-art-algorithms for Set$_3$ images, upsampling 2

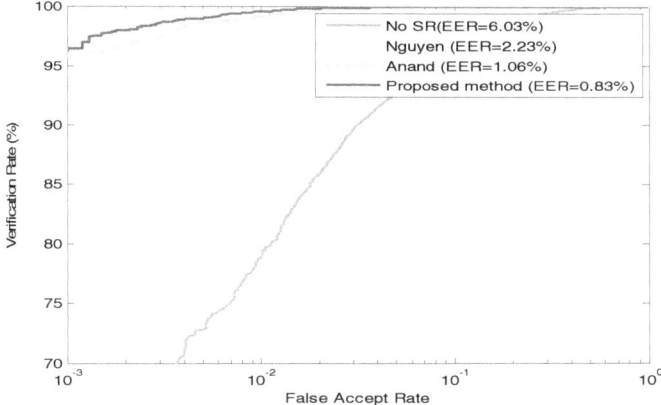

Figure 16. Comparison of the ROC curves of the proposed system with state-of-the-art-algorithms for Set$_3$ images upsampling 4

From the Figure 14, 15 and 16, it can be seen that, the EER of the proposed approach is dropped for both Set$_2$ and Set$_3$ compared to existing state-of-the-art algorithms. This shows that the performance of iris recognition with the proposed approach is better than existing methods. The average time required to super resolve the iris image is as shown in Table 2.

Table 2. Time analysis

Image Set	Up-Sampling Factor	Anand	Proposed System
S$_2$	2	3.21	4.18
S$_3$	2	2.45	3.53
S$_3$	4	1.50	3.11

From the Table 2, it can be seen that the proposed method takes more time compared to other method. But, the quality of super-resolved image and recognition accuracy is far better than other approaches.

5. Conclusion

The aim of this chapter is to recognize iris images captured at a long distance. In this chapter, we have developed a novel framework to super-resolve the long-range captured iris images based on deep convolutional neural network method. From the analyses, it can be seen that the proposed framework using deep convolutional neural network can super-resolve the iris images effectively and gives better recognition performance compared to state-of-art algorithms. In future, this work can be extended to recognize the human iris from a sequence of iris images or video. Further, work can also be extended to analyze the performance of system using handcrafted features like SIFT, SRURF, etc.

References

[1] F. Bashir, D. Usher, P. Casaverde, and M. Friedman, "Video surveillance for biometrics: long-range multi-biometric system," 2008 IEEE Fifth International Conference on Advanced Video and Signal Based Surveillance, (2008),pp. 175 -82.

[2] C. Fancourt, L. Bogoni, K. Hanna, Y. Guo, R. Wildes, N. Takahashi, and U. Jain, "Iris recognition at a distance," Lecture Notes in Computer Science, vol. 3546, (2005),pp. 1-13.

[3] Subhasis Chaudhuri, "Super Resolution Imaging," Kluwer Academic Publishers, 2002, pp.1-44.

[4] Sung Cheol Park, Min KyuPark,and Moon Gi Kang, "Super-Resolution Image Reconstruction: A Technical Overview," IEEE Signal Processing Magazine May 2003.

[5] Jianchoa Yang,Thomas Huang, " Image super resolution: Historical overview and future challenges". www.ifp.illinois.edu/~jyang29/papers/chap1.pdf - United States.

[6] J. Allebach and P. W. Wong, "Edge-directed interpolation," IEEE International Conference on Image Processing, (1996), pp. 707–710.

[7] F. N. Fritsch and R. E. Carlson, "Monotone piecewise cubic interpolation," SIAM Journal on Numerical Analysis, vol. 17, no. 2, (1980),pp. 238–246.

[8] J. Sun, J. Sun, Z. Xu, and H. Y. Shum, "Image super-resolution using gradient profile prior," IEEE Conference on Computer Vision and Pattern Recognition, 2008.

[9] W. S. Tam, C. W. Kok, and W. C. Siu, "Modified edge-directed interpolation for images," Journal of Electronic Imaging, vol. 19, no. 1, (2010), pp. 1–20.

[10] L. Wang, et. al., "Edge-directed single-image super-resolution via adaptive gradient magnitude self interpolation," IEEE Trans. Circuits Syst. Video Technol., (2013)

[11] M.Bertero,P.Boccacci, "Introduction to Inverse Problems in Imaging. (1998)

[12] K. Zhang, et al: 'Single image super-resolution with non-local means and steering kernel regression', IEEE Transaction on Image Processing, 2012

[13] X. Gao, et al.: 'Zernike-moment-based image super-resolution', IEEE Transaction on Image Processing, 2011

[14] Irani, M., Peleg, S.: Improving resolution by image registration. CVGIP Graph. Models Image Process. 53, 1991, pp.231–239.

[15] Rajan, Subhasis Chaudhuri, "An MRF-Based Approach to Generation of Super- Resolution Images from Blurred Observations," Journal of Mathematical Imaging and Vision, Volume 16, Issue 1,(2002) pp 5–15

[16] Manjunath V. Joshi, Subhasis Chaudhuri and Rajkiran Panuganti, "A Learning-Based Method for Image Super-Resolution from Zoomed Observations," IEEE Transactions On Systems, Man, And Cybernetics—Part B: Cybernetics, Vol. 35, No. 3, (2005)

[17] M. V. Joshi, S. Chaudhuri, and P. Rajkiran, "Super-resolution imaging:use of zoom as a cue," Image and Vision Computing, vol. 14, no. 22, (2004), pp. 1185-1196.

[18] Wen ChenXiang-zhong FangYan Cheng, "A maximum a posteriori super resolution algorithm based on multidimensional Lorentzian distribution," Springer Journal of Zhejiang University-SCIENCE, vol. 10, issue 12, (2009), pp. 1705–1713.

[19] Qiangqiang Yuan , Liangpei Zhang , Huanfeng Shen "Multiframe Super-Resolution Employing a Spatially Weighted Total Variation Model," IEEE Transactions on Circuits and Systems for Video Technology,Volume: 22, Issue: 3,(2012).

[20] Zemin Ren,Chuanjiang He, Qifeng Zhang,"Fractional order total variation regularization for image super-resolution," Journal Signal Processing archive Volume 93 Issue 9, September, (2013), pp. 2408-2421.

[21] Q. Wang, X. Tang, and H. Shum, "Patch based blind image superresolution," in Proceedings of IEEE Conference on Computer Vision, vol. 1, pp. 709-716,(2005),.

[22] Hertzmann, A., Jacobs, C.E., Oliver, N., Curless, B., Salesin, D.H.: Image analogies. In: Proceedings of the SIGGRAPH, pp. 327–340. Los Angeles (2001)

[23] W. T. Freeman, T. R. Jones, and E. C. Pasztor, "Example-based super-resolution," IEEE Computer Graphics and Applications, vol. 22, no. 2, pp. 56{65, 2002.

[24] Huang, T.: 'Learning based resolution enhancement of iris images', British Machine Vision Conference, (2003).

[25] Datsenko, D., Elad, M.: Example-based single document image super-resolution: a global MAP approach with outlier rejection. Multidimens. Syst. Signal Process. 18, 103–121 (2007)

[26] F. Brandi, R. de Queiroz, and D. Mukherjee, "Super resolution of video using key frames," in Proceedings IEEE International Symposium on Circuits and Systems, 2008, pp. 1608{1611.

[27] Yang, J.,Wright, J., Huang, T.,Ma,Y.: Image super-resolution via sparse representation. IEEE Trans. Image Process. 19, 2861–2873 (2010)

[28] Wang, J., Zhu, S., Gong, Y.: Resolution enhancement based on learning the sparse association of image patches. Pattern Recognit. Lett. 31, 1–10 (2010)

[29] P. P. Gajjar and M. V. Joshi, \New learning based super-resolution: Use of DWT and IGMRF prior," IEEE Transaction on Image Processing, vol. 19, no. 5, pp. 1201 { 1213, 2010.

[30] Kim, K.I., Kwon, Y.: Single-image super-resolution using sparse regression and natural image prior. IEEE Trans. Pattern Anal. Mach. Intell. 32, 1127–1133 (2010)

[31] Zhang, K.: 'Single image super-resolution with multi-scale similarity learning', IEEE Transaction on Neural Network Learning System, (2013)

[32] Y. Y. Qu, M.M Liao, Y. W. Zhou, T. Z. Fang, L. Lin, H. Y. Zhang, "Image super resolution based on data driven Gaussian process regression," Iscid, 513–520, (2013)

[33] Jianmin Li, Yanyun Qu, Cuihua Li , YuanXie, YangWu, Jianping Fan, "Learning local Gaussian process regression for image super-resolution," Elsevier Neurocomputing, (2015)

[34] Yu Zhu, Yanning Zhang, Alan L. Yuille, "Single Image Super-resolution using Deformable Patches,"Proc IEEE Comput Soc Conf Comput Vis Pattern Recognition. (2014).

[35] Chinh Dang, Mohammad Aghagolzadeh, and Hayder Radha, "Image Super-Resolution via Local Self-Learning Manifold Approximation," IEEE Signal Processing Letters, Vol. 21, No. 10, (2014)

[36] Chao Dong, Chen Change Loy, "Image Super-Resolution Using Deep Convolutional Networks," IEEE Transactions on Pattern Analysis and Machine Intelligence,Volume: 38, Issue: 2, (2016).

[37] Jingxu Chen ; Xiaohai He"Single Image Super-Resolution Based on Deep Learning and Gradient Transformation," IEEE 13th International Conference on Signal Processing (ICSP), (2016)

[38] Youngjin Yoon ; Hae-Gon Jeon,"Learning a Deep Convolutional Network for Light-Field Image Super-Resolution," IEEE International Conference on Computer Vision Workshop (ICCVW), 2015

[39] Zhaowen Wang ; Ding Liu "Deep Networks for Image Super-Resolution with Sparse Prior," IEEE International Conference on Computer Vision (ICCV), (2015)

[40] Yu Kato, Shinya Ohtani,"Image Super-Resolution with Multi-Channel Convolutional Neural Networks," IEEE International New Circuits and Systems Conference (NEWCAS), (2016)

[41] Gamal Fahmy, "Super-resolution construction of iris images from a visual low resolution face video", In Proceedings of the 9th International Symposium on Signal Processing and Its Applications, (2007), pp. 1-4.

[42] K. Nguyen, C. Fookes, and S. Sridharan, "Robust mean super-resolution for less cooperative nir iris recognition at a distance and on the move," International Symposium on Information and Communication Technology, (2010).

[43] K. Nguyen Thanh, C. Fookes, S. Sridharan, and S. Denman, "Quality-driven super-resolution for less constrained iris recognition at a distance and on the move," IEEE Transactions on Information Forensics and Security, vol. 21, no. 99, p. 1, (2011).

[44] K. Nguyen, C. Fookes, S. Sridharan, and S. Denman, "Feature-domain super resolution for iris recognition," IEEE International Conference on Image Processing, 2011.

[45] K. Nguyen, C. Fookes, S. Sridharan, and S. Denman, "Feature-domain super resolution for iris recognition," Computer Vision and Image Understanding, vol. 117, 2013, pp. 1526-1535.

[46] Nadia Othman, Nesma Houmani and Bernadette Dorizzi, "Improving Video-based Iris Recognition via Local Quality Weighted Super Resolution," International Conference on Pattern Recognition Applications and Methods, (2013).

[47] Anand Deshpande, Prashant Patavardhan, "Gaussian Process Regression Based Iris Polar Image Super Resolution," IEEE International Conference on Applied and Theoretical Computing and Communication Technology, (2016).

[48] H. He and W.-C.Siu, "Single image super-resolution using Gaussian process regression," in IEEE conference proceedings on Pattern Recognition, pp. 449-456, (2011).

[49] Anand Deshpande, Prashant Patavardhan, "Single Frame Super Resolution of Non-cooperative Iris Images," ICTACT Journal on Image and Video Processing, Volume 7, Issue 2, (2016), pp.1362-1365.

[50] Anand Deshpande, Prashant Patavardhan, "Multi-frame super-resolution for long range captured iris polar image," IET Biometrics, Vol. No.-6, Issue-2, (2016), pp. 108-116.

[51] Anand Deshpande, Prashant Patavardhan, "Super resolution and recognition of long range captured multi-frame iris images," IET Biometrics, (2017).

[52] U. Park, et. al., "Periocular biometrics in the visible spectrum," IEEE Transaction. Inf. Forens. Security, (2011)

[53] P. Viola, "Rapid object detection using a boosted cascade of simple features," IEEE Conference on Computer Vision and Pattern Recognition, (2001).

[54] Nitin K. Mahadeo, Andrew P. Paplinski, Sid Ray, "Automated Selection of Optimal Frames in NIR Iris Videos," IEEE International Conference on Digital Image Computing: Techniques and Applications, (2013)

[55] J. Daugman, "How iris recognition works," IEEE Transactions on Circuits and Systems for Video Technology, vol. 14, no. 1, pp. 21-30, (2004).

[56] J. Huan, M. Parris, J. Lee, and R. F. DeMara, "Scalable FPGA-based architecture for DCT computation using dynamic partial reconfiguration," ACM Trans. Embedded Comput. Syst., vol. 9, no. 1, pp. 1–18, (2009).

[57] M. Haque, "A 2-D fast cosine transform," IEEE Trans. Acoust. Speech Signal Process., vol. 33, no. 6, pp. 1532–1539, Dec. 1985.

[58] R. M. Haralick, K. Shanmugam and I. Dinstein, "Textural features for Image Classification", IEEE Transactions on Systems, Man and Cybernetics, Vol.3, pp. 610-621, (1973).

[59] Hu M., "Visual pattern recognition by moment invariants," IRE Transaction on Information Theory, 179–187, (1962).

[60] Christer Carlsson et.al., "Fuzzy Entropy Used for Predictive Analytics," IEEE International Conference on Fuzzy Systems, (2015).

[61] J.-D. Shie and S.-M. Chen, "Feature subset selection based on fuzzy entropy measures for handling classification problems," Appl. Intell., vol. 28, no. 1, pp. 69–82, (2008).

[62] J. Mezei, J. A. Morente-Molinera, and C. Carlsson, "Feature selection with fuzzy entropy to find similar cases," in Advance Trends in Soft Computing. pp. 383–390, Springer,(2014).

[63] K. Nozaki, H. Ishibuichi, and T. Hideo, "Adaptive fuzzy rule-based classification systems," IEEE Transactions on Fuzzy Systems, vol. 4, no. 3, pp. 238-250, (1996).

[64] Szmidt, E., Kacprzyk, J., "Entropy for intuitionistic fuzzy sets," Fuzzy Sets and Systems 118, 467–477, (2001).

[65] R. H. Abiyev and K. Altunkaya "Neural Network Based Biometric personal Identification with Fast Iris Segmentation", Journal of control, Automation, and systems, 2009.

[66] CASIA Iris Image Database [Online]. Available: http://biometrics.idealtest.org/. Last Accessed July (2014).

[67] Z. Wang, A. Bovik, H. Sheikh, and E. Simoncelli, "Image quality assessment: From error visibility to structural similarity," IEEE Transactions on Image Processing, vol. 13, no. 4,, (2004),pp. 600-612.

[68] Sheikh,H., Bovik, A., De Veciana, G. "An information fidelity criterion for image quality assessment using natural scene statistics",. IEEE Transaction on Image Processing, ,vol.14, no. 12, (2005),pp. 2117–28,.

[69] Lukes, T., Fliegel, K., Klima, M.: "Performance evaluation of image quality metrics with respect to their use for super-resolution enhancement", Qualcomm Multimedia. Exp., (2013), pp. 1-5

[70] Zhou, X., Bhanu, B., "Evaluating the quality of super-resolved images for face recognition", IEEE Computer Society Conference on Computer Vision and Pattern Recognition Workshops, (2008).

Subject Index

artificial intelligence (AI)	1, 27	hierarchical object detection	164
automatic disease detection	94	image classification	27
automatic object detection	218	image fusion	218
bag of words	137	image indexing	164
big data	177	image processing (IP)	1, 244
biometrics	244	image processing and computer	
challenges	177	vision	137
classification	194	information storage and	
computational intelligence	194	retrieval	137, 164
computer vision	244	iris recognition	244
content analysis and indexing	137	kinetic	50
content based image retrieval		machine	1
(CBIR)	68	machine learning	27
content-based analysis	164	mind	1
convolution neural network	50	neural networks	27
convolutional neural network with		principal component analysis	111
layer skipping (CNNLS)	194	radial basis function	94
convolutional neural		reinforcement learning	164
network(s)	27, 137, 164, 244	relevance feedback	68
deep belief network	50	restricted boltzmann machine	50
deep data analytics	177	security	218
deep face	218	semantic gap	68
deep learning	27, 50, 137, 177,	sketch-based image retrieval	
	194, 218, 244	(SBIR)	68
deep learning convolutional neural		SoftMax function	94
network	94	sparse filtering	194
deep multi-channel fusion	218	spatio-temporal feature	50
differential evolution extreme		sputum smear images	111
learning machines	111	stevia	94
face recognition	218	super resolution	244
feature detection	94	support vector machine	111
feature representation	137, 164	surveillance	218
feature selection	68	tuberculosis	111
gray level co-occurrence matrix	111	vehicle type recognition	194
hand gesture recognition	50	virtual reality	50

Deep Learning for Image Processing Applications
D.J. Hemanth and V.V. Estrela (Eds.)
IOS Press, 2017

Author Index

Agrawal, S.	68	Marqués, F.	137, 164
Awang, S.	194	Martin Sagayam, K.	50
Bellver Bueno, M.	164	McGuinness, K.	137
Bhatia, M.	177	Mittal, M.	177
Deshpande, A.	244	Mohedano, E.	137
Estrela, V.V.	v	Nik Azmi, N.M.A.	194
Giró-i-Nieto, X.	137, 164	O'connor, N.E.	137
Govindaraju, S.	27	Pandey, S.C.	1
Hemanth, D.J.	v	Patavardhan, P.P.	244
Henesey, L.E.	50	Pratap Singh, U.	68
Ho, C.C.	50	Priya, E.	111
Jain, S.	68	Salvador, A.	137
John, V.	218	Sivakumar, R.	94
Kumar Singh, R.	68	Srinivasan, S.	111
Lakshmi, S.	94	Torres, J.	164
Liu, S.	218	Vasuki, A.	27
Liu, Z.	218	Vedha Viyas, T.	50
Madhurima	177		

www.ingramcontent.com/pod-product-compliance
Ingram Content Group UK Ltd.
Pitfield, Milton Keynes, MK11 3LW, UK
UKHW022221170526
471099UK00001B/115